Regionalism in the Canadian Community, 1867–1967

CANADIAN HISTORICAL ASSOCIATION CENTENNIAL SEMINARS

Regionalism in the Canadian Community

1867-1967

CANADIAN HISTORICAL ASSOCIATION
CENTENNIAL SEMINARS

Edited by MASON WADE

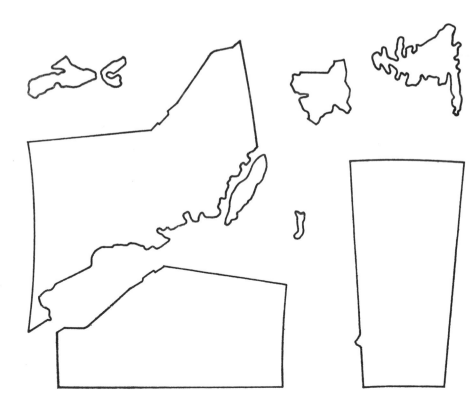

UNIVERSITY OF TORONTO PRESS

The papers in this volume were given at a series of Canadian Historical Association Centennial Seminars held at five Canadian universities in 1967. The seminars were planned by the Canadian Historical Association and sponsored by the Centennial Commission and the Association of Universities and Colleges of Canada, which provided a grant towards publication.

Foreword

THANKS TO A GRANT from the Centennial Commission and the co-operation of the Association of Universities and Colleges of Canada, the Centennial Seminars Committee of the Canadian Historical Association held five seminars during the period August 20–25, 1967, at the universities of Victoria, Saskatchewan, Laurentian, Laval, and Memorial. The participating universities provided board and room and warm hospitality; the Centennial Commission grant covered transportation and speakers' honoraria; and the AUCC, through Mr. John Banks, undertook the administrative arrangements as part of its Universities Centennial Programme. Each seminar was made up of about twenty senior scholars in Canadian history and related disciplines, junior historians, and graduate students. All five seminars discussed the same topic, "Regionalism and the Canadian Community, 1867–1967." Each was made up of representatives of the chief Canadian regions and included both French and English participants. In each case an historical geography field trip was organized to give the participants some idea of the region in which the seminar met, and perhaps inevitably, regional concerns received special attention in spite of efforts to make each seminar national in scope as well as in membership.

The Centennial Seminars were launched in 1966, with meetings at the University of British Columbia, the University of New Brunswick, and Stanley House, after being under consideration since the summer of 1964. The reactions of the participants confirmed the belief that such small gatherings, which gave junior faculty and graduate students an opportunity to discuss basic national problems with senior scholars on an informal basis, were badly needed to offset the growing depersonalization of graduate study in expanding universities, and the increasingly hectic, three-ring-circus atmosphere of the annual meetings of the Learned Societies of Canada. The seminars were conceived of from the start as interdisciplinary, since history draws upon so many other specialties and should synthetize them. Many graduate students have since borne witness how much benefit they derived from being removed from the rut of their particular historical research and forced to take a broader view of historical problems through the glasses of other disciplines. The committee is particularly grateful to those specialists in such other disciplines as geography, political science, sociology, and law who cheerfully agreed to participate in what were basically historical gatherings.

Another purpose of the seminars was to break down a still persistent regionalism by bringing together participants from all parts of the country and from both basic cultures to consider jointly their common national problems. This aim, too, has been realized, according to the testimony of participants, and many have indicated how much they gained by introduction to new points of view as well as often to new environments. It is the committee's hope that the benefits derived by the participants in the seminars will fan out to larger audiences through later teaching and writing.

The purpose of this volume is to make the papers which were given at the 1967 seminars accessible not only to the participants but also to a wider audience. The general reader as well as the specialist should find much in these pages to interest him and to give him a better idea of the wide range of Canadian opinion on basic Canadian problems. It is difficult to find any consensus in these papers, except that Canada is greater than the sum of its parts and that efforts should be made to understand and reconcile the divergent points of view which flourish so abundantly. But these papers certainly air ideas and facts which in the past have not received much attention from historians predominantly concerned with central Canada. It used to be said that there were two versions of Canadian history, the English and the French, but here is clear evidence that this observation was an unhappy simplification and that Canadian historiography is far more complicated. Believing that knowledge and comprehension are the beginning of wisdom, the committee here presents the papers which stimulated many long drawn-out seminar discussions, which rarely concluded in agreement on anything except the verdict that such efforts were eminently worthwhile.

Since I have no intention of attempting to reach conclusions which a hundred scholars were unable to attain, it remains for me to thank on behalf of the CHA Centennial Seminars Committee the Centennial Commission, and particularly M. André LeBlanc; the AUCC, and particularly its executive director, Dr. Geoffrey C. Andrew, and Mr. John Banks, whose devoted attention to administrative details did much to make the seminars successful; and the host universities for their extensive hospitality to such extra-curricular activities. For myself I should like to thank the seminar chairmen (Léopold Lamontagne, W. A. MacKay, W. L. Morton, D. C. Monroe, Gordon Rothney, John T. Saywell, and Marcel Trudel) and the speakers who responded to my appeals; and my committee colleagues, who proved so helpful in selecting topics and participants: C. C. J. Bond, Father Lorenzo Cadieux, S.J., J. M. S. Careless, Roger Graham, Léopold Lamontagne, S. R. Mealing, Margaret Ormsby, Fernand Ouellet, R. M. Saunders, Claude Thibault, Marcel Trudel, and Peter Waite.

Mason Wade, *Chairman*
CHA Centennial Seminars Committee

Contributors

Paul W. Fox, *University of Toronto*
Jean-Charles Bonenfant, *Bibliothèque de la Législature, Québec*
Marc LaTerreur, *Université Laval*
Everett C. Hughes, *Brandeis University*
Serge Gagnon, *Université d'Ottawa*
George Rawlyk, *Queen's University*
D. C. Masters, *University of Guelph*
Frank G. Vallee and Norman Shulman, *Carleton University*
Louis Courcelles, *Université d'Ottawa*
Morris Zaslow, *University of Western Ontario*
J. M. S. Careless, *University of Toronto*
Peter J. Cashin, *St. John's, Newfoundland*
Leslie Harris, *Memorial University*
Peter F. Neary and Sidney J. R. Noel, *University of Western Ontario*
G. O. Rothney, *Lakehead University*
Bernard Weilbrenner, *Archives publiques du Canada, Ottawa*
Gerald S. Graham, *King's College, University of London*

Contents

Regionalism in the Canadian Community, 1867–1967

CANADIAN HISTORICAL ASSOCIATION CENTENNIAL SEMINARS

1

Regionalism and Confederation

PAUL W. FOX

THE TERM "REGIONALISM" is very vague and subject to many different interpretations. In Canada one can think readily of geographic regions, climatic regions, economic regions, political regions, resource regions, planning regions, and no doubt many more. We have all been long familiar with the traditional conceptualizations of Canada as a country divided into geographic, climatic, economic, and political regions. With the recent attention paid to the development of natural resources and to economic planning, we are now becoming familiar also with the concepts of resource regions and economic development regions. But this elaboration adds to the confusion in the use of the term. Obviously, there may be many different kinds of "regions," and many different ways of classifying each kind. In fact, there may be as many definitions of "region" as there are persons defining it.

One can take an illustration from a recent book on regional and resource planning in Canada which reproduced a number of papers presented to the Resources for Tomorrow Conference in 1961. In it two of the authors stated: "In Canada, we may expect a system of about 400 provincial economic areas or Local Geographic Areas which can be combined into the various basic resource or Geographical Regions pointed to in the first part of this paper, or into the 241 Counties or Census Districts, 265 Economic Zones, or 66 Provincial Economic Regions."[1]

There then follows a listing of the 66 provincial economic regions that have been selected in this case as the proper subdivisions of Canada, including 10 for each of Ontario and Quebec chosen by the respective government. These are not necessarily, of course, the demarcated regions that someone else might have selected for the same purpose, nor likely the regions that the same authority would have chosen for a different purpose.

To take another example, if someone wished to talk about political regions in Canada, it would be necessary to decide immediately what it was he meant to discuss. Is he talking about regions as equivalents of provinces, groups of provinces, or parts of a province or provinces? Or selecting smaller units of government, is one discussing regions as equivalents of counties, districts, or municipalities, or any combination or part thereof? It is possible, for instance, to think of a political region in Canada that would be inter-provincial, inter-municipal, and multi-county at the same time. Professor Rowat's recent study of a federal capital territory for the Ottawa-Hull district involves that mixture.[2]

All this is put forward not to show that political scientists can be as clever as philosophers at playing the game of linguistic analysis but to indicate that at the moment in Canadian political science the term "regionalism" can mask a plethora of different forms and shapes. In a recent article on the subject of regionalism in Canada, Professor J. E. Hodgetts has remarked that "the concept of region viewed from the national perspective in Canada lacks the substance ... that may be claimed for it in the United States."[3] That is putting it modestly, as Professor Hodgetts makes clear in his elaboration:

> In Canada ... we are far less clear about the existence of regions with identifiable interests separate from the interests historically contained in and expressed through provincial units. In the First Annual Review of the Economic Council ... we find the "regions" entitled Atlantic (with a footnote to say Newfoundland is excluded), Quebec, Ontario, Prairies, and British Columbia. This nomenclature, which is quite typical, reveals how quickly we exhaust the

1/N. L. Nicholson and Z. W. Sametz, "Regions of Canada and the Regional Concept," in R. R. Krueger, F. O. Sargent, A. de Vos, and N. Pearson, eds., *Regional and Resource Planning in Canada* (Toronto 1963), 17.

2/D. C. Rowat, "The Proposal for a Federal Capital Territory for Canada's Capital," in Ontario Advisory Committee on Confederation, *Background Papers and Reports* (Toronto 1967), 215–82.

3/J. E. Hodgetts, "Regional Interests and Policy in a Federal Structure," *Canadian Journal of Economics and Political Science*, XXXII, No. 1 (February 1966), 10.

regional concept when applied across the nation: once the Maritimes and the Prairies have been mentioned, we immediately fall back on the standard political, provincial boundaries.[4]

As might have been suspected from the length of my discussion of this term "regionalism," I have had an ulterior purpose in mind. I wanted to justify its use in this paper in the way in which Professor Hodgetts explains it, in short as a near synonym for "provincialism" and "inter-provincialism." I think this use is sensible in view of the way in which the world "regionalism" is conventionally understood in Canada, and it will lead directly to the conclusions I wish to make at the end of this paper.

THE ARGUMENT

The gist of my argument in this paper is that the course of Confederation from 1867 to 1967 has been characterized by an oscillation in the assertion of political power between the federal government and the provinces; that at the present time the pendulum of power is swinging strongly in favour of the provinces; and that therefore it would be wise for us to adjust our thinking and our governmental processes to coincide with the realities of this contemporary trend. The solution for the present period is, in my opinion, to seek to achieve a flexible sort of federalism that allows the federal government to make different arrangements with different provinces according to the needs of the situation. Inevitably, this will lead to a certain amount of regionalism.

ALTERNATIONS IN FEDERAL-PROVINCIAL POWER

It is common knowledge that since 1867 there has been an ebb and flow in the assertion and exercise of power by Ottawa and the provincial capitals. It is undoubtedly true that the central government has consistently had the advantage in this flux of power. As all students of Canadian history realize, the distribution of powers made to the federal and provincial governments by the British North America Act gave the edge to the federal government. Definite psychological advantages accrued to Ottawa from this allocation as well as from the fact that the dominion government was the symbol and focus of new national ambitions and that it was staffed by the most eminent political luminaries of the day. But despite the fact that the new political system established by Confederation was tilted in favour of the federal government, there has still been an alternation in the assertion of power by Ottawa and the provinces.

4/*Ibid.*, 9.

We are all aware that Sir John A. Macdonald held the view that the provinces were little more than mere municipalities catering to local needs and that he would have preferred a legislative union, in which there were no provinces at all, to a federal system of government that gave the provinces a quasi-independent existence. Judged by the cheers in the Legislative Assembly that greeted his affirmation of this faith,[5] many of his colleagues held a similar view. In light of this and of the factors already noted that inclined the new federal system in favour of the dominion government, it is not surprising that the period following immediately upon Confederation in 1867 was marked by a vigorous display of federal activity, initiative, and power.

In the 1880's, however, the scales began to tip in the other direction. As has often been noted, a number of significant constitutional decisions rendered by the Judicial Committee of the Privy Council had the effect of enlarging the provincial grant of powers. At the same time, a number of strong provincial premiers appeared on the scene, several of whom exercized much power for rather long periods of time. Mowat of Ontario, who headed the government of that province very effectively for 24 years, was perhaps the most impressive. But one should mention also Norquay, who was premier of Manitoba from 1878 to 1887; Fielding, who was premier of Nova Scotia from 1884 to 1896; Blair of New Brunswick (premier, 1883–96); and Premier Mercier of Quebec (1887–91).

When Laurier became prime minister of Canada in 1896, the flow of power began to reverse direction again, in part because he performed one of the neatest manoeuvres in the Canadian balance of power game. He struck at the pinnacles of provincial power by persuading three leading provincial premiers – Mowat, Fielding, and Blair – to desert their local summits for positions in his federal "Ministry of All Talents," thereby deftly decapitating these prominent provincial régimes and transferring much of their strength to his government. Laurier gave additional momentum to his federal administration by reviving the image of Ottawa as the nation-builder. In a manner reminiscent of Macdonald with his National Policy, he embarked on a programme of additional transcontinental railway construction and massive immigration.

The pendulum of political power and prestige that had been swung towards Ottawa by Laurier remained fixed their during World War I by dint of the national emergency, the Union government, and the leadership and extraordinary powers exercised by Ottawa during the period of belligerency.

5/See P. B. Waite, ed., *The Confederation Debates in the Province of Canada, 1865,* Carleton Library no. 2 (Toronto 1963), 40.

With the return of peace, power began to ebb away again from Ottawa and to flow towards the provinces. The process of change took some time to run its course, yet it was apparent in a number of events. The wartime coalition government began to disintegrate. Its leader, Borden, resigned, to be replaced by Meighen, whose government was defeated in the election of 1921. King, who had been elected to succeed Laurier as the leader of the Liberal party became prime minister, but a new element had entered the federal scene. The Progressive party, recently created to speak for farmers in particular, had elected 64 members of Parliament, more than a quarter of the total membership of the existing House of Commons. In a House whose members were divided among four parties the Progressives held the balance of power and King was faced with the problem of leading a minority government. This was the first occurrence of minority government in Ottawa, but not the last. All three of the administrations that succeeded this one at Ottawa during the completion of the decade of the 1920's – King's second and third governments and Meighen's short-lived acting ministry – were minority governments also. Although minority governments are not necessarily weak by nature, the minority administrations that held office in Ottawa during the twenties were not noted either for their vigorous accomplishments or for their stability. In the decade between the beginning of July 1920 and the end of August 1930, Ottawa ran through six different governments, and none of them left much of a record.

In contrast to this instability at Ottawa, a number of provinces displayed a notable degree of constancy. Premier Taschereau had commenced his long reign of 16 years in Quebec, the local Liberal machine was digging itself solidly into power into Saskatchewan, and its counterpart in Nova Scotia was rounding out a record uninterrupted run of 43 years in office. At the same time, the farmers' parties were making even greater strides provincially than the Progressives were federally. The United Farmers of Alberta won power at Edmonton where they were destined to remain in office for 14 years. The United Farmers of Ontario gained power in that province, albeit briefly, while in Manitoba a professor of agriculture, John Bracken, headed a Progressive party government that was to rule for 21 years.

The attention of voters was attracted towards their provincial capitals, in particular in Alberta and Manitoba where the farmers felt that at long last they had elected governments sympathetic to their interests. Moreover, a great wave of popular democracy swept the West, stimulating the public's civic consciousness. Spreading into Canada from the American mid-western states, it carried with it such ideas of direct democracy as the initiative, the referendum, and the recall. These swirled about the provincial capitals rather than about Ottawa, leaving their legacy in the adoption of the single transferable voting system in provincial elections and proportional representation in some western municipalities.

During the 1920's also the powers of the provincial governments were strengthened indirectly by the Judicial Committee of the Privy Council's decisions in three important cases. In the Board of Commerce Act case, Fort Frances Pulp and Power Co., and Toronto Electric Commissioners, the Privy Council whittled down the general peace, order, and good government power of the federal government so that it was interpreted to apply only in emergencies.[6] This had the effect of extending the authority of the provinces in periods of normalcy.

The Great Depression of the 1930's brought this phase of provincial ascendancy to a halt. The bottom dropped out of the economy and the resultant economic recession had devastating political effects at the provincial level of government especially, changing the balance of power in the federal system. The provinces, which were responsible for the relief of the unemployed, were faced with paying the staggering costs of aiding the distressed in a protracted period of mass unemployment that at its peak reached one-third of the labour force. With dwindling revenues, high fixed charges on capital debts incurred during prosperity, and without benefit of an adequate existing social welfare system, the provinces were very hard hit, particularly in the West where the boom of the twenties rapidly turned into the monumental bust of the thirties, aggravated by a decline in the wheat market, crop failure, and drought. Western provincial governments teetered on the brink of bankruptcy. Alberta, in fact, went under, and its bonds had to be bailed out by the dominion government.

It is no exaggeration to say that the psychological effects of this sudden reversal of fortune were traumatic, especially in the West where the abrupt descent from the dizzy heights of prosperity to the hard rocks of depression was more precipitous than in other regions such as the Maritimes, where economic stringency was not unfamiliar and the increased misery was a matter of degree. In a province like Manitoba the collapse of its economic underpinnings instilled a dread of insecurity that is still evident in its readiness to depend on federal financial assistance today. Big Brother at Ottawa, with superior financial resources, had to be relied on to provide funds for relief cheques to keep body and soul together when the more vulnerable provincial governments had found their cupboards bare.

6/For the three cases and the judgments, see Peter H. Russell, ed., *Leading Constitutional Decisions*, Carleton Library no. 23 (Toronto 1965), 23–46.

The legacy of this circumstance is discernible in the attitude of many Canadians today, particularly of those who are more than 40 years of age and remember the depression. They tend to regard Ottawa as a more effective guardian of their welfare than their provincial government.

This umbilical attachment to the core of government has a long history in Canada, of course. It dates from the beginning of the French colonial régime with its highly centralized, absolutistic administration, carries through the period of British imperialism to Confederation, and continues to the present. In this first century of Confederation now completed, for instance, the Maritimes and the territories have continually looked for sustenance to the federal government, amply fulfilling the prediction Christopher Dunkin made in 1865, that "the legislatures ... will show a most calf-like appetite for the milking of this one most magnificent government cow."[7]

But it was the Great Depression that made the tradition into a living principle for the elder statesmen who govern Canada today. They accepted as part of the conventional wisdom of all time that the federal government is somehow inherently superior to all other governments in Canada. Since they had learned the hard way that financially it was the central government that could do things for Canadians, it was not difficult for them to believe that morally this ought to be so. Their view is still shared by many Canadians of their generation. There is something almost Freudian in the way in which mature Canadians in many provinces that are strong and in a number of respects autonomous cling with Oedipan affection to the parental image represented by Ottawa.

This image was reinforced even further by events in the 1940's. World War II gave Ottawa new prestige as the heart of the national war effort. The federal government became the physical guardian of Canadians as well as their chief economic guarantor. In view of the national emergency the provincial governments themselves acknowledged the superiority of their federal rival and abstained from exercising their full powers. As a result of this voluntary restraint and of the logic of the emergency situation, the federal government acquired and exercised great powers such as it had not had before. The provinces surrendered their rights under Sec. 92 of the BNA Act to collect direct taxes (personal and corporate income taxes and succession duties) and turned over these lucrative sources of revenue to Ottawa in return for guaranteed payments. (The first two taxes in particular are so lucrative that they alone have supplied about half of the federal government's income in recent years.) In addition, Ottawa imposed a number of rigorous controls on the populace in general;

7/Waite, *Confederation Debates*, 122.

for instance, registration of citizens, conscription, and labour direction; and on the economy in particular, for example, restrictions on wages, prices, foreign exchange, and on the manufacture, allocation, and consumption of commodities. At the same time Ottawa began to move into the field of welfare, inaugurating unemployment insurance and family allowances. It was a harbinger of things to come that the federal government established in 1944 the Department of Health and National Welfare, which was to become soon the third largest public spending agency in the country.

All of these factors meant that Ottawa was in a very strong bargaining position when the war ended and an attempt was made to readjust federal-provincial relations in accordance with peacetime conditions. Naturally, Ottawa had a somewhat different view than the provinces, especially the richer provinces, of what the respective roles of the two jurisdictions should be. The argument revolved, in particular, around the question of what the proper function of the federal government was in the fields of economic stabilization, social welfare, and tax-gathering. These fields were all interrelated, in the opinion of the federal government's senior advisers from the civil service, as became evident in the elaborate proposal they submitted for adoption to the first post-war federal-provincial conference.

Ottawa presented to the Dominion-Provincial Conference on Reconstruction in 1945 a comprehensive plan for intergovernmental relations in the new era of the welfare state that would have put the federal government in the driver's seat in the administrative machine. Without going into detail, one can say that these "Green Book" proposals incorporated some of the features of the recommendations made in the monumental Report of the Royal Commission on Dominion-Provincial Relations (the Rowell-Sirois Report), tabled in 1940 but never implemented because of the war.

The "Green Book" plan in 1945 proposed that the provinces give up all of the existing statutory subsidies that they received from the federal government and surrender permanently their right to levy income and corporation taxes and succession duties. In return Ottawa would assume all existing provincial debts, take over the cost of providing relief for all unemployed employable persons, and pay the provinces a "national adjustment grant" of $15 *per capita* based on provincial population. These proposals were similar to the major recommendations in the Rowell-Sirois Report except that in the Report the grant was to be based on need rather than on a fixed *per capita* sum.

The "Green Book," however, went far beyond the Rowell-Sirois Commission in suggesting a vastly expanded role in social welfare for the federal government. The latter now offered to pay all the costs of old-age pensions for Canadians who were 70 years of age and more, to share 50–50 with the provinces in paying pensions for those from 65 to 69, and to sponsor a joint health insurance plan for which Ottawa would pay 60 per cent of the cost. In addition, the federal treasury would contribute to provincial and municipal public works programmes if these were undertaken when Ottawa believed such pump-priming was necessary to stimulate the national economy.

The richer provinces, notably Ontario, objected strenuously to what appeared to them to be Ottawa's high-handed attitude in desiring to appropriate provincial tax fields, to invade provincial welfare jurisdiction, and to make the decisions by itself in launching public works programmes. The federal government defended itself by arguing that in the new post-war world Canada must have a minimum standard of social welfare in poorer regions as well as wealthier, that it alone could perform the task of establishing and maintaining such a national standard, and that to do so it must have the assurance of being able to manage the economy by controlling the economic levers, including the regulation of the level of taxation throughout the country and the determination of the timing of public works programmes.

It is worth dwelling on this argument because it reveals the basic problem that underlay the continual conflict in federal-provincial financial relations during the post-war period and which still persists today. The point at issue can be summed up briefly in the form of a question: is the federal government to continue to play the Big Daddy role it assumed during World War II, or are the provinces to be given more responsibility in taxing and running their own affairs and in determining the state of the economy? As for their control of social welfare, I think it is beyond dispute, constitutionally speaking, that the area belongs to the provinces. Whether or not it is best in practical terms that they should administer all welfare programmes is another question.

An important ingredient of this controversy is the element of ideology involved. The federal government's dogmatic dedication to the principle that it must have the power to control the economy stemmed largely from the Keynesian economic convictions of its leading civil servants. Many of these advisers had entered the ranks of the federal public service in the late thirties and forties as bright young men who had either studied at the feet of the great English economist John Maynard Keynes at Cambridge or had absorbed his doctrines from the definitive book he had published in 1936, *The General Theory of Employment, Interest, and Money*. Keynes argued that to avoid a repetition of the catastrophe of the 1930's it was necessary for governments to play a major role in stabilizing the economy, to control its vagaries by intervening to prime the pump with lower interest rates and taxes and greater public spending on public works in periods when recession threatened and, conversely, to drain off excessive purchasing power by means of higher taxes and interest rates and reduced governmental expenditure in periods of threatening inflation.

Keynes' disciples in Canada took this to mean that the federal government must maintain the great powers that it had acquired during World War II over the economy, taxation, welfare, and public expenditures. Since the theory fitted neatly with the recent mushroom growth of both the federal government's powers and the welfare state, it looked as though history, and maybe heaven too, were on the side of the Keynesians – and the federal government.

Perhaps it is too invidious to say that Keynes was to the federalists what Marx was to the proletariat but the impact of the ideology of Keynesianism cannot be discounted in explaining the course of Canadian federalism in the past 25 years. It accounts for the rigid and righteous obstinacy with which federal advisers, in the face of adversity, provincial opposition, and constitutional contradiction, have held to their view that Ottawa must retain the dominant upper hand in fiscal, economic, and even welfare matters. It also accounts for the inability of the provincial governments to drive home their case for a change in the balance of power. They had no effective counter-intellectual theory to displace Keynesianism, and moreover the doctrine was so convincing, pervasive, and fashionable that the provincial policy-makers believed it themselves and could not escape the haunting suspicion that the conclusions drawn in Ottawa as to the need for federal supremacy were probably correct. It is interesting to note that the most effective check to Keynesian centralism has come from Quebec. There it has taken another ideology, nationalism, to provide sufficient strength to ensure progress in the achievement of some of its goals despite the resistance emanating from Ottawa based on deductions from Keynes. But over the rest of Canada the cloud of Keynesianism still hangs. Like all great intellectual theories, Keynesianism became diffused at the public level into a popular cultural myth which few understood but most accepted, and the myth lives on in the notion that somehow, inherently, the federal government is and ought to be superior to provincial governments.

Of course, there was another reason for wanting to believe this. As the war drew to a close, everyone, provincialists as well as federalists, thought that there would be a catastrophic depression after hostilities ceased and that on the analogy of the Great Depression it would be the federal government that would have to cope with it.

The depression did not occur. Instead, the economy kept on booming and growing after the conflict ended and Ottawa, still armed with its wartime taxing powers, reaped a bountiful financial harvest. The federal government decided to spend its windfall on further incursions into the field of social welfare. In company with many other wartime governments, Ottawa had sustained military and civilian morale during the conflict by promising a new social order when victory was won. Britain had had its Beveridge Report, proposing social security from the cradle to the grave, and Canada had got its Marsh Plan, holding up much the same ideal. Now was the time to deliver. The first instalment came with the "Green Book" proposals for health insurance and improved old-age pensions submitted to the Dominion-Provincial Reconstruction Conference in 1945.

Since then the federal government has fleshed out its welfare programme even further with veterans' rehabilitation schemes, health grants, hospital insurance, disabled persons' benefits, youth allowances, contributory pensions, the Canada Pension Plan, student loans, retraining programmes, and a commitment to the introduction of a national medicare plan in the near future. In addition, the federal government during the last decade has penetrated deeply into the field of university education, subsidizing it heavily until 1967.

The first tax rental agreement entered into by the federal government with the provinces in 1942 was to last for five years. Since then Ottawa has renegotiated tax agreements with the provinces every five years as they expired. Despite the fact that there has been a progressive series of alterations that have steadily increased the amount of independence afforded to the provinces and the amount of money they receive, Ottawa has been left in effective control of the determination of the levels of income, corporation, and estate taxes and has enjoyed the lion's share of the proceeds from the first two lucrative taxes.[8]

Although the total sum of money transferred by the federal treasury to the provinces appears to be gigantic (surpassing three billion dollars in 1967), it is not by any means all a gratuitous gift from Ottawa. More than one billion of it is "tied money" in that it goes in the form of grants-in-aid to the provinces for shared-cost programmes (chiefly welfare items such as hospital insurance) which the provinces receive only if they agree to the conditions laid down by Ottawa and usually only if they pay a stipulated percentage of the costs of the programme out of their own pockets. Another large portion of the total, about $1.3 billion in 1967, consists of the amount that Ottawa turns back to the provinces as the

8/The following analysis is based on figures available in 1967, which is when the article was written.

latter's share of the combined revenues from income, corporation, and estate taxes. This sum is collected by the federal government on behalf of the provinces but it actually belongs to the latter as the proceeds of the levy of their own personal and corporation income taxes.

These arrangements have given Ottawa the initiative and control in the introduction of welfare measures. They have also given Ottawa the bulk of the revenue from direct taxes, despite the fact that the constitution clearly assigns welfare to the provinces and just as clearly gives the provinces the right to levy direct taxes. It is no wonder then that some of the provinces, especially the richer ones, have become increasingly irked by the federal government's proclivity for monopolizing the direct tax field and launching new welfare programmes, for which it takes the political credit, while calling the tune for them and paying their costs out of what the provinces claim to be their revenue resources.

Although the federal government is now trying under most recent arrangements to phase out the shared-cost welfare programmes by terminating its conditional grants and giving the provinces an equivalent in increased percentages of the proceeds from personal and corporation income taxes, some of the provincial governments are less than ecstatic, in part because Ottawa announced the change in an abrupt "take-it-or-leave-it" manner without negotiating the details with them but more particularly because Ottawa still refuses to acknowledge the provinces' need for greater revenues in general.

Some of the affluent provinces feel that this is typical of the superiority complex that Ottawa has developed during the period of its recent ascendancy since 1930. Although they resent this attitude because it injures their pride, they also have a more fundamental objection. They believe that Ottawa's claims to superiority have been considerably eroded by changing circumstances in the past decade. They are of the opinion that the scales in the balance of power between the federal and provincial governments have been moving significantly in the last 10 years in favour of the provinces and that Canada has entered into a new phase in federalism in which the recent long period of domination by the central government is coming to an end and the provinces are once again acquiring the initiative.

There are a number of reasons for believing that this assessment is correct and that we have reached a point in the transition of power at which it would be wise to adjust the federal system of government in Canada to accommodate the change. The reasons for the change may be summarized briefly and some proposals for accommodation can be suggested.

REASONS FOR THE CONTEMPORARY CHANGE IN BALANCE OF POWER

There are undoubtedly a large number of factors that account for the current swing in the pendulum of power away from Ottawa towards the provincial capitals but the following seem to be obvious. For convenience they are divided into those that have arisen within the federal sphere and those that have developed in the provincial context. Of the two, I think the provincial are probably the more important.

Federal Factors

1   For nearly a decade now we have had a series of minority governments at Ottawa. Five elections within 10 years have resulted in the election of four minority governments. While I do not agree with the common easy assumption that minority government means weak government, I think it is true to say that the repetition of minority results at least reveals that there is no great degree of popular attachment to any federal party and that there is no consensus of Canadian opinion coming to bear at Ottawa. This is in contrast to developments at the provincial level, as will be elaborated later, and it weakens Ottawa *vis-à-vis* the provinces in a fashion reminiscent of similar conditions in the 1920's, as previously explained.

2   The lack of consensus at Ottawa arises in large part from the regionalization that has developed within federal political parties in recent years. Although our parties claim to speak for the whole country, they are each confined to certain distinct regions and groups in terms of most of the members of Parliament they elect and the bulk of the support they receive.

The Conservatives under Mr. Diefenbaker's leadership have become primarily a western and rural party. Of their 97 MPs elected in 1965, 42 came from the three prairie provinces alone where the party was very strong indeed. Most of the rest of their MPs were elected from rural ridings in Ontario and the Maritimes. The party did extremely badly in large urban centres, winning no seats at all out of 18 ridings in metropolitan Toronto, none in Vancouver, and one out of 21 in the Montreal district. These results conformed to the pattern of popular electoral support given to the Conservatives in recent elections. There can be little doubt that the past decade has witnessed the transformation of the national Conservative party into a highly regionalized party somewhat similar to the "up-state" Republican party in the United States, which appeals to rural, white, Anglo-Saxon Protestants.

The Liberals have become regionalized also but in the opposite way to the Conservatives. They have done very well in recent elections in urban ridings, especially in Ontario and Quebec, but not at all well in rural and western constituencies. In 1965 the Liberals won only nine seats out of the 72 available west of Ontario. They were virtually wiped out in the prairies, in Nova Scotia, and in Prince Edward Island. Yet in urban centres they were very successful, particularly in cities with large New Canadian populations. Of the 131 Liberals elected in 1965, about 80 were from urban ridings, including 15 out of 18 possible from Toronto and 20 out of 21 from Montreal, both of which have a large number of "ethnically sensitive" constituencies. These electoral results are confirmed by voting studies of the pattern of popular support. The Liberals appear to be becoming the Canadian equivalent of the Democrats in the United States, appealing to large urban, cosmopolitan, Roman Catholic populations.

The New Democratic party is also highly regionalized. Nine of its 21 MPs elected in 1965 came from Ontario, nine from British Columbia, and three from Manitoba. Virtually all of these were from urban ridings or from ridings with a large working class component. The regionalization of Social Credit is almost too obvious to bother noting. Following the split in the party into English-speaking and French-speaking wings (which was a regional as well as an ethnic split), each faction became highly localized in terms of the MPs it elected in 1965. Social Credit's 5 MPs came from rural Albertan and British Columbian constituencies that almost adjoin across the Rocky Mountains, while the Créditistes' 9 MPs were all elected from rural ridings in Quebec.

3   A third factor weakening Ottawa's impact has been the instability that has developed in all of our federal parties during the past few years. If parties are to fulfil the role that political science traditionally assigns to them, namely the function of being a unifying force by acting as a national broker to bring diverse and opposing interests together and by securing a consensus, then each of the parties must be agreed within itself on the fundamentals of its existence. Yet internal concord is precisely what has been lacking in our national parties in recent years. It is additionally debilitating that all of our parties have been afflicted with major schisms at the same time. But perhaps it is not merely a coincidence since it may reveal the inherent weakness of the federal dimension in Canadian politics in the present period.

Whatever the cause for the general malaise, it is so obvious that one needs to mention the divisions within each party only briefly to recall them to mind.

The Conservative party, for instance, has been rent with schism over

Mr. Diefenbaker's leadership, but the roots of the conflict go much deeper than the issue of one man's tenure of office. They lie in a dispute between regions and between internal factions over what the nature and direction of the Conservative party should be. Is it to continue to be, as it has been recently, a sort of western agrarian party or is it to revert to its former long-standing posture as an upper middle class, business-oriented, eastern Canadian party? The confrontation between Mr. Diefenbaker, the prairie progressive, and Mr. Camp, the central Canadian businessman, is more than an accident.

The federal Liberal party has been plagued by divisions too which, if they are not as dramatic, are perhaps even more more numerous; for example, the so-called "right vs. left" (Sharp vs. MacEachen) conflict over the date of the introduction of medicare, the Gordon-Winters' controversy over American ownership of Canadian industry, the Thatcher-Gordon argument over curtailment of American investment of capital in Canada (a new version of the party's ancient internal battle over free trade vs. the tariff, with the westerner typically in favour of free trade and the easterner favouring protection), and the English-Canadian and French-Canadian differences in points of view on a number of issues before the cabinet.

In addition, electoral results and voting studies show that the Liberal party has gone through a great transformation in recent years, moving away from its original humble base of support in the rural and urban lower middle class to lean upon the more sophisticated and business-oriented upper middle class in larger cities.

The New Democratic and Social Credit parties have also gone through strange convolutions. Having begun 30 years ago as the CCF, which was notable as a western agrarian protest party dedicated to eradicating capitalism and inaugurating democratic socialism, the NDP from the day of its birth in 1961 has moderated its doctrines in an effort to broaden its appeal. Not much is left of its antecedent's socialistic dogmas or its support on the prairies. It has forsaken doctrinaire socialism (the word is not even mentioned in its official programmes) and it seeks avidly to win middle class support in cities. Social Credit has gone through an even more amazing somersault in the same period, swinging from a radical credo based on a highly unorthodox monetary theory to a conservative outlook which is almost indistinguishable from that of right-wing free enterprise. In the process the federal party has split into a western, English-speaking, conservative faction and an eastern, French-speaking, radical wing, which, oddly enough or perhaps it isn't odd at all, has been abetted by the premier of British Columbia. So acute is the dissention within the party that the national leader, Robert Thompson, fell victim to it and was forced to resign.

Thus all of our federal parties have become unstable lately as well as highly regionalized, and no party has been able to win a majority at Ottawa in the past five years. At the same time the provinces have been gathering strength.

Provincial Factors

There has, then, been a loss of momentum and somewhat of a vacuum of power at Ottawa, but there have been a number of significant developments at provincial capitals that have started the pendulum of power moving in their direction.

1   The most obvious of these, which probably every one thinks of first, is the nationalistic revolution that commenced in Quebec in 1960. Although it is extremely important, I cannot begin to discuss it in detail here because of lack of time and space. I would like merely to state that I think it is important not only for its nationalism but because it is a modernizing revolution – an attempt to develop in modern industrial and social terms an entire province – and that as such it is a harbinger of what is happening all over Canada in almost every other province. If this is true, it follows that even without pressure from Quebec we would have had enormous stresses and strains within our federal system at this time. The balance of power would likely have been tilted in favour of the provinces in any case for a number of fundamental reasons examined below.

2   One curious factor that may be entirely fortuitous is that while Ottawa has suffered from an absence of secure leadership, the provinces have produced an extraordinarily high percentage of able and strong premiers. One may not share their particular partisanship or approve of all their policies, but one must admit that at least nine of the ten contemporary provincial premiers are very capable, astute, and potent politicians. I am thinking of Smallwood, Stanfield, Robichaud, Johnson, Robarts, Roblin, Thatcher, Manning, and Bennett, and leaving out Campbell of Prince Edward Island because he has been in office only one year and has yet to prove himself. Perhaps he should be included too. In any event, even a 90 per cent average of proven talent is extremely high in any sector of human activity. It would raise a nice historical argument to ask if there has ever been before in Canadian history such a high percentage of skilful provincial premiers at one time. I suspect not. The closest one could come to it perhaps would be to refer to a period already mentioned

in this paper, the early 1890's, which was another era marked by strong provincial power.

3   This degree of forceful provincial leadership has coincided with the existence of very strong majorities on the governmental side of the legislatures in a number of the provinces. This no doubt accounts in part for the assurance and vigour with which some of the premiers speak and act. In any case no one can deny that Messrs. Smallwood, Stanfield, Robarts, and Manning have had in recent years more than comfortable majorities in the legislatures to lend them weight in their tugs-of-war with Ottawa. The score in favour of the government in each of these provinces in their most recent elections has been respectively 39–3, 40–6, 77–38, and 55–10. In addition, Smallwood has ruled for 18 years in Newfoundland, Manning for 24 years in Alberta, Bennett for 15 in British Columbia, Stanfield for 11 years in Nova Scotia, Roblin for 9 years in Manitoba, Robichaud for 7 in New Brunswick, and Robarts for 6 in Ontario. With these long periods in office behind them also, they are not apt to feel insecure in their own capitals.

4   The fourth factor is to my mind the most important of all in explaining why the pendulum of power is swinging towards the provinces. Since World War II concluded, there has been a dramatic upsurge in the significance of the functions of government assigned by the BNA Act to the provinces. Three, in particular, stand out: education, highways, and welfare. A fourth, health care, may be grouped with welfare. The first three, at least, are clearly provincial powers according to the constitution, and all three have undergone mushroom-like growth in the past few years.

The causes of this sudden increase are not hard to find. They are accounted for by at least the following factors. First, the rapid rise in the birth rate after the war which has brought hundreds of thousands of additional children into the educational system in recent years, necessitating enormous expenditures on the construction of schools and the provision of facilities, on the employment and training of teachers, and on the development of adequate technical, professional, and academic institutions, especially universities. Secondly, our modern society has required the construction of thousands of miles of good, hard-surfaced, and expensive highways to ensure rapid transportation for both economic and social purposes. Thirdly, citizens all across Canada have come to expect more and more benefits from the welfare state, such as hospital and medical care, higher old-age pensions, disabled persons' allowances, and more aid to students.

It is the provinces that have had to bear the burden for most of these snowballing obligations, and whatever their own personal opinions about increasing expenditures have been, the premiers have had to face a genuine demand by their own voters for such services. They have had little option but to acquiesce. After all, what politician can say "no" these days to a public outcry for such worthy goals as better and sufficient schools, university education for all who are qualified, hospital and medical care, or "a mile of blacktop"? They have become universal "goods," like peace and motherhood.

As a result of these demands, provincial expenditures have skyrocketed. Since the pattern is much the same across the country, I shall take only two examples to illustrate the general trend. Ontario spent in excess of $2 billion dollars last year (1966–67). That was about four times as much as it spent only 10 years ago, or to put it another way, it represented an increase in expenditures of approximately 300 per cent in one decade. In terms of a 20-year period it represents an increase of more than 1,300 per cent between 1947 and 1967. My other example, Alberta, presents an equally startling contrast. In the year 1944–45 the province of Alberta's total governmental expenditures amounted to $50 million. By 1966–67 they had reached $532 million, which constituted an increase of nearly 1,000 per cent. In 1966 the provincial treasurer pointed out that the current budget was "approximately equal to the combined total of all the budgets of the province from [its birth in] 1905 to 1947,"[9] or in other words, Alberta was now spending in one year as much as it had in its first 42 years.

Provincial spending *in toto*, exclusive of transfers, almost quadrupled between 1945 and 1955, and then more than trebled again between 1955 and 1965. The over-all increase in 20 years was approximately 900 per cent. In contrast, in the same period federal spending, exclusive of transfers to other governments, increased by only 68 per cent.

The reasons for these colossal increases in provincial spending are also quite similar in all the provinces. They arise from vastly increased expenditures in the three fields noted previously. Perhaps one set of examples is sufficient to depict the general point. Ontario spent $375 million on "transportation and communications" (almost all of it on highways) in 1966–67 compared to $197 million in 1956–57, which was an increase of 90 per cent, but the rise was even more evident in the other two areas. The province spent $684 million on education last year in comparison with $111 million 10 years previously, which was an increase of 516 per cent in a

9/Hon. A. O. Aalborg, Treasurer of the Province of Alberta, "Budget Speech," Third Session, Fifteenth Legislature 1966, p. 3. For data on the finances of all provinces, see Canadian Tax Foundation, *Provincial Finances, 1967* (Toronto 1967), especially chap. 15.

decade. On health and welfare Ontario expended $574 million last year compared to $103 million in 1956–57, which amounted to an increase of 457 per cent in 10 years.

If one adds together the amounts Ontario has spent on these three functions (education, highways, and health and welfare) for any one year in the last 10 and then calculates them as a percentage of the province's total expenditures for that year, one will discover that Ontario's spending on these three areas during the past decade has been running at 75 to 80 per cent of the province's total annual budget. The relevant percentages for other provinces have been near the same mark.

It is clear that the provinces, by force of contemporary developments, have become committed to enormous expenditures that are still rising and that consume a very large proportion of their total budgets. One can understand, therefore, why the provincial premiers are desperately concerned about either getting more money from Ottawa or alternatively, about obtaining control of a greater percentage of the revenues from their own direct income and corporation taxes. (They could, of course, raise their own taxes in these fields and have Ottawa collect them on their behalf, but the political repercussions from their own electorates would likely be so adverse that this policy does not appeal to them.) One can also see why the premiers are disturbed by the prospect of leaving with Ottawa the opportunity to introduce without consulting them new welfare programmes for which the provinces would have to find additional funds in part. A recent example of this concern is the appeal to Ottawa launched by all the premiers attending their annual conference at Fredericton in 1967 to postpone the introduction of medicare.

The huge growth in provincial spending since 1945 in fields that touch vitally the lives of so many citizens is, I think, the major reason for the current shift in the balance of power in our federal system from the central government to the provinces. The plain fact is that the provinces have become much more important to Canadians than they have ever been. They are no longer merely glorified municipalities, as Sir John A. Macdonald thought of them, not even "junior" governments compared to the "senior" government at Ottawa, despite the fact that these words are still used by some people who continue to think in terms of the by-gone era of the thirties and forties.

5   The unsuitability of these terms becomes evident if one studies the relevant facts and figures. The words "junior" and "senior" may have fitted the situation two decades ago when under wartime pressure the federal government's share of total government expenditures in Canada rose to as much as 87 per cent in 1944, but they certainly do not apply accurately to

the spending pattern today.[10] Indeed, the relationship is just the reverse. It is the provincial governments and municipalities (which under our constitution are, of course, the creatures of the provinces) that together have become the big spenders among Canadian governments.

The latest figures available show that in 1965 the federal government spent about $7 billion, exclusive of the $1.4 billion transferred to the other two jurisdictions, while the provinces and municipalities combined spent $9.1 billion, exclusive of transfers. In short, the so-called "junior" governments have been spending more than the "senior" government since 1961 and there is no indication that that pattern will change in the near future. A recent study predicts that by 1980 there will be a return to the pre-war position and each of the three jurisdictions will be spending about one-third of the total,[11] or in other words the provincial governments in particular will have responsibility for about two-thirds of public expenditures in Canada.

6   One important consequence of this huge expansion in provincial expenditures has been the growth in the number and quality of provincial civil servants. Between 1944 and 1964, for instance, the number of Ontario's departmental employees increased from 7,712 to 41,074. In seven years Alberta's leaped from approximately 10,000 in 1959 to more than 21,000 in 1966. Numbers in themselves are not an index of efficiency, but it is widely recognized that the quality of provincial employees has improved greatly recently as well. The governments of Quebec and Ontario especially are noted for having deliberately pursued lately a policy of recruiting able young professionals, such as economists, to plan programmes, give advice, and staff the services the provinces are now providing.

The possession of expertise is vitally important to any government in the period of complex economic and social development that we have entered into in the modern welfare state. But it is all the more important to the provinces because it enables them to cope with the recent rapid growth in their functions and also to bargain more effectively with Ottawa. The federal government for years has had an excellent civil service that has given it an edge in dealing with the provinces, which have been less well endowed in this respect. Now a new generation of young provincial "tech-

10/For quoted and relevant statistics, see *Provincial Finances, 1967*, Chapter 1, and Canadian Tax Foundation, *The National Finances, 1966–67* (Toronto 1966), chap. 1.
11/David Ivor, "General Expenditure Analysis," in Canadian Tax Foundation, *Report of Proceedings of the Fourteenth Annual Tax Conference* (Toronto 1960), 103.

nocrats" is being assembled to redress the balance. They are playing a significant role in helping to swing the pendulum of power towards the provincial capitals.

This point has been elaborated in much more detail in a very perceptive and persuasive article published in 1966 by two professors of political science from the University of British Columbia.[12] Lack of space here does not permit inclusion of their arguments, and I would merely remark in passing that they advance the same view as that expressed in this paper, namely that the cycle of federalism is bringing the provinces into the ascendancy in the present decade. Referring to this matter of the rise of provincial bureaucratic élites, they comment: "Probably the most important aspect of province-building concerns the growth of influential provincial elites in politics, administration, and resource-based industries."[13]

They also note that the opinions expressed earlier by some Canadian political scientists, for example, Professor J. A. Corry,[14] to the effect that the pressure of business élites and the requirements of national regulation of an interdependent economy would bring about a greater degree of centralization, have not been borne out by developments since then. On the contrary, as Professors Black and Cairns observe, "political integration is not an inevitable consequence of urbanization, industrialization, and rising standards of living."[15] Decentralization has been, in fact, the outcome of these trends.

7   In their comment on élites, quoted in part above, the two authors mention the importance of the growth of resource-based industries as a factor augmenting provincial powers. The point is well taken. The vigorous upsurge in the exploitation of our natural resources such as petroleum, gas, forest products, minerals, and hydro-electric power since the end of World War II has profited the entire country by contributing to the great boom in national prosperity that we have enjoyed in this period. But the political and economic benefits of this development have rubbed off on the provincial governments more than on the federal government.

There are several reasons for this. For one, natural resources are under the jurisdiction of the provinces according to the constitution and this gives the provinces the right to manage them and to tax them. There is both prestige and profit in this power. Alberta, for example, has derived a good

12/See E. R. Black and A. C. Cairns, "A Different Perspective on Canadian Federalism," *Canadian Public Administration*, IX, No. 1 (March 1966), 27–44.
13/*Ibid.*, 40.
14/See J. A. Corry, "Constitutional Trends and Federalism," in Robert M. Clark, ed., *Canadian Issues: Essays in Honour of Henry F. Angus* (Toronto 1961), 3–22.
15/Black and Cairns, "Canadian Federalism," 39.

deal of political capital out of the self-alleged shrewdness with which its government has negotiated publicly beneficial leases with private companies exploiting petroleum resources. The Alberta government has also obtained an enormous amount of revenue from natural resource industries in recent years. The latter now furnish 59 per cent of the government's total revenues, and the province is in the luxurious position of being the only province that does not have to levy a sales tax. No doubt this happy financial condition has helped the Alberta government to win friends and influence people in successive elections. In fact it probably goes a long way in explaining why the government party has remained solidly in power for 32 years.

But the advantages accruing to the provinces from the splurge in the development of their natural resources is not only a matter of dollars and cents gained in revenues. There is also the fact that the provinces profit from being identified with the glories of the resources boom. Thousands of good jobs are created in the resource industries themselves and in the service and secondary manufacturing industries that spring up locally to support them. New and valuable skills are attracted to both private and public employment in provincial centres. This expansion fosters in turn a general psychological mood of optimism, buoyancy, "good times," and excitement among voters which some provincial politicians are quick to cash in on by thumping the drum of provincial loyalty and by calling elections to endorse the government that has wrought such miracles. In the electoral activities that ensue, moreover, it is now possible for the provincial party in power to exercise a degree of independence that it did not formerly possess, since the existence in its own bailiwick of large prosperous resource industries permits it to solicit campaign funds locally without having to depend on the good offices of the national party.

If all this seems rather fanciful and exaggerated, I would invite you to review the provincial scene and to note the validity of the following observations. The provinces have become obsessed, as perhaps we all have, with the goal of rapid economic development, especially in the field of exploiting natural resources. The feverish desire to expand economically has reached the proportions of an epidemic in the provinces, like an exotic disease striking a remote people. The mania is pervasive and consuming, affecting virtually all the provinces whether they are rich or poor, large or small, or predominantly French-speaking or English-speaking. One hears on all sides of strenuous efforts and grandiose plans to develop provincial resources – dams in British Columbia, potash in Saskatchewan, iron ore in Quebec, heavy water in Nova Scotia, hydro-electric power in Labrador, etc.

Almost every province has recently created a ministry for stimulating the exploitation of these resources, in whole or in part, and a number of the premiers have themselves taken on the job of being supersalesmen of their provinces' economic potential. In typical fashion, Mr. Smallwood is his own minister of economic development and he flies about the world like a capitalist tycoon, wheeling and dealing in Newfoundland's resources. Messrs. Bennett, Thatcher, Johnson, Roblin, and even Stanfield are somewhat less peripatetic but no less interested. Messrs. Manning and Robarts are more decorous, but perhaps only because they feel that they already have it made. Backing up the efforts of the premiers and the ministers are an array of enthusiastic civil servants and a plethora of councils, boards, and agencies, public and private, devoted to economic development, planning, and productivity.

The passion of the provinces for economic development is so great that it has led a number of the governments to make bombastic, "nationalistic" (more properly stated, "provincialistic") demands upon the federal government for more money, greater powers, and sometimes quasi-independence to provide the sinews for continued growth. These assertions are perhaps not too surprising when they emanate from the more flamboyant premiers for whom they are stock in trade, but it is startling and revealing to hear as sensible and as modest an individual as the present premier of New Brunswick make a similar remark about provincial rights and natural resources. If Mr. Robichaud was quoted accurately, he said in 1967, in reference to the current controversy before the Supreme Court between the provinces and the federal government over which authority owns offshore mineral rights, "If the decision goes against us, we just won't recognize it."[16]

Summing up, I would conclude from this analysis that the rapid development since World War II of natural resources within the jurisdiction of the provinces has been a very significant factor in swinging the pendulum of power away from Ottawa towards the provincial capitals. It is probably second in importance only to the vast increase in provincial expenditures in the same period.

8   There is one final factor that should be mentioned in any explanation of the increasing stature of the provinces in the current era. It may be dealt with under the term "co-operative federalism." Although this development is very important, it is not possible for reasons of lack of space to describe it in detail here. I would refer those who wish to know more about its theoretical principles to a definitive article written by one of its

16/Quoted in the *Toronto Daily Star*, August 2, 1967.

architects, the Hon. Jean-Luc Pépin.[17] There is not yet available in published form an equally instructive and thorough review of the application in practice of its principles but several articles provide some useful information.[18]

Co-operative federalism is, in brief, the effective working together of governments in Canada to achieve mutually advantageous goals. There have been many different manifestations of this procedure in recent years. Usually it involves the meeting together of comparable officials from the federal and provincial governments for purposes of discussion and joint decision-making. A meeting may consist of those at the highest plane, prime ministers and ministers, or of senior civil servants such as deputy ministers, or of almost any rank of public servant who finds his government profits from his working directly with his opposite numbers in other governments. It is obvious that the complexities and problems of our modern professional, technological, and bureaucratic age are so great that any federal system needs a large dose of such co-operation among its federal and provincial officials if it is to function satisfactorily. Since personal consultation is a practical way of achieving this goal, it is not surprising that an extensive infra-structure of meetings on many subjects has grown up. In the last eight months of 1966, for instance, more than a hundred meetings of officials were scheduled, dealing with all sorts of subjects ranging from the federal-provincial tax structure to poultry breeding.[19]

The development of this kind of co-operative federalism in Canada has strengthened the provincial position *vis-à-vis* the federal government in at least two ways. First, it has given the provinces a greater voice in the determination of policies and practices that affect them. Although that voice is still not as influential at Ottawa as the provinces would like it to be, it provides at any rate a greater opportunity for the expression of provincial interests than anything that existed previously. The growth of federal-provincial conferences in recent years as a means of settling prob-

17/J.-L. Pépin, "Cooperative Federalism," in Paul Fox, ed., *Politics: Canada*, 2nd ed. (Toronto 1966), 79–86.
18/See D. V. Smiley, "The Rowell-Sirois Report, Provincial Autonomy, and Post-War Canadian Federalism," in *Canadian Journal of Economics and Political Science*, XXVIII, No. 1 (February 1962); D. V. Smiley, "The Two Themes of Canadian Federalism," *ibid.*, XXXI, No. 1 (February 1965); D. V. Smiley, "Public Administration and Canadian Federalism," *Canadian Public Administration*, VII, No. 3 (September 1964); E. Gallant, "The Machinery of Federal-Provincial Relations: I," *ibid.*, VIII, No. 4 (December 1965); R. M. Burns, "The Machinery of Federal-Provincial Relations: II," *ibid.*; J. R. Mallory, "The Five Faces of Federalism," in P.-A. Crépeau and C. B. Macpherson, eds., *The Future of Canadian Federalism* (Toronto 1965).
19/See the *Financial Post*, May 21, 1966, for an itemized list.

lems of mutual concern is a good example of the increased scope given to the provinces for making their views felt. These conferences are of sufficient importance that they merit greater attention here, but in the interests of brevity I shall merely remark that they have been of particular significance in the discussion and resolution of very important fiscal, welfare, and constitutional issues.

Secondly, co-operative federalism has another dimension that benefits the provinces. Although it is thought of generally in terms of the relations between Ottawa and the provincial governments, it can be interpreted to include the relations among the provincial governments themselves. There has been a vast expansion lately in the amount of consultation, co-operation, and co-ordination that goes on amongst provincial officials and departments; it is especially noticeable in such fields as education, welfare, agriculture, law enforcement, securities regulation, highway construction, etc. The exchange of information and opinion and the co-ordination of policies and standards are increasing all the time. A web of co-operative interrelations among provincial governments themselves is growing up to undergird the structure of federalism. Sometimes the provincial inter-relationship is nation-wide, as in the case of the creation in June 1967 of a Canadian Council of the Ministers of Education. On occasion it is regional, as in the instance of the holding annually of a conference of the Atlantic provinces' premiers, the establishment of an Atlantic Provinces Research Board and the Atlantic Provinces Economic Council for regional development, tri-provincial support of the Maritimes Transportation Commission, or the creation a few years ago of the Prairie Economic Council.

On the whole, however, it cannot be said that regional developments have been very significant as yet, either those among the provinces themstelves or those that stem from federal policies slanted towards a particular area. The federal government has attempted to do more for regional development than the provinces themselves. Ottawa has invested some hundreds of millions of dollars in special grants to the Atlantic provinces, in the Atlantic Development Board, and in the Agricultural Rehabilitation and Development Agency (ARDA), all of which are regional programmes and the latter of which in particular involves a large measure of federal-provincial co-operation.[20]

20/For a more detailed discussion of these programmes and of regional developments in Canada, see H. J. Whalen, "Public Policy and Regional Development: The Experience of the Atlantic Provinces," in A. Rotstein, ed., *The Prospect of Change* (Toronto 1965), 102–48; several articles in *Canadian Public Administration*, IX, No. 2 (June 1966); and J.-P. Bergevin, "Gaspé: A Case Study in Regional Planning," *ibid.*, IX, No. 1 (March 1966). See also the publications of the Department of Forestry and Rural Development, Ottawa, re rural development.

Co-operative federalism, therefore, is developing in Canada; it thus far in the main has affected and benefitted the provinces as individual entities rather than as regions.

CONCLUSIONS

1   My first and major conclusion is that for all the reasons enumerated previously it seems to me that we have entered into a period in which power is flowing away from Ottawa towards the provinces. This is part of an alternating rhythm that has characterized the history of Canadian federalism since Confederation. The present phase of growing provincial authority dates from the conclusion of World War II but has become especially significant in the last decade. It is impossible to estimate how long it will last or what its final political and economic repercussions will be, but the previous cycle of federal ascendancy prevailed for approximately twenty-five years. It is likely that we have not yet reached the zenith of the current period of provincial power.

2   Regionalism is a concept capable of many definitions, but if one adopts the common interpretation that it implies, the grouping together of provincial areas for common purposes, there is little evidence that this has yet happened on a grand scale. There are some modest attempts being made in that direction now in certain specific instances, partly as an outcome of the contemporary development of co-operative federalism, but there is absolutely no indication that we have gotten anywhere near the point of creating another significant jurisdiction of government between the federal and the provincial. As yet, regions in Canada remain very close to synonyms for provinces. At most they are administrative or economic concepts, created by political policies.

3   For these reasons the problem of federalism in Canada continues to be a problem in the adjustment of relations between the federal government and the provincial governments. At the moment, there appear to be three different ways in which these adjustments could be dealt with.

First, one might refuse to make any significant changes, adhering to present arrangements and trying to maintain the *status quo*. This appears to be in the main the policy of the present federal government of 1967, which at the federal-provincial fiscal conference in 1966 took the hard line that all provinces were to be treated equally (i.e., there was to be no "special status" for Quebec) and that the provinces were not to be given any more money or any greater voice in affairs than they now have. This course seems to me to be tempting fate by ignoring the trend in current Canadian history. It might well lead to some kind of rupture sooner or later since the dynamic forces in the provinces are, in my opinion, too strong to be contained rigidly without modifications.

Second, one might give the provinces their head and let contemporary centrifugal developments carry them out as far as they wished to go. This would be self-defeating from the point of view of the national interest since it likely would result in some kind of serious fragmentation – separatism, associate statism, or something analogous.

Third, one might review the trend in the current phase of Canadian affairs and, noting the gravitation in power towards the provinces, attempt to devise elastic policies to fit the situation. To my way of thinking, this means giving the provinces greater fiscal resources to meet their present needs and also granting to them a more significant role in determining national policies that affect the provinces; in short, expanding co-operative federalism even further. In the process it is inevitable that certain provinces will have "special (or particular) status" in certain regards, not necessarily in the same respects but in the matters that are of peculiar concern to them. Actually, we have always had a measure of "special status" in the opera-tion of Canadian federalism. The Atlantic provinces, for instance, have received special fiscal grants, Quebec has had protection of its linguistic and religious differences, the West has enjoyed special freight rates, and Ontario has had the benefit of a national tariff. I cannot see why we should now try to reverse the traditional pragmatic policies applied throughout the history of Canadian federalism, particularly when contemporary events require an even greater measure of their application. Let us make what-ever arrangements are necessary with each province to satisfy its interests and to maintain some semblance of over-all cohesion without worrying about uniformity. What does it matter how odd the pattern of Canadian federalism is so long as the components are reasonably satisfied and there is a measure of justice for all?

In conclusion, then, what I propose is a policy that could be called pragmatic, flexible federalism. How this would be applied in detail is subject for another paper.

2

Le Québec et la Confédération

JEAN-CHARLES BONENFANT

LES CANADIENS FRANÇAIS DU QUÉBEC ET LA NAISSANCE
DE LA CONFÉDÉRATION

SANS QUE NOUS EN AYONS une preuve mathématique, il semble bien que la majorité des Canadiens français aient été favorables à la Confédération lorsqu'elle prit naissance de 1864 à 1867. Certes, ils possédaient la plupart des caractéristiques qui, en Europe, depuis que s'était développé le principe de nationalité, faisaient rêver à l'indépendance, mais on peut cependant affirmer qu'à cette époque tout en voulant conserver leur identité, ils n'ont jamais songé sérieusement à cette solution.

Par ailleurs, il semble bien qu'ils aient compris que le système politique créé par l'Union en 1840, même s'il leur était devenu plutôt favorable, devait se transformer parce que les Canadiens de langue anglaise du Haut-Canada ne pouvaient indéfiniment accepter de se voir refuser la représentation selon la population. Il y eut bien à l'époque une forte tentation d'annexion aux Etats-Unis ou du moins l'impression que cette annexion serait un jour inévitable et qu'après tout, il servait de rien de lutter contre des impératifs géographiques, économiques et politiques, mais George-Etienne Cartier et le clergé catholique réussirent à convaincre la population des dangers que lui ferait courir l'annexion. D'ailleurs, on pouvait croire qu'elle était inévitable sans pour cela vouloir poser des actes précis qui la faciliterait.

Acceptant le fédéralisme comme inévitable, les Canadiens français n'en eurent cependant pas une vision théorique très élevée et ils auraient été incapables de disserter sur la plupart des problèmes qu'il pose aujourd'hui. Ces problèmes, ils ne les ont même pas soupçonnés. Comment veut-on, par exemple, qu'ils aient imaginé tout ce qu'il y avait derrière le paragraphe 13 de l'article 92 sur la propriété et les droits civils ! Comment auraient-ils pu soupçonner que l'interprétation judiciaire donnerait à cet article une portée aussi considérable ! Savaient-ils tout ce qui se cachait derrière les mots « terre publique, bois et forêts » du paragraphe 5 de l'article 92 !

Les Canadiens français s'efforcèrent de tirer le meilleur parti de solutions pragmatiques et de prévoir le mieux possible les difficultés qu'elles créeraient. Il ne faut jamais juger les événements à la lumière des faits postérieurs avec une vision que ne pouvaient posséder les contemporains. Les Canadiens français semblent avoir assez bien compris quels pouvoirs il était nécessaire de confier aux provinces pour que le Québec puisse être maître à l'époque de ses principales institutions. Ils ont pensé que le pouvoir provincial serait tellement développé dans le cas du Québec surtout qu'ils n'ont guère songé à la réalisation d'une véritable dualité canadienne au niveau fédéral. Il ne faut cependant pas oublier que la Confédération a été réalisée à l'époque où le Canada était une colonie anglo-saxonne et où le meilleur gouvernement était celui qui intervenait le moins possible dans la vie de ses habitants. Il était donc beaucoup moins grave, il y a cent ans, que l'état fédéral soit presque entièrement anglo-saxon puisque le Canada n'avait pas de statut international, puisqu'il n'intervenait pas dans la vie économique et puisqu'alors il n'existait pratiquement pas de mesures de sécurité sociale.

On peut cependant reprocher aux Canadiens français du Bas-Canada de ne pas avoir vraiment tenu compte des minorités françaises du Haut-Canada et des provinces maritimes. Ces minorités n'étaient malheureusement pas représentées au point de vue politique. D'ailleurs, à l'époque, les problèmes d'éducation étaient beaucoup plus centrés sur la religion que sur la langue et c'est ce qui explique que la protection qu'on réclama pour les minorités le fut en fonction de la première plutôt que de la seconde.

Les Canadiens français ont été an majorité favorables à la Confédération, il y a cent ans, parce que c'était la seule solution réaliste qui s'offrait à eux et même ceux qui s'y opposèrent se contentèrent d'affirmer qu'elle était prématurée et n'offrirent pas une solution de rechange. La

Confédération s'est réalisée parce que les Canadians anglais avaient besoin que les Canadiens français en soient, et que ceux-ci ne pouvaient alors devenir indépendants.

LE PREMIER QUART DE SIÈCLE

Il me semble que les historiens n'ont pas suffisamment étudié le fait que pendant les premières années de la Confédération, le Québec a manqué de dynamisme et ne s'est guère occupé de son autonomie. Les premières luttes, surtout juridiques, ont été menées par l'Ontario et son premier ministre Oliver Mowat. Pendant ce temps, le gouvernement et la législature du Québec contrôlés et dominés par le puissant parti conservateur n'osaient se dresser contre l'hégémonie fédérale. C'est aussi à cette époque que l'Ontario a accentué son avance industrielle et commerciale sur le Québec qui se contentait de sa vocation agricole traditionnelle et qui par ailleurs laissait partir vers les Etats-Unis des milliers de ses fils. Certes, en 1887, on assista à un réveil du Québec sur le plan politique avec Honoré Mercier, et les revendications des provinces s'épanouirent dans le Manifeste de la première conférence interprovinciale de 1887, mais on peut affirmer que cet éveil fut lent à se concrétiser en des mesures fécondes.

Par ailleurs, le Québec essaya alors de rationaliser son impuissance et il est révélateur qu'un de ses maîtres à penser à la fin du premier quart de siècle de la Confédération ait été Mgr L.-A. Paquet qui prononça le fameux sermon sur la vocation de la race française en Amérique, dont on a voulu pendant longtemps faire le bréviaire des patriotes canadiens-français.

Je pense que pour bien étudier l'arrière-plan historique de la situation actuelle du Québec dans le fédéralisme canadien, il faudrait mieux étudier les répercussions durables et lointaines qu'ont eues dans la province certaines attitudes fondamentales comme celle exprimée de cc sermon sur « la vocation de la race française en Amérique » prononcé par Mgr Paquet près du monument Champlain, à l'occasion des noces de diamant de la société Saint-Jean-Baptiste, le 23 juin 1902. Certes, le prélat avait pris la précaution de dire à ses auditeurs qu'il ne méprisait pas « ces bienfaits naturels de la Providence » et qu'il n'allait pas « jusqu'à prêcher à [ses] concitoyens un renoncement fatal aux intérêts économiques dont ils ont un si vif soin », mais il reste qu'a longtemps retenti aux oreilles des jeunes pour les consoler de leur sort ce conseil : « N'allons pas descendre du piédestal où Dieu nous a placés, pour marcher au pas vulgaire des générations assoiffées d'or et de jouissances. Laissons à d'autres nations, moins éprises d'idéal, ce mercantilisme fiévreux et ce grossier naturalisme qui les rivent à la matière. »

A-t-on suffisamment étudié les oppositions qui, dès le début du xxe siècle, se sont dressées contre la plupart des entreprises de développement de l'éducation, comme la fondation de l'Ecole des hautes études commerciales et l'entrée du secteur public dans les domaines autres que celui du primaire ? A-t-on suffisamment étudié les réactions de certaines élites à l'augmentation de l'activité gouvernementale comme, au lendemain de la première guerre, l'étatisation du commerce de l'alcool et l'établissement de l'assistance publique ? A-t-on suffisamment étudié les réactions ultra-conservatrices d'une grande partie de la population en face des premières tentatives d'établissement de mesures de sécurité sociale comme la loi des pensions de vieillesse ?

En d'autres termes, je me demande si des études plus poussées sur la politique interne du Québec et sur les influences qu'elle a subies ne seraient pas aussi révélatrices pour expliquer la situation présente que l'étude du Québec à l'intérieur du fédéralisme canadien. Mais je veux revenir en arrière pour essayer de brosser un tableau d'une autre période que j'appellerais volontiers celle de l'autonomie négative, c'est-à-dire la période qui s'étend de 1900 à 1954, ou plus précisément de la guerre de 1914 à l'après-guerre de 1939.

DE 1900 à 1954

Après 1900, sous le règne de Sir Wilfrid Laurier, les relations fédérales-provinciales semblent d'abord devoir se réaliser sans heurt. Pendant long-temps la vie politique du Québec est dominée par la puissance intangible du parti libéral qui, sous la direction successive de deux chefs, Lomer Gouin et Alexandre Taschereau, ne se sentit jamais menacé. Le premier gouverna de 1905 à 1920; le second, de 1920 à 1935. Tous les deux avocats, amis de l'ordre, respectueux des puissances financières sur qui ils comptaient pour développer la province, furent avant tout de grands commis, improvisateurs prudents, ennemis à la fois de l'aventure et de la planification, mais sachant parfois tenter des innovations étonnantes. Ils ne mesurèrent pas toujours très bien la portée ultime de certaines décisions et ne comprirent qu'après coup la transformation profonde d'une société rurale qui s'industrialisait. Par instinct de défense et par crainte de l'inconnu, ils furent autonomistes mais commencèrent en même temps à saisir l'importance des minorités françaises des autres provinces. Ils représentè-rent assez bien, pendant longtemps, les idées et les sentiments de l'immense majorité de la population, et le parti conservateur provincial, affaibli surtout pour des motifs de politique fédérale ne réussit jamais à cristalliser les sentiments d'opposition qui naissaient au gré des événements.

Le problème qui a permis aux gouvernants du Québec d'entre les deux guerres d'adopter sa politique la plus constante et la plus rationalisée fut celui des relations fédérales-provinciales. Après les années d'accalmie du régime Laurier et même du début du régime Borden que ne virent pas troubler les premiers mois de la guerre de 1914–18, ni même la création de l'impôt fédéral sur le revenu, la lutte reprit en décembre 1917 à la suite de l'adoption par le cabinet canadien d'un arrêté-en-conseil décrétant que toute émission pour emprunts par les gouvernements provinciaux devait être approuvée par le ministre des finances. Le cabinet de la province de Québec riposta par un arrêté-en-conseil niant au gouvernement fédéral le droit de contrôler les finances provinciales et affirmant que Québec ne se croyait pas lié par le nouveau règlement. Cette attitude causa une profonde impression, et le ministre fédéral des finances, Sir Thomas White, déclara que si le gouvernement du Dominion n'avait aucun pouvoir de contrôler les émissions des gouvernements provinciaux, il n'avait aucun pouvoir non plus de contrôler les émissions des municipalités et des compagnies ayant obtenu leur charte de l'autorité provinciale, ce qui était de nature à diminuer sérieusement la juridiction du Dominion dans les questions de défense nationale. Les règlements furent cependant adoucis et en définitive, la province de Québec eut gain de cause.

Le gouvernement fédéral sorti affaibli de la guerre et les provinces virent s'ouvrir devant elles une décennie d'activité intense. Dans le Québec, l'état organisa tout un système d'assistance publique ; il développa les forces hydrauliques, construisit des routes et des ponts. Malgré sa puissance, il continua à redouter l'intervention du gouvernement fédéral. Dans un discours qu'il prononçait en novembre 1920, Alexandre Taschereau qui venait de succéder à Lomer Gouin comme premier ministre, dénonçait l'intervention du gouvernement fédéral dans les domaines de l'agriculture, de la voirie et de l'instruction publique et accusait Ottawa de tarir les sources de revenus des provinces.

M. Taschereau continuera à s'opposer aux empiètements du gouvernement fédéral, même si ce fut avec un peu moins de véhémence lorsque ses amis libéraux détinrent le pouvoir. C'est ce qui explique en grande partie son attitude en face du système des pensions de vieillesse créé par la loi fédérale de 1927. Pour profiter de cette loi, les provinces devaient verser elles-mêmes la moitié des pensions, part qui, en 1931, fut réduite au quart. Québec n'accepta pas cette offre et prétendit même que la loi fédérale était inconstitutionnelle. Son gouvernement ne se sentit guère ébranlé par le cinquième rapport de la Commission des assurances sociales du Québec qui, en 1933, après avoir critiqué la loi fédérale parce qu'elle ne décrétait pas l'assurance contributoire, recommandait son acceptation comme mesure transitoire malgré, ajoutait-on, « les dangers de paternalisme qu'elle comporte ». Ce ne fut qu'en 1936 que la province de Québec décide de profiter de la loi fédérale des pensions de vieillesse, ayant ainsi perdu une somme de $25,000,000.

Lors de la conférence fédérale-provinciale, tenue à l'automne de 1927, en l'année du 60e anniversaire de la Confédération, pour examiner toutes les questions qui pouvaient se poser entre le Dominion et les provinces, M.Taschereau déclara : « Pour que le Canada soit heureux et prospère, il faut que les provinces soient heureuses et prospères, et ces dernières font plus pour le Canada que les autorités fédérales. Les autorités provinciales sont plus en contact avec le peuple car elles l'instruisent, construisent ses chemins et s'occupent de sa santé. » Il ajouta que les provinces avaient cependant continuellement à combattre pour sauvegarder leurs droits et demanda une délimitation plus précise des pouvoirs d'imposition.

En 1929, le parlement de Québec adopta une loi relative à la radiodiffusion, loi plutôt générale qui donnait au lieutenant-gouverneur-en-conseil le pouvoir d'ériger une station d'émissions radiophoniques et qui fut suivie d'une autre loi qui ne devait entrer en vigueur que sur proclamation et qui établissait le contrôle provincial sur la radiodiffusion. Le Premier Ministre du Québec échangea alors avec le Ministre fédéral de la Marine des lettres dans lesquelles était discuté le problème constitutionnel du contrôle de la radio que finalement les tribunaux déclarèrent être exclusivement du ressort du pouvoir fédéral.

C'est évidemment la crise économique et le chômage qu'elle provoqua qui ébranlèrent le plus toute la structure des relations fédérales-provinciales en plongeant certaines provinces pauvres dans des situations sans issue. La province de Québec accepta l'aide d'Ottawa, mais elle vit ses municipalités conduites au bord de la faillite. Aussi, son premier ministre, M. Taschereau, déclarait-il en 1935 à la Conférence du Dominion et des provinces : « Nos municipalités sont aux abois. » Il précisait que la situation financière de Québec était assez bonne, mais il demandait que sa province fût placée sur le même pied que les autres provinces. « On ne peut pas exiger », disait-il, « plus de la province de Québec que des autres. »

Les gouvernants du Québec furent à ce point partisans de l'autonomie provinciale qu'ils la placèrent souvent au-dessus de l'autonomie du Canada que favorisait l'évolution du statut international des Dominions. Ils souhaitèrent le maintien des appels au comité judiciaire du Conseil privé en qui ils voyaient plus de garantie pour les droits des provinces qu'en la Cour Suprême. En 1921, M. Taschereau déclarait à Toronto : « Dans un pays favorisé comme le nôtre de minorités, le Conseil privé est la sauvegarde de ces minorités. Enfin, lors de l'élaboration du Statut de Westminster, les provinces de Québec et d'Ontario firent des représentations auprès d'Ottawa pour que les conséquences de la nouvelle loi ne nuisent pas à leur autonomie. » C'est à cette occasion que le premier ministre d'Ontario, M. Howard Ferguson, formula *the compact theory* qui avait déjà été esquissée par des hommes politiques canadiens-français et qui devait connaître dans la province de Québec une grande popularité.

Le sentiment autonomiste traditionnel du Québec s'exaspéra à quelques reprises lorsque des événements comme la conscription et la formation du gouvernement d'union en 1917 firent que les Canadiens français cessèrent presque de participer au fonctionnement du fédéralisme canadien. Il connut sa plus forte pointe officielle en 1918 lorsque fut présentée à l'Assemblée législative de Québec la motion Francœur dont le texte se lisait ainsi : « Cette Chambre est d'avis que la province de Québec serait disposée à accepter la rupture du pacte fédératif de 1867 si, dans les autres provinces, on croit qu'elle est un obstacle à l'union, au progrès et au développement du Canada. » La motion ne fit que provoquer un débat académique et elle ne fut pas adoptée mais dans presque tous les discours qui furent alors prononcés, on note ce fort sentiment autonomiste qui semble être la dominante la plus certaine et la plus constante de la vie politique québécoise de 1910 à 1935.

Cette recherche plutôt négative de l'autonomie provinciale n'empêche pas le Québec de regarder au-delà de ses frontières et de se préoccuper du sort des minorités françaises dans les autres provinces, mais c'est là une autre question que nous n'avons pas le temps d'aborder ici aujourd'hui.

En 1936, avec M. Duplessis, l'orientation semble au début différente, mais en réalité le chef de l'Union Nationale continuait la politique de ses prédécesseurs libéraux. Il le fait avec plus de vigueur parce qu'il représente une autre génération et aussi parce que l'intervention d'Ottawa est plus profonde. Ajoutons que les inimitiés politiques favorisent considérablement l'opposition du Québec.

DE L'IMPÔT SUR LE REVENU DE M. DUPLESSIS À L'AVÈNEMENT
DE M. LESAGE

Pendant longtemps, le Québec tout en se montrant autonomiste, en particulier de 1937 à 1939, à l'occasion de l'enquête Rowell-Sirois, ne revendiqua pas expressément un statut particulier. Ce n'est qu'au début de l'automne de 1954 qu'on affirma que « le Québec n'est pas une province comme les autres ». Ce sont les mots mêmes qu'utilisa Gérard Filion dans un éditorial du *Devoir*, le 11 septembre 1954, à la suite d'un discours que le Premier Ministre du Canada, M. Louis Saint-Laurent, avait prononcé quelques jours auparavant à bord du *Saxonia*, pour dire que rien ne pourrait frêner l'influence d'Ottawa. Le 18 septembre, parlant au Club de Réforme de Québec, M. Saint-Laurent, tout en se défendant d'être centralisateur, déclarait qu'il ne partageait pas l'opinion de M. Filion, et il ajoutait « que la province de Québec peut être une province comme les autres ».

Le Premier Ministre du Québec, M. Duplessis, et ses partisans reprirent ce thème d'un Québec qui n'est pas une province comme les autres, phénomène qui d'ailleurs s'affirmait davantage dans les faits depuis qu'en 1947 Québec avait refusé de conclure avec Ottawa les ententes fiscales apportant aux autres provinces de généreuses subventions. Le statut particulier du Québec se précisa encore lorsqu'en 1954, son parlement créa un impôt sur le revenu pour lequel un abattement fut en partie accordé sur l'impôt fédéral. La même année, dans un livre consacré à la dualité canadienne, Michel Brunet écrivait : « Des journalistes, des historiens et des économistes ont reconnu que, dans la fédération canadienne, la situation du Québec était différente de celle des neuf provinces anglaises. »

Dans son rapport, publié en 1956, la Commission royale d'enquête sur les problèmes constitutionnels, la Commission Tremblay, sans utiliser l'expression de « statut particulier », en esquissait tout de même la théorie sous le titre de « situation spéciale » au chapitre de la situation constitutionnelle du Québec. Après avoir montré que jusqu'à un certain point « la situation constitutionnelle du Québec ne diffère pas de celle des autres provinces », le rapport exposait « ce qui rend la province distincte des autres à l'intérieur de la Confédération » et expliquait que « l'Acte confédératif fait au Québec une situation exceptionnelle », pour conclure que « Québec, non seulement occupe une position particulière et distincte, mais possède aussi la seule autorité qui puisse la modifier. »

LE STATUT PARTICULIER

Lorsque M. Jean Lesage prit le pouvoir au Québec en juin 1960, un de ses premiers gestes fut de faire distribuer aux représentants du gouvernement fédéral et des autres provinces des exemplaires du Rapport de la Commission Tremblay, semblant ainsi épouser les idées qu'il contenait. D'ailleurs, la plupart des réclamations qu'il fit par la suite conduisaient à un statut particulier. Ce fut le cas de la demande de ne pas adhérer aux programmes conjoints, faculté que le gouvernement fédéral a reconnue à toutes les provinces, mais dont seul le Québec a vraiment profité.

Une des premières réclamations tapageuses d'un statut spécial pour le Québec fut formulée en octobre 1963 par le Secrétaire de la Province du Québec, M. Bona Arsenault, lorsqu'il affirma à Ottawa que « le Canada ne se tirera pas de la crise actuelle à moins de consentir au Québec un régime particulier à l'intérieur de la Confédération » et qu'il était « urgent d'entreprendre une réforme de la constitution canadienne qui tendra vers cet objectif, seul compromis acceptable aux Canadiens français entre l'indépendance et le *statu quo* ». En mai 1964, M. Lesage déclarait à Moncton que le Québec n'avait pas à quitter la Confédération pour faire reconnaître son statut distinctif.

Par ailleurs, M. Daniel Johnson, dès le 4 juillet 1963, déclarait que « l'élaboration d'une constitution nouvelle pour le Canada exige que l'on reconnaisse que le Québec n'est pas une province comme les autres » et il ajoutait que pour y arriver, il faudra qu'on se débarrasse du faux principe « voulant qu'en régime fédératif ou confédératif, tous les Etats membres ou toutes les provinces doivent nécessairement être coulés dans le même moule constitutionnel, avec les mêmes droits, les mêmes responsabilités et les mêmes sources de revenus ».

Plus tard, dans le dernier chapitre de son livre *Egalité ou Indépendance*, M. Johnson écrivait : « Certains parlent d'un statut particulier pour le Québec, en se gardant bien de définir ce qu'ils entendent par là. Voilà un terme fort commode, qui peut contenir n'importe quoi... Il existe de nombreux exemples de fédérations où certains Etats membres bénéficient d'un statut particulier. Mais je connais aucun cas qui puisse s'appliquer exactement à la situation canadienne. Car cette situation est unique. »

C'est en juin 1964, à Charlottetown, que Me Jacques-Yvan Morin formula pour la première fois d'une façon lucide et élaborée la théorie du statut particulier pour conclure que « dans l'avenir prévisible, le seul régime qui permettrait, d'une part, de réconcilier les thèses Rowell-Sirois et Tremblay et, d'autre part, de favoriser le progrès social, demeurera, à notre avis, un statut particulier du Québec au sein d'une nouvelle confédération ».

Au cours de 1965, alors que la solution du statut particulier devint de plus en plus populaire dans tous les milieux, Me Morin continua de s'en faire l'apôtre. Il eut en particulier comme allié, lors d'une journée d'étude organisée par la société Saint-Jean-Baptiste de Montréal, le R. P. Richard Arès qui, dans la livraison de juin précédent de l'*Action Nationale*, avait publié, sous le titre de « Le Statut particulier minimum vital pour le Québec », l'exposé qu'il avait fait le 25 avril 1965 à la Journée de la Ligue d'Action nationale.

A la suite des interventions de Me Morin et du Père Arès et à la suite de quelques reprises du thème par le Premier Ministre Jean Lesage pendant son voyage dans l'Ouest canadien, au début de l'automne, M. Claude Ryan consacra, le 30 novembre 1965, son éditorial dans *Le Devoir* à « La formule du statut particulier ». L'éditorial plutôt favorable au « thème qui semble devoir réaliser un accord assez large de l'opinion québécoise » éveilla l'attention du Canada anglais. Il provoqua dans le *Globe and Mail* du 11 décembre un éditorial qui, sous le titre de « A Positive Approach from Quebec », était loin de rejeter la thèse du statut particulier.

Mais la proclamation la plus politique de la nécessité d'un statut particulier pour le Québec, on la trouve dans le discours que M. Jean Lesage prononça, le 14 décembre 1965, devant la Chambre de commerce de Ste-Foy. « Pour répondre aux vœux de notre population », déclara M. Lesage, « nous chercherons à obtenir tous les pouvoirs nécessaires à notre affirmation économique, sociale et politique. C'est là un objectif logique, sain et positif. Dans la mesure où d'autres provinces, pour des raisons tout à fait acceptables, n'ont pas besoin de se fixer le même objectif, et il semble bien que ce sera le cas – le Québec verra, par rapport à elles, son statut se différencier davantage. » Le professeur Donald Smiley prétendit, avec un peu d'exagération, dans *Le Devoir* du 14 février 1966, que le discours de M. Lesage, à Ste-Foy, dans lequel il avait fait sienne l'option du statut particulier « apparaîtra peut-être à l'avenir comme un important virage dans les relations entre Québec et le reste du Canada ». Le statut particulier est demeuré depuis une formule à la mode assez « ondoyante et diverse » pour satisfaire tous ceux qui ne veulent ni de l'indépendance ni du *statu quo*.

Dans le mémoire que le Premier Ministre, M. Daniel Johnson, déposa à la conférence fiscale, en septembre 1966, on ne trouve nulle part l'expression « statut particulier », mais il est difficile de ne pas l'imaginer derrière l'intention « de faire reconnaître juridiquement et politiquement la nation canadienne-française, entre autres moyens, par l'élaboration d'une nouvelle constitution, qui reconnaisse dans notre pays des droits collectifs égaux aux Canadiens de langue anglaise et aux Canadiens et langue française et qui confie au Québec toutes les compétences nécessaires à la sauvegarde de l'identité québécoise ». Aussi M. Claude Ryan pouvait-il écrire dans *Le Devoir* du 14 septembre 1966 : « Le mémoire de M. Johnson à la conférence fiscale donne un sens concret à l'idée du statut particulier qui s'est fait jour dans le Québec depuis quelques années. »

Le statut particulier a trouvé des adversaires venant de milieux divers.

Les indépendantistes y sont opposés parce que, pour eux, comme le disait Pierre Bourgault aux étudiants du Séminaire de Sainte-Thérèse, « le statut particulier que propose M. Lesage consacre l'état de réserve du Québec » et que « le statut particulier, c'est payer deux fois pour obtenir la même chose ».

Comme un statut particulier pour le Québec peut constituer un affaiblissement des liens fédératifs, on comprend qu'interviewés à la télévision par le journaliste Pierre Berton, deux députés fédéraux, MM. Pierre-Elliot Trudeau et Gérard Pelletier, aient déclaré qu'ils ne voulaient pas pour le Québec « un statut trop particulier ». Par ailleurs, le professeur Donald Smiley, intitula « Plutôt qu'un statut particulier, étape vers la séparation, mieux intégrer le Canada français au système fédéral » un des deux articles qu'il publia dans *Le Devoir* les 14 et 15 février 1966. A la Chambre des Communes, en février 1966, deux députés, MM. G. W. Baldwin et Warren W. Allmand, s'opposèrent aussi au statut particulier. Enfin, dans une lettre que publia *Le Devoir* du 16 mars 1967, M. Eugene Forsey, tout en reconnaissant que « le Québec possède déjà un statut particulier », ajouta : « Le statut particulier préconisé par M. Johnson et M. Lesage, si je les ai bien compris, est inadmissible pour ceux qui veulent que le Canada reste quelque chose de plus qu'une simple expression géographique. »

Enfin, le dernier épisode de l'histoire du statut particulier a été la prise de position du NPD lors de sa réunion en mai 1967. Le NPD de Québec a opté pour le statut particulier et il tentera de faire adopter son point de vue par l'ensemble du parti lors des assises nationales du mois de juillet. Le chef fédéral du parti, M. Douglas, a déclaré que « pour résoudre les graves problèmes de l'heure, il faut que la constitution reconnaisse que le Québec n'est pas une province comme les autres ». Quelques jours auparavant, lors du débat sur l'adresse en réponse au discours du trône, M. Douglas avait proposé un sous-amendement dans lequel on reprochait au gouvernement de ne pas avoir préparé une conférence constitutionnelle nationale « en vue de prévoir un statut spécial approprié pour la province de Québec ». Le sous-amendement fut rejeté, mais il fallait beaucoup d'imagination pour y voir un vote de la Chambre des Communes contre le statut particulier du Québec.

La recherche par le Québec d'un statut particulier est depuis cent ans la manifestation du jeu de ceux principes que connaissent bien les théoriciens du fédéralisme et dont le professeur Georges Scelle a naguère analysé le fonctionnement : la loi de participation et la loi d'autonomie. Dans le Québec où les origines ethniques s'ajoutent à la géographie et à l'histoire pour créer des particularismes, on éprouve par suite des difficultés de participer pleinement à l'activité fédérale le besoin de chercher chez soi une expression plus autonome du pouvoir que constitue le statut particulier.

LE STATUT PARTICULIER DE FAIT

Quelles que soient les attitudes en face du statut particulier, il existe de plus en plus dans les faits et j'oserais dire que même ses adversaires l'acceptent, ne serait-ce que comme instrument de négociations politiques. On comprend que les hommes politiques canadiens-français fédéraux ne prisent guère un tel statut qui est de nature à réduire leur importance dans le gouvernement canadien, mais, par ailleurs, même tout en refusant de l'accepter en théorie, ils se voient obligés de le reconnaître dans les faits. Le fédéralisme qui, par sa nature, est un système « ondoyant et divers » peut s'accommoder d'un « statut particulier » pour le Québec, mais il est sûr qu'un certain degré ne peut être dépassé sans mettre en danger l'état fédératif lui-même. Il y a là un vaste domaine ouvert à l'imagination et à l'ingéniosité des théoriciens et des praticiens et, dans votre cas, à des discussions qui me permettront de préciser mon exposé et surtout dans certains cas de le développer.

Pour le moment, je me refuse à conclure si ce n'est qu'au strict point de vue historique un siècle de fédéralisme a été pour le Québec beaucoup plus un siècle de tâtonnements, de piteuses improvisations, qu'un siècle d'injustice.

3

La Confédération canadienne et son centenaire: « Variations sur un thème connu »

MARC LATERREUR

DOIS-JE AVOUER, *ex abrupto*, que j'aurais aimé que l'année qui marque le centenaire de la Confédération canadienne a mis l'accent sur la réflexion et la recherche de solutions concrètes à nos problèmes actuels et futurs d'existence comme nation ? Mes vœux n'ont pas été comblés. 1967 entend un tapage retentissant, contemple d'innombrables cortèges de majorettes, s'étourdit enfin dans le gigantisme prémédité des manifestations outaouaises du 1er juillet. On se demande si le directeur du *Journal of Canadian Studies* n'avait pas raison d'écrire que les activités de la Commission du Centenaire étaient imprégnées d'un esprit peu raffiné (il emploie le mot « vulgar ») destiné à plaire surtout aux couches inférieures de la société[1]. Bref, c'est dans le bruit et le confetti qu'on a voulu célébrer cette unité canadienne qui nous échappe depuis un long siècle. Ajoutons, pour être juste, que ces colloques auxquels nous participons représentent l'élément sérieux, substantiel, des projets commandés du centenaire, et ne me faites pas dire que même ces colloques servent à prouver ce que je viens d'avancer.

1/Robert D. Chambers, « Editorial », *Journal of Canadian Studies/Revue d'Etudes canadiennes*, I, No 3 (novembre 1966), 2.

Cette année du Centenaire a débuté de façon caractéristique : l'on s'est rendu compte, le soir du 31 décembre 1966, que les francophones du Québec réagissaient froidement à l'idée même de marquer dans la joie l'anniversaire de l'Acte de l'Amérique du nord britannique. Un représentant de la Commission du Centenaire a cependant souligné, au réseau français de la télévision d'Etat, qu'il ne fallait pas se méprendre sur ce manque apparent de ferveur, que les Canadiens français étaient aussi emballés que quiconque face à la Confédération, mais qu'ils manifestaient leur joie « d'une façon intérieure ». Naïf que j'étais d'avoir toujours cru que les Français, d'origine latine, étaient plus exubérants que les flegmatiques Anglo-Saxons ! Le premier ministre du pays, lui, put à peine contenir son indignation lorsque les journaux rapportèrent que les Québécois n'avaient pas déployé autant d'entrain dans leurs réjouissances nocturnes du 31 décembre que le reste du Canada. M. Pearson faisait évidemment allusion aux célébrations officielles (car la presse ne s'arrête pas, ni au Québec ni ailleurs, aux « cérémonies » individuelles qui saluent l'aube d'une nouvelle année, et personne ne regrette, que je sache, ce manque de publicité !). Toujours selon le premier ministre, ces nouvelles étaient erronées car il croyait, lui, que le Québec célébrait le centenaire de la Confédération « d'une façon particulière ». Je suis, pour cette fois, entièrement d'accord : le Québec célèbre d'une façon bien particulière, en empochant l'argent d'Ottawa, en construisant centres civiques et culturels, mais en ne soufflant mot du centenaire commémoré. Que voulez-vous ? On a toujours dit que le Québec n'était pas une province comme les autres.

Que les Canadiens anglophones ne se fassent pas d'illusions : la population française du Québec n'a jamais eu l'intention de s'associer au reste du pays pour célébrer le centenaire de la Confédération. C'est un euphémisme que le modéré Claude Ryan a employé en écrivant que « few French-Canadian leaders share the enthusiasm of their English-speaking counterparts as the approaching centenary of Confederation[2] ». Le gouvernement de la belle province a d'ailleurs symbolisé sa réaction, en quelque sorte, dans l'affaire des plaques d'immatriculation d'automobiles de 1967. L'administration Lesage, comme vous le savez, avait maintenu sa décision de conserver les deux inscriptions « Expo – 1967 » et « 1867 – Confédération – 1967 », la première pour les plaques allant à l'avant, la seconde pour les plaques allant à l'arrière des véhicules. L'Union Nationale a gardé les plaques mais en laissant entendre que l'une des inscriptions (on devine laquelle !) ne lui plaisait pas. Un ministre a même déclaré que, sur sa propre voiture, il ajouterait peut-être le slogan « Confédération – Connais

2/Claude Ryan, « The Enigma of French Canada », *Saturday Night*, vol. 82 (janvier 1967), 21.

pas ». Le moment venu, en janvier 1967, de rappeler aux automobilistes qu'il fallait procéder au changement annuel, on a trouvé un moyen subtil d'éviter la simple mention du mot abhorré ; dans les annonces des journaux, la plaque « Expo – 1967 » était photographiée de façon à cacher entièrement à la vue de la population québécoise l'exécrable mot inscrit sur l'autre plaque. Tempête dans un verre d'eau ou signe des temps, que l'on juge !

N'empêche qu'une publicité monstre – pas toujours raffinée – et que des sommes d'argent royalement dépensées n'ont pas suscité l'enthousiasme ni même éveillé l'intérêt des francophones québécois face à ce centenaire. Ceci me rappelle le mot d'Albert Lévesque en apprenant que le gouvernement canadien dépenserait $250,000 en 1927 pour fêter les noces de diamant de cette même Confédération.

Les noces de diamant auxquelles le gouvernement canadien convie son peuple, ressemblent fort à ces noces de diamant familiales où les jubilaires, privés d'une postérité reconnaissante, seraient contraints d'organiser eux-mêmes leur fêtes, au risque d'être seuls à célébrer[3].

Mon propos n'est cependant pas, aujourd'hui, d'attaquer ou d'analyser cette constitution de 1867, décrite récemment comme un « antiquated piece of mid-Victorian plumbing ». Je voudrais plutôt grouper sous deux chefs mes remarques. La population des provinces maritimes et du Canada-Uni voulait-elle vraiment du système fédéral échafaudé par les politiciens, en 1864–67 ? Et, présentement, quels sont les arguments traditionnels de la population francophone du Québec contre l'Acte de l'Amérique du nord britannique ?

Il n'est pas aisé de connaître les sentiments véritables d'une population sur une question constitutionnelle. A cent ans de distance, c'est chose impossible dans le cas de l'acceptation par le peuple de l'Acte de l'Amérique du nord britannique. Aucun référendum, aucune consultation électorale ne nous venant en aide, il faut recourir au contexte de l'époque et aux faits que l'histoire a enregistrés.

Le Haut-Canada (nous délaissons les désignations Est et Ouest, peu usitées en français) était entièrement favorable au système de gouvernement proposé qui instaurerait, enfin, la représentation proportionnelle et qui le dégagerait, enfin, de l'emprise du Bas-Canada. George Brown évoque cette approbation en termes emphatiques :

J'ose affirmer... qu'aucun projet d'une égale importance qui ait jamais été soumis au monde, n'a été reçu avec de plus grands éloges, avec une approbation

---

3/Albert Levesque, « La Confédération et la jeunesse canadienne-française », dans *L'Action française*, XVII, No 5 (mai-juin 1927), 403.

plus universelle, que la mesure que nous avons maintenant l'honneur de soumettre à l'acceptation du parlement canadien[4].

Vous remarquez l'emploi des mots « monde » et « universelle » : dans l'esprit de Brown ils ne peuvent signifier autre chose que Haut-Canada. Il apparut bientôt, en effet, qu' « approbation... universelle » n'incluait pas tout le Bas-Canada. Dès le 7 novembre 1864, Antoine-Aimé Dorion, le chef des réformistes délibérément écartés des conférences de Charlottetown et de Québec, déclara que son parti s'opposait au projet. L'argument avait peu de poids aux yeux des artisans des résolutions de Québec qui avaient décidé que l'année 1865 verrait la mise en œuvre de « leur » constitution. Le gouverneur-général prédisait dès lors que les gouvernements provinciaux procéderaient avec tellement de diligence que le parlement britannique pourrait étudier le projet de fédération à sa prochaine session. Cette prédiction de Lord Monck est du 11 novembre 1864[5].

Ce caractère d'urgence ne plaisait pas aux Rouges. Véritables démocrates, ils proclamaient que « lorsqu'il ne s'agit de rien moins que de refaire la constitution, de poser de nouvelles bases de l'édifice politique, le peuple dont l'intérêt et la postérité sont affectés doit être consulté[6] ». Selon eux, cette innovation était due « aux exigences des partis, et non pas à un désir spontané et général du peuple de faire des changements radicaux dans ses institutions ou dans ses relations politiques[7] ». Ils affirmaient même que la population bas-canadienne – lui eût-on demandé son avis – aurait accordé la représentation proportionnelle au Haut-Canada mais aurait refusé le projet de Confédération[8]. Avant l'introduction de l'Acte d'Union, le gouvernement impérial avait consulté les gens qui devraient vivre sous ce nouveau régime et il semble aux réformistes de 1865 « que le peuple doive être traité avec moins de respect, moins d'égards par ses propres mandataires qu'il ne l'a été par le parlement anglais en 1840[9] ». Ils soulignent enfin que les assemblées tenues dans le Bas-Canada démontrent, sinon l'hostilité *vis-à-vis* des résolutions de Québec, du moins un désir net d'être renseigné à fond sur la teneur et les implications d'un projet aussi important[10]. En un mot, les Rouges désirent simplement que le projet de Confédération soit soumis à l'assentiment populaire. Ils

4/*Débats parlementaires sur la question de la Confédération des provinces de l'Amérique britannique du Nord* (Québec 1865), 83.
5/Donald Creighton, *The Road to Confederation* (Toronto 1964), 187.
6/Antoine- Aimé Dorion, « Manifeste à ses électeurs d'Hochelaga », cité par J. C. Bonenfant, *Les Canadiens français et la naissance de la Confédération.* Brochure No 21 de la Société historique du Canada (Ottawa 1966), 5.
7/*Ibid.*, 10.
8/*Débats parlementaires*, Luc Letellier de St. Just, 9.
9/*Ibid.*, A. A. Dorion, 273.
10/*Ibid.*, L. A. Oliver, 137.

savaient sans doute, comme devait plus tard l'écrire Lord Bryce, que l'espérance « is one of the cardinal virtues and Democracy will never perish till after Hope has expired », parce qu'ils ne cessèrent de réclamer que l'on consultât la population. Les Rouges possédaient au moins une vertu cardinale !

Mais les promoteurs du projet n'étaient pas férus de principes démocratiques. Cartier, le patriote de 1837 qui avait pris les armes pour la défense des libertés politiques, évoqua les loyaux chefs canadiens-français de 1778 qui ne s'étaient pas laissés leurrer par les principes républicains des Américains ; ces chefs loyaux « savaient qu'au fond de la démocratie est l'abîme[11] ». Ecoutons maintenant John A. Macdonald.

Submission of the complicated details to the country is an obvious absurdity... If by petitions or public meetings parliament is satisfied that the country does not want the measure, they will refuse to adopt it. If on the other hand, parliament sees that the country is in favour of the federation, there is no use in an appeal to it[12].

Deux mois plus tard, en présentant les fameuses résolutions de Québec à l'Assemblée, il déclara:

Si cette mesure reçoit l'approbation de la chambre, il n'y aura pas de nécessité de la soumettre au peuple. [Notons, en passant, que la coalition de juin 1864 assurait nécessairement une majorité parlementaire favorable à la Confédération.] D'un autre côté, si la mesure est repoussée, il appartiendra au gouvernement de juger s'il doit y avoir un appel au peuple ou non[13].

On peut comprendre le peu d'empressement des conservateurs Cartier et Macdonald devant les exigences démocratiques, mais l'attitude des réformistes du Haut-Canada apparaît plus étrange. Pour le *Globe*, parler de consultation du peuple équivaut à parler de plébiscite ; or, un plébiscite n'est autre chose « qu'une épouvantable hérésie républicaine... qui violerait tous les principes du gouvernement parlementaire[14] ». Quant à Fergusson Blair, il exécute des prouesses verbales pour éluder la question.

L'on a beaucoup parlé de soumettre le projet aux électeurs, mais ce serait évidemment causer un délai que rien ne saurait compenser ; cependant, si plus tard il s'opère dans le public un mouvement important, si de nombreuses pétitions sont signées en faveur d'un appel au peuple, alors la question se présenterait sous un aspect différent ; ou bien si la majorité se prononçant pour le

11/*Ibid.*, G. E. Cartier, 58.
12/John A. Macdonald à Amsden, 1er décembre 1864. Cité par Creighton, *The Road to Confederation*, 189s.
13/*Débats parlementaires*, John A. Macdonald, 17.
14/Toronto *Globe*, 5 novembre 1864. Cité par Creighton, *The Road to Confederation*, 189–90.

projet dans l'autre branche de la législature (l'Assemblée Législative), était très faible, ce serait à vrai dire une raison suffisante pour le soumettre au pays[15].

Le gouvernement ne put expliquer, en vérité, son refus d'accéder au désir de l'opposition et l'un de ses partisans accueillit fraîchement la proposition d'Antoine-Aimé Dorion de tenir des élections où le peuple accepterait ou rejetterait les résolutions de Québec.

Tous les ans, cet honorable monsieur [Dorion] se plaint que notre loi d'élection est défectueuse, que l'argent l'emporte sur le mérite dans nos luttes électorales. Comment peut-il donc demander qu'une question aussi importante que celle de l'union des provinces soit soumise à l'épreuve du vote populaire sans autres espérances que d'entraîner le pays dans le trouble et dans une dépense de quelques centaines de mille piastres[16].

Cet étalage de logique laisse supposer ce que l'on pense des pétitions contre le projet de confédération signées par nombre de citoyens du Bas-Canada. On les écarte, simplement, en prétendant qu'elles ont été endossées par des femmes et des enfants et qu'elles ne revêtent donc aucune signification[17]. Ou, on affecte de ne pas les juger sérieuses, ce qui évite une réponse directe.

Mais on sait ce que valent ces pétitions ; – on sait ce que sont les rouges. Et l'on sait qu'ils signeront des pétitions partout et toujours, pourvu que ce soit contre le gouvernement ou sa politique. L'opposition est aujourd'hui comme ces enfants à qui l'on refuse un jouet et qui pleurent pour l'avoir, mais qui ensuite le refusent à leur tour si on veut le leur donner[18].

En fait, le gouvernement ne trouva que deux arguments pour justifier son attitude. Tout d'abord, il y a eu des élections sur cette question, « des élections générales et spéciales, depuis 1858 » dit Cartier[19] ; cinquante circonscriptions électorales ont eu à se prononcer sur le projet de confédération « et quatre candidats seulement se sont hasardés à y faire de l'opposition », proclama George Brown[20]. Un examen plus attentif, cependant, démontre que nulle élection générale n'a présenté la confédération comme le régime qui remplacerait l'Acte d'Union. Quant aux élections partielles dont parle propriétaire du *Globe*, elles n'ont pas de signification réelle après l'entente de juin 1864 qui stipulait que les comtés détenus par les libéraux et les conservateurs, respectivement, ne devaient pas changer d'allégeance politique pendant le temps que durerait la mise en œuvre du

15/*Débats parlementaires*, A. J. Fergusson Blair, 12.
16/*Ibid.*, J. H. Bellerose, 481.
17/Creighton, *The Road to Confederation*, 256.
18/*Débats parlementaires*, J. Dufresne, 558s.
19/*Ibid.*, G. E. Cartier, 53.
20/*Ibid.*, G. Brown, 83.

projet de confédération[21]. En guise de second argument, le gouvernement prétendit qu'il considérerait les prochaines élections générales comme « l'approbation ou la condamnation de notre initiative[22] ». Nous savons, évidemment, que le Québec approuva en 1867 et l'Acte de l'Amérique du nord britannique et le gouvernement qui l'avait fait adopter. Mais il ne faut pas oublier qu'à ce moment l'episcopat québécois avait approuvé publiquement la loi votée par le parlement britannique ; il ne faut pas oublier, non plus, que les Canadiens français devaient dorénavant s'accomoder de ce nouveau régime ; pas plus qu'il ne faut oublier que le parti ministériel fit campagne contre les libéraux en disant que ces derniers ne pouvaient administrer le pays au moyen d'un système gouvernemental auquel ils ne croyaient pas et auquel ils s'étaient farouchement opposés.

Il semble assez évident que le gouvernement ne voulait pas consulter la population sur son projet de confédération. Le procédé est étrange ; et ce qui l'est encore plus, c'est la fièvre témoignée pour faire approuver les résolutions de Québec par le parlement du Canada-Uni, sans que ces résolutions puissent être amendées d'une quelconque façon. Dès l'ouverture du débat, le 3 février 1865, Macdonald établit clairement la position du gouvernement.

Si le projet ne passe pas tel que présenté, il faudra, une fois les changements introduits, recommencer la conférence, et je crois que cette occasion manquée, nous n'en aurons pas d'autre dans le cours de ce siècle[23].

La discussion battait son plein, au début de mars, quand l'on apprit que l'électorat du Nouveau-Brunswick avait rejeté sans équivoque les résolutions de Québec. L'on vit alors un John A. Macdonald encore plus désireux de faire adopter derechef le projet de confédération.

Aussi, puis-je déclarer que, malgré le résultat de ces élections, le gouvernement canadien n'est nullement disposé à modifier sa politique en ce qui regarde le projet. Le gouvernement désire, au contraire, qu'il soit bien entendu, qu'au lieu de modifier son action il est déterminé à agir plus que jamais avec énergie et promptitude[24].

Energie et promptitude assurément ! Macdonald continue :

Non seulement nous ressentons que l'obligation de presser l'adoption de la législature existe toujours, nous ressentons qu'il importe d'avantage [sic] de la remplir. Voilà pourquoi, et sans plus tarder, le gouvernement demande que la chambre, tout en observant les procédures parlementaires usuelles, de décider le plus tôt possible si elle approuve ou non ce projet[25]. [sic]

21/Toronto Globe, 29 septembre 1865. Cité par Creighton, The Road to Confederation, 312.
22/Débats parlementaires, J. Cauchon, 589.
23/Débats parlementaires, John A. Macdonald, 16.
24/Ibid., 652s.   25/Ibid.

Pour minimiser leur attitude cavalière vis-à-vis des droits d'expression du peuple, les conservateurs bas-canadiens se rangèrent derrière le support que leur accordait le clergé.

On a fait allusion à l'opinion du clergé. Eh bien ! Je dirai que l'opinion du clergé est favorable à la confédération... Nous avons tous les hommes modérés, tous les hommes respectables et intelligents, y compris les membres du clergé, qui sont favorables à la confédération[26].

Cartier, qui présentait ainsi comme acquis l'appui du clergé, savait fort bien que ce dernier n'aurait pu collaborer avec les rouges, hostiles à la confédération mais anticléricaux par tradition. Il reste qu'aucune étude n'a pu encore prouver que le haut-clergé, seulement, était favorable au nouveau régime. Le contraire serait peut-être plus près de la vérité. Pour une fois, le haut-clergé observa un silence total (j'allais dire religieux !) et ne se prononça en faveur de la confédération – en y mettant parfois des réticences – qu'après son adoption par le parlement britannique. Ici encore, l'argument avancé par le gouvernement m'apparaît peu valable.

Les remarques qui précèdent indiquent assez clairement – du moins, je l'espère – que l'on a fait certains accrocs aux procédés normaux de la démocratie en 1864 et en 1865. J'aurais d'ailleurs pu ajouter les fameuses résolutions Galt qui ne furent pas présentées à l'Assemblée législative qui les aurait rejetées mais qui furent néanmoins insérées dans la nouvelle constitution. On peut rétorquer que les résolutions de Québec ont facilement reçu l'approbation des députés, mais il ne faudrait pas oublier que les représentants canadiens-français, soumis à la férule de Cartier, n'ont donné qu'une majorité de quatre voix au projet de confédération. On s'explique alors pourquoi le gouvernement ne s'empressait pas de consulter la population bas-canadienne : il craignait un refus. Clifford Sifton, qui s'y connaissait en questions électorales, écrit avec candeur qu'à l'époque de la Confédération « the most prudent method of ascertaining the people's wishes was not followed[27] ». Il ne pouvait faire allusion qu'au Canada-Uni puisque, dans les Maritimes, la voix du peuple se fit entendre.

A Terre-Neuve, le problème fut vite réglé : la force de l'opinion publique fit rejeter l'idée de Confédération. Le même phénomène se produisit à l'Ile du Prince-Edouard. Le premier ministre J. H. Gray supportait les résolutions de Québec. Il demanda, assez poétiquement il faut l'avouer, à ses députés : « Vous rangerez-vous, par vos voix, au nombre de ceux qui se satisfont de végéter comme des loirs[28] ? » L'état végétatif n'a pas semblé

26/*Ibid.*, G. E. Cartier, 60.
27/Sir Clifford Sifton, « Some Canadian Constitutional Problems », *Canadian Historical Review*, III, No 1 (mars 1922), 3.
28/Creighton, *The Road to Confederation*, 198.

repoussant aux représentants de cette tranquille population : Gray dut démissionner et c'est en 1873 seulement que l'Ile du Prince-Edouard s'unit au Canada.

Comme chacun sait, le Nouveau-Brunswick est entré dans la Confédération dès 1867. Il n'est peut-être pas superflu, cependant, de résumer les événements tumultueux qui ont précédé cette entrée. Le gouvernement Tilley, favorable à la Confédération, dut se présenter devant l'électorat à l'expiration de son mandat, et subit la défaite. La nouvelle administration, dirigée par Smith et Wilmot, avait vertement dénoncé le projet élaboré à la conférence de Québec. Mais, à une élection partielle dans le comté de York, un ancien premier ministre, Fisher, porta l'étendard fédératif ; Tilley prévint John A. Macdonald que huit à dix mille dollars assureraient la victoire de Fisher[29]. L'argent canadien, puis la crainte savamment entretenue des Féniens, firent élire Fisher et, du même coup, minèrent le prestige du gouvernement Smith-Wilmot. Ce n'était pas suffisant aux yeux du gouverneur-général, Gordon, qui voulait la tête d'Albert Smith pour le plus grand bien de la Confédération. Or, à ce moment précis, le juge-en-chef Parker agonisait. Gordon entrevit la solution de son problème et, le 17 novembre 1865, il persuada Smith d'accepter la position de Parker. Mais ce dernier, de façon peu élégante, ne se soumit pas au désir autocratique de Gordon et ne rendit l'âme que le 28 novembre. Dans l'intervalle, Smith avait pu se ressaisir et consulter ses collègues : il refusa d'être juge-en-chef. Gordon fut abasourdi, mais pas pour longtemps, car il était maintenant décidé d'imposer lui-même la Confédération à ces rustres coloniaux du Nouveau-Brunswick. Fort de cette décision, il dépêcha triomphalement à son secrétaire d'Etat : « I am convinced I can make (or buy) a union majority in the legislature[30]. » Après mainte péripétie, le 4 avril 1866, Gordon télégraphiait à Lord Monck que « son » gouvernement venait de démissionner. Une nouvelle élection, en juin 1866, règlerait le sort de la Confédération au Nouveau-Brunswick.

Cette fois, il ne fallait pas que se répète la malencontreuse expérience de l'hiver 1865 : le parti fédéraliste devait l'emporter à tout prix. « A tout prix », remarquons-le, n'est pas employé au figuré. Tilley quémanda presque l'assistance pécuniaire du Canada-Uni pour aider son parti favorable à la Confédération à remporter l'élection et il mentionne « $40,000 to $50,000 to do the work[31] ». Les Canadiens s'impressèrent de satisfaire les vœux de Tilley et, par le fait même, d'encourager les bonnes tactiques

29/S. L. Tilley à Macdonald, 13 septembre 1865, dans Creighton, *ibid.*, 319
30/Gordon à Cardwell, 20 novembre 1865, cité par Creighton, *ibid.*, 334.
31/Tilley à Macdonald, 17 avril 1866. Cité par Chester Martin « British Policy in Canadian Confederation », *Canadian Historical Review*, XIII, No 1 (mars 1932), 12.

démocratiques au Nouveau-Brunswick[32]. Le procédé n'est-il pas encore le moyen le plus sûr d'assurer le triomphe des idéaux patriotiques et parlementaires ? La menace fénienne fut aussi utilisée à bon escient pour influencer les loyaux électeurs ; certains devinrent si inquiets qu'au moment de proclamer, par leur vote, leur choix de l'un ou l'autre candidat, ils ne purent que dire : « Je vote pour la Reine[33]. » L'histoire ne rapporte pas si ces votes furent inscrits au compte du candidat fédéraliste ou au compte de son adversaire, mais il est permis de supposer ! Quoi qu'il en soit, l'argent canadien vint au secours des procédés démocratiques usuels pour faire élire le parti de Tilley et, partant, pour faire entrer le Nouveau-Brunswick dans la Confédération canadienne.

La pratique utilisée au Nouveau-Brunswick ne fut cependant pas répétée en Nouvelle-Ecosse. Et ceci pour une bien simple raison : le gouvernement de Charles Tupper, acquis à l'idée fédérale, pouvait attendre jusqu'à mai 1867 pour déclencher des élections. Le péril d'une consultation populaire n'était donc pas imminent mais n'empêche que, d'ici là, le parlement devait se réunir. Or, à l'automne de 1864, il s'avérait impensable de présenter les résolutions de Québec à l'approbation des députés. Tout d'abord, le gouverneur MacDonnell y était opposé. « I shall certainly not allow the question to be carried through the existing legislature which was elected without reference to the question », écrivait-il[34]. De plus, Tupper se rendait compte que l'opinion générale, dans sa province, était hostile au projet de Confédération, projet qui pourrait peut-être devenir réalité avec le support adroit du gouvernement britannique[35].

Il fallait nécessairement tenir une session au cours de l'hiver 1865. Telles étaient les craintes de Tupper qu'il déclara que le projet de Confédération n'était pas une mesure qui liait son gouvernement ; et, d'ailleurs, le projet ne fut même pas présenté à la députation. Dans une lettre à Macdonald il avoua avoir dû employer toute son « ingénuité » pour empêcher que l'on votât une motion hostile à la Confédération[36]. Et il dut se contenter, pour opérer une diversion, de proposer le vieux plan d'union des provinces de l'Atlantique « since for a time at least, the federal union of all British America has become impracticable[37]. » A la session de 1866,

32/Donald Creighton, *John A. Macdonald, The Young Politician* (Toronto 1952), 434s; aussi, G. E. Wilson, « New Brunswick's Entrance into Confederation », *Canadian Historical Review*, IX, No 1 (mars 1928), 235.
33/Creighton, *The Road to Confederation*, 374.
34/MacDonnell à Gordon, 10 décembre 1864. Cité par Creighton, *The Young Politician*, 209.
35/Creighton, *ibid.*
36/Tupper à Macdonald, 9 avril 1865. Cité par Creighton, *ibid.*, 265. 265.
37/Creighton, *ibid.*, 267.

les augures sont encore plus sombres, la formidable opposition de Joseph Howe semble devoir faire échouer le projet d'union fédérale[38]. Tupper doit déclarer que son gouvernement n'a aucune politique relative à ce projet, mais à Macdonald il dévoile son plan. « We *must* obtain action during the present session of the imperial Parliament or all may be lost[39]. » Il avait raison. Le projet de Confédération qui liait l'avenir de la Nouvelle-Ecosse ne fut pas soumis au parlement de cette colonie qui l'aurait assurément rejeté. C'est à Londres et non à Halifax que, sans mandat du peuple et sans approbation de ses représentants, le gouvernement Tupper entra la Nouvelle-Ecosse dans la Confédération. Quand ce gouvernement dut enfin se présenter devant l'électorat pour faire ratifier sa conduite, un seul (sur dix-neuf) de ses candidats fut élu.

L'on peut résumer brièvement ce qui précède de la façon suivante ; l'Acte de l'Amérique du nord britannique ne fut pas soumis à l'approbation de la population du Bas-Canada parce que ses avocats craignaient une réaction négative ; d'autre part, une seule des quatre législatures des Maritimes (le Conseil législatif du Nouveau-Brunswick) entérina les résolutions de Québec, et encore, cet assentiment porte-t-il fortement l'empreinte du gouverneur Gordon. Ceci revient à dire que les Pères de la Confédération – ceux du Canada-Uni, au moins – saturés des rivalités partisanes et de l'impasse parlementaire, furent si soulagés et si heureux d'avoir trouvé une solution à leurs maux qu'ils employèrent tous les moyens pour imposer à la population cette solution qu'eux, ils avaient trouvée. Ou encore que des hommes politiques ont fait fi de l'opinion publique pour obtenir un système gouvernemental qu'eux, ils jugeaient désirable. Nous avons là la cause de cette atmosphère de conspiration qui entoure parfois les tractations et les procédures qui ont conduit à l'adoption de l'Acte de l'Amérique du nord britannique.

Je ne prétends pas que les événements subséquents n'ont pas donné raison aux Pères de la Confédération ; car, en définitive, la constitution élaborée de 1864 à 1867 a généralement donné satisfaction aux provinces canadiennes. Il y a cependant une exception à cette règle : cette exception est celle de la province – maintenant appelée état – qui refuse systématiquement cette année de s'associer à ses consœurs dans les célébrations qui marquent le centenaire de la Confédération canadienne. Cette province, d'ailleurs, semble entretenir avec une évidente complaisance les griefs qu'elle nourrit contre le régime fédératif instauré en 1867 et dont elle s'était assez bien accomodé jusqu'en 1885.

38/*Ibid.*, 357.
39/Tupper à Macdonald, 17 juin 1866. Cité par Creighton, *The Young Politician*, 390s.

Loin de ma pensée l'intention d'énumérer tous ces griefs que les francophones québécois entretiennent contre notre système fédéral. Dès 1867
ils ont vu – il serait plus juste de dire qu'ils ont voulu voir – dans la nouvelle
constitution une alliance entre deux partenaires ethniques : « Avec la
confédération, il n'y aura pas de domination d'une race sur l'autre, et si
une section voulait commettre une injustice envers une autre section,
toutes les autres s'uniraient ensemble et l'en empêcheraient[40]. » C'est
Langevin qui professe cet optimisme. Mais la grande victoire pour les
Canadiens français de l'époque c'est la souveraineté provinciale du Québec et la reprise d'un contrôle assez complet de l'existence des francophones comme entité ethnique distincte. La confusion va plus tard surgir
du fait que les hommes politiques québécois perdront de vue la sécurité
qu'ils possèdent sur le plan provincial pour essayer d'établir, sur le plan
fédéral, une alliance à part égale entre les deux groupes ethniques aux
niveaux administratif et gouvernemental, alliance qui n'était même pas
entrevue en 1867. Il ne faut pas s'illusionner : l'Acte de l'Amérique du
nord britannique n'a pas accordé, aux francophones, des droits égaux à
ceux de la majorité en dehors du Québec, du parlement fédéral et des
tribunaux de juridiction fédérale. C'est se berner que d'écouter Macdonald
dire que « nous avons maintenant une Constitution qui fait à tous les sujets
britanniques une situation d'absolue égalité, qui leur garantit les mêmes
droits en matière de langue, de religion, de propriété ou de droits per-
sonnels[41] ».

Si le texte de notre constitution ne peut, en toute vérité, permettre de
conclure à l'alliance à part égale des deux groupes ethniques, les Canadiens
français, eux, ont fait découler cette égalité de « l'esprit de la Confédération ». On retrouve cette idée chez les nationalistes de Bourassa au début
du siècle et, surtout, on la rencontre établie en principe dans *l'Action
française*.

L'idée dominante dans la Constitution de 1867 c'est celle d'un contrat, d'un
traité entre deux races, la française et l'anglaise, deux communautés religieuses,
l'une catholique, l'autre protestante. La base de cette union fut l'égalité parfaite
de traitement entre les deux groupes ethniques consentant à signer cette
convention politique[42].

A cette formule des deux nations, l'on ajoute une dimension nouvelle à la
loi de 1867 : « Consacrer la *dualité nationale du peuple canadien dans
l'union politique d'un seul Etat*, voilà toute la signification morale de l'Acte

40/*Débats parlementaires*, Hector L. Langevin, 374.
41/A la Chambre des Communes en 1890. Cité par Antonio Perrault, « Déceptions
et griefs », *L'Action française*, XVII, No 5 (mai-juin 1927), 388.
42/*Ibid.*, 387.

fédératif de 1867[43]. » On peut alors, avec une abondante facilité, relever les si nombreux cas où la majorité anglo-saxonne a rompu « le pacte d'honneur » conclu avec les Canadiens français en 1867. Mais, depuis le début des années 1930, les courants d'idées ont évolué au pays du Québec. A l'heure actuelle on peut déceler parmi les théories plus ou moins séparatistes, parmi les politiques diverses et parfois contradictoires que l'on préconise, on peut déceler un dénominateur commun : c'est le mécontentement général des francophones à l'endroit de cette constitution telle que conçue il y a un siècle et telle qu'appliquée maintenant. La plupart désirent déchirer ce document ou, à tout le moins, le modifier de façon à le rendre méconnaissable. On pourrait presque parodier ce qu'Israël Tarte disait, d'une autre problème cependant, en 1893 : « Nous ne demandons pas plus, mais nous ne nous contenterons pas de moins. » Ce sentiment général est un fait tangible, qu'on le veuille ou non. On peut mettre en doute le bien-fondé de cette demande de changement constitutionnel ; on peut en attaquer les motifs, la nécessité ou l'utilité. Personne ne peut, par contre, nier l'existence de ce vœu général de changement chez les francophones du Québec. Que l'Acte de l'Amérique du nord britannique soit une loi, un contrat entre deux cultures, une entente entre des provinces : cela n'importe plus dans les discussions présentes. L'une des composantes de l'union de 1867 – que ce soit la province de Québec, la culture ou la race françaises – estime avoir reçu un traitement injuste et manifeste à voix très haute son mécontentement. Sa voix, cette fois-ci, devra être entendue.

Un reproche traditionnel que l'on adresse à la Confédération demeure le traitement réservé aux minorités françaises depuis 1867. On a beau jeu d'énumérer les cas du Nouveau-Brunswick en 1871, du Manitoba en 1890, de l'Ontario en 1912 où l'on a aboli, en pratique, l'enseignement du français dans les écoles publiques. Je ne prétends pas que la Confédération elle-même ait été responsable directement de ces actions. Les hommes politiques – en certains cas ceux que le Québec envoyait à Ottawa – doivent recevoir une bonne part de blâme pour avoir laissé autant de fanatisme l'emporter sur la justice. Mais la constatation que je veux dégager est la suivante : sous le régime fédératif, les groupes français en dehors du Québec ont perdu la plupart de leurs droits et ce qu'ils ont pu en conserver fait figure de privilèges ou de faveurs ; à tel point que ces minorités s'assimilent rapidement avec anglophones et que les îlots clairsemés qui sont demeurés français le doivent à leur opiniâtreté et à leurs sacrifices. J'admets que les préjugés qui ont causé cette situation appartiennent heureusement au passé. Mais que l'on admette avec moi que ces injustices peuvent

---

43/Levesque, « La Confédération et la jeunesse canadienne-française », 408 (les soulignés sont de l'auteur).

expliquer l'hostilité latente qui prévaut au Québec contre un régime politique qui a permis – même de façon légale – qu'un tel état de choses se développe et puis subsiste. La bonne volonté (car c'est de la bonne volonté) manifestée aujourd'hui par les gouvernements de l'Ontario et du Manitoba pour corriger les erreurs du passé ne pourra jamais effacer ce premier grief que l'on fait à la Confédération.

En second lieu, les Canadiens français estiment qu'ils n'ont jamais eu au sein du gouvernement d'Ottawa et de la fonction publique fédérale l'influence que leur nombre justifie et que leur langue n'a jamais été l'égale de l'anglaise dans l'administration. Ce reproche, à mon sens, est valable. Toutefois, je m'inscris en faux contre le principe courant de revendication qui voudrait qu'un individu sur trois, dans les organismes de ressort fédéral, soit francophone. Le problème en est un de compétence et non de proportion mathématique. Certaines constatations sommaires laissent cependant songer. Depuis 1867, environ 20 pour cent des portefeuilles dans les cabinets fédéraux ont été détenus par des francophones, la proportion étant plus élevée dans un ministère libéral que dans un ministère conservateur. Le pourcentage, en toute décence, pourrait être plus élevé. Mais ce qui frappe, c'est que les portefeuilles d'importance-clef échappent systématiquement aux francophones. Ceux des finances, du commerce, de l'agriculture et de la défense depuis le XIXe siècle, sont invariablement détenus par des anglophones. Faut-il conclure qu'au cours de tout un siècle il ne s'est jamais rencontré un Canadien d'expression française assez compétent pour devenir ministre des finances ou ministre du commerce ? Que, depuis 1896, aucun francophone n'avait les qualifications requises pour être titulaire des ministères de la défense ou de l'agriculture ? La même chose se reproduit dans la fonction publique : les postes de commande, comme greffier du Conseil privé ou sous-ministre des finances, ou les présidences des grandes corporations de la Couronne, n'échoient pas à des francophones. Serait-on encore en face d'un manque systématique de compétence ? De plus, le nombre de francophones aux échelons supérieurs du fonctionnarisme est remarquablement peu élevé. En 1961, sur 163 fonctionnaires qui gagnaient plus de $14,000, six étaient de langue française, soit 4 pour cent ; la proportion est montée à 11 pour cent en 1967. Parmi ces haut fonctionnaires qui constituent le 4 pour cent ou le 11 pour cent que je viens de mentionner, il serait intéressant d'apprendre combien viennent de la province de Québec et combien sont de culture authentiquement française. Je ne parle pas de complot ou de machination pour exclure les francophones des postes de commande au sein du gouvernement ou de la fonction publique : mais l'on peut néanmoins trouver étrange l'incapacité historique des Canadiens français à accéder à des fonctions d'importance stratégique tout en demeurant authentiquement fidèles à leur culture. Ici encore, on ne peut imputer à la Confédération cet état de choses ; mais n'empêche qu'on a longtemps déploré cette inégalité de traitement, source de revendication constante pour obtenir plus d'influence, et qu'on a attribué cet état de choses au système fédéral. J'ai sciemment, ici, employé le passé parce que, dans le contexte actuel, on se moque royalement de cette inégalité. Tout francophone québécois qui va à Ottawa perd son influence – de façon assez automatique – dans sa province natale et reçoit l'étiquette de « vendu ».

L'hostilité qu'on a manifestée à l'endroit des Canadiens français, à certains moments de notre histoire, n'a pas été sans créer une tension dont on peut malaisément effacer les vestiges du revers de la main. L'exécution de Riel, la loi indemnisant les Jésuites, la participation mitigée des Canadiens français aux deux conflits mondiaux, ont suscité chez certains anglophones canadiens des explosions de mépris assez évident. Que le Québec chahute la reine d'Angleterre et ouvre les bras au président de la République française : et on entend encore parler de refaire la guerre de la conquête ! La correspondance politique des premiers ministres canadiens, d'autre part, est remplie de requêtes d'associations ou de protestations individuelles contre toute mesure qui tient le moindrement compte des particularités culturelles du Canada. La simple instauration du bilinguisme sur les mandats de poste du réseau ferroviaire d'Etat, dans les années 1930, amena les habitants de Régina à aller systématiquement acheter leurs mandats aux bureaux du Pacifique Canadien où – Dieu merci ! l'on ne pourrait voir aucune inscription française[44]. Dans les années 1940, on rapporte que le chef intérimaire du parti conservateur refusait même de lire la traduction des articles originairement écrits en français : un écrit important aurait d'abord été rédigé en anglais, maintenait-il[45]. La conscience d'une certaine supériorité raciale jointe à une arrogance assez intempestive trop souvent manifestée par les Anglo-Saxons canadiens ont conduit les francophones à douter de l'estime que leur prodiguaient verbalement leurs « partenaires de 1867 ». Cet état de choses – est-il nécessaire de le préciser ? – a été créé par une poignée d'individus, mais la logique humaine démontre malheureusement que l'on conclue souvent du particulier au général. Ces tensions ethniques laissent des cicatrices : elles n'ont pas été causées par la Confédération, mais la co-existence au sein d'un régime fédéral y a contribué. Aujourd'hui, pour

44/F. W. Turnbull à R. B. Bennett, 25 août 1933. *Papiers R. B. Bennett*, vol. 493, M-154.
45/John R. Williams, *The Conservative Party of Canada: 1920–1949* (Durham, N.C. 1945), 65, n. 87.

les Canadiens français, l'antagonisme latent entre les deux groupes linguistiques qui puise ses racines dans notre passé commun se concrétise dans l'ensemble des erreurs que l'on attribue à notre système de gouvernement.

Ajoutons que ce régime isole réellement la province de Québec en temps de crise ; qu'il n'a pas fonctionné de façon à ce que le Québec puisse développer harmonieusement ses aspirations culturelles ; que le Québec doit scruter toute législation émanant d'Ottawa de crainte d'y trouver de possibles empiètements sur ses droits provinciaux ; que les francophones n'ont eu que très rarement une influence déterminante dans les affaires du pays. Ces motifs de ressentiment des francophones québécois vis-à-vis de la Confédération peuvent sembler faibles : mais ce ressentiment et cette frustration sont authentiques et doivent être acceptés comme tels. Bref, l'Acte de l'Amérique du nord britannique sert de bouc émissaire aux griefs présents et passés de la province de Québec qui, selon Laurier, n'était pas menée par des opinions, mais par des sentiments.

Pour ma part, je ne suis pas surpris outre-mesure de constater cette réaction québécoise dans une société disposée à remettre en question, depuis sept ou huit ans, tout l'héritage social et culturel « conservé si jalousement par nos ancêtres ». Par ailleurs, la société anglocanadienne a, elle aussi, considérablement évolué. Je ne retiens qu'un aspect de changement, mais je le considère important dans les relations entre les deux « nations » canadiennes : c'est le détachement progressif du Canada anglais de la Grande-Bretagne et de sa politique. Il nous semble que les professions de foi monarchistes et britanniques viennent surtout maintenant de M. Diefenbaker qui, en passant, n'est pas un Anglo-Saxon ! L'épouvantail impérialiste, source de conflits profonds pendant une bonne quarantaine d'années, est passablement effacé. L'époque des « what we have, we hold, what we don't have, we take », du « Britannia rules the waves » et du « Blood is thicker than water » est heureusement révolue. D'autre part, l'électorat plus informé que jadis n'obéit pas aussi strictement aux considérations partisanes ; le manque de fidélité à un parti rend les scrutins plus aléatoires et oblige les groupements politiques à plus de sérieux dans leurs programmes. Enfin, un régionalisme grandissant et le dynamisme de la plupart des premiers ministres provinciaux ont affaibli la structure de l'édifice fédéral, miné par les animosités personnelles et dominé trop longtemps par des politiciens suffisamment âgés pour avoir participé à la guerre 1914–18. L'instabilité gouvernementale, au niveau fédéral, et la recherche fiévreuse de solutions ont résulté de ce contexte de changement.

Dans cette atmosphère, l'unité nationale et l'identité canadienne si chères aux Canadiens anglais se sont heurtées au mur solide du Québec.

Ses habitants francophones estiment, précisément, qu'ils constituent une nation qui possède son identité propre, basée sur trois siècles d'occupation du même sol, sur une langue, un système d'éducation, un droit civil, une religion et des coutumes différents de ceux du Canada anglais. Les Québécois croient qu'ils possèdent une civilisation bien à eux. Cette identité est peut-être d'un caractère inférieur à l'insaisissable identité canadienne (« La province de Québec n'est pas une province comme les autres, elle est plus bête ! » a déjà écrit Gérard Filion), mais elle nous appartient et nous ne voulons ni la tronquer ni la troquer. Le francophone du Québec ne veut pas être englobé dans le grand tout canadien, il est québécois avant d'être canadien. Il est grand temps que, là-dessus, les Canadiens anglais perdent leurs illusions et cessent de rêver : il leur faut accepter – ou rejeter – le Canada français tel qu'il est et non pas tel que l'on voudrait qu'il soit ; et il leur faut s'accomoder de ce que le Canada français désire, à condition que ces désirs soient enfin clairement exprimés.

Jusqu'à présent il me semble que la pierre d'achoppement des relations entre anglophones et francophones canadiens est le manque de synchronisme dans leur idéologie et dans leurs réactions. Prenons le cas de Henri Bourassa. Dès 1899, il prêche le nationalisme canadien tel que le Canada français l'acceptait *alors* et tel que le Canada anglais l'accepte *aujourd'hui*. Les anglophones ont dénoncé Bourassa comme un traître et l'ont considéré comme un rebelle : certains ont même proposé, à la Chambre des Communes, qu'il soit livré aux Allemands durant la première guerre mondiale. Maintenant, le Canada anglais vit et prêche le nationalisme de Bourassa alors que les francophones québécois ont dépassé le stade de la philosophie ou du patriotisme du fondateur du *Devoir*. Ils ont abandonné ces idéaux rejetés par les « partenaires de 1867 » et ils se sont tournés vers d'autres objectifs. Ces objectifs – statut particulier, association d'Etats plus ou moins souverains – ne seront-ils acceptés qu'après une période de réflexion d'environ cinquante ans, comme ce fut le cas du nationalisme de Bourassa ? La réponse n'appartient pas au Canada français. Il me semble, quant à moi, que le Canada anglais (ou du moins le gouvernement d'Ottawa) érige l'attentisme en principe, espérant de façon implicite que la tempête cessera de souffler au Québec et que l'on pourra revenir au bon *statu quo* de jadis. Ainsi, depuis à peu près cinq ans, une forme d'unanimité prévaut chez les francophones du Québec : le minimum que chacun exige, c'est une revision complète de la constitution canadienne de façon à enlever les vestiges de colonialisme qu'elle renferme, à consacrer le principe des deux nations fondatrices, à redonner l'exercice de certains droits aux provinces, etc. Après cinq ans, dans l'atmosphère carnavalesque du Centenaire, le gouvernement canadien a réussi à nommer deux légistes anglophones – dont l'un seulement, paraît-il, est bilingue – pour étudier la question. Cette grave décision, fruit des lentes cogitations de notre (?) ministre de la justice, est tout simplement enfantine et reflète le peu de compréhension des politiciens fédéraux devant des problèmes graves qui nécessitent des solutions sérieuses. Si le Canada anglais – par son porte-parole, le gouvernement d'Ottawa – ne se met pas, pour une fois, à l'heure du Québec, s'il ne prend pas conscience de l'état d'esprit qui prévaut chez les francophones de la belle province, il se retrouvera aux prises avec une situation qui lui fera perdre plus que son rêve d'unité nationale.

4

Regionalism in French Canada

EVERETT C. HUGHES

THIS IS A TITLE which would never have occurred to me. Mason Wade gave it to me in a letter. I assumed, and he agreed, that I might interpret it as I like. It does have a certain appropriateness to what is happening in Quebec, but not in Quebec alone, for similar changes are occurring throughout a good part of the world. I refer especially to those changes which affect the balance between what is local and what is regional, and what in modern social life, economy, and politics is played out on some larger scenes – province-wide or state-wide, nation-wide, or one even larger.

Regionalism, both as a doctrine and as a method of study, has emphasized folklore, dialects, local fêtes and customs and beliefs. Usually there was an implied or explicit plea for preservation of the regional culture against the encroaching outside world. In the time prior to World War I, European movements of minority peoples tied regionalism to their claim for national independence. Were they not there first? Were not their way of speaking, their customs, their method of cultivation indigenous to the area, and somehow linked to climate and terrain? In his *Traité des nationalités* (Paris 1919) the ethnologist Arnold van Gennep noted this connection, but rejected the notion that a particular language is in some mysterious way the product of climate and geography. In North America regionalism of this kind occurred mainly in Quebec, in the Pennsylvania German country, and in the southern United States. I think study of the lore of a region will not be used so much in the future to defend a claim for survival or independence. In Quebec the claim now being made is for a better place in the new urban-industrial order: progress, not survival, is the keynote. I hope the search for lore, dialect, and local arts will not slacken. My guess is that in the future it will be pursued in the name of aesthetics and cultural enrichment.

The geographers have also had their part in developing the concept of regions. Raoul Blanchard is said to have done his geography of Quebec on foot; he reported it in volumes named after regions. Each region, as he described them, had its characteristic terrain, type of soil, watershed, and flora. Local agriculture and industry were closely related to these characteristics. Anyone who has had occasion to use those volumes will join me in testifying as to their great usefulness. How useful they would be in talking of the present and future of the economy and society in the same territory is another question. The last volume was published, *sauf erreur*, in 1938. There have been fantastic changes since then, changes which have made life much less local. Life and social institutions still vary greatly from New Quebec, the Gaspé, the North Shore below Tadoussac to Quebec, Montreal, Three Rivers, the Eastern Townships, and those few remaining truly rural counties on the south shore. But the differences are not so much those of local separate ways of living in different environments as of functions within and adaptation to the new industrial system.

Of course the first great change has been the drop, relatively and absolutely, in the agricultural labour force and population. Nathan Keyfitz has analysed this phenomenon in his "L'exode rural dans la Province de Québec, 1951–1961" (*Recherches sociographiques*, III, 303–15). In that decade alone the agricultural labour force of the province fell by 43 per cent. Thus in the year 1961 only 8 per cent of the total labour force of the province was engaged in agriculture, as against 11 per cent of the labour force of all Canada. The corresponding figure for the United States was 9 per cent, but of men under thirty-five years of age only 5 per cent were engaged in agriculture.

The figure for young men points the way to the future; it is probably the same for Quebec as for the United States. Thus a slow trend, a slope downward ("une pente douce") has become a fall over a cliff, an avalanche. Keyfitz carefully shows how the drop is distributed over the counties of the province; it is a regional distribution, save for the distortions created by the growth of industries and cities.

Only four counties still have as many as half of their working people in agriculture. Even in such counties the rural population is thinning out. I have not seen figures on the number and size of farms. There was a fairly long period in Quebec in which the number and the size of farms did not change greatly, in spite of constant new settlement on the frontiers. Now that such settlement is definitely at an end, and now that many farms are being abandoned, it is likely that farms are larger. The farm enterprise is becoming much larger in the more fertile agricultural regions of the continent, and the capital requirement is much greater. I am not familiar enough with agricultural affairs to know how large the Quebec farming enterprise is, or what new forms of such enterprise are being developed in the better parts of the province. It may be that there will not be anything comparable to the large farming enterprises of Wisconsin or parts of Ontario.

Whether there are such enterprises or not, the thinning-out of the rural population has many features and consequences which should be studied. Keyfitz thinks that one son less stays at home to help on the farm. Certainly rural families are smaller than they used to be. If farms are larger and the farm population of humans and animals is smaller, and if production per acre is greater, then an ever smaller portion of the farm's produce will be used on the farm. And the same may be said of the children of the farm; they are less in demand not only as help in house and field, but as those who will perform functions for the rural society. The society, in this sense, becomes less dense. I refer not to the number of people per square mile, but to the web of social relations and to the social orbits in which people move. A society of family-owned and operated farms, each producing a large number of children, develops a dense web of social relations on a quite local base.

Guy Rocher, in an unpublished document, tells us that, generations ago, something like one hundred convents in the province gained the right to train teachers for the elementary schools. The pupils in these normal schools were certainly not far from home; when they went to teach in an *école de rang* for a year or two, it was not far from the *rang* where they were born and reared. The nuns who taught them were not far from home. And when the young teacher married, the bridegroom was probably no stranger either. Likewise, the diocesan seminary, with its *collège classique*, or *petit séminaire*, trained the élite of town and country to step into the small business enterprises of the region; to go on to the priesthood in the seminary itself and hence back into the secular clergy of the region; or to go on to the medical and law schools in Quebec or Montreal, and then – some of them – back into the notarial or law practices, the pharmacies, and medical practices of the region. Some of the youngsters, perhaps of less favoured classes than those who went to the *collège*, somehow got into the religious brotherhoods and so came back to teach in public schools of the towns or in schools run by the religious communities themselves. "Frère Untel" gives the key to how the system worked in the autobiographical parts of his *Sous le soleil de la pitié*: "Je suis fils de bûcheron et de cultivateur; fils de journalier, fils de pauvre, fils du cours public" (p. 93). Perhaps that rather cultivated mother of his "cultivated" – along with the brothers who taught him – the vocation which put him into the teaching orbit. His years of reading when physically immobilized by tuberculosis put him into a higher intellectual orbit and gave him a wider vocation.

I would like to see someone do a thorough job on the occurrence and function of vocations in the Quebec countryside. It appears to have been, in effect, that feature of Catholic culture which led to the detection and cultivation of talents, both small and great, and to the selection and training, at lower and higher levels, of those who would then perform the essential services of the society. I should like also to have someone study the history of the students of classical colleges, as to their social origins, their staying in or dropping out, and their subsequent careers. I think that, especially in the more rural region, one would find a good many youngsters were encouraged to start the classical college and then later dropped out, or were encouraged to drop out, so as to pursue some sort of lesser vocational course. I suspect that a good many of the artisans and smaller *entrepreneurs* had some such history in which there was a vague notion of a religious vocation. I am suggesting that this concept of vocation was a great integrating force in rural French Canada, and that it mobilized young people of various backgrounds into a variety of occupations, religious and secular, which provided services to the community. Although this system operated on a strongly local basis, putting some young people into the regional orbit as teachers, nurses, priests, professionals of various kinds, and public functionaries, it also provided a low road which could lead to the high way. A "Frère Untel" could have remained a "local," but he became a "cosmopolitan." A son of St-Germain de Grantham could go to his diocesan seminary at Nicolet, back to his home parish as priest, then to the large, growing, and troublesome St-Frédéric of industrial Drummondville, thence to the bishopric of Chicoutimi, a still larger and more industrial "parish."

To be sure, this dense web was never closed; there were connecting threads with the outside world. But I think the evidence is that there was a high degree of social self-sufficiency in the more highly agricultural parts of Quebec. This whole complex has certainly been weakened. The relationships have loosened and there are fewer of them. Life is less local.

When I wrote something about a corner of Quebec about thirty years ago, I noted that the shadow of a city did not reach so far into the country-side as in other parts of North America. Keyfitz says that this is no longer the case. Rural life has become more like urban life. Children go farther to school, in order that there may be enough children gathered in one place to allow more efficient and more specialized teaching. Teaching is more and more a "career" profession. The teacher must go farther from home to be trained, and study for a longer time. This situation has led to a demand that the rural teacher be paid the same as the teacher in the towns and cities, which can happen only if the schools are given subventions from funds other than those from local real-estate taxes.

Fewer and fewer of the young people will work in agriculture, which traditionally did not require much formal schooling. Nor will the emigrant from the farms find unskilled work in industry. Industry no longer needs many unskilled workers. Somewhere on the road this emigrant must get more schooling than any previous generation. This point is made clear in the *Parent Report*. Professor Marcel Daneau in his paper, "Evolution économique du Québec, 1950–1965" (prepared for Le Congrès des Caisses Populaires, June 1965), analyses in a clear and detailed fashion the changes in the structure of the labour force in this period of great increase in production. More than half the labour force is now engaged in the tertiary sector of the economy; entry to this sector requires more schooling that any rural community could possibly provide. In short, local schooling will give way to a more regional organization of education. This is precisely what has happened in most of North America, and is happening in Quebec as well.

Both the *Parent Report* and Professor Daneau plead for regional plan-ning, not to preserve tradition and lore (although the long months of unemployment in the less favoured regions may serve to preserve local lore and turn it bitter), but to equalize income and opportunity.

This new regionalism will be a creation of professional workers. The teachers will study longer and farther from home. They will teach more specialized subjects in schools also farther from home. Most of them will be town or city born. Physicians of the several specialities and members of the many para-medical professions will deliver medical services and health education in regional hospitals and clinics.

I do not know what will or has happened to the small-town notary who kept the records of family properties, drew up marriage contracts and wills, administered estates, and had time left to write parish and county histories. A propertyless, mobile population of professionals and bureaucrats will have little need of the notary, especially in a welfare state. Even the functions of the priest are more and more specialized; indeed, bureaucratized, as was evident in my favourite Quebec industrial town thirty years ago. It is evident in the Catholic Church in the United States, where the staff of specialists which works in a given parish includes assistants who will never be pastors, and who are restless and somewhat obstreperous. A long editorial in *Le Devoir* in the summer of 1967 dealt with this very problem of the specializing and bureaucratizing of the functions of the priest and noted what I have long suspected, that the regular clergy are more specialized and perhaps more cosmopolitan than the seculars. The regulars move in wider orbits than the diocese, and are thus further removed from the web of local life.

This specialist priest has two sets of colleagues: his religious colleagues and his professional colleagues, who are laymen in religion. It appears likely that it is he who is least content with the celibate life. He is, as the editorial noted, a part-time priest. I would add that he is part-time in the sense that he spends most of his time at work which is not especially the function of the church in our day. He is of interest to us because he represents the bureacratizing and secularizing of services which were once performed by natives of a region through the familiar institutions of parish, town, county, and region.

But what of Quebec as a whole, considered as a region? It is one of the most highly industrial and urban regions of its size in the world. Forty per cent of its people live in one metropolitan area. Its growing frontiers are industrial, while its agricultural frontiers are drawing inward. It is clear that the emigrants from the land and villages are not leaving the province, but are coming into the cities of the province itself. It is also evident that if they find work, it will more and more be work in the tertiary sector of the economy. In Montreal, as in other cities of its kind, a great number of people are re-tooling themselves for more specialized, more professional work. The Université de Montréal has become a huge enterprise of precisely this kind. It has added training schools for nearly all of the new North American professions – or quasiprofessions if one does not like to extend that sacred term. The English-speaking Sir George Williams University has long been engaged in providing this sort of re-tooling, but perhaps not in so wide a range of special occupations. The Catholic School Commission provides training for thousands of adults. These self-upgraders are part of the great masses who are engaged in this effort in North America; not all of them are enthusiastic about what they are doing, but they must get on with it. A person can no longer be sure that his trade will last as long as his own working life. Change is no longer a respecter of the human life-cycle. These people who are working to up-grade themselves, or simply to keep up with change are, however, not people recently come from farms. They are, according to such scraps of evidence as I have seen, people who already were in the lower ranks of the white-collar services. I do not have before me as I write this the results of a study of the origins of students of l'Université de Montréal made a few years ago by Professor Jacques Brazeau; hardly any of them had ever lived on a farm. (The Brazeau study was circulated in ditto form and has never been published.)

But, we must ask, where will these students go? To other cities still larger; or if not larger, at least large enough to have a demand for people of their skills and of their readiness to learn new skills? Will they be deployed out through the province to teach, to work in industry and in the public services? It apparently is assumed that these young, or even older people, of advanced training in new specialties will be deployed throughout the province to staff the new regional institutions and the industries. If they stay in Montreal, what sorts of careers are open to them and how far can they climb upwards in the various hierarchies of business, communications, education, and the professions?

And there we meet head-on the problems of an ethnic and linguistic minority highly concentrated in a small territory and in a few smaller and one immense city. That city, Montreal, is doubly a headquarters city. It is the headquarters city for all of Canada, as well as the headquarters of finance, industry and certain professional services for the whole province. Time was when the Université de Montréal was a branch of Laval, and when the archbishop of Quebec was *de facto* the head of the church in the province. The phenomenal growth of institutions of higher education throughout the western world has operated to decentralize dominance in that field. I will not comment on the delicate question of the relative dominance of the two main archbishoprics of the province. However that may be, Montreal's predominantly French institutions have as their hinterland mainly the province of Quebec. English institutions – including McGill University, hospitals, banks, industries – have had as their hinterland all of Canada. They have not had all of Canada to themselves, of course, but their field of operation has been half a continent, not a province.

This has meant that the urban, specialized French Montrealer has operated in a smaller orbit, territorially and in other respects, than his English counterpart. We may have some findings on the measure of these orbits when the projects done for the Royal Commission on Bilingualism and Biculturalism are available. It is, of course, common knowledge that the larger of the industrial enterprises of the province have been initiated, operated, and controlled by English-speaking people rather than by French. Another way of putting this is that the English-speaking middle class of the province has been more fully industrialized than the corresponding class of French-speaking. French-owned industries are smaller, more local in the area from which they draw labour, and are more likely to be owned by a family. But these are precisely the features of earlier economic life on this continent which are rapidly becoming things of the past. Industries are being merged into ever larger units of production and control. They are quick to move from one site to another if it appears profitable to do so. As John K. Galbraith says – or is said to say – in his newest book, industry is more and more controlled by a technistructure of specialists who make the important decisions. It seems to be the fate of French Canada, and more especially of the French-Canadian middle classes to be entering the industrial lists just at the time when family ownership and the small independent operation are in a parlous condition. The merger of newspapers has been going on in North America for a long time; it has now hit the French press of Quebec. Utilities have been merged into huge systems. Firms which formerly were engaged in a single line of production now diversify their operations and their holdings.

As these changes proceed, technologists, managers, and crucial research personnel appear to become more and more detached from any fixed home base and succeed by being ready to move. What is called "brain drain" is merely an aspect of this movement of specialized personnel in ever larger orbits. What regional boundaries can be effectively drawn to determine the movement of such personnel in the future I do not know. Of course, it is quite possible that a high degree of industrialization can be achieved with much less movement of personnel than industries have been accustomed to believe necessary. I do not believe our knowledge of this matter is especially strong. It will become more adequate only to the extent that we study intensively not merely the Quebec case of a huge modern city that has two languages, two peoples, and two hinterlands, but also other cases which share some of its characteristics and are different from it in various respects. The nature of the changes in the organization of industry and services will, I suspect, be much the same in countries of equivalent development. The political and social accompaniments will no doubt vary greatly.

5

Le Régionalisme au Canada:
le cas du Québec, une société pas comme les autres

SERGE GAGNON

IL Y A SANS doute bien des façons de comprendre la signification du thème général des Colloques du Centenaire. Autrement, notre essai serait bien déroutant. Le régionalisme au Canada ! Qu'est-ce que cela signifie dans le cas du Québec ? On a affirmé ici et là que cette province était différente des autres. Très peu, par contre, ont tenté de la définir. Or pour nous, c'est par ses institutions et sa structure sociales que la province française du Canada diffère de ses voisines. Réduire la « question canadienne » à ses aspects linguistique et culturel au sens restreint de ce terme, c'est se méprendre grandement sur les dimensions réelles de la crise que nous traversons. Derrière la langue, il y a les valeurs, les genres de vie, les traits de mentalité, les philosophie de l'existence qui confèrent au Québec une identité qui le distingue du reste du Canada. C'est dire que notre vision du problème ne pouvait pas marquer davantage les tendances régionalistes de la communauté québécoise. D'aucuns trouveront qu'il n'est ni original, ni convenable de souligner de cette manière le centenaire d'un événement politique. A ceux-là nous disons qu'il nous semblait inutile de présenter un autre éventail des options politiques éventuelles du Québec, en un temps où le reste du pays s'interroge sur ses aspirations profondes. C'est pourquoi nous avons tenté d'éclairer les arrière-plans du débat constitutionnel[1].

LE PASSÉ : UNE SOCIÉTÉ TRADITIONALISTE

Comme toutes les provinces françaises d'ancien régime, la Nouvelle-France comptait une élite laïque et ecclésiastique à qui l'on doit l'orientation de la colonie, abstraction faite des limitations du contexte colonial. De même qu'en France aux XVIIe et XVIIIe siècles, l'Eglise et l'Etat y jouissaient de pouvoirs concurrents : les intérêts de l'Etat étaient ceux de l'Eglise, et celle-ci souscrivait avec zèle aux conceptions théocratiques dont Bossuet s'était fait l'écho et le défenseur. Aussi était-il normal que l'épiscopat de la Nouvelle-France siégeât au Conseil Souverain, au même titre que les administrateurs civils de la colonie.

A la suite de la conquête, les assises du pouvoir temporel de l'Eglise subirent de profondes modifications. Fidèles des églises réformées, les nouveaux fonctionnaires en charge de l'administration civile vont d'abord conclure à l'incompatibilité de la double allégeance au pape et à la couronne d'Angleterre. Mais très tôt, par souci de réalisme politique, ils se mirent à composer avec l'élite autochtone : le clergé, les seigneurs, et ce qu'il restait d'un groupe encore mal connu de la bourgeoisie coloniale. Si, tout comme avant la conquête, l'Eglise s'en trouvait asservie sur le plan spirituel, en revanche, elle retirait de cette collaboration une garantie officieuse de ses privilèges d'Ancien régime. La fidélité à l'Angleterre qu'elle encouragea plus ou moins ouvertement durant l'invasion américaine de 1775, était une manifestation non équivoque de sa loyauté envers George III. Par contre, quand la hiérarchie sentit ses positions menacées, comme au moment où fut projetée l'érection d'une université neutre et bilingue, en 1789, les dirigeants de la colonie saisirent qu'ils devaient payer d'un recul la loyauté du peuple que leur assuraient les élites de la colonie. Le projet avorta au moment où les événements qui, en France, ébranlaient l'union du Trône et de l'Autel, firent apprécier les bienfaits des libertés britanniques. Le spectacle de la nationalisation des biens de l'Eglise de France et la constitution

1/Notre essai doit beaucoup, dans sa partie historique, aux travaux d'histoire sociale du professeur Fernand Ouellet qui a renouvelé la recherche au plan des méthodes. Nous avons tenté d'y intégrer l'interprétation de l'historiographie néo-nationaliste, dont les représentants les mieux connus sont les professeurs Michel Brunet et Maurice Séguin. Quant à l'influence française, dont nous avons voulu signaler l'importance au niveau de l'imagination des idées et des hommes, nous la devons à un vieux courant historiographique renouvelé par les historiens Claude Galarneau, Elzéar Lavoie, Pierre Savard et Philippe Sylvain, engagés dans l'histoire intellectuelle et l'histoire de l'éducation du Québec. Ce qui concerne le XXe siècle est le reflet plus ou moins fidèle de la sociographie du Québec.

civile du clergé scellaient des liens définitifs entre les conquérants et la hiérarchie catholique. Il s'en fallait de peu pour admettre que la conquête avait providentiellement préservé le pays des affres de la révolution de 1789. Or c'était l'époque où l'Angleterre autorisa quelque 45 prêtres, victimes de la révolution, à passer dans la colonie. Contingent important puisqu'il représentera, au début du xIxe siècle, le tiers des effectifs cléricaux du Canada français. Au surplus, Edmund Burke n'était-il pas dans la voie de Bonald et De Maistre pour condamner les horreurs de la révolution française ? Monseigneur Plessis saisit toute l'importance qu'il y avait à encourager un sentiment de méfiance à l'égard de l'ancienne mère-patrie. Et il l'incarna avec d'autant plus de conviction que la philosophie des Lumières avait laissé des traces dans son diocèse.

Car, au début du xIxe siècle, une nouvelle élite canadienne-française, abondamment nourrie de la pensée des Encyclopédistes, affichait, à l'endroit de l'Eglise, des attitudes semblables à celles qui avaient préparé la chute du monarque français. Formée d'avocats, de médecins, d'arpenteurs et de petits marchands, cette nouvelle composante de la hiérarchie sociale professait un libéralisme anti-clérical qui menaçait de rompre l'union séculaire de l'Eglise et de l'Etat. La constitution de 1791, en accordant aux Canadiens un régime représentatif, apparaissait comme l'instrument fondamental de sa lutte pour l'obtention du leadership de la collectivité. Expliquer comment elle est parvenue à supplanter pour un temps l'Eglise, c'est rappeler les transformations profondes de l'économie canadienne à l'orée du xIxe siècle.

La seconde génération du régime britannique assista au déclin de l'économie de la fourrure relayée par celle du blé et du bois que l'Angleterre importa de ses possessions d'Amérique jusqu'au milieu du xIxe siècle. Or la classe paysanne du Bas-Canada ne profita guère de la vague de prospérité liée aux ventes de blé sur le marché métropolitain. A la détérioration des sols s'ajouta une pénurie de terres arables qui accentuait les tensions démographiques liées à un taux de natalité exceptionnellement élevé. C'était le temps où la spéculation foncière dont les Cantons de l'Est faisaient l'objet, favorisa une perception nationaliste du péril collectif. Plusieurs éléments s'ajoutèrent pour déterminer les fondements de la thèse selon laquelle la collectivité était livrée à un vaste programme d'assimilation. Le flot d'immigrants britanniques qui, à partir de 1815, déferla sur la province, l'épidémie de choléra qui l'accompagna un moment, les malversations de certains hauts fonctionnaires anglais étaient autant de justifications de l'idéologie nationaliste définie et diffusée par la bourgeoisie des professions libérales.

Cette élite, elle s'accroissait à un rythme inversement proportionnel aux besoins de la société paysanne. Acculée à la pauvreté, elle aurait pu s'allier aux grands intérêts du capitalisme commercial anglophone, risquant peut-être d'ouvrir la voie la plus sure de l'assimilation, mais elle préféra subordonner sa conscience de classe à ses réflexes ethniques, en optant pour la défense d'une population qu'elle jugeait opprimée et dont les ressentiments la rendaient prête à accepter n'importe quelle explication de ses malheurs ; en ce faisant, la bourgeoisie canadienne-française voulait s'assurer de l'appui paysan dans son désir de promotion sociale. C'est dans cette perspective qu'il faut saisir sa lutte en vue d'obtenir le gouvernement responsable, et sa prétention d'organiser la nation sur le modèle des grands états bourgeois engendrés par les révolutions américaine et française. En luttant contre les prérogatives de l'Eglise qui pactisait avec les détenteurs du pouvoir politique et économique, elle s'assura de la faveur populaire, en dépit des mandements de l'épiscopat.

Son appel aux armes fut entendu par les habitants de la région de Montréal en 1837. Curieux revirement chez un peuple, qui, selon une image récente du Canada français, n'aurait jamais fait défaut aux exhortations de ses chefs spirituels. Mais si l'on tient compte du faible recrutement du clergé durant le siècle qui suivit la conquête, on n'est pas surpris de voir une élite laïque se substituer au leadership clérical. Ainsi, à mesure que le clergé diminuait en nombre, la phalange toujours plus nombreuse des avocats sans cause assiégeait la scène politique avec l'arsenal idéologique de son époque : libéralisme, nationalisme, démocratie.

On aurait pourtant tort de croire que leur vision séculaire du destin collectif s'articulait à un plan de réformes sociales en profondeur. Chez eux, comme chez tous les nationalistes extrémistes qui les suivront, les désirs de changement furent obnubilés par l'instinct de survivance caractérisé par un conservatisme sans demi-mesure. Ainsi s'explique leur désir d'asseoir la nation sur la seigneurie et l'agriculture. Réflexe explicable du reste, car la mise en place de nouvelles structures sociales n'eût certes pas eu pour effet de transférer le pouvoir économique entre les mains de la collectivité qu'elle prétendait libérer.

L'échec de la rébellion allait raffermir l'alliance de l'Eglise avec les élites du Canada anglais. Alliance où la première trouvait l'assurance du contrôle des institutions sociales, et où la seconde, à défaut d'assimiler les conquis, obtenait la garantie de leur consensus par la voie du traditionalisme clérical. Forte de cette entente tacite, l'Eglise allait de nouveau assurer, et pour un siècle, les modalités de la survivance. La vision ecclésiastique qui prévalut dès lors dans la société canadienne-française avait pour programme d'action la colonisation soutenue par le cadre paroissial qui sacralisait l'accomplissement temporel de la nation dans l'agriculture.

L'Ecole primaire passa sous le contrôle à peu près exclusif de l'Eglise. L'épanouissement de l'enseignement classique intégra définitivement la bourgeoisie au traditionalisme, si bien qu'en 1875, le gouvernement du Québec décréta l'abolition du ministère de l'éducation créé en 1867, au moment où naissait l'Etat canadien. En somme, à la faveur d'un accroissement considérable des effectifs cléricaux, imputable autant au recrutement interne qu'à l'immigration de communautés françaises, la pensée théocratique d'Ancien régime, dont l'ultramontanisme est une version moderne, reprit la place qu'elle occupait au XVIIIe siècle. Et l'on transposa à un plan supposément religieux, le souci de développement économique commun aux sociétés occidentales. Vers 1900, l'activité missionnaire deviendrait pour le Canada français une forme d'émigration de capitaux. Le nationalisme ecclésiastique avait lui aussi une conception du progrès. Mais il s'agissait du progrès moral et spirituel qui devait l'emporter sur les impératifs de développement économique. Ce dernier, c'était l'affaire des Canadiens qui pouvaient construire sans contestation de la part de la minorité culturelle, l'armature économique du Canada contemporain.

La mise en œuvre de ces conceptions sociales n'a pourtant pas suscité une sanction unanime. Malgré les efforts déployés pour écarter le libéralisme de la province, celui-ci survécut à l'épopée révolutionnaire, vivant en communauté de pensée avec la France d'Auguste Comte et de Jules Ferry. A tel point qu'en 1897, le régime libéral de Gabriel Marchand tenta de ressusciter le ministère de l'éducation. Mais en vain. Dans l'ensemble, le Québec évoluait comme le prolongement de la France d'ancien régime. Mieux encore, il avait remplacé la France contemporaine qui avait défailli à son rôle de fille aînée de l'Eglise. N'était-ce pas d'ailleurs l'époque où un clergé persécuté de la IIIe république émigra au Québec, et contribua au triomphe de la lutte contre la « Ligue de l'enseignement » de Montréal ?

Au début du XXe siècle, le Canada français était le théâtre de changements importants. Grâce à l'entrée de capitaux américains, une seconde vague d'industrialisation allait accentuer le processus d'urbanisation. Le relèvement du niveau de vie qui s'opéra dans l'ensemble de la collectivité, tout autant que la pénétration de l'*American way of life* inquiétèrent le clergé sur les conséquences morales de cette évolution. De fait, ces changements socio-économiques suscitèrent, dans l'ensemble, une certaine indifférence des milieux ouvriers à l'égard d'une pastorale encore largement inspirée du mode de vie rural. Le clergé accepta toutefois l'inévitable, et prit sa part des bienfaits matériels que procurait la révolution industrielle. Néanmoins, le divorce de l'école et de l'organisation socio-économique continua de s'opérer. Quelques individus évoquèrent la nécessité d'accroître les pouvoirs de l'Etat en cette matière, mais ces vœux de réforme avortèrent devant les pressions de l'épiscopat. Le contrôle de l'Eglise sur les institutions sociales était si bien enraciné qu'il faudrait attendre 1960, avant de voir apparaître un régime politique assez audacieux pour tenter la révolution sociale dont le Québec est dorénavant l'objet.

S'il fallait réduire à une formule l'évolution sociale du Canada français, on pourrait dire qu'elle fut conforme aux données de l'idéologie traditionaliste. Le traditionalisme, c'est le rejet de la pensée libérale et démocratique et l'incarnation de conceptions sociales à l'image de la société féodale idéalisée. C'est le refus de toute réforme et bien plus encore de toute révolution. Car pour les traditionalistes, la révolution détruit le déroulement naturel de l'histoire. Chez les peuples qui l'ont vécue, un retour au passé est la seule voie du véritable progrès, le progrès spirituel et moral, garantie de la victoire des valeurs du cœur sur les empiètements de la raison. Le rationalisme et l'individualisme, telles sont, pour les traditionalistes, les grandes plaies de la révolution industrielle. C'est pourquoi ils étaient agriculturistes, et qu'ils ont fait, sous une forme ou sous une autre, le procès du déracinement auquel ont été soumises les populations rurales. Néanmoins, en dépit de leurs conceptions communautaires de l'organisation sociale, ils repoussent tout autant l'égalitarisme de la pensée socialiste. Il lui préfèrent une hiérarchie paternelle qui unit le pouvoir et le peuple par des liens de confiance, au lieu que par les impératifs de productivité de la société industrielle qui évalue les hommes en fonction de leur efficacité. Née en Europe, à la suite des grandes révolutions bourgeoises, cette idéologie fut importée au Québec par le canal du collège classique d'où est sortie l'élite de la collectivité canadienne-française. Or la disparition de ce type d'école, du moins dans sa formule traditionnelle, constitue, au plan des institutions, l'aspect majeur de la révolution présente.

LE PRÉSENT : UNE SOCIÉTÉ EN RÉVOLUTION[2]

Pour comprendre l'évolution cahotique de la société québécoise, il peut paraître utile d'échafauder une certaine phénoménologie de la révolution, puis, à l'aide de ce modèle, de décomposer les aspects marquants de ce que tout le monde appelle la révolution tranquille. Au préalable, il est bon

2/Cette seconde partie, le lecteur le constatera facilement, est en retard d'au moins un an par rapport à la situation présente. Ce texte a été écrit en 1967. Depuis lors, la fusion des mouvements indépendantistes, la disparition de certains périodiques comme *Parti Pris*, la contestation étudiante ont sensiblement modifié les données concrètes de l'enjeu. Mais dans l'ensemble, nous croyons que le découpage social que nous avons plus ou moins improvisé, demeure encore valable.

de noter que notre tableau n'est pas le fruit d'une analyse méthodique, mais plutôt le résultat d'une réflexion globale et intuitive comparable à celle de l'éditorialiste de la presse.

Fondamentalement, toute révolution s'opère par un conflit d'élites, l'une en émergence, l'autre en régression. Les élites nouvelles se chargent de formuler un arsenal idéologique qui s'avère à la fois un programme de réformes et un procès des institutions traditionnelles et des élites dont elles sont l'expression et le produit. Saper leur autorité, miner leur prestige et les utiliser comme boucs-émissaires susceptibles d'engager les classes laborieuses dans la liquidation de l'ordre ancien, voilà l'essentiel de la stratégie déployée par le leadership en devenir. Au conflit idéologique s'articulent d'autres perturbations d'ordre économique, démographique et politique qui constituent un terrain propice à l'enracinement du message dans les classes « exploitées. » Après quoi, viennent les modifications au niveau des structures mentales qui préparent à l'acceptation, par la masse, des institutions nouvelles à la tête desquelles s'installent progressivement les nouveaux chefs de file. Comment l'évolution du Québec correspond-t-elle à ce schéma dynamique ? C'est ce que nous allons tenter de déterminer, en donnant un aperçu fragmentaire des tendances au niveau de la société globale. Vérifions d'abord comment se présentent les conditions préalables à l'implantation de l'idéologie révolutionnaire.

L'explosion démographique de l'après-guerre constitue le phénomène central d'où découle l'effervescence actuelle. Celle-ci se traduit par un rajeunissement de la population, contexte éminemment favorable à l'incarnation d'idées nouvelles. C'est pourquoi on peut remarquer qu'au Québec, même s'il s'agit d'un malaise aux dimensions de l'Occident, la jeunesse démolit avec enthousiasme les conceptions qui ont nourri son éducation familiale et religieuse. Dans une large mesure, elle fait souvent face à de graves problèmes d'accessibilité aux études au sein d'une société qui, par incapacité ou par négligence, n'a pas transformé ses cadres scolaires en fonction des exigences de la société industrielle. Situation pénible d'où découle une certaine rancœur, à l'âge des espoirs terrestres et de la société d'opulence, situation propice à la remise en question d'un régime socio-économique qui ne parvient pas à combler ses aspirations matérielles ou autres.

Au point de vue économique, le Québec est relativement développé grâce aux investissements étrangers et canadiens-anglais. L'entreprise canadienne-française, pour sa part, joue un rôle marginal, compte tenu de ses dimensions et de la mentalité particulière de l'homme d'affaires canadien-français. Ce dernier n'a jamais vraiment joué le jeu du libéralisme économique, peut-être en raison, comme certains l'affirment, de la colonisation anglaise qui l'a livré sans défense aux mains du traditionalisme. D'autre part, l'ouvrier de cette entreprise autochtone connaît une sous-syndicalisation qui le rend peu sensible aux condamnations de la libre entreprise proférées par le leader syndical. La conscience de classe y est relativement absente de même que la conscience ethnique, puisque le patron fait partie de la même collectivité culturelle. En revanche, la véritable entreprise capitaliste, l'anglaise, subit les assauts des élites nouvelles. Et c'est dans ce secteur que l'on tente d'implanter la conscience d'une nation prolétarisée. Néanmoins, et c'est peut-être l'indice de l'impuissance de la collectivité québecoise en face du grand pouvoir économique, les attaques contre la grande firme, ne dépassent guère l'explosion verbale. En revanche, c'est au sein des services publics que se manifestent les taux d'agressivité les plus élevés du monde du travail, parce que c'est dans ce secteur que l'action des élites syndicales conduit à des conflits très graves. Dans la population agricole, par contre, le procès de l'Etat bourgeois n'a pas une grande emprise, et la chose n'étonne guère si l'on tient compte de la lenteur normale de l'évolution des mentalités en milieu rural.

Mais les véritables acteurs du conflit, la population révolutionnaire active, ce sont les élites nouvelles, cette nouvelle classe moyenne qui essaie de rejoindre les masses à l'aide des techniques de diffusion contemporaines. Elles sont en face de l'élite clérico-professionnelle avec laquelle elles se sont parfois coudoyées sur les bans de l'école secondaire. Le collège classique qui a engendré celle-ci et qui disparaît ou se modifie peu à peu, affaiblit considérablement son prestige et porte une atteinte directe à ses privilèges. Elle se sent du reste de moins en moins associée aux transformations en cours. Par contre, l'école de science sociale qui a produit celle-là, joue un rôle primordial dans la redéfinition des objectifs de la collectivité québecoise. Enfin, bien que ce réflexe de solidarité repose davantage sur une communauté d'intérêts que sur une même vision de la société à bâtir, d'autres couches sociales, dont font partie les ingénieurs, les techniciens et les enseignants, lui manifestent, de façon sporadique, un appui moral non équivoque.

Quel est donc le crédo social de cette élite ? Au départ, elle préconise un accroissement des pouvoirs de l'Etat, opération relativement aisée, en raison de l'absence d'une grande bourgeoisie d'affaires franco-québécoise. Elle veut engager une désintégration de la culture traditionnelle qui avait jusqu'ici conféré à la masse une remarquable docilité envers le pouvoir économique, largement anglophone, accepté par les clercs et les membres des professions libérales. A la fois socialiste et nationaliste, elle sabote les valeurs bourgeoises tout en travaillant à l'instauration d'un ordre socio-économique nouveau. Et son accroissement numérique que l'on peut sommairement évaluer par le nombre grandissant des diplômés de science sociale, laisse soupçonner qu'elle livrera, à la longue, une lutte sans merci pour se substituer à l'élite clérico-petite-bourgeoise. Est-il besoin d'ajouter que ses conceptions sociales doivent fort peu aux traditions de recherche américaines ? La sociologie québécoise a beaucoup emprunté aux courants intellectuels européens, de tendance philosophique, et peu à l'école américaine de sociologie, plus positiviste. Du reste, les sociologues du Québec sont plus souvent à l'emploi de l'Etat qu'au service de l'entreprise industrielle et commerciale. Les grandes entreprises, celles qui sont anglaises, élaborent leur publicité à l'aide de cadres anglophones, et la petite entreprise canadienne-française n'a pas toujours les moyens financiers de recourir aux services de cadres qualifiés. La même affirmation s'applique en gros à l'économiste et au spécialiste en relations industrielles, ce dernier devant, en tout cas, accepter très souvent le milieu de travail de la grande firme anglaise. D'ailleurs que pourrait-on faire d'un technicien de l'économie et de la société qui semble mieux préparé à critiquer le régime économique qu'à lui insuffler un regain de vitalité ! Aussi, n'est-on pas surpris de constater que les récentes enquêtes sur la consommation dont le Québec a été le laboratoire, n'ont pas pour but de rationaliser la mise en marché mais portent sur les modalités de « l'exploitation » du consommateur. D'autres recherches menées en milieu urbain portent la même étiquette. Ces exemples sont l'illustration d'un phénomène plus global où les tendances sont érigées en principes, les postulats de recherche, en outils de travail.

Grâce à l'existence d'une télévision d'Etat fortement engagée, les nouvelles conceptions sociales sont diffusées sur une grande échelle. On peut même avancer que le réseau français de la télévision canadienne joue un rôle d'animation sociale sans lequel il serait impossible de modifier les structures existantes. Car les animateurs des émissions d'affaires publiques jouent un rôle capital dans la mesure où ils engagent les masses à accepter les grandes politiques définies par les technocrates de la législature québecoise. On y voit se quereller tour à tour le clerc et le sociologue, le capitaliste des deux langues et le chef syndical, en somme les deux élites au cœur du conflit social. La création artistique elle-même joue un rôle analogue. Tel téléthéâtre qui offre une caricature de la collusion du clergé et des notables en face des défaites mémorables du monde du travail durant l'ère duplessiste; tel roman-fleuve qui met en scène la misère des quartiers ouvriers de Montréal ou des régions sous-développées de la province ; tel long métrage dont le héros est un anarchiste qui prêche l'indépendance du Québec sont autant de tentatives propres à soulever les masses contre le rôle historique du clergé et l'opulence des classes bien nanties. N'y a-t-il pas là toutes les caractéristiques d'une révolution culturelle ? A ceux qui pensent que ce phénomène est négligeable, on pourra rétorquer que si la presse écrite a été une arme importante des révolutions bourgeoises, combien plus efficaces peuvent être les techniques de diffusion audio-visuelles.

Néanmoins, l'imprimé continue de jouer un rôle important comme expression des forces en présence. Avant 1960, il n'y avait, pour ainsi dire, qu'une seule revue pour faire face au duplessisme. *Cité libre*, fondée dans les années '50, groupait alors les pionniers du leadership syndical québecois entraîné à l'école des encycliques sociales qui occupaient encore une place privilégiée dans l'enseignement des sciences humaines. Elle servait de foyer de rayonnement à la gauche et dénonçait ouvertement la répression des conflits sociaux de l'après-guerre. Le clergé, à cause de son approbation implicite ou explicite des décisions gouvernementales, était la cible préférée de ces jeunes intellectuels. Toutefois, pour avoir vu le duplessisme identifier la nation à la stagnation, ces ouvriers de la première heure parviennent difficilement à s'intégrer au nationalisme de croissance du Québec contemporain. Ils craignent, du reste – et peut-être ont-ils raison – que l'effervescence nationaliste ne compromette la mise en place des institutions nouvelles, en particulier dans le champ de l'éducation. Quoiqu'il en soit, d'autres publications, dont la naissance coincide avec la fin du régime de l'Union nationale première manière, ont relayé la revue *Cité libre* parfois coiffée de l'étiquette conservatrice par les nouvelles venues.

Parmi celles-ci, *Le Magazine Maclean* détient une place à part, en raison des moyens financiers qui lui permettent une vaste diffusion. Depuis sept ans, ce périodique populaire fait la chasse à l'ordre établi, à l'aide d'une technique d'interview analogue à celle qui caractérise la télévision d'Etat. Plus sensible au réformisme social qu'à l'idéologie nationaliste – n'est-ce pas une publication financée par des capitaux anglais – il contribue à donner une grande publicité aux initiatives récentes dans le domaine de l'éducation. La revue *Parti Pris*, pour sa part, est l'expression de la jeune génération montréalaise dont le souci est de réconcilier la révolution sociale et les questions dites nationales. Depuis 1964, *Socialisme*, périodique au ton plus sérieux, en raison du nombre d'universitaires qui y collaborent, veut fournir un bilan et un programme d'engagement social à l'intelligentsia en gestation.

A côté de cette presse passablement anticléricale, apparentée au Mouvement laïque de langue française, se profilent d'autres imprimés qui n'ont pas rompu avec la tradition chrétienne dans la formulation des questions profanes. C'est le cas de la revue *Maintenant* qui veut promouvoir l'instauration du socialisme au Québec. C'est le cas de *Témoins*, organe d'un groupe de jeunes intellectuels catholiques, qui s'adresse à la jeunesse étudiante restée fidèle au christianisme, à l'heure où Vatican II et *Populorum progressio* rejettent le libéralisme en matière économique et invitent les croyants à une nouvelle forme d'engagement social et politique. En somme, deux revues qui tout en définissant leur vision des réformes à entreprendre, dénoncent, comme leurs consœurs, le pacte officieux des clercs de la vieille génération et de la petite bourgeoisie canadienne-française.

Au palier politique, de nouvelles factions viennent seconder les efforts de cette presse engagée. Le Rassemblement pour l'indépendance nationale promet, s'il accède au pouvoir, de faire du Québec un Etat indépendant et socialiste. Quant au Ralliement national, reflet assez fidèle des aspirations des élites traditionnelles, il tente de faire échec aux tendances radicales du RIN, et c'est probablement pour mieux sauvegarder l'ordre établi qu'il préférerait imprimer une orientation différente aux réformes du système scolaire. Quant au Parti socialiste du Québec, il exerce une influence négligeable par rapport à la Confédération des syndicats nationaux, l'exemple le plus clair du syndicalisme politique dit apolitique. Car comment expliquer son appui inconditionnel aux grèves retentissantes qui ont affecté les services publics, sinon par une volonté bien arrêtée d'édifier, selon l'expression de son président, une société bâtie pour l'homme. Comptant sur l'appui des travailleurs et sur celui de corps intermédiaires comme l'Union générale des étudiants du Québec, elle entend donc, par l'intermédiaire de son puissant organe *Le Travail*, enraciner dans les milieux ouvriers l'idée d'une réforme radicale des structures socio-économiques. C'est ainsi que ses dirigeants brandissent ce temps à autre le spectre du plafonnement des prix, et se font les défenseurs de la gratuité scolaire à tous les niveaux.

Devant cette percée de la gauche, au sein de laquelle la jeunesse joue un rôle de premier plan sans égard à ses origines sociales, les élites traditionnelles ont formé une résistance soit au sein des corps intermédiaires traditionnels comme les Sociétés Saint-Jean-Baptiste ou la revue *L'Action nationale*, soit encore dans de nouveaux organes d'expression comme *Aujourd'hui Québec*, publication financée par la bourgeoisie canadienne-française qui distribue les excommunications aux cadres de la télévision d'Etat, aux leaders du monde ouvrier et à certaines vedettes politiques de gauche qu'elle accuse tous ensemble de mépriser les principes chrétiens dont est pétrie l'âme de la nation. Les factions réactionnaires protestent encore contre les mauvais professeurs qui préparent la jeunesse à la révolution, et elles s'appuient sur les associations parents-maîtres où se retrouvent presque invariablement les notables issus du collège classique du temps des humanités gréco-latines. Et si elles ne donnent pas leur appui entier à des groupements nationalistes comme les *Etats généraux du Canada-français,* opinant que cette formation politique semble recéler des éléments radicaux, elles souscrivent par contre sans hésiter aux propos de l'*Association Professionnelle des Industriels* ou encore aux déclarations des *Chambres de Commerce du Québec,* lorsque l'un ou l'autre de ces organismes déclare que la province n'a pas les moyens de payer les frais de l'assurance-santé.

LES CHEMINS DE L'AVENIR

Il peut paraître imprudent d'extrapoler sur l'issue de la révolution québecoise, d'autant plus que le tableau précédent fait abstraction d'autres facteurs susceptibles de l'engager dans des voies nouvelles. Au niveau politique déjà, la prise du pouvoir par l'Union nationale, en mettant l'accent sur l'enjeu constitutionnel, a déjà imprimé un rythme différent au processus de révolution interne. En outre, il n'est pas rare de constater ici et là de brusques réalignements idéologiques qui rendent encore plus précaire la possibilité d'une analyse articulée à notre schéma général d'interprétation. Ainsi du Ralliement national qui semble vouloir reviser sa pensée sociale. Ainsi de la revue *Aujourd'hui Québec* qui manifeste de temps à autre le désir de se dissocier de l'élite clérico-professionnelle pour s'aligner davantage sur la pensée progressiste de Vatican II. Autre source de difficulté ; la révolution québecoise s'accompagne de contradictions internes propres à dérouter celui qui voudrait en présenter le déroulement dans une seule direction. Sur le plan démographique, pour ne citer qu'un cas, le fléchissement de la natalité n'augure rien de bon pour la survie de la collectivité. Enfin, les conflits de générations qui divisent des groupes apparemment homogènes, comme c'est le cas du clergé, en particulier, interdisent des conclusions prophétiques. Quoi qu'il en soit, ne pouvant bénéficier du recul de l'histoire, il est possible de déterminer approximativement les effets durables et les initiatives irréversibles du Québec en marche.

LE RÔLE DU CLERGÉ

Les attaques dirigées contre le clergé à propos du contrôle des institutions sociales ont eu pour conséquence du nuire à son recrutement et à son prestige. Bien plus, elles sont responsables, dans certains cas, des défections dont souffre spirituellement l'église québécoise. En fait, le statut social des clercs n'est plus celui que lui conférait la société de notables. Et tout indique que cette tendance va continuer de s'accentuer. Aussi, les institutions sociales du Québec vont se séculariser dans la mesure où un clergé moins nombreux va tendre à occuper des fonctions strictement pastorales. C'est dorénavant à titre de citoyens à part entière que des individus-clercs vont s'engager dans des tâches profanes, ce qu'une fraction du jeune clergé a du reste commencé de faire.

LE RÔLE DE LA BOURGEOISIE

Quant on parle de la bourgeoisie québécoise, il faut établir une distinction très importante entre la bourgeoisie des professions libérales et la bourgeoisie d'affaires. La première a passé par le collège classique. Pour la seconde, ce n'est généralement pas le cas. Il en découle une absence de solidarité qui est très caractéristique de la société canadienne-française. Il y a, bien sûr, certains rapprochements au sein d'organismes comme l'Ordre des Chevaliers de Colomb, pour citer un cas typique, mais les liens qui en résultent sont souvent factices et superficiels.

Bien qu'il représente un poids négligeable au niveau du pouvoir économique, l'homme d'affaires canadien-français qui doit son ascension au laisser-faire du régime duplessiste, représente encore auprès de l'Etat provincial un groupe de pression passablement écouté. La Société générale de financement est l'un de ces organismes de nature à contrebalancer les initiatives socialisantes qui menacent la prospérité de la petite entreprise québécoise. Néanmoins, il est difficile de prédire quel rôle lui est dévolu dans le Québec de demain. Pour l'instant, elle lutte à armes inégales contre la concurrence de la grande firme et les demandes syndicales qu'elle ne peut satisfaire en raison de ses dimensions.

Quant à la bourgeoisie des professions libérales, on peut prévoir que, règle générale, son rôle va se limiter à des activités strictement professionnelles. On en voit déjà l'indice dans son déclin numérique au niveau du personnel politique, et bien plus encore dans la disparition du collège classique traditionnel dont elle soutient encore moralement la survivance. Moralement, par le truchement des associations d'anciens, mais non financièrement, parce qu'elle n'est plus en mesure de s'en faire l'avocat auprès des pouvoirs publics, et surtout parce que rien n'indique qu'elle est disposée à assumer personnellement ses besoins financiers, comme cela se pratique dans les grandes institutions privées de l'Amérique du Nord. C'est pourquoi on peut avancer que si la position changeante du clergé joue en faveur de la sécularisation de l'enseignement, le nouveau statut des professions libérales favorisera le mouvement en faveur d'une mainmise de l'Etat dans ce domaine. Mouvement universel, si l'on veut, mais qui a des chances d'avoir des suites plus immédiates au Québec qu'ailleurs parce que celui-ci n'est pas doté d'une bourgeoisie riche et puissante.

LES ÉLITES NOUVELLES

Cette nouvelle composante de la structure sociale constitue le seul grand changement que le Québec ait connu depuis l'après-guerre. La phase d'industrialisation et d'urbanisation qui a coincidé avec le début du siècle continue de s'opérer selon le même processus qu'auparavent. Mais cette nouvelle couche sociale qui forme les cadres de la bureaucratie québécoise, de ses mass média, de ses universités et de ses syndicats, dirige et oriente le renouveau d'aujourd'hui. Comme toutes les classes en émergence, elle tente de bâtir une société qui correspond à ses valeurs aussi bien qu'à ses désirs d'ascension dans l'échelle sociale. Elle se fait le porte-parole, au sein de la société québécoise, de la pensée socialiste internationale. Et si elle est largement séparatiste, c'est parce qu'elle considère l'indépendance du Québec comme une condition prélable à l'instauration de la société soi-disant égalitaire. En outre, ses tentatives pour rejoindre la jeune géné-ration du clergé québécois, plus sensible que ses prédécesseurs au catho-licisme social post-conciliaire, ne sont qu'une manifestation de la stratégie qu'elle met en œuvre pour gagner l'appui des masses. Jusqu'ici, ses succès sont minimes. Car si elle rejette les valeurs de la société bourgeoise, il n'est pas certain que les masses ouvrières qu'elle tente de séduire soient sur le point de répondre à son appel. A long terme pourtant, il est possible qu'elle parvienne à enraciner l'idée d'une société originale par le truchement de l'école nouvelle dont elle a pensé les structures et le fonctionnement. A long terme également, elle peut compter sur l'appui plus global du clergé qui s'est toujours réconcilié avec les nouveaux régimes dans le déroule-ment de l'histoire, pour la raison qu'il ne peut assurer autrement le mode de présence des valeurs religieuses.

Mais l'école nouvelle aura-t-elle atténué le clivage social que l'élite ne pourra pas pour autant réaliser ses idéals socialistes au plan de la structure économique. Car les grandes réformes sociales n'auront pas pour effet le transfert du pouvoir économique aux mains de la collectivité québécoise. Celle-ci continuera de demeurer, dans une large mesure, aliénés aux in-vestissements étrangers duquel dépend un niveau de vie qu'elle n'est pas prête à sacrifier. Les élites nouvelles tenteraient-elles ce suprême effort d'abnégation qu'elles se rendraient odieuses aux yeux du prolétariat, à moins que celui-ci ne soit brusquement transformé ou encore que l'édifice américain ne s'écroule. Rêves chimériques qu'elles caressent peut-être, mais revenues à la réalité, il y a de fortes chances que ses réalisations sur le plan économique n'aillent guère au-delà de l'économie mixte où le capitalisme d'Etat et la formule coopérative joueront un rôle complémentaire aux côtés du capitalisme étranger.

ET L'UNITÉ CANADIENNE ?

Ce sous-titre nous reporte au thème de ce colloque. Sur quelle option politique la révolution québécoise va-t-elle déboucher ? Formulons la question autrement : le régionalisme québécois l'engage-t-il résolument dans la voie de l'indépendance ? sinon comment envisager une nouvelle alliance des deux sociétés qui composent le pays ?

Aussi longtemps que le Québec s'inspira des principes traditionalistes, il fut relativement facile de préserver l'unité canadienne. N'ayant pu assimiler les vaincus, le Canada anglais y vit probablement le moyen de bâtir le pays sans tenir compte de la présence française. De son côté, la population canadienne française évoluait docilement derrière les notables à qui elle doit sa survivance, et ces derniers pouvaient incarner à leur aise les aspirations du catholicisme conservateur issu des révolutions bourgeoises. De la sorte, les conflits ethniques ne pouvaient avoir de suites dangereuses pour l'unité canadienne, puisque deux conceptions différentes du « nation building » évoluaient côte à côte sans se heurter. Lorsqu'une crise sévissait, les concessions symboliques de la majorité suffisaient à satisfaire le nationalisme romantique de la minorité. Le néo-nationalisme québécois n'a pas perdu le caractère émotif de la conscience collective traditionnelle. Le rôle considérable qu'accomplit l'œuvre littéraire écrite et chantée dans la diffusion du message libérateur, en est une preuve irréfutable. Il n'en demeure pas moins que les nouvelles élites ont une vision différente du destin de la collectivité. Le refus d'en tenir compte, au moment où l'on s'apprête à renégocier le pacte des deux peuples fondateurs, risque de mener à une rupture définitive, au grand malheur des deux sociétés canadiennes. De son côté, l'élite québécoise fera bien de reconnaître le rôle efficace des structures économiques canadiennes dans le contexte nord-américain. Elle devra porter plus d'intérêt aux problèmes de croissance qu'aux beaux discours sur l'épanouissement de la nation. Telles nous apparaissent les conditions essentielles à la survie des deux Canadas menacés l'un et l'autre par la marche implacable de l'impérialisme américain. Vœu de Centenaire, il est vrai. Car un fait demeure : c'est que les nouvelles élites québécoises auxquelles nous avons attaché tant d'importance, ne se sentent plus solidaires, comme leurs prédécesseurs, du sort des Canadiens français de la diaspora. C'est là un phénomène nouveau capital dans l'histoire du nationalisme canadien-français.

6

The Viability of French Groupings outside Quebec*

FRANK G. VALLEE AND NORMAN SHULMAN

INTRODUCTION

THERE IS MUCH TALK today of plural societies, as though these were unusual kinds of structure. A moment's reflection persuades us that most societies are plural. In the sense that they contain different kinds of sub-cultures, whether these are based on generation, social class, religion, language, region of origin, or whatever. In this paper, we regard Canada in its aspect as an *ethnically* plural society. For purposes of the paper, we equate society with sovereign state: the population of a territory which makes its own foreign policy, determines the inflow of newcomers, and has a monopoly over the legitimate use of force. Within the society, an ethnicity is ascribed to, or is assumed by, persons. Ethnicity is determined by descent from ancestors who shared a common culture based on national origin, language, religion, or race, or a combination of these. In short,

*This is a report on a research project which was launched in the spring of 1967 and which should be completed by late 1969. Because we are not yet at the half-way point of the study, many conclusions are stated tentatively and some hypotheses have not been tested at all. Nevertheless we felt this preliminary report worth making because of its relevance to ethnic pluralism and regionalism.

ethnicity is determined primarily by kinship. An ethnically plural society is one in which two or more ethnic categories co-exist and in which the cultures of the people in these categories differ significantly from one another in some respects.

The great majority of modern states are ethnically plural, although they did not all get ethnically plural in the same way. Some got that way through conquest by one group over others; some got that way because groups from different backgrounds invaded the same relatively unpopulated territory or because they have become immigrant-receiving societies, inviting people from many backgrounds.

No matter how they got that way, ethnically plural societies have one thing in common: they all face the problem of how to accommodate the different ethnic groups to one another is such a way that social order and cohesion are maintained. What principles of social and political organization are used in this endeavour depends on circumstances. In the short term, oppression is used in some places to keep conquered ethnic groups in their place and to keep the system going. We say in the short term, because this solution usually gives way in the long run to a break-up and re-formation of states, or to the acceptance of the situation by the oppressed groups and a rationalization of the whole system through mythology and religion, as happened in caste-like societies.

More typically, the different ethnic groups have regional bases which once enjoyed some political autonomy as states, dukedoms, and so on, but which currently are geared into a strong central government, there being one language which almost everyone speaks, although local and regional dialects and languages are still used. Britain, Holland, Germany, France are examples of this type in which regional diversity subserves societal unity.

A variant of this type of regionally based ethnicity is that in which the ethnic groups have statutory guarantees for their survival. We refer here to the federal type of ethnic integration in which each ethnic group is both a regional and a political segment. Switzerland is often held up as the classical example of this type of ethnic integration, in which the groups which are autonomous and differentiated from others at one level are united at another, higher level, through a formal political machinery. The survival of each ethnic group is guaranteed by this formal machinery.

Finally, we note another kind of ethnically plural situation in which the ethnic groups are dispersed and do not have mutually exclusive regions as bases. Clusters of people in given ethnic groups occur in such societies, but there is no formal or official recognition that ethnicity defines a region for important purposes. The United States of America is perhaps the best example of this type of ethnically plural society, where the ethnic groups are very much interspersed, and where the appeal for consensus is made by emphasizing national unity, in effect creating a new kind of ethnic group – the "American" – to which all owe prior allegiance.

The situation in Canada is a blend of the federalist and interspersed kinds of ethnic integration. Strictly speaking, the regional or federal type of integration applies in Canada officially only to the French and English in Quebec and to some Indian groups which are "protected" spatially and culturally by the Indian Act. The great majority of French-Canadians are gathered in one massive region, although French-Canadians are dispersing increasingly over other parts of the country. The majority of Canadian Indians live in hundreds of autonomous communities all over the country, but they too are dispersing increasingly among non-Indian communities. Except for some small religious communities, like the Hutterites, the remaining ethnic groups are dispersed in varying degrees and do not have an officially recognized region of identification, even though we all know that certain parts of the country are unofficially recognized as predominantly Ukrainian, Icelandic, Scottish, German, and so on. Although there is no official sanction guaranteeing the survival of these sub-cultures, there appears to be considerable official and non-official sentiment in favour of recognizing the right of each ethnic group to maintain at least some distinction.

We need to know much more than we do about the conditions under which particular ethnic groups maintain, or fail to maintain, distinctiveness in the different regions of Canada. It is the purpose of this paper to suggest a way of studying ethnic viability or strength and to apply this method to the study of people of French origin living in places outside the province of Quebec. We select the French for initial attention because information about them is relatively abundant, although not nearly as abundant as we would like it to be, and because the position of the French element in Canada is so very much a cause for concern in the country.

In examining the position of an ethnic group in Canada or in a locality within the country, the following kinds of information are usually sought: (*a*) a history of settlement of the group;[1] (*b*) statutory provisions for

1/For brief summaries of the history and present position of French-speaking groups in various regions of Canada, see Paul E. Gosselin, *L'Empire français d'Amérique* (Quebec 1963); and essays by various authors in Mason Wade, ed., *Canadian Dualism* (Toronto 1960). Our examination of the historical dimension in communities with substantial French-Canadian populations will concentrate not only on the evolution of the French-speaking component as such, but also on the relations between this component and the non-French, especially as these are made manifest in such issues as French-language instruction in schools, French language usage in the mass media, and the like. For a recent example of this approach, see John D. Jackson, "A Study of French-English Relations in an Ontario Community," *Canadian Review of Sociology and Anthropology*, III, No. 3, 1966.

recognition of the special status of the group, if any; (c) attitudinal data from group members and from "outsiders" among whom they live; (d) demographic patterns and trends for the group; (e) the extent of and the kinds of organization in the group; (f) the kinds of group and individual resources possessed by members. In this paper, we concentrate on the latter three kinds of information as they apply to French-speaking Canadians outside Quebec.

A brief comment is in order on the theoretical rationale for concentrating on demography, organization, and resources. Bierstedt gave us a simple formulation which owes much to Marx and other writers, and which is useful as a conceptual framework within which to assess the strength of ethnic groups.[2] Very briefly put, the argument is that, all other things being equal, the group which is most numerous has more social power than the numerical minority; but that a numerical minority can control a majority through superior organization and through superior access to valued resources; and that the social group with most power will be that which enjoys a favourable combination of advantage in those three factors. Using this simple scheme, it should be easy to determine which ethnic groups in which regions are most powerful or viable. In our study group resources such as newspapers, radio, and TV facilities are grouped with organization and treated separately from such "individual" resources as income and education.

Before proceeding with more detailed discussion of the methods and kinds of information sought we list four of the most general hypotheses to be tested in the study:

1   The lower the social power "score" of the grouping in a region, the higher will be the rate of assimilation as measured by numbers of French origin who are reported as non-French in language, non-Roman Catholic, and having non-French origin marital partners.

2   The higher the social power score of the grouping in a region, the lower will be the average standing of its members in terms of such "individual" resources as income and education.

3   French-Canadian claims to special status will be most widely recognized where their social power score is relatively high and where their claim to charter membership in a *region* can be substantiated.

4   Where the grouping's social power score is relatively low and claims to regional charter-membership weak, the spokesmen for French-speaking organizations will direct their pressures for special status to the federal, rather than to the provincial or municipal, level.

2/Robert Bierstedt, "An Analysis of Social Power," *American Sociological Review*, xv, No. 3, 1950.

The research programme requires information on the following topics:
1   Population data on French-speaking population outside Quebec with a view to (*a*) identifying the regions within Canada [but outside Quebec] with the highest percentage density of French-speaking people; (*b*) regional figures on language usage, religious affiliation, inter-marriage, income, education, occupation, recency of settlement, per cent urban and rural.
2   Organization strength and group resources for each of the fifteen regions.
3   Attitudes on the part of non-French in each region as to the claims for special status; attitudes and approaches of French-speaking spokesmen in each region with reference to achieving group goals as they perceive them.

Population Data
Much of the required demographic data has been gathered during the first phase of the programme. Of extreme value have been the studies done by Henripin and others on behalf of the Royal Commission on Bilingualism and Biculturalism.[3] However, we still require a considerable amount of data on intermarriage, religious affiliation, and recency of settlement, which we are getting either directly or indirectly through the Dominion Bureau of Statistics.

Assessment of Organization Strength and Group Resources
This forms the major component in the programme. The following aspects of group life are taken into account in assessing the strength of French-speaking organization and group resources in the various regions and provinces outside Quebec: institutional completeness, institutional activity and participation, group resources, representation in political and administrative structures. We simply assess the various regions and provinces relative to one another on these four aspects of group life and combine the assessments into an over-all "score" for each region and province, the score being based on a five-point scale ranging from very weak to very strong. Comments on each of the aspects noted will clarify our data gathering procedures:

3/Jacques Henripin, *Etude démographique des groupes ethniques et linguistiques au Canada,* monograph for the Royal Commission on Bilingualism and Biculturalism, publication forthcoming. Henripin's data appear in Book I of the Commission's report, *The Official Languages,* Ottawa, October 1967. See especially chap. II.

Institutional completeness. We borrow this term from Raymond Breton, who used it in a study of the integration of immigrants into Canada.[4] In our study we are interested only in those institutions the affairs of which are carried out entirely or to a considerable extent in French. Furthermore, we are concerned not only with the *numbers*, but also with the *range* of institutions present in a community or region. Thus, a community with a French-speaking parish, school, *caisse populaire* (credit union), recreational club, local political "cell" and a branch of a patriotic society would be regarded as relatively complete institutionally, whereas another community with, say, four recreational clubs but none of the other institutions listed, would be relatively incomplete on this score. The institutions for which we seek information are the following:

(*a*) *Economic and Mutual-Benefit* – Co-operatives, *caisses populaires*, mutual-benefit and other foundations, farmer's unions, etc.

(*b*) *Educational* – Primary and secondary schools, colleges, educational associations, teachers' associations, etc.

(*c*) *Patriotic* – Some of these are explicitly patriotic, for example, *La Société nationale des acadiens*; but there is much overlap in this category, for most of the educational and religious associations are also "patriotic."

(*d*) *Religious* – Here we are primarily interested in French-speaking parishes and associated religious associations.

(*e*) *Miscellaneous* – For example, broadcasters, youth, women's associations.

Institutional activity and participation. We are interested in more than the mere existence of institutions, for they could be of hardly any significance if inactive or if the members are few or indifferent. It has proved difficult to get reliable information on membership and activity. We have managed to get membership information on almost all *caisses populaires* outside Quebec and have calculated the proportion of people of French origin in provinces and regions who are members. We also know the assets of each *caisse populaire* and have calculated assets per capita and an indication of group commitment to the *caisse populaire*. However, for other institutions listed above we have insufficient information on activity and participation.

Group resources. In this category we include institutions which contribute to French language and cultural maintenance, but are not institutions to which people belong in the usual sense of the word. We intend to

4/Raymond Breton, "Institutional Completeness of Ethnic Communities and the Personal Relations of Immigrants," *American Journal of Sociology*, LXX, No. 2, 1964.

include eventually French-speaking companies (stores, factories) welfare agencies, etc. Initially we have concentrated on communications. We intend to collect information on libraries and book stores, and have begun to do so, but the information so far collected is most complete for regular publications, radio, and television.

Representation in political and administrative structures. We are gathering information on French-speaking membership in political and civil service structures and diocesan hierarchies, as indicators of the extent to which French-speaking elements are taken into account in decision-making processes and in the allocation of honorific positions, such as the Senate. Our information is most complete for the dioceses, Senate, House of Commons, and provincial Legislative Assemblies. The most serious gaps in our information pertain to civil services and local government units.

Attitudinal Data. In order to test some of our hypotheses we shall need to know how French-speaking persons in each region view their positions *vis-à-vis* the non-French and how the latter in turn view certain French claims, complaints, and aspirations. A certain amount of information is already available through representations made by spokesmen to the Royal Commission on Bilingualism and Biculturalism and through various polls carried out by the Canadian Institute of Public Opinion. However, this information is far from adequate for our purposes. For one thing, we need systematically collected data based on interviews focussing on specific questions in which we are interested, interviews carried out with specified populations in mind. For some purposes the sample populations may be selected on a random basis; for others on a quota basis; for still others, we want to interview only those people who are defined as spokesmen. This part of the project will be carried out during the final phase of the programme.

THE RESEARCH FINDINGS

Population Density

In terms of provincial populations, people of French origin outside Quebec have their highest proportions in New Brunswick, Prince Edward Island, Nova Scotia, and Ontario, their lowest in British Columbia and Newfoundland, as will be seen in Table I. Mere numbers and percentages per province are not very useful in our attempt to assess the social power or viability of a category of the population. In order to make such assessments we must also know the extent to which the populations are dispersed or are clustered. A clustered population provides a more feasible numerical

TABLE I

PERCENTAGE OF POPULATION WHO ARE OF FRENCH
ORIGIN, CANADA AND THE PROVINCES, 1961

Province	Number of French origin	Percentage of French origin in population
Quebec	4,241,354	80.6
N.B.	232,127	38.8
P.E.I.	17,418	16.6
N.S.	87,883	11.9
Ontario	647,941	10.4
Manitoba	83,936	9.1
Saskatchewan	59,824	6.4
Alberta	83,319	6.2
B.C.	66,970	4.1
Newfoundland	17,171	3.8
Canada	5,540,346	30.4

Source: Census, 1961.

and spatial opportunity for the maintenance of organizations than does a dispersed one. In the remainder of this paper we concentrate on those regions within provinces which have the highest percentage density of people of French origin outside Quebec.

An analysis carried out by Jacques Henripin of population by census tract and division reveals that the highest clusterings of people of French origin occur in the twelve localities listed in Table II.[5] Henripin endeavoured to discover the association between such demographic variables as density and urbanization, on the one hand, and rate of assimilation on the other. He uses only one measure of assimilation, namely: the proportion of those who report their origin as French who also report French as their mother tongue. In our study we use language retention as only one measure of assimilation, combining it with rates of marriage with non-French partners and proportion of French origin reported as having a religious affiliation other than Roman Catholic. However, because we have not yet completed our analysis of marriage and affiliation statistics, for purposes of this paper we use only Henripin's index of assimilation, that of language retention.[6]

5/Henripin, *Etude démographique*. In chap. II of *The Official Languages,* only seven of these twelve regions are discussed in detail.
6/This is far from being a perfect index of assimilation for several reasons. In the census, there is no measure of actual language capacity in French or English. The question on ethnic origin implies a considerable degree of arbitrariness. Finally, the published census reports do not link directly those who report a given origin with those who report a given language usage. Recognizing the limitations in the census handling of correlations between origin and language usage, in our study we supplement these measures of assimilation by others, as noted on page 87.

TABLE II
REGIONS OUTSIDE QUEBEC WITH HIGHEST PERCENTAGES FRENCH ORIGIN

Region	Population of French origin	Percentage of French origin in region
Northern and eastern N.B. (Gloucester, Kent, Madawaska, Northumberland, Restigouche, Victoria, Westmoreland)	207,974	61.0
Southern and western N.S. (Yarmouth and Digby)	19,787	45.5
Northern Ontario (Cochrane, Nipissing, Sudbury, Timiskaming)	159,098	40.8
Northern N.S. (Inverness, Richmond, Cape Breton Island)	11,560	38.4
Eastern Ontario (Carleton, Glengarry, Prescott, Renfrew, Russell, Stormont)	185,813	32.1
Northwestern P.E.I. (Prince)	11,073	24.6
Southern Saskatchewan (Assiniboia, Gravelbourg, Lafleche)	6,052	21.4
Southern Ontario (Essex and Kent)	66,351	19.0
Northern Alberta (Bonnyville, Grande Prairie, Lac la Biche, Peace River, St. Paul's)	23,227	18.6
Northern Saskatchewan (bounded by Lloydminster, North Battleford, Prince Albert)	19,765	12.7
Southeastern Manitoba (South of Lake Winnipeg)	62,520	9.9
Edmonton and surroundings	28,836	7.0

Source: Adapted from Jacques Henripin, *Etude démographique des groupes ethniques et linguistiques au Canada.*

If population density or clustering were an infallible predictor of resistance to assimilation, we would expect a perfect correlation between language retention and French population density. However, this is not the case, as will be seen by an examination of Table III.

Not surprisingly, the regions most resistant to assimilation, New Brunswick and northern Ontario, border on Quebec. However, proximity to Quebec does not correlate perfectly with rate of assimilation; for instance, the region of southern Saskatchewan has a slightly lower rate of assimilation than does eastern Ontario, which also borders on Quebec.[7]

Among several other demographic factors which we would take into account if we had the time and the data, we mention here only that of

7/After this article had been prepared and presented in the form of a paper at the University of Saskatchewan, we learned of a parallel investigation conducted by Richard J. Joy, in which demographic trends are highlighted. Joy concludes that the linguistic lines between French and English in Canada are being sharpened and that French has little hope of survival as a viable tongue outside the area bounded by Moncton on the east and Sault Ste Marie on the west side. See Richard J. Joy, *Languages in Conflict*, published by the author, Ottawa 1967.

TABLE III
INDEX OF ASSIMILATION BY PERCENTAGE OF FRENCH ORIGIN
IN 12 REGIONS, 1961

Region	Percentage of French origin in region	Index of assimilation*
Northern and eastern N.B.	61.0	4.4
Southern and western N.S.	45.5	22.7
Northern Ontario	40.8	13.2
Northern N.S.	38.4	15.4
Eastern Ontario	32.1	16.3
Northwestern P.E.I.	24.6	39.8
Southern Saskatchewan	21.4	14.5
Southern Ontario	19.0	51.2
Northern Alberta	18.6	30.7
Northern Saskatchewan	12.7	31.8
Southeastern Manitoba	9.9	24.1
Edmonton and surroundings	7.0	47.1

Source: Jacques Henripin, *Etude démographique des groupes ethniques et linguistiques au Canada.*
*This index was calculated by Jacques Henripin in the following manner. The difference between the population of French origin and the population whose mother tongue is French was divided by the population of French origin, the result multiplied by 100 to obtain a percentage. The higher the percentage, the greater the degree of assimilation as measured by 'language loss.'

rural-urban settlement. Henripin argues that the more urban the French population outside Quebec, the higher the rate of assimilation as measured by proportion of French who report English as their mother tongue. He shows that in such centres as Windsor, Winnipeg, and Edmonton, the rate of French language loss is quite high when compared with the rate of language loss in rural and small town localities. In urban centres the social and economic worlds, as well as the communications media, are so dominated by English language usage that the pressure to adopt that language is apparently overwhelming. Note that the two regions with the highest index of assimilation (Table III) are southern Ontario and the Edmonton area, two of the most highly urbanized regions in our sample.

Organization and Resources
Given the importance of demographic factors, we argue that resistance to assimilation is highest where the French element possesses the most complete set of institutions and a large measure of control over the kinds of resources which contribute to group autonomy. In this section we present

what material we have been able to collect so far in our research programme on certain French institutions, political representation, media of communication, etc.

To avoid burdening the text with details about particular organizations and group resources, such as newspapers, schools, *caisses populaires*, and so on, among the populations of French origin outside Quebec, we present here only an over-all assessment of organizations and group resources for each region, based on the information we have gathered so far. We put into perspective the assessments of the twelve regions of the highest French concentrations designated by Henripin, by providing information for other regions and for provinces not included in Henripin's list. Assessments are based on the extent to which there exist autonomous French-language organizations, such as *caisses populaires*, mutual benefit and other associations, French-language parishes; French as the language of instruction in schools; French-speaking representation in diocesan and politico-administrative spheres; accessibility to French-language newspapers, radio, and television; informal and statutory recognition of French as an "official" language.

Our thinking about French-Canadian and Acadian communities outside Quebec had to be ordered in such a way that we could compare them with one another, even in the crudest fashion, in terms of group strength. This was done by assessing the strength of the particular group (region, province, local) in certain institutions for which we have been able to gather information, media of communication, juridical rights and politico-administrative representation, combining these assessments in our judgment about the overall organizational and resource strength of the group as expressed in a five-point scale comprising the following categories: (1) very weak; (2) weak; (3) moderate strength; (4) strong; (5) very strong. These terms are relative: a group which we regard as "very strong" organizationally, in comparison with other French-language groups in the country, might be regarded as weak by an observer who compares the group with one from the heartland of Quebec.

Here we give just one example of our procedure, comparing Newfoundland with New Brunswick. In Newfoundland there is a clustering of Acadian people around Baie St. Georges and St. Georges itself, an area which contains more than half of Newfoundland's population of French origin (17,171). This population is represented by one member of the legislative assembly, but is merely an unorganized category of the population, without their own parishes, mutual benefit associations, etc. No French language newspapers, radio, or TV programme pervade the homes of these people. Thus they are classified as "very weak" in terms of organization and group resources. The New Brunswick Acadians, on the other hand, have a French-speaking premier, an archbishop and four bishops who are French-speaking, a university, three colleges, a normal school where French is the language of instruction or where it shares equal status with English. About 40 per cent of the French-speaking population belongs to the *caisse populaire*; French-speaking insurance companies and fraternal societies have large memberships; a daily paper and two weeklies, two radio and one television station transmit messages in French. Needless to say we classify the New Brunswick French-speaking as very strong in organizational and group resources.

According to our assessment of organization and group resources, the strongest regional grouping of French-speaking Canadians outside Quebec is that of New Brunswick, the weakest that of Newfoundland and British Columbia. Our assessments of the different provinces and regions are presented in Table IV.

In this table we find a clear association between organizational strength on the one hand and degree of assimilation on the other. The regions with above-average assimilation indices are located in the lower part of the scale of organizational strength. It should be noted that the assimilation indices for British Columbia and Newfoundland are for the entire prov-

TABLE IV
STRENGTH OF FRENCH-SPEAKING ORGANIZATION AND
GROUP RESOURCES AND ASSIMILATION

Assessment of organization and group resources	Province or region	Assimilation index for province or region* (in per cent)
Very Strong	Northern and eastern N.B.	4.4
	Eastern Ontario	16.3
	Northern Ontario	13.2
Strong	Manitoba	24.1
	Southern and western N.S.	22.7
	Southern Saskatchewan	14.5
Moderate	Northern N.S.	15.4
	Northern Alberta	30.7
	Northern Saskatchewan	31.8
	P.E.I.	39.8
Weak	Edmonton and surroundings	47.1
	Southern Ontario	51.2
	B.C.	66.0
Very Weak	Newfoundland	85.1

Source: Authors' data and Henripin, *Etude démographique des groupes ethniques et linguistique au Canada.*
*For method of computing, see Table III.

inces and not for French regions within them. We have not yet had the opportunity to calculate regional rates for such French districts as Maillardville in British Columbia and Baie St. Georges in Newfoundland. No doubt when this is done we shall find assimilation rates for such regions to be lower than for entire provinces, but still we expect those regional rates to be the highest in our sample.

Individual Resources

It will be recalled that we differentiated between group resources, such as communications media, and individual resources, such as income and education. We felt that group resources would be positively related to group strength and resistance to assimilation, and that individual resources would be negatively related to these.

It has been suggested that the more a minority group turns in upon itself and concentrates on making its position strong, the more it costs its members in terms of their chances to make their way as individuals in the larger system.

The argument is that the more energy and resources an ethnic minority group puts into the provision of its own set of institutions, particularly educational ones, and the more these institutions give priority to the maintenance of language, religions, and other differences, the smaller the amounts of energy and resources available to transmit the educational and other skills required to cope with the social and economic requirements of the larger system. Furthermore, among ethnic minority groups which strive to maintain language and other distinctions, motivation to aspire to high-ranking social and economic positions in the larger system will be weak unless, of course, it is characteristic of the ethnic group to put a special stress on educational and vocational achievement, as is the case with the Jews. Bouvier[8] shows the cost in individual achievement, in terms of education and income, for Franco-Americans compared with other ethnic groups in the United States which have less institutional distinctiveness.

Unfortunately we have not yet completed our analysis of income and education by ethnic origin for the twelve regions within which we seek to test the hypothesis that, the higher the score on organizational strength and group resources, the lower the individual income and educational position. We must be content at this stage with citing figures for the provinces.

Because averages in educational attainment and income vary considerably by province, we saw little point in comparing the French-speaking in

8/Léon-F. Bouvier, "La stratification sociale du groupe ethnique canadien-français aux Etats-Unis," *Recherches sociographiques*, v, No. 3, 1964.

each province with the national average. Instead, we try to control for inter-provincial variations by comparing the French with the non-French *within* each province, deriving from this comparison a measure of the extent to which the French differ from the average within the province of residence. In no province are the French average income and years of schooling as high as the average for all origins. That is, the French are at a disadvantage on these counts in every province. But our interest here is in the *extent* of their being disadvantaged within each province. Where the French are many percentage points lower than the provincial average in educational attainment and income, we say they are highly disadvantaged; where the French are few percentage points lower than the provincial average on these counts, we say that they are relatively advantaged. Note again that judgments about being advantaged or disadvantaged do not refer to a grouping's position with reference to the *national* picture. For instance, the French in Newfoundland are only 5.1 per cent below the income average for their province and so we say that they are heavily advantaged; the French in Saskatchewan are 8.2 per cent below the income average for *their* province, and so we say that they are only relatively advantaged. These judgments are made in the full knowledge that average income for the Saskatchewan French is substantially higher ($3,049) than the average income for the Newfoundland French ($2,531), implying that on the national scene the Saskatchewan French are in a better income position (i.e., advantaged) than the French in Newfoundland.

Eventually we shall devise a refined index of *over-all* advantage and disadvantage of the French in different localities in terms of these "individual" resources. For the purposes of this preliminary report we use the crude device of coupling percents of income and education averages in order to arrive at a rough measure of how the French in the different provinces compare with one another. The third column of Table V shows the French in Newfoundland and Alberta to be "most advantaged" in terms of income and education combined, the French in New Brunswick and Prince Edward Island to be the least advantaged on these counts.

Because we are not yet in a position to assess income and educational position for regions within provinces, we must be content with data for French populations in provinces considered as wholes. For the purpose of testing hypotheses about association between group and individual resources, then, we must make assessments about group strength on a provincial basis rather than on a regional one. This awkward task can only be done by arriving at some rather arbitrary average group strength for the French in some provinces within which there are marked differences in

TABLE V
PERCENTAGE OF FRENCH ORIGIN, OUTSIDE QUEBEC, BELOW AVERAGE INCOME
AND NUMBER OF YEARS OF SCHOOLING BY PROVINCE, 1961

Province	Percentage below provincial annual income* (I)	Percentage below provincial average beyond grade 8** (II)	Combined (I) and (II)
Newfoundland	5.1	6.9	6.0
Alberta	7.1	5.6	6.3
B.C.	6.6	8.0	7.3
Saskatchewan	4.4	12.1	8.2
Ontario	11.6	12.2	11.9
N.S.	11.1	15.2	13.1
Manitoba	7.9	18.9	13.4
N.B.	13.2	14.4	13.8
P.E.I.	16.7	11.4	14.0

*These percentages represent the extent to which French-origin annual income from wages and salaries falls below the annual income average for all origins. Derived from a 1 per cent sample of the 1961 census.
**These percentages represent the extent to which French-origin fall below the average for all origins in proportion having completed Grade 8 or higher. Derived from 1961 Census.

group strength by region. For instance, the French in eastern and northern Ontario are substantially stronger in group organization and resources than are the French in southern Ontario, whom we judged to be relatively weak (see Table IV). All averages have a certain arbitrariness about them, but to combine such categories as *very strong* and *relatively weak* and derive a category of simply *strong* for Ontario as a whole is being more arbitrary than we would like to be. However, at this preliminary stage of our research we are forced to perform such an operation if we are to test hypotheses with a view to opening up avenues of research and discussion, the chief purpose of this paper.

If we arrange the French-origin populations of the provinces on a five-point scale in order to compare advantage and disadvantage in terms of "individual" resources of income and education and compare these with the equally crude measure of organization and group resource strength of French origin by province, we find a suggestive inverse correlation, which we do not attempt to make statistically precise for obvious reasons, between organizational and group resource strength, on the one hand, and individual resources, on the other. In other words, the stronger the group in its environment, the lower tends to be the individual resources of income and education of its members. Table VI illustrates these tendencies and shows, as well, the association with provincial rates of assimilation as

TABLE VI
FRENCH ORIGIN OUTSIDE QUEBEC: GROUP RESOURCES, INDIVIDUAL RESOURCES,
INDEX OF ASSIMILATION (LANGUAGE) BY PROVINCE

Province	Organization and group resource strength*	Individual resources (income and education)**	Provincial index of language assimilation
N.B.	Very strong	Heavily disadvantaged	12.4 (very low rate)
Manitoba	Strong	Relatively disadvantaged	32.8 (low rate)
Ontario	Strong	Relatively advantaged	38.6 (low rate)
N.S.	Mod. strong	Relatively disadvantaged	57.2 (high rate)
Saskatchewan	Mod. weak	Relatively advantaged	45.5 (moderate rate)
P.E.I.	Mod. weak	Heavily disadvantaged	55.5 (high rate)
Alberta	Mod. weak	Heavily advantaged	53.2 (high rate)
B.C.	Very weak	Heavily advantaged	66.3 (very high rate)
Newfoundland	Very weak	Heavily advantaged	85.3 (very high rate)

*See Table IV.
**See Table V, Column 3.

measured by language retention. There are, of course, exceptions, such as the French in Prince Edward Island who are moderately weak on organization and group resources, most disadvantaged compared to the non-French in Prince Edward Island in terms of income and education, and with a fairly high index of assimilation in terms of language "loss." However, the inverse relation between group and individual resources for most provinces appears to bear out Bouvier's findings for the Franco-Americans.

Thus far we have been considering variables which can be measured without too much difficulty. However, the picture which emerges from the analysis of this kind of "hard" data is skeletal and rather static. To get at underlying dynamics of ethnic viability, we need to show how other variables, more difficult or impossible to measure, must also be taken into account. We have to consider, for instance, the views and tactics of French Canadian leaders and spokesmen outside Quebec with reference to the goals of cultural survival and the means to reach these goals. These views and tactics will vary according to group strength which, in turn, will be dependent not only on the factors already discussed, but also on the extent to which French claims to charter membership are regarded as legitimate in a particular region. A certain amount of documentation on regional variations in attitudes to such matters is already available and the forthcoming publication of some of the studies carried out under the auspices of the Royal Commission on Bilingualism and Biculturalism will certainly be useful for our purposes. However, in order to test hypotheses pertaining to the views of French and non-French outside Quebec on matters such as "special status" we have to supplement this material with information gathered through interviews in each region. As we have said earlier, this interviewing will be conducted during the final phase of the research programme.

It was the purpose of this paper to bring before the seminar tentative conclusions from the material gathered so far on demography, organization and resources, both group ond individual. We reserve for future papers consideration of the more dynamic aspects of ethnic viability.

7

The Maritimes and the Canadian Community*

A Brief Study of Nova Scotia Regionalism:
"Come near at your peril – Canadian Wolf!"

GEORGE RAWLYK

IN LATE JUNE I returned to Nova Scotia from the "fleshpots of Upper Canada." Within a few days of my arrival, I seriously wondered whether Nova Scotia's major Centennial project had been the revival of the "Repeal Movement" and the concomitant growth in intensity of anti-"Upper Canadian" sentiment. Almost the first thing I heard on the radio was an impassioned attack on the federal government by a former Halifax Conservative MP. He denounced Ottawa for spending millions of dollars to provide ice-breaker service for various St. Lawrence ports, thereby assuring the further decay of Halifax as an ocean port. He also questioned the spending of vast sums of federal money on further improvements on the Welland Canal while Nova Scotia continued to be an economic backwater of despair. He concluded his emotional address by declaring that the time had come for all true Nova Scotians to take the initiative and save their own province from the indifferent if not hostile Ottawa Liberal administration. The banner of "Repeal" had apparently been raised once again in

*This paper appeared in the *Queen's Quarterly*, LXXV, No. 1 (Spring 1968), under the title "Nova Scotia Regional Protest, 1867–1967."

Joseph Howe's province and Sir Charles Tupper once again was without question spinning wildly in his grave!

The following day, before I had time to recover fully from the virulence of the radio broadcast, I heard this strange fragment of conversation while researching at the Public Archives of Nova Scotia. "I did not know how he would use the material – so I was particularly careful – you know he might have been an Upper Canadian." At that moment I expected the Archives staff to burst out singing their own version of the old Newfoundland anti-Confederate folk song:

Would you barter the rights that your fathers have won,
No! Let them descend from father to son,
For a few thousand dollars Canadian gold,
Don't let it be said that our birthright was sold.
Nova Scotia's face turns to Britain
Her back to the Gulf
Come near at your peril
Canadian wolf!

Any "Canadian wolf" should realize that since 1867 two important ingredients in Nova Scotian regionalism have been an often profound dislike of Upper Canada and "Upper Canadians" and also a basic distrust of Confederation itself. Often these two attitudes have blurred into one another, and have been further strengthened by the widespread parochialism and inbreeding of the population. The dislike of "Upper Canadians" was cogently expressed in an 1886 editorial in the Halifax *Morning Chronicle*:

The people of Nova Scotia know the Ontario or Quebec man but we know him principally in the shape of the commercial traveller. He comes here to sell, but he buys nothing but his hotel fare and in this respect he makes a rather ostentatious display. He is usually a genial enough sort of person, has a diamond ring, smokes fair cigars, "sets them up with the boys" in an off-hand way, and generally conveys the impression that in his own estimation he is a very superior being, whose condescending patronage it is a great privilege to enjoy. He spreads himself periodically throughout this province, in number he equals the locust and his visit has about the same effect. He saps our resources, sucks our money and leaves a lot of shoddy behind him. He has been able – at least the people whose agent he is – to have laws passed that compel us to buy his wares or submit to a tremendous fine, if we purchase from John Bull or brother Jonathan.[1]

This editorial undoubtedly articulated the prejudices of many Nova Scotians in 1886, but it also reflected the anti-"Upper Canadian" bias of a large number of Nova Scotians in the period both before and after 1886.

1/Cited in D. Creighton, *Dominion of the North* (Boston 1944), 356–57.

No one who has studied Nova Scotia in the nineteenth and twentieth centuries and no one from outside the province who has lived in Nova Scotia for any length of time can possibly come to a different conclusion. Modern communications may be breaking down some of the barriers but many of them still exist today.

Nova Scotia's distrust of Confederation can be seen in numerous statements made by a host of provincial patriots. Most of these declarations have two important characteristics in common. First, Confederation is considered to be directly responsible for the economic decline of Nova Scotia since 1867. Second, it is contended that "Repeal" or "Secession" would bring back the never-to-be-forgotten, glorious "Golden Age" of the Reciprocity period of 1854–66. H. W. Corning, the MLA for Yarmouth, enunciated these classic arguments on April 21, 1923 at the beginning of the "Maritime Rights Movement":

Restore our province as an independent, self-governing British dominion, make us once more free and independent in the matter of trade and commerce, competent to protect ourselves sanely and wisely from the products of Ontario and Quebec as well as other lands, then there would undoubtedly be a great revival in business and local manufacturing in this province. Instead of decreasing, as at present, our population would increase. In a comparatively short time, in my opinion, we would have a million people in Nova Scotia. Farming would become remunerative. Manufacturing, commerce and foreign trade would quickly and actively develop. Enterprise would flourish. Distributing houses, banks and other institutions would quickly spring up.[2]

It may be argued that the anti-"Upper Canadian" and anti-Confederation attitudes have combined to produce what may be called the "Paranoid Style in Nova Scotia Regionalism." Such a "Paranoid Style," of course, is not unique to the Atlantic province. The "Paranoid Style" approach could also be used to examine regionalism in other areas of Canada as well as Canadian attitudes towards the United States.

The "Paranoid Style" approach to Nova Scotia regionalism has numerous fascinating research possibilities. Like Professor Richard Hofstadter, I would argue that when I refer to the "Paranoid Style" I am using the term in a rather vague unclinical manner. In the Nova Scotia context, the spokesmen of the regional "Paranoid Style," men such as Joseph Howe before "Better Terms," William Annand, H. W. Corning in the 1920's, Edmund Morris, the former Halifax MP in the 1960's, felt that the hostile and almost conspiratorial world of "Upper Canada" was directed specifically against their beloved Nova Scotia. Their extreme political rhetoric reveals a great deal about the nature of their regional protest movements.

2/*Halifax Herald*, April 23, 1923.

The vast reservoir of political rhetoric in every area of Canada must be seriously examined and analysed and will without question add much to our understanding of "Canadian political pathology."

Confederation was seen by the "Paranoid Style" spokesmen as a blatant example of the vicious power of a hostile enemy. It was argued that the British North America Act had brought to a sudden end the material and cultural growth of Nova Scotia. Almost overnight Nova Scotia was transformed into an economic, political, social, and cultural backwater. The province was carefully bypassed by the flood of immigrants to Canada; old industries left the province because of the advantages of Upper Canada and new industries never came. Young Nova Scotians were compelled to emigrate and old Nova Scotians became increasingly bitter and disillusioned subjects. They usually remained sullen and quiet until those periods of extreme economic crises when the embers of their discontent and suspicion were fanned into the flames of regional protest by the propagandists of the "Paranoid Style."

Of course, there was some truth in the charges made against Ottawa by the proponents of Nova Scotia "Rights." Until the time of Diefenbaker, Nova Scotia's special problems were seldom dealt with in a constructive manner by the federal authorities in spite of numerous persuasive submissions made by various provincial administrations. A few palliatives were made available when the cry from Nova Scotia became too shrill, but few fundamental issues were dealt with. There is and was, therefore, some justification for the "Paranoid Style." But this political rhetoric, which came in waves of decreasing intensity after Confederation, was also an attempt to explain away the province's unfortunate lack of adequate natural resources in the post-Confederation period as well as the end of Nova Scotia's "Golden Age" – the age of "Wooden Ships and Iron Men." Moreover, and this is of some consequence, the "Paranoid Style" was effectively used by the Nova Scotia economic, social, and political establishment to channel the deep-rooted and sometimes violent frustrations of the ordinary farmers, fishermen, and workers against Ottawa rather than against Halifax. In periods of economic crises, as in 1868–69, 1885–86, 1922–25, movements emphasizing provincial rights have been organized and "Upper Canadian interests" singled out for blame and abuse. In some respects, therefore, the "Paranoid Style" of Nova Scotia regionalism has played a key role in preserving the *status quo* in the province.

An examination of the three major outbursts of Nova Scotian regionalism – that of the immediate post-Confederation period, that of 1886 and that of 1922–25 – should throw further light on the development of the "Paranoid Style." But of course this concept in itself, it must be stressed, does not explain these outbursts. Nova Scotia regionalism should be seen in its proper geographical and historical context. Only then can perceptive generalizations be made.

Nova Scotia, only 21,068 square miles in area, is like a giant disfigured foot kicking out towards Newfoundland. Most of the soil is of low fertility and the province has not been blessed with an abundance of natural resources. No point in Nova Scotia is more than fifty miles from the sea, the province's most important natural resource. In many respects it has been the sea that has given Nova Scotia its special character and the sea that has played a significant role in conditioning the province's historical development. As D. C. Harvey perceptively observed in 1934, the Atlantic Ocean was:

the first heritage of the Maritimes and their first contribution to the Dominion. It was seen in the primary interest of Europeans in our fisheries, which coloured all our early history; in the privateering industry of the Napoleonic wars and the War of 1812; in the struggle with the United States for control of the West Indian trade; in the shipbuilding industry which dominated our golden age; and it still lives in countless families whose homes contain muniments of ships and men who roamed the seven seas and brought home momentoes of their distant voyages. It lives today in the heart of many a retired sea-captain in the Canadian West who contemplates ruefully the "prairie schooner" and swaps stories in the Cutty Sark Club in Winnipeg. Its power in transforming the lives of men may be studied with profit in the story of Lunenburg, Nova Scotia, where a community of land-loving immigrants from Hanover have in less than two centuries become the finest deep-sea fishermen in the North Atlantic.[3]

Unfortunately D. C. Harvey never developed his argument regarding the "transforming power" of the sea on Nova Scotians. In certain respects, the Atlantic can be considered Nova Scotia's frontier. One does not have to be a maritime disciple of Frederick Jackson Turner to pursue the fascinating possibilities of such a thesis. Surely life at sea, whether as a fisherman or as a deckhand, encouraged the development of the so-called frontier traits. Furthermore, the Atlantic provided an escape-valve for those disenchanted with the *status quo*. It was also of great consequence in the psychological sense because it was always there if needed. It always promised excitement and possible wealth, and added much therefore to the myth of potential abundance – a myth that was destined to play havoc with any radical political or economic movement in the province.

The influence of the "maritime frontier" on the historical development of Nova Scotia should not be underestimated. Until well into the nine-

3/D. C. Harvey, "The Heritage of the Maritimes," *Dalhousie Review*. XIV (April 1934), 29.

teenth century naval power politics in the North Atlantic affected Nova Scotia. Moreover, sea communications tended to strengthen the area's ties to Great Britain on the one hand, and to New England on the other.

From the founding of Acadia in the first decade of the seventeenth century until the Confederation period, it was Nova Scotia's misfortune to be ground between the millstones of contending imperial forces in North America. Until the end of the Seven Years' War, Nova Scotia had been sandwiched between the imperial thrusts of France and Britain. During the period from the outbreak of the American Revolution until Confederation, it can be argued that the Americans appropriated the earlier British thrust while the Anglo-Canadians took upon themselves the old French imperial thrust into the continent. However, during most of these two periods, British naval power was supreme in the North Atlantic. This fact was destined to be more important than any other in determining Nova Scotia's response to hostilities.

In time of war, the inhabitants of the region, often torn between contending loyalties as well as being aware of military and economic realities, chose to walk the knife-edge of neutrality. It is noteworthy that the vast majority of Acadians were neutral when France was at war with Britain. This was certainly the case during King William's War, 1689–97, Queen Anne's War, 1702–13, King George's War, 1744–48, and the French and Indian War, 1754–63. Not knowing which side would eventually win and eager to make a profit from both sides if necessary, the shrewd and pragmatic Acadians found in neutrality a perfect answer to their perplexing problem. The Acadian answer would be the one given by the "Neutral Yankees of Nova Scotia" during the American Revolution. Most of them, it seems certain, would have joined the Revolutionaries if they had been completely free. But the isolation of the Yankees and British seapower persuaded them to choose neutrality. During the War of 1812, the Nova Scotians – Scots, Acadians, pre-Loyalists, and Loyalists – once again adopted virtually a neutral stance. Of course, Nova Scotian privateers were active but their activities can be regarded as business operations rather than as military manoeuvres. There was no fighting in the colony and the Nova Scotia merchants eagerly provided both sides in the dispute with badly needed supplies. A kind of Nova Scotian pragmatism had developed by the War of 1812. Matters of principle would almost always take second place to military and economic realities – this was particularly the case with Nova Scotia's ruling élite.

If the sea is regarded as the most important single formative force in the pre-Confederation history of Nova Scotia, the influence of New England is probably the second. From the early seventeenth century,

New England exerted a powerful influence on Nova Scotia. Certainly until the Revolutionary period, the latter area was the north-eastern frontier of New England; it was "New England's Outpost." Even after the Revolution had shattered permanently the British American colonial empire, there were still surprisingly strong economic, social, religious, and cultural ties between Nova Scotia and New England. In the post-Revolutionary period, many Nova Scotians, descendants of pre-Loyalists and Loyalists, were not absolutely certain that choosing to remain part of the British Empire had been a wise decision. These people apparently had serious second thoughts when they unfavourably contrasted the slow economic growth of Nova Scotia with dynamism of nineteenth-century industrial and commercial America. The ease with which Nova Scotians could compare their society with that in the United States helped to raise many embarrasing questions. Because of the various close ties to New England, it is not surprising that for a significant number of Nova Scotia residents what New England offered was much more attractive than anything offered by "Upper Canada." This same point of view would also exert some influence in the post-Confederation period, especially in the latter part of the nineteenth century.

The British connection can be considered the third formative force in the historical development of pre-Confederation Nova Scotia. After the American Revolution, the Loyalist migration, reinforced by economic, strategic, and constitutional considerations, drew Nova Scotia closer to Britain. The increasingly strong ties with Britain effectively neutralized the New England impact on Nova Scotia.

The fourth force in the evolution of pre-Confederation Nova Scotia and by far the weakest, was "Upper Canada." Events occurring there did not go unnoticed in Nova Scotia and, as J. S. Martell has effectively demonstrated, by 1867 "Intercolonial Communications" had "provided the facilities for closer relations between the Canadians and their fellow colonists down by the sea."[4]

The interplay of these four major formative forces has to be examined in order to place historical events in their proper perspective, not only in pre-Confederation Nova Scotia but also in post-Confederation Nova Scotia. The interplay of the influences of New England, Britain, and "Upper Canada" in Nova Scotia should provide the basis for any examination, however superficial, of Nova Scotian regionalism after Confederation.

4/J. S. Martell, "Intercolonial Communications, 1840–1867," Canadian Historical Association *Report*, 1939, 61.

JOSEPH HOWE AND REPEAL

As Professor J. Murray Beck has perceptively observed, there were two major qualities that apparently determined Howe's conduct and generally shaped his career. There was a "restless, agitating uncertainty" and also a "reverential, almost mystical attitude towards the British connection."[5] In addition, Howe possessed an unusual grasp of Nova Scotian public opinion and his opposition to Confederation, for example, reflected the general mood of his province.

He opposed Confederation vigorously for three main reasons. He felt that Confederation was not in the best interests of his concept of the New British Empire. Second, it was not in the best interests of his native province. And third, the people of Nova Scotia had not been consulted. That Howe did not want to play "second-fiddle" to Tupper was of little actual consequence in moulding his thinking concerning Confederation.

His attitudes were succinctly expressed in a letter to Sir John C. D. Hay, written in November 1866:

I am a dear lover of Old England, and to save her would blow Nova Scotia into the air ... With an enormous amount of shipping at sea Nova Scotia must belong to a great sea power. When England throws her off her destiny is inevitable and nobody with the eye of a statesman in his head can suppose that she will choose Ottawa for a capital when she has lost London and can have New York ... We go in for "the Empire one and indivisible" but when the old ship is broken up we are not such fools as to trust our lives in a crazy craft in which we are certain to be drowned.[6]

The gist of Howe's argument is not difficult to follow. He sincerely believed that Nova Scotia's economic and political future was dependent upon closer ties with the mother country. He also considered Nova Scotia to be superior in most respects to "Upper Canada" and he did not want to be associated with "a nation with a helot race within its bosom."[7]

Howe was also aware of the attractions of closer ties with the United States. He once complained that "Placed between two mighty nations, we sometimes feel that we belong to neither."[8] This may help to explain why Howe was compelled to work so hard at being more British than the British. Subconsciously, it seems that he sometimes questioned the decision

5/J. M. Beck, *Joseph Howe: Voice of Nova Scotia* (Toronto 1964), 12.
6/Howe to Sir John Hay, November 12, 1866. PAC JHP IX, 199–210.
7/J. A. Chisholm, *The Speeches and Public Letters of Joseph Howe*, II (Halifax 1909), 26. Howe to Moffatt, May 8, 1849.
8/Quotation in R. A. MacLean, "Joseph Howe and British-American Union" (unpublished PHD thesis, University of Toronto 1966), 99.

of his father to become a Loyalist. He was fully aware of the "swelling surges of Republicanism"[9] as they affected himself and Nova Scotia, and he did everything in his power to become an "Imperial Zealot."

Nova Scotia's attitude towards Confederation was accurately expressed in the provincial and federal elections of 1867. In the former, 36 out of 38 anti-Confederates were elected and in the latter 18 out of 19. It would be distorting historical facts to contend that Howe was solely responsible for the strength of the anti-Confederation movement, which probably reached its zenith in 1868. There were at least four important forces which appear to have converged in 1868 to bring about the intensity of this movement.

First, Confederation ushered a serious economic recession into the province. A good example of the impact of the recession can be seen in the trade figures of the town of Yarmouth. In 1865 the total trade was worth $23,212,355; but in 1868 it was only worth $13,655,147.[10] In such a period of economic crisis and adjustment there was bound to be considerable discontent. Something had to be blamed and Confederation became a kind of scapegoat.

Second, the old business élite, especially those people in Halifax closely tied to the old commercial system, were hard hit by the changes Confederation introduced. These men had invested a great deal in the old system and they naturally resisted the necessary major readjustment in their thinking and policies.[11]

Third, there was a widespread feeling, especially among the old business élite, that the mother country had sacrificed Nova Scotian interests on the altar of political expediency. Because of their previous dependence on Britain and because of the strong emotional ties, the change in British policy precipitated a violent reaction in Nova Scotia. Like the St. Lawrence merchants during the temporary aberration of the Annexation Manifesto period, many Nova Scotians – "the leading bankers and merchants, the wealthiest farmers, and the most independent gentlemen in the province,"[12] – felt that they had been betrayed by the mother country; and like children made aware for the first time of an adulterous parent, they were bitterly disillusioned.

Fourth, and this was particularly the case in the southern part of the province, pro-New England sentiment became increasingly important. Such sentiment had been effectively neutralized by the anglophilic tendencies in Nova Scotian development until the "betrayal of 1867."

9/Chisholm, I, 610. Howe to Lord John Russell, 1846.
10/*Yarmouth Herald*, November 11, 1869.
11/Archbishop MacDonnell to Cardwell, February 16, 1865. PANS, CO, 217.
12/*Ibid.*

It is clear that Joseph Howe did not create the profound anti-Confederation sentiment in Nova Scotia. He unsuccessfully attempted to harness and use it to obtain repeal from the British authorities. When he realized that the British would not grant repeal, he decided instead to seek "Better Terms" for Nova Scotia. When he entered John A. Macdonald's Cabinet on January 30, 1869, the repeal movement received a fatal blow. Conceived in frustration and economic discontent, it had a relatively short life in Nova Scotia and when signs of an economic upswing appeared in 1869, the movement withered.

Why did Howe leave the movement? He simply realized that repeal was impossible if Nova Scotia hoped to remain a part of the British Empire. He did not want annexation and reacted violently to the proponents of such a view in the repeal movement. He could not advocate warfare against his beloved Britain and he was also fully aware of British military power and the hopelessness of the cry of the Digby *Bluenose*: "The remedy lies in our own legislation, but most of all in our stout hearts and strong arms. The only power that will ever repeal the Stamp Act of '67 is the power that repealed the Stamp Act of '76."[13]

From 1867 to 1869, repeal had a great deal of emotional appeal in Nova Scotia. The practical problems involved in actually bringing it about may have added to this appeal. Independence was the only solution and independence was impossible when British military power and American indifference were taken into account. Howe clearly saw the *cul-de-sac* before him and jumped off the "Repeal Waggon" just before it ground to a halt.

W. S. FIELDING AND "SECESSION"
1885–86

The "Better Terms" agreement negotiated by Howe provided only minor concessions and did not adequately deal with the fundamental objections Nova Scotia had concerning Confederation. The "Better Terms" were deliberately and narrowly financial in nature, but they gave Howe and other anti-Confederates some valid justification – or so they rationalized – for accepting what was in fact inevitable. The anti-Confederation feeling in Nova Scotia, however, lingered on in Nova Scotia, reappearing as a political force usually during periods of economic stress. As Professor R. A. MacLean has contended, "Had the economic resources of the province been more viable and marketable, such attitudes would have weakened sooner than they did."[14]

13/Digby *Bluenose*, March 4, 1868.   14/MacLean, "Joseph Howe," 480.

More than anything else, the secession movement of 1885–86 was the product of the acute financial embarrassment of the government of Nova Scotia in the 1870's and early 1880's. As early as 1878 the Conservative Holmes-Thompson administration felt compelled to adopt a policy of retrenchment, made necessary in part by the expiration of the "Better Terms" agreement of 1869 and also by an economic recession. Apparently John A. Macdonald underestimated the extent and significance of Nova Scotia's grievances and in the provincial election of 1882 the Liberals swept into power with 24 out of 38 seats.

Almost immediately, the Liberals began to stress provincial rights and continued to make political capital by attacking the indifferent if not hostile Ottawa authorities. Macdonald's National Policy received most of the Liberal salvos. The tariff was blamed for most of the province's woes as was western expansion "to keep up that conglomeration of rocks [British Columbia] and Digger Indians."[15]

On February 24, 1885, the Liberal MLA, James A. Fraser, gave notice of a motion respecting the separation of Nova Scotia from Canada and the establishment of a Maritime Union. On March 12, Fraser finally moved his resolution by declaring that: "Since the financial and commercial condition of the Province was in a very unsatisfactory state, and there was no prospect of improvement while it remained part of Canada, the interests of the people of Nova Scotia, New Brunswick, and Prince Edward Island, would be advanced by withdrawing from the Canadian Federation and forming a Maritime Union."[16] If the other Atlantic Provinces refused to accept the scheme, Nova Scotia was to return to the status of an independent province of Great Britain.

On March 25, W. S. Fielding, the close-lipped Liberal premier, moved an amendment which reflected government policy:

That if the Government and Parliament of Canada fail to make provision, during the present session of said Parliament, to place the Province of Nova Scotia in a better financial position in the union, this House affirms that it will be necessary to consider the advisability of taking steps to secure a severance of the political connection between the province and the Dominion of Canada.[17]

Fielding was endeavouring to pressure the federal government into providing more financial aid to Nova Scotia but he had little actual bargaining power. Secession was impossible within the framework

15/*Halifax Morning Chronicle*, April 22, 1886.
16/P. R. Blakeley, "Party Government in Nova Scotia, 1878–1897" (unpublished MA thesis, Dalhousie University 1945), 94.
17/Quoted *ibid*.

of the British Empire and only a few Nova Scotians wanted annexation – most Americans did not! But threat of secession was part of the political game in the federal system, and Fielding realized that in tapping the almost limitless reservoir of hostility to "Upper Canada" and Confederation, he could not lose politically in Nova Scotia. The threat of secession had already become a part of the political ritual. In the Speech from the Throne in 1886, Fielding had to admit that Macdonald had called his bluff by declaring that the Dominion had made a final settlement of the province's financial objectives to the British North America Act in 1869. No further concessions would be made!

This refusal aroused a storm of protest both in the legislature and throughout the province. Fielding endeavoured to take advantage of this wave of discontent and was also eager to control it effectively in order to strengthen his political position. On May 8, 1886, he therefore moved his famous "Repeal Resolution":

That if it be found impossible, after negotiations ... to secure the co-operation of the respective Governments of the sister provinces in withdrawing from the Confederation and entering instead into a Maritime Union, then this Legislature deems it absolutely necessary that Nova Scotia, in order that its railways and other public works and services may be extended and maintained ... its industries properly fostered; its commerce invigorated and expanded; and its financial interests placed upon a sound basis, such as was the case previous to Confederation, should ask permission from the Imperial Parliament to withdraw from the Union of Canada and return to the status of a Province of Great Britain with full control over all fiscal laws and tariff regulations within the Province, such as prevailed to Confederation.[18]

The debate lasted only one day, since Fielding wished to go to the people as quickly as possible for their endorsement of his policy.

In general, there were three main issues in the provincial election of 1886 – repeal, the progressive administration of the Fielding government, and both provincial and federal railway policy. It would be a serious mistake to argue that repeal was the only issue. Most Nova Scotians must have realized that repeal was a constitutional impossibility. Certainly most Liberal politicians were aware of this fact. But the "Paranoid Style" served a useful purpose as an emotional outlet for many frustrated Nova Scotians. The secession threat was little more than political blackmail. In the past, John A. Macdonald had often been willing to purchase support or quell discontent when the cries of protest became too shrill for his sensitive ears. It was a well-known fact that all provinces had their grievances, and it was also realized that they also had their price!

18/Nova Scotia Assembly, *Journal* 1886, 147–49.

The election results pleased Fielding; the Liberals increased their number of seats to 29, the Conservatives dropped to 8, and there was one Independent. Conservative strength was restricted to northeastern Nova Scotia where the industrial areas were bound by the advantages of the National Policy to the dominion. The residents of this region were convinced that repeal and closer ties with the United States would probably destroy their struggling steel industry and lower the price they could receive for their coal. Two commercial systems were therefore in conflict and in 1886 it appeared that the advocates of the "Golden Age" were still in the ascendancy provincially. The election also was an opportunity for patriotic Nova Scotians to reassert their intense love and pride in their province. A vote for Fielding was a vote for Nova Scotia; a vote for the Tories was a vote for "treason."

Fielding now had more than an adequate mandate for his policy of repeal. But he refused to do anything until the 1887 federal election. His point of view was expressed in the *Nova Scotian* on February 19, 1887:

Without a decisive and overwhelming vote now for repeal, the great victory of last summer will amount to nothing. Every man who voted for repeal then is bound by every obligation that can have influence upon an intelligent, consistent, and patriotic citizen, to repeat it now, and not only that, but to exercise all legitimate influences to persuade his neighbour to do the same ... Let the victory of February 22nd [1887] be a perfect Waterloo for Tupper and his fellow conspirators.[19]

On February 22nd the "conspirators" won 14 seats and the Liberals 7, the same as in 1882. Apparently, the support for repeal had lost some of its fervor between the two elections. Fielding's procrastinations fooled few people. Furthermore, on the whole, the Liberals ran their best candidates provincially while the Conservatives ran their federally. This might help to explain the shift in voting behaviour.

The results of the federal election gave Fielding the excuse he so desperately needed. He maintained in the Nova Scotia House:

I have felt, since the February election, that the hands of the government were tied ... I am persuaded that our true policy is to tell the people of Nova Scotia that they had the matter in their own hands, that they had a glorious opportunity of asserting their desires on this question, and of placing themselves in a fair position to secure the accomplishment of those desires, that they lost that opportunity, and that, until they are prepared to take up the question again with greater firmness, and repair the damages of the February election, this repeal movement can have no reasonable hope of success.[20]

19/*Nova Scotian*, February 19, 1887.
20/Nova Scotia *Debates*, 1887, 254–55.

Repeal had failed in 1886–87, because it was never really a viable political issue. It was of course an emotional election issue, but only in the sense of being the vehicle of anti-Upper Canadian and anti-Confederation feeling. Once some Nova Scotians got this venom out of their systems they were content to accept the *status quo*. Their ties were gradually being strengthened with "Upper Canada" and they had no other future but that as a "Maritime Outpost of Upper Canada."

MARITIME RIGHTS AND THE HALIFAX HERALD

In 1920 the Nova Scotia Conservative party was humiliated at the polls and was replaced as the official opposition in the legislature by the new Farmer-Labour movement. In the 1920 provincial election, the Conservatives won 3 seats, Farmer-Labour 11, and the Liberals 29. For the first time in Nova Scotia's history fundamental socio-economic reforms were being advocated by the official opposition.

The post-war recession, agricultural and labour discontent, and the disorganization of the Conservative party had all helped to give rise to the Farmer-Labour movement. But even before the election, the farmers and industrial workers were at each other's throats. The movement began to disintegrate soon after the election, disintegration accelerated by the sudden revival of Nova Scotian regionalism as expressed by the desperate Conservative party.

The Conservatives realized that if they hoped to continue as a viable force in provincial politics they would have to absorb the protest movement that had brought forward the Farmer-Labour movement. Furthermore, there were many substantial Nova Scotians who were disturbed with the reforms advocated by the new political movement and they wished to check its further growth. They wanted to continue to operate under the old accepted ground rules.

Internal disintegration of the Farmer-Labour movement, the dynamic Conservative re-organization activity, and the clever use of the "Maritime Rights" issue all played key roles in the gradual rebuilding of the provincial Conservative Party. In the "Maritime Rights" movement, leading Conservatives, particularly those associated with the Halifax *Herald*, saw the emotional issue to ensure not only the survival of their party, but also eventual electoral success.

Although the serious post-war depression would have made life difficult for any party in power, it was the ringing cry of "Maritime Rights" that rallied the discontented to the banner of the new-look Conservatives against both federal and provincial Liberals. Despite the election of the so-called "solid sixteen" Liberal MPs from Nova Scotia, Mackenzie King neglected the province. He tended to take Nova Scotia for granted.

The birth of the "Maritime Rights" movement in Nova Scotia occurred publically on the editorial page of the Halifax *Herald* on July 27, 1922:

We want to say that it is time for the people of the Maritime Provinces to put shoulder to shoulder and fight for their rights. And cease not until those right(s) are acquired. We have the lesson of the Western Members of Parliament who stand like a rock and compelled the government to DELIVER THE GOODS. Our "Solid Sixteen" marched up the hill and then marched down again.

What did they bring home to Nova Scotia? Frothy assurances and fulsome promises are the only things they offer the people. We have had enough of these. Now we want action and practical rational results ... be no longer humbugged by claptrap.[21]

W. H. Dennis, owner of the *Herald*, and H. S. Congdon, editor of the Dartmouth *Patriot*, were the vociferous propagandists of "Maritime Rights" in Nova Scotia. They worked hand-in-glove with the Maritime Board of Trade – an organization intimately involved with the rise of the new "protest movement" in all three Maritime provinces. The important speech made on April 19, 1923, by H. W. Corning, house leader of the Conservatives, outlined the case for Nova Scotia "Rights," and was prepared by Dennis, Congdon, and others. This address was used by the Conservatives to show that "Maritime Rights" had become the cornerstone of their party policy. It was a calculated gamble and it apparently worked.

The effectiveness of "Maritime Rights" as an election issue was demonstrated in a federal by-election in Halifax late in 1923. The Conservatives emphasized "Maritime Rights" to the exclusion of any other issue and won an unexpected victory. This victory acted as a catalyst in the reorganization of the provincial Conservatives and gave them a badly needed psychological lift. Always swift to adjust to changing public opinion, the Liberals soon became ardent advocates as well of "Maritime Rights." The Liberals maintained that the tariff was responsible for Nova Scotia's woes, thus endeavouring to force the Conservatives to support protection against free trade. The Conservatives refused to fall into the trap but instead wisely discussed "Maritime Rights" in a vague and emotional manner. The issue of "Maritime Rights" played a significant role in the 1925 provincial election, when the Conservatives won 40 seats and 60 per cent of the vote and the Liberals only 3 seats and 36 per cent of the vote, and in the federal elections of 1925 when the Conservatives almost annihilated the federal Liberals.[22]

21/*Halifax Herald*, July 27, 1922.
22/A good description of the "Maritime Rights" movement in Nova Scotia is to

In the Conservative party platform of 1925 are to be found three planks dealing with "Nova Scotia Rights":

(8) Promotion and maintenance of Nova Scotia rights and equalities in national enterprises and undertakings ...
(13) Removal of economic injustice and disabilities under which the province is found to be labouring and in the event of failure to obtain redress, to submit the question directly to the people of the province, to obtain the will of the electors in regard to the injustices complained of, and in particular to mandate and empower the Provincial Administration to petition and request the Dominion Government to modify or relax its arrangements on the subject of taxation, trade, and the fisheries which may be found to prejudice the business and industrial interests of the people and province of Nova Scotia.
(14) If, after such action, the Federal authorities will not meet our fair demands with respect to freight rates, trade adjustments and the fisheries, then we must carry our case to the British Government for such amendments to the British North America Act as may be necessary to ensure the welfare and existence of the people of the province.[23]

No mention was made of the words repeal or secession. The Tories simply demanded certain financial concessions in spite of the ritualistic shibboleths of regional protest. The rhetoric of "Nova Scotia Rights" was good political propaganda, and if successful could be carefully put away until the next election. Emotional demands did not require action – only votes!

The cap could always be dusted off, the cup polished, and rich Mr. Ottawa approached for a little "conscience money." Full equalization could be demanded by some Nova Scotia politicians in the 1960's, but most Nova Scotians could not understand, so they would not listen. They were satisfied with small mercies – a post office here, a wharf there.

In the Canadian federal system each section, in theory at least, is supposed to have its interests looked after by its representative in Ottawa. But as Professor Beck has observed:

This raises the question whether Nova Scotian members of Parliament have been more concerned with maintaining party solidarity than with safeguarding provincial interests. While the western Canadian Provinces have undoubtedly found it to their advantage to return third-party representation in strength, the Maritimes have rarely deviated from old-party lines to the extent of more than a single member, and the political leaders at Ottawa have had no difficulty in keeping them in line by what might be alleged to be little more than temporary sops.[24]

be found in E. R. Forbes, "The Rise and Fall of the Conservative Party in the Provincial Politics of Nova Scotia 1922–33" (unpublished MA thesis, Dalhousie University 1967).
23/*Ibid.*, 205–6.
24/J. M. Beck, *The Government of Nova Scotia* (Toronto 1957), 338–39.

Mere political rhetoric, however paranoid, was and is no adequate substitute for power politics. Nova Scotia may be experiencing the "Stanfield Revolution," but most citizens are content with federal "sops." In the last federal election the party that enthusiastically advocated full equalization grants to Nova Scotia received less than 9 per cent of the popular vote and no seats. "Upper Canada" is still often blamed by Nova Scotians for their plight, but they nevertheless seem content to have their disenchantment expressed in words rather than in effective action. Is there any other choice for a dependent, "colonial" society?

8

Aspects of Metropolitanism in Atlantic Canada

J. M. S. CARELESS

I

METROPOLITANISM, the pattern of reciprocal relations whereby large urban communities focus broad areas on themselves, is intimately associated with regionalism. For regions usually centre on metropolitan communities, which largely organize them, focus their views, and deal with outside metropolitan forces on their behalf. Indeed, much of what is often called regionalism may be better expressed in terms of metropolitan relations and activities. In that belief, this discussion of metropolitanism in Atlantic Canada is offered. Because the subject is so large, it has been limited to the period from the mid-nineteenth to the early twentieth centuries, and to a selective consideration of the metropolitan roles of the three principal Atlantic cities, Saint John, Halifax, and St. John's during that period.

This time span is long enough to allow a considerable process of change to be examined, still highly significant today. Although its limits are inevitably imprecise, there is some validity in starting with the 1850's, after the end of the Navigation Acts and the old imperial system, and closing before the First World War brought striking new developments to the Maritimes and Newfoundland. As for the subject-matter, there seems no less validity in studying the three largest communities of the Atlantic region in themselves: both as regional leaders, and because we might well pay more regard to urban history in Canada.

The fact is that, land of vast frontiers and wilderness or not, urban communities long have played a large part in Canadian development and this is no less true for the Atlantic region. Nor need the cities in question be huge and teeming by modern standards. It is far more the proportion of their population to the total in their regional community that has meaning. In 1861, for instance, Saint John had a population of 27,315 to 252,045 for all New Brunswick, or a proportion of close to 1 in 9; Halifax had 25,025 to 330,885 in Nova Scotia, or roughly 1 in 13; St. John's 30,475 to 122,635 in Newfoundland, or a remarkable proportion of almost 1 in 4. A century later, by the Canadian census of 1961, Saint John stood at something over 1 in 8, Halifax at about 1 in 8, St. John's around 1 in 9. Plainly then, even by present standards, each city has represented a decided concentration of population in its own provincial community; not to mention a concentration of capital and labour that would enable it to fulfil metropolitan functions.

These functions or attributes of metropolitan stature have broadly been held to comprise, first, the provision of commercial facilities for the import and export trade of the city's dependent region or hinterland (on which, of course, it in turn depends); second, the establishment of industries to process products of, or imports for, the hinterland; third, the development of transport services to channel traffic to and from the urban centre; and fourth, the creation of financial facilities for investment and development in the region. All these attributes can be seen in greater or less degree within the three cities under inquiry. But to these economic characteristics might also be added those of political power or military authority often centred in the metropolis; and, quite as frequently, the exercise of religious, educational, and intellectual leadership for the regional community, along with press influence over its opinion.

Indeed, to a great extent a metropolitan system is inherently a system of communications, whether this carries goods, people or money, orders or ideas. As a result, it may be deeply affected by changes in technology; a point as true for the age that experienced the introduction of the steamship, railway, and telegraph as for that of automobility, jet transport, and television.

The effect of technological change on communications is notably clear in the case of Atlantic Canada. Although in assessing it, this general survey must to some extent put together material that is far from new, yet it is hoped that a restructuring in terms of metropolitan patterns and pulls will make the data more meaningful. And it is thought that a comparative analysis of the development of the three major Atlantic centres can promote new queries concerning their regional functions. The procedure will be to start with Saint John, then move out to sea, so to speak, in a properly Toronto-centred view of the globe.

II

In the mid-nineteenth century, Saint John held a prominent role in an Atlantic communications system extending to Liverpool and London in one direction, Boston and New York in another. It was the commercial metropolis for much of New Brunswick, exporting the timber wealth of the Saint John River from its position at the entrance to that long waterway, importing the British manufactures or American provisions needed for a hinterland heavily based on forest production. It was a focus of industry also, that utilized the chief product of its hinterland region in large-scale wooden shipbuilding. And through wealth acquired from the timber trade or the sale of Saint John ships in England, the city's business community was able to provide significant financial services, including by the later fifties three locally owned banks and four local marine, fire, or general insurance companies.

Yet Saint John's metropolitan stature had clear limits. First, although New Brunswick was past the frontier expansionist stage, the province was relatively poor and undiversified in depending on its forest staple. Second, since the whole region was largely composed of a series of separated river valleys, Saint John's sway over its own river and Bay of Fundy area by no means extended to the province's north shore. And third, since the city was not the seat of government, it could not enjoy the pervasive influence of a centre of political authority. Nor did it really exercise social or cultural headship, which remained with the genteel society of little Fredericton up-river.

Saint John's own leading elements composed a substantial, overlapping business élite of import merchants, timber traders, shipbuilders, and shipowners. The same individuals reoccurred in lists of the directors of banks, insurance firms, and other joint stock enterprises such as the Saint John Gas, Light, Electric, Telegraph, or South Bay Boom Companies: men such as William Parks, President of the Commercial Bank, or shipbuilders and shipowners such as Wright, DeVeber, and Zebedee Ring.[1] Nor did this Saint John business community lack strong political ties. Out of its

1/See *Saint John Business Directory and Almanac for 1857, et seq.* (Saint John 1857).

background came such major political figures as R. L. Hazen and R. D. Wilmot, W. H. Steeves, a father of Confederation, G. E. King, provincial premier of the seventies – or Samuel Leonard Tilley himself, partner in the prominent firm of Peters and Tilley, merchants.

The business élite of Saint John was perhaps more limited in its outlook than its counterparts in either Halifax or St. John's. The New Brunswick port's outside connections largely ran to Portland as an intermediary for Boston, or else focussed on Liverpool; hardly a city of light. A scion of the mid-century élite (son of the president of the Bank of New Brunswick) recalled that Saint John businessmen would cross to Liverpool and Manchester twenty times "without ever going on to London."[2] Yet the sober, workaday masters of Saint John were lively and enterprising enough when it came to the city's main industrial activity, shipbuilding.

In the prosperous fifties, stimulated by the gold rush to Australia, Saint John yards turned out a splendid succession of large sailing vessels for Liverpool owners. There was James Smith's famed *Marco Polo*, hailed as the fastest ship in the world, after her 68-day voyage from Liverpool to Melbourne in 1852; or the *Morning Light*, of over 2,300 tons, launched by William and Richard Wright in 1855, which remained for twenty years the largest ship constructed in British North America. By 1858, of 100 major vessels over 1,200 tons sailing out of Liverpool, 32 had been built in Saint John and the pace continued through the sixties.

Successful as it was in ocean transport, the city entered a whole new phase of problems when it looked to railways to improve its land communications in the prosperous mid-century years. Saint John interests were deeply involved in the scheme to build the European and North American Railway, which would link the Bay of Fundy port overland with the Atlantic shore at Shediac, and in the other direction with Portland, Maine, there connecting with the rails to Boston and with the Atlantic and St. Lawrence to Montreal, open since 1852. Saint John was thus to become the focus of a great international overland route between coasts close to Europe, New England, and Canada. It was a bright vision, often more appealing than the alternative Intercolonial Railway project from Nova Scotia through New Brunswick to Quebec – though, conceivably (in the brightest moments of vision) both lines might be built, and tied together at Saint John. Of course, John A. Poor, the Portland capitalist who expressed his own city's metropolitan ambitions, had other hopes as to the final focal point of the railway scheme he was promoting. But in any case it did not succeed.

Neither Portland nor Saint John could organize the capital for so large

2/J. W. Millidge, "Reminiscences of Saint John from 1849 to 1860," *New Brunswick Historical Collections*, no. 10 (Saint John 1919), 135.

a design, and construction problems had been underestimated. The European and North American was completed only between Saint John and Shediac by 1860, and then as a publicly owned road. Moreover, Saint John was not really well placed to dominate overland routes to the interior of the continent, a fact of growing ominous significance in the spreading railway age. When again in 1865, an attempt by a new company under William Parks shortly failed to build the "Western Extension" from the city to Maine, it was no wonder that many in Saint John viewed with disdain the coming of Confederation, and its concomitant bargain to build the Intercolonial, but via New Brunswick's distant north shore. Indeed, they might sense that an oceanic metropolitan system in which their city had flourished was passing away, to be replaced by new continental patterns with which they were less equipped to deal.

Yet Confederation was more coincident than causal in regard to changes that affected the whole functioning of Saint John as a metropolis. In fact, the changes did not plainly reveal themselves until after the depression of 1873 began. Most vital was the shift from wood to iron technology in transport. It was not the steamship that drastically affected Saint John's shipping industry, but the iron-built vessel. British yards had begun turning out cheap, capacious iron and steel steamships in quantities. They doomed Saint John's Liverpool sales and attacked the lucrative charter business of wooden sailing craft, secure while the steamship itself had been limited to fairly small wooden hulls, carrying fuel as well as cargo on a relatively few high-cost ocean runs. And while it had once been economic to build wooden ships in New Brunswick instead of England, now the great British iron and steel capacity made it increasingly uneconomic to do so. The effects came gradually. A peak year for Saint John yards was 1873, and as late as 1888, 2,000 men were still employed there.[3] But through the seventies and eighties, the city's major industry inexorably declined.

One should recall, of course, that the sweep of technological change also affected wealthier adjacent American centres. Thus New England's magnificent but costly clippers could not compete, and the region failed to build an iron ship industry. This in part was because Boston capital had turned from marine to railway investment, in efforts to organize and dominate continental routes west that proved only somewhat less abortive than Saint John's hopes of the European and North American. Portland declined. Boston itself was not so well placed to collect the traffic from the ever growing continental hinterland. It could be the chief regional metropolis of New England, but not a great deal beyond.[4] Railways, which had made inland western development so much more feasible and

3/F. W. Wallace, *Wooden Ships and Iron Men* (London n.d.), 309.
4/A. P. Langtry, ed., *Metropolitan Boston* (New York 1929), 1067.

valuable, had shifted the emphasis from ports chiefly well located for the exchange of water-borne coastal and ocean traffic to those which also offered the most effective land access to broad continental territories.

All this was true for Saint John in the advancing railway age – itself another aspect of triumphant steel technology. Again the city was not in a position to benefit. Its own hinterland did not provide fuel or raw material for new heavy industry. And along with the relative down-grading of its timber resources went a decline in their quality, as the best pineries were cut over. Even in the 1860's it was becoming difficult to get good timber for large ships at Saint John yards.[5] Hence these underlying changes, affecting the commercial position, industrial enterprise, and even hinterland supply of the New Brunswick metropolis, were much more basic than any effects of Confederation, the National Policy of 1879, or the long depression of the later nineteenth century.

No doubt the lean depression years made the impact of change harder, especially for a city swept by the disastrous fire of 1877 that destroyed two-fifths of Saint John and $27,000,000 in property.[6] No doubt the protective tariff offered little to the business enterprises of a community largely geared to primary production, except for a declining industry tariffs could not protect. But world depression created none of Saint John's essential problems. And National Policy or not, the smaller business units of the Maritime centres would surely have faced powerful competition from much larger aggregations of capital and labour, once the age of overland communication by rail had tied them into major continental traffic systems. Here indeed lay the essential significance of the later nineteenth-century years for Saint John and its region; it was the difficult era when the old Atlantic system was failing and the New Brunswick metropolis had not yet adjusted to the new forces of continental dominance.

That adjustment came in the early twentieth century. It was, perhaps, only relatively successful, in that it could not restore all Saint John's vanished eminence, but it has largely endured to the present. Its effect was economic, yet it was achieved largely by political means for political reasons: not in spite of, but because of, the Atlantic region's membership in Canada. And it was built on the advantage the Atlantic region had to offer within that membership, year-round access to the ocean.

The Canadian federation had a political, national, need for winter ports of its own. In a sense, the process of developing them was a valid complement to the National Policy. For that programme, as Professor R. C. Brown has emphasized, must truly be seen as an expression of

5/Millidge, *loc. cit.*, 131.
6/D. R. Jack, *Centennial Prize Essay on Saint John* (Saint John 1883), 151.

national aspirations, however much it might also enhance central Canadian metropolitan power.[7] If the federal state could pursue nation-building by tariffs, it could equally do so by railway and port development, by subsidies and preferential rail rates, to aid enterprises and areas disadvantaged by distance or tariffs. It was all a natural response to the problem of integrating regions within a Canadian continental entity.

The process of adjustment for Saint John really began when in 1887 business leaders in its Board of Trade opened a campaign to shift the winter terminus of the Dominion-subsidized mail steamers from Portland to the New Brunswick city. Then in 1890 the completion of the Canadian Pacific's Short Line from Montreal across Maine to Saint John meant that the Fundy port now had fairly direct access to central Canada, as well as by the more circuitous Intercolonial, intersected by the Saint John–Shediac line at Moncton. Now there indeed was hope that Canadian winter traffic still moving via Portland could be diverted to Saint John. Hence that city invested in building large ocean docks, to the extent of $1,000,000 by 1895.[8]

Late that year came the key political step. When city delegations repeatedly had failed to bring the federal government to grant a mail subsidy to a Saint John-based steamship line, the city's two MPs, J. D. Hazen and J. A. Cheslay, bluntly indicated they would resign their seats if nothing were done.[9] The Conservative cabinet, already in turmoil, and nearing highly doubtful elections, forthwith provided an annual subsidy of $25,000 to the Beaver Line for fortnightly service between Saint John and Liverpool. The Donaldson Line quickly followed in shifting its terminus from Portland; others soon did the same. Almost in months in 1896 Saint John emerged as a major winter port.

Thereafter, as the western Canadian boom developed, prairie grain flowed out of the port and imports for central Canada came in. Both the city and the CPR repeatedly enlarged the harbour facilities in a veritable race to keep up with cargoes. In 1910, the federal government entered directly into building ocean berths itself.[10] And though Saint John's old shipbuilding industry did not re-emerge, it gathered repair yards, railway shops, sugar refineries and lumber mills. Finally, another technological change benefited it and its provincial hinterland. The development of wood-pulp mills gave a new significance to forest resources, especially those that had been inferior, such as spruce.

7/See R. C. Brown, "The Nationalism of the National Policy," in P. Russell, ed., *Nationalism in Canada* (Toronto 1966), 155–63.
8/F. W. Wallace and I. Sclanders, *The Romance of a Great Port* (Saint John 1935), 37.
9/*Ibid.*, 44.   10/*Ibid.*, 46.

By 1914, accordingly, the New Brunswick city had moved far in adjusting to continental pulls, and had succeeded in making connections inward to share in western and central Canadian hinterlands. Its commercial future as a Canadian outlet and gateway would still largely depend on deliberate political policy, as in the provision of preferential railway rates. Industrial – and financial – pre-eminence had decisively moved to central Canadian metropolitan centres. Yet in the national continental system that had replaced the colonial and Atlantic one, Saint John clearly continued to play a metropolitan role within its own region.

III

Halifax and St. John's can be dealt with more briefly – not in any way as less significant, but as variations on a theme that has been established. The theme, of course, is the role of these communities in an Atlantic metropolitan system, and the effects technological change and continental pulls had upon them. However, there is more to say of Halifax during the period to be covered, since the changes in question affected St. John's later and more slowly.

The Nova Scotian city of the mid-nineteenth century did not have as full commercial control of an immediate hinterland area as did its New Brunswick neighbour. There was no long Saint John Valley to dominate; the open Atlantic coasts of the Nova Scotian peninsula enabled many lesser places to share in Halifax's importing or exporting functions, although at the same time no part of the province was wholly remote from its influence. Moreover, Halifax did not develop industry on the scale of Saint John; either wooden shipbuilding, or later enterprises. On the other hand, it was a notably larger focus of shipping interests and financial power. It was also political capital, intellectual centre – and perhaps social arbiter – as Saint John was not. Finally, Halifax, of course, was an imperial citadel and naval base: a transatlantic bastion of British metropolitan power that had strong ties to sustain and pounds sterling to spend. Still closely akin to Boston, despite the breach of the Revolution, the Haligonian descendants of Loyalist and pre-Loyalist New Englanders were happy to view London in their midst, in the fashionable society of the garrison.

As Saint John had grown with timber and the large shipbuilding it fostered, so Halifax had grown with the fishing staple and the schooners it required. The location of Halifax's superb harbour, at the corner of the continent adjacent to the main northwest Atlantic fishing grounds made it an excellent base for a fishing fleet. It was also well placed as a first main-land port of call for ships bringing imports on the great circle route from Europe to America; and for trading fish to the West Indies, in return for tropical products to be re-exported by coastal or transatlantic shipping. This extensive trading pattern, well settled by the mid-century, had made Halifax a major centre of shipping rather than shipbuilding, a commercial and financial emporium, and the wealthiest, most advanced metropolitan city in the British Atlantic provinces – focus of a fairly diversified regional society matured beyond the frontier phase.

The metropolitan stature of Halifax was evinced in the wealth and power of its merchants, notably its West Indies merchants, and in its bank-ing institutions. In the 1850s and 1860s these included the long-estab-lished Halifax Banking Company, the Bank of Nova Scotia, the Union Bank, and the Merchants Bank, begun in 1864, which would become the Royal Bank of Canada. Again their directors and those of Halifax insu-rance, gas, and water companies formed a business élite interwoven with wholesale merchants, shipping magnates, and steamship operators.[11] Men such as Enos Collins, Samuel Cunard, W. A. Black, and M. B. Almon were prominent. Their political pedigree was evident also. Although the old days of the Halifax oligarchy and the Council of Twelve had vanished, other potent names like Uniacke, Fairbanks, Kenney and Tobin also revealed the strong connections of the Halifax business world with Nova Scotian politics. As for wealth, Collins died in 1871 worth $6,500,000; Cunard in 1865 worth $5,000,000; and many others amassed sizeable fortunes.[12]

Cunard might have moved to England to direct his burgeoning steam-ship line, but the foundations of his fortune had been laid in Halifax. He had no less benefited his native city by establishing his "ocean ferry" (steamships running to schedule as sailing ships could not), and making it the first port of call in the regular steam service from Liverpool to Boston, begun in 1840. Boston was thoroughly grateful for the Cunard Line, with good reason; Halifax had reason also.[13] At the same time Halifax and Cunard could thank the British metropolitan concern for improved Atlan-tic communications that produced the vitally needed imperial mail con-tract and subsidy. Still further, Cunard might thank the imperial dock-yard at Halifax for a lucrative coal contract to supply steam warships.[14]

11/See *Beecher's Farmers Almanack for 1850, et seq.* (Halifax 1850).
12/A. W. H. Eaton, *Chapters in the History of Halifax* (New York 1915), 839.
13/F. L. Babcock, *Spanning the Atlantic* (New York 1931), 48.
14/P. H. Watson, "The Two Hundredth Anniversary of the Halifax Dockyard," *Occasional Papers of the Maritime Museum* (Halifax 1959), 21.

And all the Halifax merchants could appreciate the dockyard contracts for provisions, or the imperial expenditures on Halifax defences which exceeded £170,000 in the later sixties.[15] These investments in steam communications or improved facilities at Halifax were aspects of British metropolitan influence wholly beneficial to the Nova Scotian centre.

Yet the wooden paddlewheeler was the forerunner of the iron screwsteamer, which in the seventies began to exert its effects on Halifax. No longer need the larger iron vessels call at the port for fuel after crossing the ocean; the tendency was to concentrate through runs at larger ports. Thus even in 1867 the main Cunard route ceased its stop at Halifax: an unfortunate coincidence with the inception of Confederation. And although Halifax had no major wooden ship industry to suffer, its functions as a wholesale centre did. For the ubiquitous iron tramp steamer could readily take cargoes direct to hinterland ports, instead of via Halifax warehouses. In fact, by the 1880's the ease of ordering goods direct by telegraph and the speed of steamship delivery was seriously affecting Halifax as an *entrepôt*.[16] Moreover, the decline in the West Indies sugar economy increasingly harmed Halifax shipping and fishing interests.

Again, the old oceanic trading pattern was failing, while the Nova Scotian capital was being opened to rising continental influences. The Intercolonial was completed through to Halifax in 1876; the National Policy came three years after. Far from gaining the flow of western trade that had been hoped for, Halifax firms seemed chiefly to have acquired increasing competition from larger central Canadian firms – all this, and world depression, and the British government reducing expenditures on the Halifax base.

Nevertheless, the wealth and power of Halifax business were such that it was a case of slowed growth rather than absolute decline. New industries were started, some aided by tariff protection: cotton mills, shoe factories, sugar refineries.[17] But the important response was as that of Saint John: to make the city an effective part of the Canadian continental system as a winter port. The work began as early as 1882, when indeed the dominion government built a grain elevator at Halifax. But more important were the building of the big Halifax drydock in 1887–89, and the steady development of the Intercolonial's deep water terminus, which by 1899 could handle twelve large ocean steamers at once.[18]

With first-class port facilties and improving rail connections, Halifax was now equipped to take its own considerable share of the Canadian

15/*Ibid.*, 32.
16/P. R. Blakeley, *Glimpses of Halifax, 1867–1900* (Halifax 1949), 24.
17/*Ibid.*, 38–45.   18/*Ibid.*, 28.

boom of the early twentieth century. It prospered vigorously, able to hold its own with Saint John – and hold as well the Atlantic margins of New Brunswick, more susceptible to its own rail connections. In fact, it made little difference when in 1905 a long era ended for Halifax, and Britain, concentrating her naval forces, gave up the Halifax naval base. Formal transfer of the naval dockyard to a largely store-keeping Canadian regime came in 1910, to mark another aspect of advancing continental dominance. Still another sign of that advance came in the financial field. In 1900 the general manager's office of the Bank of Nova Scotia was transferred to Toronto, in 1907 that of the Royal Bank to Montreal, and in 1903 the august Halifax Banking Company became part of Toronto's Bank of Commerce as it invaded the Maritimes.[19]

Still, if Halifax was thus being incorporated in the continent, it retained its essential strategic importance as a focal point for transatlantic communication. That was made abundantly plain only a few years thereafter, when the port was again called upon to prove its significance in naval war, as it had not been required to do since 1814. But that is another story.

IV

To conclude with St. John's: its metropolitan role might seem the least significant of the three Atlantic cities. Certainly its own hinterland was thinly populated and scarcely developed but for the fringe of fishing outports; it had virtually no industrial base apart from the cod and seal fisheries; and its financial services were limited by the backward state of the Newfoundland region in general. And yet, in other respects, St. John's had a decidedly powerful metropolitan role, as the great commercial and shipping *entrepôt* of the island. Its merchants and shipowners financed the fishing staple, marketed dried cod from the West Indies to the Mediterranean, imported and distributed foodstuffs and manufactures for the outports and through the use and abuse of the credit system tied the fishing population closely to the business houses of Water Street. Here was a compact urban élite, notably internationally minded, whose social predominance was unrivalled. One cannot doubt the enduring influence of the great dynasties of the St. John's business world, the Bowrings, Job Brothers, the Ayres, Newman and Company.[20] And one need scarcely assert the political ascendancy of St. John's figures like Charles Fox Bennett and Ambrose Shea, Robert Thorburn and Robert Bond, when all the

19/See *McAlpine's Halifax City Directory for 1907–08* (Halifax 1907).
20/See *Year Book and Almanack of Newfoundland, 1913* (St. John's 1913); also C. R. Fay, *Life and Labour in Newfoundland* (Toronto 1956), 13–37.

class and religious friction of the province found its focus in politics at the capital.

The city, moreover, was well integrated in the old Atlantic nineteenth-century system, traditionally linked with Liverpool, London, and Bristol, increasingly with the Maritimes and Boston. Yet it was still remote from the continent, buying supplies rather than selling there, and little affected by continental forces – as the flat rejection of Confederation with Canada might show. The state of the fishing and sealing catches also affected it far more immediately than the world process of technological change. Indeed, for much of the later nineteenth century St. John's was generally flourishing. It had four banks by the mid-seventies, direct steam service with England from 1869, the Atlantic cable since 1866, and regular steamship sailings to Halifax.[21] The eighties brought the beginning of railway building with the line to Harbour Grace and stimulated many small-scale industrial enterprises, of which Colonial Cordage survived.

But the well-being of St. John's continued to rest ultimately on the uncertain fortunes of the fisheries; its metropolitan ventures into industrial and transport development proved shaky and premature. After the Great Fire of 1892, that burned out most of the city's commercial firms and left 11,000 homeless, the whole strained overextended financial system was in deep trouble.[22] The bank crash of 1894 that followed, the failure of renewed Confederation negotiations with Canada the next year, left the city in financial chaos and considerable bitterness over apparent Canadian indifference to the gravity of the problem. When recovery came, with prosperous world trade in the new century, and a Newfoundland boom based on railway building and the development of pulpwood and mineral resources, it seemed that St. John's had again decisively turned its back on Canadian continental connections.

But had it? With hindsight, one could say that the connections had only been delayed; or rather, that they were so far premature for an island community which, in remoteness, had not yet felt the full impact of technological change in its communications system. The decline of the old-style Newfoundland fishery in face of modern big-ship operations would not become fully apparent until the bad years between the two world wars. Commission government might then be regarded as a final, reluctant exercise of British metropolitanism; the establishment of American and Canadian bases on the island in the Second World War as a function of extending continental metropolitan dominance – to be consolidated politically in the Confederation settlement of 1949.

21/P. Toque, *Newfoundland as it was and is* (London 1878), 76–87.
22/A. B. Perlin, "St. John's," *Atlantic Advocate* (June 1960), 47.

Furthermore, again with hindsight, one may note the growth of continental pulls upon St. John's even from the 1890's; above all, the fact that Canadian banks took over in the city after the collapse of its own financial institutions.[23] Also, the very Newfoundland railway boom was shaped, if not captured, by R. A. Reid, fresh from his building for the CPR. And the pulpwood and iron-mining developments that began at last to diversify the Newfoundland region were largely in accord with Canadian continental interests. The real point is that St. John's, like its sister cities of the Atlantic region, was going to join the continent; each in varying ways, perhaps, but decisively – with changes in metropolitan patterns of communications which involved them all. What remain are questions. There is no intention here to put forward technological change as a kind of simplified economic determinism – but how far did it relate to the decision-making processes both of business and of government? How far was it the factor that made urban business élites in the Atlantic metropolitan centres aware of their own need to respond to change and make adjustments? How far did they utilize political influence to do so, and what were the reactions in their own regional communities? We need a great deal more study of the role of these urban élites, in the Atlantic region as elsewhere in Canada: more urban history, more business history, more study of the political and social interweavings of these entrepreneurial elements – which will inevitably carry us further into regional socio-cultural history as well. In sum, the restructuring in this inevitably sketchy paper (that still leaves so much out) of things we already know, should only make us aware of how much we do not know, when we look at regionalism in terms of metropolitanism.

23/R. A. MacKay, ed., *Newfoundland* (Toronto 1946), 459.

9

The English Communities in Winnipeg
and in the Eastern Townships of Quebec

D. C. MASTERS

I

TO DESCRIBE THE fortunes of the English communities in Winnipeg and the Eastern Townships, I am using the terms "English" and "Anglo-Saxon" to denote English-speaking Canadians of English, Scottish, Irish, and Welsh descent. This is a bit hard on the Scots, the Irish, and the Welsh, but there is no completely satisfactory blanket term to cover these four groups. The other possible alternative, "British," would displease many Canadians who dislike the term as smacking of colonialism.

To begin with, a brief description of Winnipeg and the Eastern Townships is essential. Most Canadians are at least vaguely aware of the location of Winnipeg, but I have encountered westerners who have never heard of the Eastern Townships. Winnipeg, a city with a population of some 265,000 in Winnipeg proper, and 476,000 in the metropolitan area of Greater Winnipeg,[1] is situated at the confluence of the Red and Assiniboine Rivers, on the flat plain which covers most of southern Manitoba. The city has an area of thirty-one square miles.

The Eastern Townships is an area in southeastern Quebec, lying between the St. Lawrence Lowlands and the United States border, extending

1/*Census of Canada, 1961*, I, Part II, Tables 38 and 39.

from Dorchester County in the northeast to Mississquoi County in the southwest. It includes fifteen counties: Arthabaska, Bagot, Beauce, Brome, Compton, Dorchester, Drummond, Frontenac, Megantic, Mississquoi, Richmond, Shefford, Sherbrooke, Stanstead, and Wolfe. The region is somewhat elevated, with an area of 9,120 square miles, about 77 per cent of which is occupied. It had a total population in 1961 of about 610,000. The region is said to have been given the name Eastern Townships in the early British period to distinguish it from the townships west of Montreal, in what is now Ontario.

In discussing the fortunes of the English in the two areas, one is struck at the outset by certain similarities and certain differences. In each case the English under consideration form an urban group. In the case of Winnipeg, they all, of course, live in one city; in the Townships, they live largely in a number of urban centres such as Sherbrooke, Granby, Drummondville, and Thetford. The English in the Townships are not completely urban, but mainly they are urban and suburban, and are becoming more so. Both groups of English are in the economic hinterlands of Montreal and Toronto, the largest Canadian metropolitan centres.

Both the English in Winnipeg and the English in the Townships were majority groups to start with. Each has now become a minority group confronted by a larger number of non-Anglo-Saxons. Yet the position of the English in the two areas respectively, vis-à-vis the non-English, is not the same. In the Townships, the English are a comparatively small minority group, living among a French-Canadian majority which composed 90 per cent of the total population in 1961.[2] In Winnipeg, the English, though not a majority, form the largest group, 113,000 out of 265,000, according to the 1961 census. In Greater Winnipeg, also, the English are the largest group but not a majority, 213,000 out of 475,000. They are confronted by a comparatively small French group, 13,000 in Winnipeg, and 13,000 in St. Boniface. The French total for Greater Winnipeg is 39,700. There are other large non-Anglo-Saxon groups: Ukrainians, 36,000; Germans, 30,000; Poles, 16,000 in the city; and in Greater Winnipeg, Ukrainians, 54,000; Germans, 50,000; and Poles, 25,000.[3] However, these groups are rapidly becoming anglicized and do not consciously challenge the dominance of Anglo-Saxon culture, as do the French in the Townships. I taught some of the second generation of these New Canadians at United College and can testify to the great extent to which they had become assimilated to English culture.

There are noticeable differences in tone between the two groups. Partly

2/*Ibid.*, I, Part II, Table 37.
3/*Ibid.*, Tables 38 and 39.

because Winnipeg is more of a metropolis than Sherbrooke, and partly because the English in Winnipeg are closer to a majority position, they appear more confident and expansive. The Eastern Townships English are a quieter, more restrained element, although not without considerable economic power. The managerial element in large industry in the Townships is still Anglo-Saxon. Although the English in Winnipeg are for the most part nationalist in the sense of being proud of Canada as a whole, some Anglo-Saxons in the Townships share the pride of the French in Quebec and are in their loyalties Quebecers first, and Canadians second. Others of the English in the Townships are worried by the fear of French dominance. The nationalist speeches of M. René Lévesque and others have taken their toll. The question by a French-Canadian resident of Lennoxville on a visit to Bishop's University, "Why do the minority rate all these new buildings?" created something of a sensation. So did the sudden appearance of French shelf-labels in the Lennoxville chain stores. They cater to a predominantly English population. English teachers are worried about their pensions in the light of the French educational revolution. An English executive in the Bell Telephone Company was worried by the hostility of French Canadians working under him, asked for a transfer to Ontario and received it.

In 1963, during the FLQ disturbances, I had a talk with an automobile sales manager in Sherbrooke. This man was of Loyalist stock and came from a family which had lived in Brome County (the most English area in the Eastern Townships) since the time of the American Revolution. He said that he did not see what grievances the French had. Their educational system had steered all the bright boys into the Church or the legal profession; so why should they blame the English because they had not done well in business? He declared that the French said he could stay in Quebec, but that he must speak French. He had no desire to speak French and was contemplating departure. This man was typical in his attitude to the French language. As in other parts of the province, the English in the Townships have not made a great effort to learn French. For example, in the town of Lennoxville, 20 per cent of the English are bilingual compared with 50 per cent of the French.[4] The English in the Townships are aware of the fact that they are part of a large Anglo-Saxon group in Canada as a whole and fear Quebec separatism because its success would deprive them of the support of their English compatriots from outside Quebec.

There is a striking contrast between the tone of the English in the Townships and the Winnipeg group, who are still on top of the heap, proud

4/W. G. Ross, "Lennoxville" (mimeographed study produced at Bishop's University 1966), 9.

of their position in Winnipeg and in Canada. They are very different from the English in the Townships, a minority-minded group, which feels its way of life threatened by a dynamic and triumphant French majority. I personally found it a shock, having always regarded myself as a Canadian, to find, on moving to the Townships, that I had ceased to be a Canadian and had instead become "English."

II

The present position of English-Canadians in Winnipeg and the Eastern Townships can better be understood if one begins with a survey of their previous fortunes.

In the Townships, settlement developed in a country which was dominantly a producer of agricultural products and lumber down to the turn of the century, after which it became an important manufacturing centre, producing textiles, machinery, paper, and furniture. These industries secured power from developments on the St. Francis, as well as from Shawinigan Falls north of the St. Lawrence. The development of transportation facilities played an important role in the opening up of the Townships. The St. Lawrence and Atlantic Railway, later part of the Grand Trunk, connected the Townships with Montreal and Portland in 1853. By a process of construction and the use of older lines, the CPR established connections across Maine between the Eastern Townships and the Maritimes in 1890. The era of good roads began during World War I, with the paving of the Sherbrooke-Stanstead highway in 1914–15.

The earliest settlers in the Townships were the French, who settled in the Beauce during the French régime.[5] English Loyalists arrived during the last fifteen years of the eighteenth century. Between 1792 and 1812 the pioneers were mainly from New England, Loyalists and others anxious to secure good land. A number of groups came in, operating on the leader principle, by which members of a group, each permitted to purchase 1,200 acres, assigned their holdings to a leader. Between 1814 and 1830 the settlers were chiefly from Great Britain, although the main stream of English settlers was going to Upper Canada. The British-American Land Company was largely responsible for settlement in the Townships in the 1830–50 period. Formed in 1833, the Company bought 1,324 square miles of crown reserve land and brought in many Scottish and Irish settlers, especially to Compton and Megantic Counties.

The invasion of the English counties by the French from Dorchester and

5/Esdras Minville, ed. *Etudes sur notre milieu* (Montreal 1942), chap. III, 79–106, Bénoit Brouillette, "La Région des Appalaches."

Beauce Counties commenced early in the nineteenth century, but half-way through the century the English part of the Townships still had an English majority: 60,000 out of a total population of 94,000.[6] At this time the French-Canadian leaders were bewailing the fact that so many French Canadians were going to New England and so few to the Townships. In 1850 a group of French clergy wrote a pamphlet in which they urged the Quebec French-Canadian to "admire, in the days of harvest, the riches and the fertility of the soil of the Eastern Townships," and to "say whether our efforts to people the most important section of our beautiful country do not deserve our utmost zeal."[7] This plea was not destined to fall on deaf ears.

French migration continued apace, stimulated by the economic development of the Townships. Some migrants came in as labour when the railroads were built and then settled permanently.[8] Woods-work brought in some of the French, chiefly around Lake Megantic. Asbestos, discovered in the Townships in 1876, brought the French to Thetford Mines and Asbestos.

While the French influx continued, the English exodus began. As early as the 1850's the Scots and the Irish began to leave the countryside and to emigrate toward the United States and Upper Canada. In 1871 the French were in a majority in the part of the Townships originally settled by the English, 71,500 to 67,191.[9]

The 1961 Canadian census indicated the extent to which the population of the Townships had become French. Out of a total population in the fifteen counties of 609,628, the French had 550,075 and the English, 49,278.[10] The city of Sherbrooke had a total population of 66,555 of which 58,259 were French and 6,585 English.[11] Population statistics of other Eastern Townships cities in the 1961 census show a pattern as indicated in Table I. The pattern of settlement in the Townships makes clear the tendency of the English to concentrate in certain areas. Partly this is the result of the fact that they are town-dwellers, but it also reflects their desire to live in areas which are dominantly English. Of the 50,000 English Canadians in the Townships, nearly 46,000 or 92 per cent lived in eight counties (Brome, Compton, Drummond, Mississquoi, Richmond, Shef-

6/*Census of the Canadas, 1851–2*, I, 106–7.
7/Printed in *First and Second Reports of the Special Committee appointed to inquire into the causes which retard the Settlement of the Eastern Townships of Lower Canada* (Quebec 1851), 17.
8/Raoul Blanchard, cited in E. C. Hughes, *French Canada in Transition* (Chicago and Toronto 1943), 19.
9/*Notre Milieu*, 97.
10/*Census of Canada, 1961*, I, Part II, Table 37.
11/*Ibid.*, Table 38.

ford, Sherbrooke, and Stanstead). Brome and Mississquoi accounted for 11,467 or 22 per cent of the English total. Sherbrooke, Granby, and Drummondville made up another ten thousand or 20 per cent.[12]

TABLE I
POPULATION, EASTERN TOWNSHIPS, 1961 CENSUS

	Total	English	French
Drummondville	27,909	1,207	26,351
Granby	31,463	2,048	28,751
Thetford Mines	21,618	863	20,487

Source: *Census of Canada* 1961, I, Part II, Table 38.

In his two valuable studies of the Eastern Townships, W. G. Ross has noted the tendency of the English to form enclaves in certain towns and villages which have either maintained or increased their English element.[13] Lennoxville is a notable example of the English enclave. Its population was 67 per cent English in 1961; in 1911 it was only 56 per cent English. During the fifty-year period, English stock in Lennoxville had increased 3.7 times and French population only 3.5 times.[14] The same applied to other villages. Hatley was 100 per cent English, Huntingville 92 per cent and Massawippi 83 per cent. The desire to be in an English environment was not the only factor which impelled English Canadians to move to these villages. Opportunities for employment were another factor. All these villages are within commuting distance of heavily industrialized Sherbrooke. Environment was more important to retired people, whereas opportunities for employment were stressed by heads of households.[15] Even when the prospective English settler wished to select an area within commuting distance of Sherbrooke, he still had the option of choosing villages where there was a concentration of English, and of ignoring purely French villages.

Within Sherbrooke itself the English have shown the same tendency to congregate. The North Ward is more heavily English. The East Ward used to have an English Protestant school, but it has recently been closed because there were no longer enough English children to justify its existence. Table II indicates the ethnic distribution of the Sherbrooke population in 1965.

12/*Ibid.*, Table 37.
13/W. G. Ross, "Lennoxville"; "A Century of Change in Selected Eastern Townships Villages" (mimeographed report, Lennoxville, 1967).
14/Ross, "Lennoxville," 8–9.
15/Ross, "A Century of Change in Selected Eastern Townships Villages," 27–30.

TABLE II
ETHNIC DISTRIBUTION OF THE SHERBROOKE POPULATION IN 1965

	French	English and other non-French
East Ward	20,006 (89.2%)	2,422 (10.8%)
South	3,693 (80.2%)	912 (19.8%)
West	21,258 (87.3%)	3,092 (12.7%)
Centre	2,124 (92.4%)	175 (7.6%)
North	12,694 (69.1%)	5,677 (30.9%)

Source: City of Sherbrooke, *Annual Statistics*, 1965, p. 10.

During the period of comparative English dominance (down to 1892), the English in the Townships made an important contribution to Canadian life. Politically the area contributed A. T. Galt, one of the Fathers of Confederation, an aggressive politician and railway promoter, who was Canadian Minister of Finance 1858–62, 1864–66; and John Henry Pope, not a first-rate orator, but an effective member of the Conservative party, who was Minister of Agriculture 1871–73, 1878–85 and Minister of Railways and Canals (1885–89). The British-American Land Company, in which local men such as A. T. Galt and R. W. Heneker had a great deal of influence, was an important factor in the life of the community. The St. Lawrence and Atlantic Railway was largely a local enterprise in its inception, although most of the capital came from outside the Townships. The Eastern Townships Bank, chartered in 1855 with its head office in Sherbrooke, played an important role in the province of Quebec, where it had eighty branches. In 1898 it began an expansionist policy and established ten branches in Western Canada prior to its absorption by the Canadian Bank of Commerce in 1911. In the field of higher education, Bishop's University, which began teaching in 1845, and Bishop's College School, which originated in 1837, were important focal points for the development of Anglo-Saxon culture in Quebec.

The beginnings of Winnipeg may be traced to the establishment of the Red River Settlement by Lord Selkirk in 1811–12. At first the settlement was largely dependent on the Hudson's Bay Company. The establishment by 1849 of a connection with the United States traders and St. Paul, Minnesota, made possible the rise of Winnipeg as a commercial centre. It was incorporated as a city in 1873.

Its greatest rise occurred in the 1880–1914 period. The great migration to the Canadian west began about the same time as the construction of the CPR which reached Winnipeg in 1881. Building of the railway provided the city with a vast hinterland, making it the commercial centre of

Manitoba and of the entire Northwest. George Ham, who was a journalist in Winnipeg in the 1875–91 period, suggested the atmosphere of the early boom period: "Then came the boom of 1881–82 … one continuous joy-ride."[16] The Winnipeg Grain Exchange was incorporated in 1887. The movement of nearly the whole western grain crop was financed by the Winnipeg branches of Canadian banks. The city developed a wholesale structure capable of distributing throughout the Northwest the manufactures of central Canada.

During the early boom period, Winnipeg remained dominantly British in ethnic composition. The population of the city in 1881 was 83 per cent English-Irish-Scottish in ethnic composition.[17] After 1896 a large immigration into the West occurred. Great numbers of the immigrants came from central Europe as a result of the policies of the Hon. Clifford Sifton, Laurier's vigorous Minister of the Interior. Sifton's policy was indicated by his famous assertion, "I think a stalwart peasant in a sheep-skin coat, born on the soil, whose forefathers have been farmers for ten generations, with a stout wife and a half-dozen children, is good quality."[18] By 1911, when Winnipeg had a total population of 136,000, the population included 33,000 who were "foreign-born." The largest groups of these New Canadians were those born respectively in Austria-Hungary, 10,096; Russia, 8,577; Germany, 1,866; Iceland, 1,640; and Sweden, 1,406.[19] In addition to these European groups, the city included another large block of *uitlanders*, for more than 20,000 Winnipegers had been born in Ontario. The city, in common with much of southern Manitoba, seemed to assume the character of an Ontario colony in the years between 1880 and 1914.

By 1961, the polyglot character of Winnipeg was much more pronounced than in 1911. This is indicated by Table III. The mixed character of the Winnipeg population can also be indicated by the following succession of names, selected at random from the 1966 telephone directory:

Andrews, Andrewshko, Andreychuk, Andreyczuk, Andrianopoulos, Andriaschuk, Andriash, Andrich, Andrichuk, Andries, Andrieshyn, Andriessen, Andriniuk, Andronak, Andronick, Andros, Androusick, Andruchuck, Andrukow, Andruschak, Andrusco, Andrushak, Andrushiw, Andrushko, Andrushuk, Andrusiak, Andrusiw, Andruski, Andrusko, Andruson, Andrusyk, Andrusyshyn, Andryc, Andrychuk, Andryjowich, Andrykow, Andrya, Andryslak, Andrzejewski, Andy etc.

Like their counterparts in the Eastern Townships, the English in Winnipeg have shown a tendency to congregate in dominantly English areas, and

16/George H. Ham, *Reminiscences of a Raconteur* (Toronto 1921), 51.
17/*Census of Canada, 1881*, I, 296–97.
18/John W. Dafoe, *Clifford Sifton in Relation to His Times* (Toronto 1931), 142.
19/*Census of Canada, 1911*, II, Table 16.

TABLE III
WINNIPEG POPULATION STATISTICS, 1961 (IN THOUSANDS)

	City of Winnipeg	Metropolitan area
Total	265.4	475.9
British Isles	113.6	213.9
French	13.9	39.7
German	30.2	50.2
Italian	4.2	5.7
Jewish	11.6	18.3
Netherlands	6.8	14.8
Polish	16.5	24.9
Russian	2.5	4.1
Scandinavian	10.09	17.8
Ukrainian	35.9	53.9

Source: *Census of Canada* 1961, I, Part II, Tables 38 and 39.

to evacuate areas when other ethnic groups begin to move in. North Winnipeg, originally English, is now a polyglot area. Many of the English left the north end of the city to settle in the newer areas, such as River Heights and Tuxedo. There was also a heavy concentration of English in St. James, 24,486 out of a total of 33,977 in 1961.[20] St. James has the same relation to Winnipeg which Lennoxville has to Sherbrooke.

In moving to new areas, the English in Winnipeg often moved out of the confines of the city proper; but they still live within the confines of Greater Winnipeg. The Metropolitan Corporation of Greater Winnipeg was incorporated in 1960. In addition to the City of Winnipeg, it includes those of East Kildonan, St. James, St. Boniface, and West Kildonan, and a number of other municipalities and villages which I list in a footnote.[21]

III

I shall now discuss the economic fortunes of the English in the Townships and Winnipeg.

In the Eastern Townships, finance and the large industries are mainly under English control, but English control from outside the Townships. This is the case with the banks (Montreal, Commerce, Royal, and so on), and also with the other financial institutions: insurance companies, investment firms such as Greenshields and Company, and the Royal Trust Com-

20/*Ibid., 1961*, Table 39.
21/Assiniboia, Brooklands, Charleswood, Fort Garry, Kildonan North, Old Kildonan, St. Paul, St. Vital, Transcona, Tuxedo. St. Vital, Charleswood, and Assiniboia have large portions within the Metropolitan area, but are not completely within it.

pany. The Sherbrooke Trust Company is partially under local control, some French and some English. The president is a prominent French Canadian from Montreal.[22]

Large industry, controlled mainly from outside, consists chiefly of the Canadian Johns-Manville Company, Canadian Ingersoll Rand, and a number of textile companies, all with head offices in Montreal: Canadian Celanese Ltd., Domil Ltd., the Dominion Textile Company Ltd., and the Paton Manufacturing Company Limited. The Asbestos Corporation of Thetford is under local control.

In the Townships the managerial positions in large industry are dominantly held by the English. The work force is almost completely French. This is indicated in E. C. Hughes' description of Drummondville, a textile town. An analysis of the personnel of a textile mill in 1937 indicates that of the twenty-five executives, only one (the company physician) was French. Of the foremen, 57 were English and 25 were French. Of the workers engaged in textile production 123 were English and 1,882 were French.[23]

Table IV, listing the names of managers of companies employing more than 100 workers each, indicates that the pattern in Sherbrooke was similar to that in Drummondville. Except in large industry, the French had a virtual monopoly of most occupations. Those in the professions and the proprietors of small businesses were dominantly French, as is indicated in Table V, which shows the distribution of French and non-French in non-industrial occupations in Drummondville in 1938. An analysis of the owners and managers of business and service units in Drummondville in 1938 gave further evidence of French dominance: 457 were French; 10 were English; and 20 were Jewish or other.[24] An analysis of the legal profession in Sherbrooke, a city in which the English composed 10 per cent of the population in 1961, gave a further indication of the increasing dominance of the French. Sherbrooke is the county town and the site of the law courts for the St. Francis district. English lawyers played an important role in its legal history. Bishop's University had a law faculty in Sherbrooke in the 1880's and 1890's. Yet by 1965, out of 48 *avocats* listed in the Sherbrooke telephone book, there were only two English-Protestant lawyers. I personally knew an able and ambitious Anglo-Saxon lawyer who tried it in Sherbrooke for a few years, and then moved to Montreal where the openings for Anglo-Saxons were less restricted.

In discussing the fortunes of the English in Winnipeg, it should be noted that they are functioning in a city which is more of a trading centre,

22/*Financial Post Directory of Directors* (Toronto 1967).
23/E. C. Hughes, *French Canada in Transition* (Chicago and Toronto 1943), 55.
24/*Ibid.*, 68.

TABLE IV
FIRMS IN SHERBROOKE EMPLOYING MORE THAN 100 WORKERS

Company	Products	Manager	Workers
American Biltrite Rubber Co. (Canada) Ltd.	rubber goods	C. E. Joslin	564
Bruck Mills Limited	nylon	P. E. Boudreault	435
Canadian Ingersoll Rand Co. Ltd.	heavy machinery	J. H. Daly	1068
Canadian Unitcast Steel Limited	machinery	L. N. McEntush	188
Combustion Engineering Superheater Ltd.	superheaters	R. J. Scholes	439
Domil Ltd.	rayon goods	A. F. Burgess	991
Dominion Textile Co. Ltd.	rayon and cotton	G. McD. Shaw	545
Hooper & Co. Ltd.	papermill machinery	N. Hanson	145
Kayser Roth of Canada Ltd.	silk stockings	H. S. Peterson	308
Walter M. Lowney Ltd.	chocolate	B. R. McGregor	766
MacKinnon Structural Steel Co. Ltd.	structural steel	F. C. McDougall	188
Paton Mfg. Co.	woollen goods	K. F. Jackson	379
Prospect Shoes Ltd.	shoes	M. W. Rothschild	130
Rubin S. Clothing	clothing	P. H. Martin	188

Source: City of Sherbrooke, *Annual Statistics*, 1965.

TABLE V
DISTRIBUTION OF FRENCH AND NON-FRENCH IN
NON-INDUSTRIAL OCCUPATIONS IN DRUMMONDVILLE IN 1938

	Non-French	French
Professional and quasi-professional	9	101
Proprietors and managers of business concerns	13	238
Agents and clerks	10	463
Proprietors and persons engaged in service shops and trades	7	445
Servants	—	295
Rentiers and public functionaries	2	111
Labourers	—	617

Source: E. C. Hughes, *French Canada in Transition*
(Toronto 1943), 67.

and comparatively speaking less occupied with manufactures, than is the case with the Eastern Townships cities. Winnipeg retains its traditional functions as a distributing and financial centre and grain market. Its position has changed since the rise of Vancouver and other western cities after 1914; but it remains essentially a trading centre. An advertisement placed by the Winnipeg *Tribune* in eastern newspapers in 1938 to advertise Winnipeg and the *Tribune*, is a fair indication of the character of the city. The ad reads in part:

Greater Winnipeg is truly the market-place of Western Canada. Products of agriculture, its millions of bushels of grain, its livestock, its dairy products, flow through the Greater Winnipeg area, and here are concentrated the commercial and financial transactions involved in the marketing of vast quantities of primary products. Here is located one of the world's greatest grain markets and here are the vast stockyards and packing establishments through which pass livestock products from a large area in the West.

But Greater Winnipeg does more than receive and market the products of Western agriculture. Manufactured goods, farm machinery, supplies of all descriptions required by the agricultural industry of Western Canada, the fishing industry of the northern lakes, the mining industry of northern Manitoba and western Ontario, flow through Winnipeg to consumers in these areas. Goods of every description are distributed from Greater Winnipeg from where 45 per cent of Canada's railway mileage (over 19,000 miles) radiates to the vast area it serves.

Greater Winnipeg is the strategic centre of western business in all its many phases. It is the nerve centre of western affairs. It responds to western conditions. It is the richest, most concentrated market in the Prairie Provinces. It offers opportunities to those who desire to profit by the progress of Western Canada.[25]

Despite the expansive spirit of the Winnipeg business community, it must be realized that Winnipeg, like Sherbrooke, is largely under outside control, although to a somewhat lesser extent. The same great banks (Montreal, Commerce, Royal, *et al.*) operate in Winnipeg. The difficulties of James Coyne in establishing the Bank of Western Canada indicate the obstacles to the maintenance of genuinely western banking ventures. The financial houses are mainly controlled from outside, with some notable exceptions such as the three insurance companies: the Great West Life, the Monarch Life, and the Canadian Premier Life. The Winnipeg Stock Exchange, and the complicated marketing organization for grain, centring on the Winnipeg Grain Exchange, the Canadian Wheat Board, and marketing companies such as the Manitoba Wheat Pool, the United Grain Growers, James Richardson and Sons, Limited, and the Searle Grain Company, give Winnipeg some control over its own economy. The large stores and the meat packing companies are subject to outside control. Among the companies under local control are the J. H. Ashdown Hardware Company, a large wholesale and retail establishment and the Beaver Lumber Company.[26]

25/From *The West Marches On*, announcements published in leading daily newspapers of eastern Canada by the Winnipeg *Tribune* Autumn 1938.
26/*Financial Post Directory of Directors* (Toronto 1967).

Since Winnipeg is largely a distributing centre, many Canadian companies maintain distributing agencies in Winnipeg. The *Manitoba Trade Directory* of 1966 contains a section of 178 pages, listing the distributors and the products being distributed. The list includes agricultural equipment and accessories, aircraft accessories, alcoholic beverages, aluminum products, automotive parts and accessories, and so on.

Although Winnipeg is largely under the control of the eastern metropolitan centres, the positions of leadership in Winnipeg itself are still largely in the hands of the English. The leading railway officials, the bank managers, and members of the Board of Grain Commissioners are mainly English. Most of the distributing companies operating in Winnipeg have head offices in Montreal, Toronto, or Hamilton, but in most cases the local manager has an English name.

Winnipeg is rather more of a metropolis than Sherbrooke, and in so far as it is a metropolis it is under English control. There is more feeling against the large eastern metropolises in Winnipeg than in Sherbrooke, perhaps because Winnipeg is more of a metropolis itself.

IV

The English world is dominantly Protestant, both in the Townships and in Winnipeg. In the Townships, the Anglican, Baptist, Presbyterian, and United Churches comprise 86 per cent of the English population.[27] The same four denominations have 82 per cent of the English population in the City of Winnipeg, and 83 per cent of the English population in Greater Winnipeg.[28] English-speaking Catholics (Scottish and Irish in Winnipeg, Irish in the Townships) account for a considerable part of the remainder of the English-speaking community. In 1961 there were about 12,000 "English" Catholics, over 9 per cent of the "English" total in the City of Winnipeg, and over 22,000, or 10 per cent of the English total in Greater Winnipeg.[29] In Sherbrooke, out of 6,585 "English," 2,285 were Catholics, no doubt mainly Irish.[30]

In the Townships, as well as in Winnipeg, the Protestant churches and the schools are focal points of the English-speaking community, but the churches and the schools are of more vital significance as rallying points for the English in the dominantly French society of the Townships. The churches are rallying points, not only on account of their religious func-

27/*Census of Canada, 1961*, I, Part II, Table 44.
28/*Ibid.*, I, Part III, Tables 112 and 113.
29/*Ibid.*
30/*Ibid.*, Table 112.

tions but also through their related activities: women's organizations, Boy Scouts and Cubs, badminton clubs, and other parish associations. Even in Sherbrooke-Lennoxville, the largest Anglo-Saxon concentration, the churches and the school organizations give to the Anglo-Saxon community the character of a medium-sized town in which each member can know a large part of the group if he has lived in the community for very long. Another organization, the Snowshoe Club, a social club composed of English Protestants, provides the spectacle of Anglo-Saxon Sherbrooke in a fraternizing mood.

Socially, the English-speaking Catholics tend to participate in the activities in the Protestant churches. Hughes describes the manner in which the English-speaking Catholic ladies participate in activities in the Anglican parish hall in Drummondville.[31]

The function of the church as a rallying point for the English is even more important in some rural areas. The English community at Hereford near the Vermont border is an example. An English community of perhaps 200 people has continued to exist in isolation at least 15 miles from other Canadian Anglo-Saxons. Geographic isolation and association with English-speaking people across the line have helped the group to survive as a homogeneous unit, but a principal factor has been the fact that they all attend the local Anglican church and participate in its social activities. It is, of course, true that as the English rural population continues to shrink, Protestant churches are gradually abandoned. Some, like the Anglican church at Kingsey, are deserted except for an occasional service.

Because the English constituency is shrinking in the Townships, and because the older denominations have long since abandoned any idea of converting the French, they serve a limited constituency. Table VI indicates the minority position of the principal Protestant churches in the Townships. This table indicates that the Anglican Church had more than 1,000 members in only seven of the fifteen counties (Brome, Compton, Mississquoi, Richmond, Shefford, Sherbrooke, and Stanstead). The United Church had more than 1,000 members in the same seven counties respectively. In some counties there were scarcely any Protestants. Bagot County, with a total population of 21,390, had 13 Anglicans, 6 Baptists, 15 Presbyterians, and 23 members of the United Church. Protestants made their best showing in Brome where the English were almost a majority. Out of a total of 13,691, Brome had 3,602 Anglicans, 243 Baptists, 117 Presbyterians, and 2,308 members of the United Church.

The failure of Protestantism to expand, even in areas where a sizeable Protestant group remained, is indicated by the record of Sherbrooke.

31/Hughes, *French Canada in Transition*, 119.

TABLE VI
PRINCIPAL RELIGIOUS DENOMINATIONS IN THE EASTERN TOWNSHIPS
(IN THOUSANDS OF MEMBERS)

County	Total	Anglican	Baptist	Presbyterian	Roman Catholic	United Church
Arthabaska	45.30	.06	.01	.04	45.10	.01
Bagot	21.39	.01	.006	.01	21.29	.02
Beauce	62.26	.04	.04	.04	62.05	.01
Brome	13.69	3.60	.24	.11	7.00	2.30
Compton	24.41	2.17	.22	.26	19.72	1.83
Dorchester	34.71	.06	—	.01	34.58	.002
Drummond	58.22	.78	.05	.09	56.33	.71
Frontenac	30.60	.09	.007	.06	30.33	.05
Megantic	57.40	.69	.017	.10	56.11	.36
Mississquoi	29.52	2.99	.05	.08	23.91	1.98
Richmond	42.23	1.67	.079	.42	37.65	2.04
Shefford	54.96	1.74	.19	.13	50.76	1.64
Sherbrooke	80.49	4.03	.30	.91	71.00	2.99
Stanstead	36.09	3.04	.37	.16	28.57	3.93
Wolfe	18.33	.18	—	.01	17.90	.19

Source: *Census of Canada*, 1961, I, Part II, Table 44.

TABLE VII
RELIGIOUS GROUPS IN SHERBROOKE

	1941	1951	1961
Total Population	35,965	50,543	66,554
Anglican	2,667	2,384	2,344
Baptist	206	172	183
Jewish	200	197	181
Presbyterian	931	735	554
Roman Catholic	30,151	44,736	61,092
United	1,421	1,851	1,468

Source: *Census of Canada*, 1941, II, Table 40; 1951, I,
Part II, Table 42; 1961, I, Part II, Table 45.

Sherbrooke had 1,270 Anglicans out of a total population of 7,227 in
1881;[32] and in 1961, when the population had risen to 66,554, there were
only 2,344 Anglicans.[33] The static position of the Protestant churches in
Sherbrooke, is indicated by Table VII.

In spite of an increase of over 20,000 in population, between 1941 and
1961, and a comparable increase of Roman Catholics, the Protestant and

32/*Census of Canada, 1881*, I, 136.
33/*Ibid., 1961*, I, Part III, Table 112.

Jewish groups all had fewer members in 1961 than in 1941, with the exception of the United Church, which had some 40 more members.

The drop in Protestant churches was even more apparent in the rural and rural-suburban areas, with the exception of the English enclaves. In the rural area around the village of Compton, the Anglicans had 576 members in 1881. Now the parish of Compton has practically ceased to exist, and is kept going merely because the rector is also the chaplain of King's Hall, a residential girls' school in Compton. The United Church in Compton has been taken over by a group of French Baptists. The rural area of Leeds had 754 Presbyterians in 1881.[34] Now there is a plaque on a building in the village of Leeds indicating that a Presbyterian church once stood there.

Two Protestant groups have shown substantial progress in the modern period, the Plymouth Brethren and the more evangelical Baptists. Both of these groups have made gains in the Townships. They have not only expanded their work among the English, but have done significant work among the French as well. Both groups, the Brethren, particularly, have taken pains to avoid a challenge to French linguistic culture. They have attempted to convert the French without making them English-speaking. The result has been the establishment of a number of French-Protestant congregations in the Townships.

A striking example of an expanding Protestant church has been the career of Grace Chapel, the leading English Brethren Assembly in the Townships. Established in Sherbrooke by two devoted physicians in 1940, Grace Chapel became the centre and inspiration for a significant religious movement in the Townships. In addition to maintaining a growing work in Sherbrooke, Grace Chapel established additional English groups at Albert Mines, Stanstead, Cherry River, Ayers' Cliff, Huntingville, and Brookport. Two of the groups, those at Huntingville and Brookport, took over church buildings previously occupied by moribund Protestant congregations. Grace Chapel conducted a Sunday radio broadcast for twenty-five years; established a thriving youth camp, "Frontier Lodge," in 1944; an old people's home, Grace Christian Home, in 1958; and in 1960 an orphans' home, "Maplemount." In 1946, Grace Chapel entered the French field with the establishment of a French Assembly in Sherbrooke. Eventually the French work was extended to Thetford Mines, Drummondville, Granby and Farnham in the Eastern Townships, and to other areas beyond the Townships including Valleyfield, Sorel, Montmagny, Cap de la Madeleine, and Shawinigan.

Relations between the clergy of the larger Protestant churches and the

34/*Ibid.*, *1881*, I, 133 and 134.

Roman Catholic clergy in the Townships, particularly in Sherbrooke-Lennoxville, are closer than ever before. This is a result of the ecumenical movement in the Protestant churches and of the increased cordiality of Roman Catholics toward Protestants as a result of the lead given by Pope John XXIII. I suspect that it is also a reflection of Roman Catholic fears of increasing anti-clericalism in political circles in Quebec. In Sherbrooke-Lennoxville the Roman Catholic and Protestant clergy have recently participated jointly in public services. Archbishop Cabana entertained the Sherbrooke Ministerial Association at lunch. The sermon preached by the Anglican Archdeacon in Lennoxville at the Convocation service at Bishop's University in 1967 was a vigorous plea for closer co-operation between the Anglican and Roman Catholic churches.

TABLE VIII
RELIGIOUS GROUPS IN THE WINNIPEG AREA. 1961 (IN THOUSANDS)

	City of Winnipeg	Greater Winnipeg
Total Population	265.42	475.98
Anglican	37.04	70.97
Baptist	5.96	9.7
Greek Orthodox	9.51	13.9
Jehovah's Witnesses	1.17	
Jewish	12.58	19.37
Lutheran	22.42	35.91
Mennonite	6.71	13.59
Pentecostal	2.15	3.7
Presbyterian	9.08	15.19
Roman Catholic	58.23	112.69
Salvation Army	.81	
Ukrainian Greek Orthodox	19.74	27.79
United Church	71.33	134.4
Other		18.71

Source: *Census of Canada*, 1961, I, Part III, Tables 112–13.

In Winnipeg, where the atmosphere is more relaxed, religion is not identified with conflict between ethnic groups to anything like the same extent as in the Townships. This has not always been so, as was indicated by the controversies over education which will be discussed in the next section. Table VIII suggests the size of religious groups in the City of Winnipeg and in Greater Winnipeg in 1961. Analysis of the ethnic composition of each denomination provides evidence of the process of anglicization of the European ethnic groups. The United Church in Winnipeg contained sizeable groups of New Canadians. Out of a total of 71,330, some 19,000 were non-English. The non-English part included: German, 3,675; Netherlands, 1,877; Polish, 1,343; Scandinavian, 2,661; Ukrainian, 3,491. In Greater Winnipeg, out of a United Church population of about 134,000, some 35,000 were non-English, including German, 6,762; Netherlands, 4,018; Polish, 2,369; Scandinavian, 5,280; and Ukrainian, 6,082.[35]

The Anglican church included a considerable, although smaller number of New Canadians, as shown in Table IX. The English communities in Winnipeg and the Townships are both heirs to educational systems which have been produced through the interaction of English and French groups. In Winnipeg the schools are part of the Manitoba system which stems from the period of English dominance in the 1890's. In Quebec and the Townships the school system was developed in the middle and later nineteenth century at a time when the French were in the majority, although the English were a politically effective group.

TABLE IX
PRINCIPAL NON-ENGLISH GROUPS IN THE ANGLICAN CHURCH

	City of Winnipeg	Greater Winnipeg
Total Anglicans	37,043	70,972
English	31,382	60,123
German	845	1,653
Netherlands	331	817
Polish	478	930
Scandinavian	876	1,724
Ukrainian	867	1,692

Source: *Census of Canada*, 1961, I, Part III, Tables 112–13.

Manitoba between 1870 and 1890 maintained a system of public schools (called "Protestant Common Schools") and Roman Catholic Schools, with each given state support. Although the Roman Catholic schools in the province as a whole were mainly French, those in the Winnipeg area were English-speaking. Of the twenty-one Catholic schools listed in the *Report* of the superintendent of Catholic schools in Manitoba in 1876, all of the twenty-one Catholic schools were presided over by French Canadians except five, three of them in the Winnipeg area. The superintendent reported that in the Winnipeg Boys' School, under the direction of Reverend F. McCarthy, the English language predominated. The Catholic Girls' School in Winnipeg, although presided over by Sister Marie de Dieu, was an English-speaking institution, the forerunner of St. Mary's Academy. The report of the superintendent's visit to St. Boniface Girls' School suggests that the curriculum in the French schools was an orthodox programme of the three R's combined with a good deal of instruction in the Catechism.[36]

35/*Ibid.*, I, Part III, Tables 112–13.
36/*Report of the Superintendent of Catholic Schools of the Province of Manitoba, 1875–76.*

In 1890, when English Protestants had a majority in Manitoba, the administration of Thomas Greenway abandoned state aid to Roman Catholic schools and began a policy of monolithic, non-sectarian schools. Six years of bitter controversy followed. The Catholic minority appealed for assistance from the federal government, but failed to secure it. The views of the Protestant majority in Winnipeg were expressed by Principal J. M. King of Manitoba College, a Presbyterian institution.

If a purely secular system of education is deemed in the highest degree objectionable, and a denominational or sectarian system only less objectionable, what is it proposed to establish in their place? I answer, a system of public, unsectarian but not non-religious schools. It is admitted on all hands that the main work of the school ought to be instruction in the various secular branches. Its primary aim is to fit those in attendance for the active duties of life. But as not inconsistent with this aim, rather as in a higher degree subservient to its attainment, it is desired that the religious element should have a definite place assigned to it in the life of the school ... A system of public education of this kind, in which religion has a definite but at the same time strictly guarded place assigned to it, ought to be acceptable to the great majority of the people of this province.[37]

The return of the Liberals to power at Ottawa in 1896 meant that the Manitoba Schools Act was upheld. Sir Wilfrid Laurier, the new prime minister, negotiated a settlement with the Roman Catholic Church and the Manitoba Government which resulted in the compromise provincial bill of 1897. The new legislation still denied separate schools, but permitted some religious instruction in public schools and provided for bilingual schools in districts in which there was a sizeable French or other non-English-speaking element. After the influx of New Canadians to Manitoba between 1896 and the First World War, the latter clause became unworkable and was repealed in 1916. As a result Manitoba and Winnipeg secured the system of schools which the Anglo-Saxon majority desired: non-sectarian and with no religious instruction, except for the reading each morning of a brief, non-controversial passage from the Bible which the teacher was forbidden to explain or expound. In 1959 the Report of the Manitoba Royal Commission on Education, under the chairmanship of R. O. MacFarlane, proposed the introduction of extensive programmes of religious instruction (Catholic, Protestant, and Jewish) into the school curriculum; but the objections to this proposal were so great that the Roblin administration did not venture to implement it.

In the Townships the English Protestant minority, in common with their compatriots throughout Quebec, fared better than did the Catholic and largely French minority in Manitoba. The English in Quebec and the

37/Quoted in Dafoe, 69.

Townships enjoyed a separate and definitely Protestant system of education. This was the result of a combination of factors, two in particular. One was the concern of English-speaking Protestants, outside as well as inside Quebec, for the rights of the Protestant minority in the province. This helped to produce the safeguards for religious minorities contained in Section 93 of the BNA Act. The other factor was the desire of the French Roman Catholic bishops to control their own schools. In order to maintain this control, they were willing to allow Anglo-Saxon Protestants to control their own schools.

Quebec and the Townships thus acquired in effect two systems of separate schools, set up originally in 1846 and from 1859 nominally presided over by a Council of Public Instruction. Between 1867 and 1875 Quebec maintained a Ministry of Education; but it was abandoned in 1875, mainly because the Roman Catholic bishops disliked the idea of state control of education.[38] Anglo-Saxon Protestants supported the Catholic bishops in this policy. After 1875 Quebec acquired an even more divided system of education under Roman Catholic and Protestant Commissions respectively. Thus in the Townships the Anglo-Saxon minority was able to operate its own school system, insulated from contact with the French. The difficulties of English-speaking Catholics and Jews in adjusting themselves to this system is a complicated story which can only be mentioned here.

The curriculum of the Protestant schools in Quebec and the Townships has had a much larger religious content than is the case in the public schools of Manitoba, Ontario, and other provinces. This is indicated by the *Protestant Teachers Handbook*.[39] From Grade 1 to Grade 7 the students were given a good deal of Bible teaching. The tone and character of the course is indicated by the list of topics, all concerned with the life of Jesus Christ and with the early church:

Grade 1   The Home in Bethlehem and Nazareth
Grade 2   A Boy in Galilee
Grade 3   Jesus and His Work
Grade 4   Stories of the Nation to which Jesus Belonged
Grade 5   The Life of Jesus according to St. Mark
Grade 6   The First Christians
Grade 7   The Story of God and man

The Bible Study for Grades 8 to 11 was more critical, but still contained a heavy religious content. Actually there were wide variations in the

38/K. D. Hunte, "The Ministry of Public Instruction in Quebec, 1867–1875" (unpublished PHD thesis; McGill University).
39/*Handbook for Teachers in the Protestant Schools of the Province of Quebec* (Quebec 1957), 129–42.

amount of scripture actually taught in the schools in the Townships, but in some schools much of the programme was taught.

Into this comparatively placid picture of separate English, Protestant schools came the Lesage administration and the Quiet Revolution. Among those dedicated to reform none was more ardent than M. Paul Gérin-Lajoie, the Minister of Youth and Welfare. The Parent Commission, appointed by the Lesage Government, recommended policies of far-reaching reform. The first part of the *Parent Report*, which appeared in 1963 asserted:

Like every other country throughout the world, the Province of Quebec must examine the educational problems confronting it in the light of objectives which originate in its own economic and social development and from modern trends in education generally. While taking full account of the special problems arising from its own traditions and history, the Province must seek with clarity of vision and practical good sense to endow its educational system with a structure suited to its present needs.[40]

The *Report* recommended a thorough revision of the Quebec system of education, beginning with the appointment of a minister of education, "to promote and co-ordinate educational services at all levels, including the private and public sectors."

Publication of the *Parent Report* was followed by a vigorous programme of reform, including the establishment of a ministry of education. M. Gérin-Lajoie became the minister of education. Reorganization of the Department of Education abolished the previous separation of the French and English sections. This was followed by a policy of setting up single school boards, in place of the Catholic and Protestant boards in various districts. Proposals were made to establish "Institutes" for both English and French students, to cover Grade XII of the school system and at least the first year of university work.

The English in the Townships, as well as in other parts of the province, were alarmed at the potentialities of this programme. Some feared loss of the defence previously afforded English culture by a separate school organization. They feared that the introduction of a single system, although it meant a raising of the standard of education for the French, would mean a lowering of the standard for the English. Some insisted that the English should not be blamed for the problems faced by the French. Their views were similar to those expressed by the Quebec Federation of Home and School Associations in a brief to the Commission on Bilingualism and Biculturalism:

French Canadian isolation, insecurity and insularity spring from certain factors

40/*Parent Report*, I, 75.

which French Canada chose as being necessary or desirable for its own particular development or its way of life. It created its own walls within which it lived. It created a rigid religious hierarchy, a narrow classical educational system, a refusal to mingle with the outside world in order to preserve those values which it held dear to itself. This was voluntary; this was not imposed ... a feeling of guilt should not result in placing false blame on innocent parties.[41]

Although the English in the Townships feel that they should not be blamed for the previous inadequacy of the French schools, some have an uneasy feeling that the French have been badly treated in other parts of Canada, notably in Manitoba and Ontario. Some recall the Manitoba school question, Circular Seventeen, and the Ottawa City school case in Ontario. They are pathetically anxious that their English compatriots elsewhere in Canada shall be more conciliatory to the French. They are distressed by the indifferent ("We won't bail you out") attitude of some of these other Anglo-Saxons.

VI

Politically, French Canadians dominate the picture in the Eastern Townships. There has been a steady transfer of control from English-speaking to French-speaking Canadians. This is true at all levels of government: federal, provincial, municipal. Dr. Aileen Ross of McGill has described the process by which the French gradually swamp the English in the municipal field:

The stages by which the French gradually take over political control of the Townships can perhaps be most clearly seen in the turn-over of the municipal council from English to French. Thirteen of the municipalities of Compton County were settled by English Canadians and began with English mayors and councillors. These have now been either completely taken over by the French or are in process of becoming French. The first step of the transfer is the election of a councillor to represent the French population. He will be either an English Catholic or a bilingual French Canadian who has lived long enough in the vicinity for the English to consider him "almost English." As the French buy more property they gradually get to the position where they can elect more representatives from their own group, and at last the stage is reached when they are strong enough to elect a French mayor. The well-known gentleman's agreement is then introduced whereby the office of mayor will alternate between the two groups, one year being filled by a French Canadian and the next by an English Canadian. By this time the French are numerous enough to introduce their own language at council meetings. Both French and English will be spoken, and the agenda and minutes will be written in the two languages. The next stage is reached when the gentleman's agreement to alternate the office of mayor is overlooked. By this time the English will have lost the right to use

41/Montreal *Star*, November 29, 1965.

their language at council meetings. The last stage arrives when the sole remaining English representative on the council is "pushed" out (in the words of the English) by the French, and the use of English as an official language comes to an end.[42]

Sherbrooke provides a striking example of increasing French dominance. The city's development is symbolized by a comparison between its first MP in 1867, A. T. Galt (English-speaking, Anglican, and born in Great Britain) and its most recent MP, Maurice Allard (French-speaking, Roman Catholic, and born in Sherbrooke). Until 1892 Sherbrooke had English-speaking members in the federal and provincial legislatures. In 1892 occurred what Gordon Rothney has described as the most crucial election in Sherbrooke in the last hundred years.[43] According to Rothney it "settled forever the question as to whether the district's members should be elected on the basis of language." The Scottish immigrant, Joseph Gibb Robertson, who had been a member of the provincial legislature since 1867, was defeated by Edmond Panneton, whose campaign was based on the proposition that Sherbrooke should be represented by a French Canadian.

The period from 1891 to 1940 was that of the *bonne entente* in Sherbrooke, with English-speaking representation at Ottawa and with French-speaking members in the Quebec legislature. With the election of Maurice Gingues to the federal house in 1940, the period began in which there are French Canadians at both levels of government.

In the municipal government the last of the three stages described by Dr. Ross has been reached. The city council is entirely French and French is the sole language of discussion. The progress of French influence in Sherbrooke may be traced in the list of mayors. From 1868 to 1879 they were all English. From 1880 to 1896 there were some French but more English mayors (10 English, 6 French). In 1897 the gentleman's agreement began, with English and French mayors alternating. This lasted until 1955, when Armand Nadeau succeeded J.-E. Lévesque as mayor.[44]

In Drummondville the indigenous English population has disappeared from political office and the new industrial English population shows no sign of competing for office.[45] All candidates in local, provincial, and dominion elections have been French for years. Everett Hughes reported

---

42/Aileen Ross, "French and English Canadian Contacts and Institutional Change," *Canadian Journal of Economics and Political Science* (August 1954), 287.
43/Paper presented to Canadian Political Science Association, reported in *Sherbrooke Daily Record*, June 11, 1966.
44/See table, "Mayors of Sherbrooke 1868 to 1967," in City of Sherbrooke, *Annual Statistics*, 4–5.
45/Hughes, *French Canada in Transition*, 86.

in 1943 that, so far as local politics were concerned, the English confined themselves mainly to adverse criticism, expressed in ethno-centric terms. They charged the French politicians with inefficiency, graft, and unfairness to the English and to English-controlled industry. The chief local issue discussed by the English industrialists was taxation of companies. In municipal elections the English rated candidates according to the current impression as to whether they were "nationalistic," i.e., whether they would raise the assessed valuation of property and whether they would take the side of labour.[46]

The record of the Townships as a whole demonstrates the extent to which English representation has been obliterated. According to the 1961 record all representatives of the fifteen Eastern Townships constituencies in the Quebec legislature were French except Glendon Brown, the member for Brome.[47] In the federal election of 1965 all the members elected in the Townships were French except Heward Grafftey, the member for Brome-Mississquoi. It would be inaccurate to say that the English have no political influence in the Townships. No doubt English industrialists are able to exert influence behind the scenes to secure tax concessions, etc. In Sherbrooke where the English are 10 per cent of the population they were able to secure a judgeship for an Anglo-Saxon Anglican in 1948. The English in Drummondville never speak in public on any local political issue. Managers of plants in Drummondville identify themselves with the companies for whom they work, but as they are not of sufficient rank to make company policy, they can do nothing but stand for the position of industry in general. If they have political objectives to secure, they make their representations privately.

Although they are not entirely devoid of political influence, the English are excluded from formal politics and must deal with French-Canadian politicians to get what they want. Hughes' assertion about Drummondville applies, with the exception of Brome, to the Townships as a whole:

One of the common functions of politics is to give the individual the release of participating in conflicts that mean something to him. Related to this function is that of giving the individual a sense of identification with the institutions of government. Politics do not perform these functions for the English of our community. The zest of political struggle belongs to the French alone, as completely as if the English were not present.[48]

Because the English had so little part in politics they were frequently ignorant of the realities of local politics. As a resident of the English

46/*Ibid.*, 86–87.
47/*Quebec Statistical Year Book*, 1961, 34.
48/Hughes, *French Canada in Transition*, 91.

community in Lennoxville, I noticed a tendency on the part of my compatriots to back the provincial party in power just when the French were getting ready to desert it. Thus they supported Bourque and the Union Nationale in the election of 1960 which the Union Nationale lost, and in 1966 they supported Lesage and the Liberals. It seemed to be a process of climbing on the band-waggon just before the band stopped playing.

In Winnipeg, where the confrontation between French and English is not the primary fact of life, the English community regards itself as Canadian rather than as English. However, it is not beyond regarding recent arrivals in Canada as not quite Canadians, but still hyphenated citizens: New Canadians, Ukrainian-Canadians, and so on. Probably because the English do not yet feel themselves seriously challenged, the political atmosphere is not characterized by the idea of a competition between various ethnic groups. An examination of representation in public life indicates that the English still do well.

From 1873, the year of Winnipeg's incorporation, until 1956 all the mayors were English.[49] The election in 1956 of Mayor Stephen Juba, a Ukrainian, was an indication of the increasing influence of New Canadians in Winnipeg public life. Juba, a colourful personality, was a new type of mayor for Winnipeg. Robert Collins wrote in 1957:

If Juba's supporters were dismayed [at his antics] his critics were shattered. To them the new mayor was a lowbrow. He owned a wholesale business and drove a Cadillac but the car was flashy yellow, not sincere black. He liked western music and even yodeled, within the sanctuary of his home. He lived in a four-room bungalow half a block from a railway track on William Avenue West, one of Winnipeg's least fashionable districts.
He didn't belong to the better clubs, sometimes lunched at the CPR station, and had once raced his own stock car at a local speedway.[50]

The English have maintained a proportion of representation on the city council higher than their proportion of the population of the city. Of the eighteen aldermen, ten are Anglo-Saxons.[51] The English, too, have a fair representation in the provincial legislature.[52] Of the twelve Winnipeg representatives in the Manitoba legislature six are Anglo-Saxons.

In the federal House of Commons, Winnipeg South, Winnipeg South Centre, and Winnipeg North Centre have always had English representatives. Winnipeg North Centre has a large New Canadian population and yet it elected J. S. Woodsworth 1941–42 and since then Stanley Knowles

49/See table of mayors of Winnipeg from *City of Winnipeg Municipal Manual*, 1967, 33–34.
50/*Maclean's*, November 23, 1957.
51/*City of Winnipeg Municipal Manual*, 36–39.
52/*Ibid.*, 213.

1942–67, except for the interlude 1958–62 when J. MacLean was the member. Until the election of D. Orlikow in 1962, Winnipeg North always had English-speaking representatives in the federal field, although they usually had qualifications calculated to appeal to the non-Anglo-Saxon elements in the constituency. A. A. Heaps (1926–40) was of English-Jewish descent. Alistair Stewart was a superb organizer. In my opinion, the English were able to get elected in Winnipeg North Centre and Winnipeg North because race is less important as an element in elections than in the Townships. Woodsworth, Knowles, and Stewart were elected mainly because they were CCF.

The dominant element in Winnipeg in Liberal federal and provincial political circles was for long a little group of Anglo-Saxon Liberals to whom Harry Sifton, the publisher, gave the term "the Sanhedrin." It included J. W. Dafoe, A. B. Hudson; the Honourable T. A. Crerar; Frank Fowler, a prominent grain merchant; E. J. Tarr, President of the Monarch Life Assurance Company; H. J. Symington, who began his career as a junior partner of Hudson and who was later the President of Trans-Canada Airlines; and J. B. Coyne, an acute and brilliant lawyer. George Ferguson wrote in his book on Dafoe:

The Sanhedrin, like the UN Security Council today, was in continuous session; a quorum could be gathered together any day on half an hour's notice. But its chief sessions were Saturday luncheons at the Manitoba Club, where the politically minded Tories of that great institution watched sourly as this strictly unofficial but powerful board of Liberal strategy gathered to swap stories and discuss tactics.[53]

In general the influence of the Eastern Townships English on federal and provincial politics since 1900 has been slight. The influence of the Winnipeg English on national parties has been and probably still is extensive. J. W. Dafoe, E. J. Tarr, and Stuart Garson exercised great influence in the counsels of the Liberals; the Honourable Robert Rogers in the period 1911–17 and the Honourable Gordon Churchill in the period since World War II on the Conservative party; Woodsworth, Knowles, and others on the CCF–NDP since 1921.

VII

In the field of what might be called political thought, there have been obvious differences in the attitudes of the English in Winnipeg and in the Townships. The Winnipeg group has been far more positive in its attitude to the problems and potentialities of Canadian nationalism. In many ways

53/G. V. Ferguson, *John W. Dafoe* (Toronto 1948), 60.

Winnipeg is the least provincial city in Canada. The dominant element in the city, while proud of its role as the capital of Manitoba, has always thought in genuinely national and international terms. Several reasons may be suggested for this breadth of outlook. The central position of the city about half-way between the Atlantic and the Pacific has tended to make Winnipeggers conscious of the roles of both East and West in Canadian development. The economic history and present position of the city has fostered a broadly national and international viewpoint. The CPR and later the other transcontinental railways were national projects, dependent for construction on outside capital; and because they continued to be so important to Winnipeg its citizens were drawn by the railways into the arena of national politics. Winnipeg's dependence on the western wheat industry made it constantly aware of Canada's relations with the outside world and particularly with Great Britain, the principal market for Canadian wheat.

I remember being impressed by the breadth of outlook displayed in Winnipeg in 1937. I had been spending the year in Minneapolis, which was quite amazingly narrow and self-centred. The only foreign news which I recall in the Minneapolis papers during my whole year there was the report of the abdication crisis in Britain in December 1936 ("Why won't they let him marry the girl?"). In Winnipeg I entered a community which was infinitely aware of the forces and political cross-currents of the outside world – particularly in their bearing on the western wheat industry.

The English in Winnipeg have been self-appointed spokesmen for the interests of western Canada. The *Rowell-Sirois Report* of 1940 was in large part an expression of the Winnipeg viewpoint. One of the three members of the Rowell-Sirois Commission was J. W. Dafoe. G. V. Ferguson, Dafoe's close associate on the *Free Press*, and Adjutor Savard, the French-speaking secretary of the commission, have testified to the importance of Dafoe's influence.[54]

The *Report* stressed a view widely held in the West – the fatal influence which wide disparities in income between regions would have on Confederation. The *Report* asserted in the introduction to the volume of recommendations: "We are fully alive to the importance of maintaining, and of expanding as rapidly as possible, the national income which is woefully inadequate for the standards of well-being which Canadians have come to adopt ..." The *Report* also asserted that the national income must be better distributed among income groups, and continued: "There is a second aspect of the distribution of the national income which is of great

54/*Ibid.*, 91; Savard is quoted in R. Cook, *The Politics of John W. Dafoe and the Free Press* (Toronto 1963), 228.

importance in a federal system, and of particular importance in Canada. The unequal distribution of the national income as between the people of different regions may excite feelings quite as dangerous to national unity as those aroused by gross inequalities between different income groups."[55] The Commission sought to correct these divergencies by recommending that inequalities be ironed out by the federal government, which would give extensive financial assistance to the provinces in return for the surrender of provincial income and corporation taxes and succession duties.

Winnipeg was also a principal source of strength for the movement toward Canadian autonomy. In the twenties and thirties, when Canada was moving toward autonomy, its great advocates were Dafoe, Ferguson and A. R. M. Lower, who came to United College in 1929. The controversy in Canada and particularly in Winnipeg about Lord Halifax, in 1944, was indicative of the thinking of the Winnipeg advocates of autonomy. On January 24, 1944, Lord Halifax made a speech in Toronto in which he appeared to advocate greater centralization of the empire. This provoked a storm of protest in Canada, where the speech was regarded as the first step in depriving Canada of its control over foreign policy. The *Free Press* was particularly vigorous, publishing many news stories and a number of editorials critical of Lord Halifax. It advocated instead a renewed League of Nations organization, in which presumably Canada would have more independence. In its editorial on January 26, 1944, the *Free Press* asserted:

Lord Halifax in summing up saw but two alternatives. The Commonwealth must either be centralized so that it may take equal rank with the other two great powers in ruling the world, or the traditional trend toward complete equality under the crown must take the form of isolation, with each of the British nations going its own way.

We suggest that there is a third course which offers the best hope not only for the Commonwealth but for all nations. That course will only become possible when the balance of power obsession is banished and when the peace-loving nations of the world form themselves into a society or community and collaborate for all the purposes of the good life ... In such a world society, the British Commonwealth will find its highest opportunity for service, and Canada a destiny befitting her stature.

On other occasions the *Free Press* took an independent line, that is, independent of party considerations. To some extent this was a result of the personality of Dafoe, but in a sense Dafoe personified the independence of Winnipeg and he spoke for the city. This was never more apparent than in 1938 after the Munich settlement which was widely acclaimed

---

55/*Report of the Royal Commission on Dominion Provincial Relations*, Book II, 9–10.

in Canada as well as in Great Britain. Dafoe wrote a famous editorial on September 30th entitled *What's the Cheering For?* He began:

> While the cheers are proceeding over the success which is attending the project of dismembering a state by processes of bloodless aggression, some facts might be set out for the information of people who would like to know what the cheering is about and who ought to be taking part in it.

After a devastating examination of the story of broken Nazi promises given to Austria and Czechoslovakia, Dafoe concluded,

> The doctrine that Germany can intervene for racial reasons for the "protection" of Germans on such grounds as she thinks proper in any country in the world which she is in a position to coerce, and without regard to any engagements she has made or guarantees she has given, has now not only been asserted but made good; and and it has been approved, sanctioned, certified and validated by the governments of Great Britain and France, who have undertaken in this respect to speak for the democracies of the world.
> This is the situation, and those who think that it is right will cheer for it.

The English in the Townships have little of the dynamic concern shown by Winnipeg for Canadian nationalism, and by the French, including those in the Townships, for French-Canadian nationalism. The main political problem of the English in the Townships is to preserve good relations with the French on their doorstep. Willy-nilly, they are advocates of the *bonne entente*, anxious to work out a *modus vivendi* with the French which will preserve as much as possible of their own way of life. They are too worried and obsessed with the menace of Quebec politics to see further west than the Ontario border. Prior to the Liberal defeat in 1966 M. Lévesque was shouting "Quebec is not asking, from now on it is *demanding* respect for its jurisdiction."[56] After succeeding to office in June 1966 M. Johnson continued the same crusade. In the face of such onslaughts the English in the Townships were diverted from much concern for the broader conception of "a dominion from sea to sea." The demands of the local situation proved more engrossing and also more alarming.

VIII

How shall we compare Winnipeg and the Townships? After living five years in Winnipeg and twenty in the Townships, I should say the English in Winnipeg are a vigorous, self-confident, and effective force, perhaps a little past the peak of their influence and basking in the afterglow of Dafoe and Sifton, but still optimistic and still dominant; whereas the

56/Discussion period after speech at McGill University, January 25, 1966 (CBC transcription).

English in the Townships compose a cautious, rather defeatist minority, still with power which they are afraid of losing.

Winnipeg was for long in the mainstream of Anglo-Saxon expansion in Canada, a process particularly apparent in the West in the years between 1880 and the first world war. George Ham somehow caught the spirit of the city when he wrote:

The doors of vast opportunity lay wide open and Canada's adventurous sons flocked to Winnipeg to have a part in the great expansion – the building of a newer and greater Canadian West. They were big men, come together with big purpose. Their ideas were big, and they fought for the realization of them. They struggled for place and power and advantage, not with regard to the little, isolated village which was the field of their activities and endeavours; but always with an eye to the city that now is and to the great plains as they now are.[57]

The city reflected the spirit of the frontier and in its attitude to eastern dominance still does. A. J. McPhail, the President of the Canadian Wheat Pool, spoke for Winnipeg during stormy negotiations with eastern farmers in 1930 when he wrote: "It was a wonderful exhibition of the type of men in charge of the financial affairs of the country. God help the country if these are the kind of men who carry such large responsibility."[58] This anti-eastern attitude has been shown in the efforts of Winnipeg to compete with Montreal for control of Air Canada facilities, and the gallant but unavailing efforts of James Coyne to establish a genuine western bank.

The Townships passed through their frontier stage in the early and middle nineteenth century, but in a sense the region was a backwash from the beginning. Even in the 1830 to 1850 period, when the Townships received considerable immigration from Great Britain, it was a side-show compared to Upper Canada. The Townships have meant more to the French because they did not think in east-west terms and were more prone to settle down in the Townships, unattracted by the pull of westward expansion.

57/Ham, *Reminiscences of a Raconteur*, 30.
58/H. A. Innis, ed., *The Diary of Alexander James McPhail* (Toronto 1940), 216.

10
Problèmes scolaires dans l'Ouest

LOUIS COURCELLES

INTRODUCTION

UNE DES PRÉOCCUPATIONS majeures du Canadien-français, surtout celui qui habite hors du Québec, a été de conserver intactes deux valeurs qu'il considère comme un précieux héritage : sa langue et sa foi. A plusieurs reprises, certaines personalités politiques de même qui certaines sectes fanatiques ont tenté de lui enlever cet héritage, comprenant mal qu'un Canadien-français pouvait être en aussi bon citoyen que n'importe lequel autre Canadien. Dans leur intolérance, ils s'acharnèrent surtout à détruire le système scolaire de caractère catholique et français qui perpétuait jusque dans les confins de l'Ouest canadien cet héritage religieux et culturel.

Le récit des conflits scolaires qui surgirent dans cette partie du pays au tournant du vingtième siècle fera l'objet du présent travail. Notre attention se portera d'abord sur le problème des écoles du Manitoba, puis sur celui des écoles des Territoires du Nord-Ouest au moment où le Parlement fédéral sanctionnait l'entrée dans la Confédération des provinces de l'Alberta et de la Saskatchewan. Deux hommes jouèrent un rôle prépondérant sur la scène fédérale lorsque ces questions furent débattues : Sir Wilfrid

Laurier et Henri Bourassa. Nous exposerons leur pensée ainsi que leurs faits et gestes à cet égard, tentant de démontrer que Laurier aussi bien que Bourassa poursuivaient une politique logique et consistante. Bien qu'il ait défendu les droits des minorités de l'Ouest avec moins de verve et d'éclat que son jeune protégé, Laurier n'avait pas moins à cœur les intérêts de ses compatriotes ; plutôt, il entrevoyait la possibilité de constituer un Canada uni, où Canadiens-anglais, Canadiens-français, catholiques et protestants seraient tous des citoyens canadiens à part entière.

MANITOBA

Avant d'aborder la crise scolaire que Laurier et Bourassa eurent à régler en 1896, il est utile, sinon nécessaire, de retracer l'historique du problème scolaire au Manitoba. Quelques temps avant que le Manitoba n'entre dans la Confédération, en 1870, le gouverneur du temps, Sir John Young, avait fait la promesse solennelle de sauvegarder les droits de la minorité canadienne-française de ce territoire : « Par l'autorité de sa Majesté, je vous assure qu'après votre union avec le Canada, tous vos droits et privilèges civils et religieux seront respectés[1]. » De fait, le Manitoba Act de 1870 consacrait, à l'article 22, les prérogatives de la religion et de la langue des minorités. Cet article reprenait à peu près en entier l'article 93 de l'Acte de l'Amérique du Nord britannique sauf qu'il ajoutait aux termes « by law », celui de « by practice », de sorte qu'aucune législature provinciale ne pouvait changer un système scolaire qui existait avant l'Union, de fait sinon de droit[2].

Cette précaution s'avéra inutile pourtant puisque dès 1890, sous l'instigation de D'Alton McCarthy et du procureur provincial Joseph Martin, une nouvelle loi scolaire était votée le 31 mars. Les chapitres 37 et 38 de cette loi – le Public Schools Act de 1890 – stipulait que le Conseil de l'Instruction publique, créé le 3 mai 1871 et comprenant une section catholique et une section protestante, serait désormais remplacé par un Département d'Education sous contrôle gouvernemental auquel on adjoignit un « Advisory Board » dont les membres seraient tous protestants. Le Département d'Education allait élaborer les programmes, engager les

1/Sir John Young, cité dans Lionel Groulx, *L'Enseignement français au Canada*, II, *les écoles des minorités* (Montréal 1933), 148:
« Les droits religieux et civils des minorités s'appliquent à toutes les minorités sans distinction, les droits linguistiques à l'anglais et le français seulement. Bien que nous restreignons l'application de ces droits uniquement aux Canadiens-français dans ce travail, ils s'étendent indifféremment à toutes les minorités. »
2/Parlement du Canada, *Actes de l'Amérique du Nord britannique et Statuts annexes* (Ottawa 1962), 202.

professeurs, choisir les manuels, prélever les taxes devant servir exclusivement aux écoles publiques. On tolérera l'existence des écoles séparées mais on refusera de leur accorder des subventions. Les exercices religieux étaient également tolérés pourvu toutefois, qu'ils soient d'un caractère « non-sectarian » et se fassent après 3:30 PM[3]. Fait plus grave : on révoqua le certificat des enseignants catholiques[4].

Les catholiques en appelèrent tour à tour à la Cour du Banc de la Reine du Manitoba, à la Cour Suprême du Canada et au Conseil privé[5]. Après cinq années de tergiversations, le Conseil privé rendit finalement un jugement favorable à la minorité et permit ainsi au Ministre de la Justice, Sir Charles Hibbert Tupper, de rédiger (21 mars 1895) un ordre-en-conseil qui intimait au gouvernement manitobain de restaurer les droits de la minorité. Israel Tarte, stratégiste machiavélique, confia alors à Dafoe : « The government is in the den of lions ; if only Greenway will now shut the door[6]. » Peine d'en fut donc, car le gouvernement manitobain refusa de s'y contraindre. Il allégua que les écoles catholiques étaient inefficaces et que, également, le fait de distribuer des subsides aux catholiques, aux anglicans et aux mennonites parsemés dans un si vaste territoire, serait inconséquent. De plus, il demanda au gouvernement fédéral de faire une investigation de la situation avant de légiférer de quelque manière que ce soit.

Laurier fut pleinement d'accord avec cette dernière proposition. Une fois les faits trouvés, il fallait tenter de concilier les protagonistes : « If that object is to be attained, it is not to be attained by imperious dictation nor by administrative coercion. The hand must be firm and the touch must be soft...[7] » Pour le moment, et avant que toute législation ne soit proposée, Laurier refusait de prendre position. Le 8 octobre 1895, prononçant un discours à Morrisburg, il déclara :

I want to give my views, but remember that war has to be waged in a certain way. When the Duke of Wellington was in Portugal... he withdrew at one time within the lines of Torres Vedras, and there for months he remained, watching the movements of the enemy... Gentlemen, I am within the lines of Torres Vedras[8].

Le 11 février 1896, Mackenzie Bowell, ex-grand-maître de la loge

---

3/Lionel Groulx, *L'Enseignement français au Canada*, II, 92.
4/Joseph Schull, *Laurier, the First Canadian* (Toronto 1965), 287.
5/Barrett and Brophy cases.
6/Israel Tarte, cité dans J. W. Dafoe, *Laurier, a Study in Canadian Politics* (Ottawa 1967), 36.
7/Laurier, cité dans Oscar D. Skelton, *Life and Letters of Sir Wilfrid Laurier*, II, No. 22, The Carleton Library (Toronto 1965), 155.
8/*Ibid.*, 156.

orangiste de l'Ontario, eut la noblesse et le courage des présenter un « bill réparateur » qui réquisionnait du gouvernement manitobain la restitution aux catholiques de leurs privilèges. Le bill exigeait la nomination d'une commission catholique chargée de veiller au maintien de leurs écoles ; de plus, le bill incitait le gouvernement à verser des subsides aux écoles séparées sans toutefois l'y obliger[9]. Laurier entendit la lecture de ce bill avec soulagement. En fait, le gouvernement s'était placé dans une position plus que difficile puisque le bill présentait un maximum de coercition de la province, non compensé par une aide réelle et effective à la minorité. Sans subsides provinciaux, les écoles séparées des municipalités rurales ne pouvaient ni maintenir leur efficacité ni même leur existence. Laurier était donc fort aise de proclamer à nouveau le slogan des droits provinciaux, « Hands off Manitoba », et de blâmer le gouvernement de ne pas suffisamment connaître les faits avant de préconiser des mesures législatives de coercition. Dans un autre domaine, c'était Laurier lui-même qui était menacé de coercition. L'épiscopat canadien tenta de lui dicter une ligne de conduite sur la question du bill réparateur. Ce fut le vieux Père Lacombe qui s'en fit l'interprète. Le 20 janvier, il écrivit en effet :

It is in the name of our bishops, of the hierarchy and the Catholics of Canada, that we ask the party of which you are the worthy chief, to assist us in settling this famous question, and to do so by voting with the government on the Remedial bill... If... you do not believe it to be your duty to accede to our just demands, and if the government... is beaten and overthrown... I inform you, with regret, that the episcopacy, like one man, united with the clergy, will rise to support those who may have fallen in defending us[10].

Laurier donna réponse à cette lettre dans son discours du 3 mars 1896, alors qu'il discuta les mérites du bill réparateur :

No, I am a Liberal of the English school. I believe in that school which has all along claimed that it is the privilege of all subjects, whether high or low, whether rich or poor, whether ecclesiastics or laymen, to participate in the administration of public affairs, to discuss, to influence, to persuade, to convince – but which has always denied even to the highest the right to dictate even to the lowest[11].

Laurier sountint à nouveau que le gouvernement agissait sans connaissance de cause parce qu'il n'avait pas procédé à une enquête. Selon lui, toute la cause s'en trouvait dans le fait que la position prise par les catholiques en matière d'éducation n'était pas comprise. Les protestants ne

9/Robert Rumilly, *Henri Bourassa, la vie publique d'un grand canadien* (Montréal 1954), 28.
10/Père Lacombe à Laurier, 20 janvier 1896, cité dans Skelton, *Life and Letters*, II, 159–60.
11/Laurier, *Débats de la Chambre des Communes*, le 3 mars 1896, 3034.

comprenaient pas l'importance que l'Eglise attachait à l'enseignement dogmatique. Les protestants ne voulaient pas d'écoles athées, mais il ne voulaient pas, non plus, d'enseignement moral et, en imposant aux catholiques les mêmes restrictions qu'ils s'imposaient à eux-mêmes, ils ne se rendaient pas compte qu'ils étaient coupable d'un acte d'intolérance. « C'est là le premier préjugé qu'il y a à faire disparaître. C'est là le premier point sur lequel il faut faire la lumière, et jusqu'à ce que ce point soit rendu lumineux, la question est insoluble[12]. »

Pour justifier son opposition au bill, Laurier dit que si le Parlement avait adopté ce bill ou tout autre semblable, la province du Manitoba en aurait certainement contesté la validité et il s'en serait suivi une longue période d'agitation et de tourmente au grand détriment de la minorité catholique dans les autres provinces. « La croyance que toute législation de ce genre n'apporterait pas un règlement final dans la question, justifiait amplement l'opposition que le parti libéral fit au bill du gouvernement[13]. » Il rétorqua à tous ceux qui s'empressaient de l'affubler du nom de « traître à sa race et à sa religion[14] » que l'aide apportée aux minorités catholiques par ce bill ne se mesurerait que de loin avec les concessions volontaires qu'il obtiendrait du gouvernement manitobain en recourant à ses « sunny ways ».

Dans le discours mentionné plus haut, Laurier avait suggéré qu'on ne procédât pas plus avant avec l'étude du bill mais que, plutôt, on remette l'étude du projet de loi à six mois. Cette motion fut mise au vote le 20 mars, mais le gouvernement s'en tira avec une majorité de 24 voix. Il s'ensuivit de la part des libéraux et des McCarthystes une obstruction systématique qui tint la Chambre en session presque jour et nuit pendant sept semaines. Sproule y lut la loi scolaire de la Nouvelle-Ecosse ; John Charlton, les passages bibliques prescrits dans les écoles d'Ontario et Tyrwhitt, des passages de l'*Histoire du Canada* de Bibaud, de sorte que, le 15 avril, Bowell se vit dans l'obligation de retirer son projet de loi et de déclarer des élections pour le 23 juin.

La campagne pour la justice scolaire qu'avaient menée jusque-là les évêques – Mgr Langevin, archevêque de Saint-Boniface, en tête – prit des tons encore plus impérieux. Une lettre pastorale collective des évêques

---

12/Lettre de Laurier à Charles-Eugène Pouliot, citée dans Groulx, *L'Enseignement français au Canada*, 117.
13/Documents pour servir à l'intelligence de la question des écoles du Manitoba, avec quelques notes explicatives, cité dans Groulx, *L'Enseignement français au Canada*, 117.
14/Thomas Chapais : « Cette attitude est celle d'un traître. » Cité dans Groulx, *L'Enseignement français au Canada*, 116.

des provinces ecclésiastiques de Québec, Montréal, et Ottawa traçait la ligne de conduite à suivre :

Si les évêques, dont l'autorité relève de Dieu lui-Même, sont les juges naturels des questions qui intéressent la foi chrétienne... il leur appartient lorsque les circonstances l'exigent, non pas seulement d'exprimer vaguement leurs vues et leurs désirs en toute matière religieuse, mais encore de désigner aux fidèles ou d'approuver les moyens convenables pour arriver à cette fin...[15]

Le moyen convenable, selon Mgr Langevin, eut été de voter avec le gouvernement pour le bill réparateur. Le 17 mars, il avait en effet écrit une lettre à l'Hon. Larivière, mais le véritable destinataire était Laurier : « Aucun évêque ne diffère ; ils sont tous de mon avis. Les catholiques qui opposent le bill trahissent la minorité catholique[16]. » Quelques temps après, il avait déclaré publiquement à Montréal : «moi je dis, en ma qualité d'évêque et avec la pleine autorité qui s'y attache, que le catholique qui n'obéit pas à la Hiérarchie sur la question de l'école, cesse d'être catholique[17] ».

Commentant la prise de position de Laurier selon laquelle il agirait « non pas au point de vue du catholicisme, non pas au point de vue du protestantisme[18] » mais selon les principes de la justice, de la liberté et de la tolérance, Mgr Laflèche déclara en pleine cathédrale des Trois-Rivières : « L'homme qui parle ainsi est un libéral rationaliste. Il formule une doctrine entièrement opposée à la doctrine catholique. C'est dire qu'un catholique n'est pas tenu d'être catholique dans sa vie publique. C'est une erreur fondamentale et qui peut mener aux plus déplorables conséquences[19]. »

Pour compléter le tout, les évêques obligèrent les fidèles à voter pour celui des candidats qui déclara publiquement son allégeance à la prise de position épiscopale : « Un électeur qui est sincèrement catholique et qui veut obéir aux évêques ne peut dire, sans pécher gravement et se rendre indigne des sacrements : c'est mon opinion qui est de même, je dois voter selon ma conscience[20]... » Laurier aurait sans doute pu appliquer à

15/Lettre pastorale collective, cité dans André Siegfried, *Le Canada, les deux races* (Paris 1906), 54.
16/Lettre de Mgr Langevin à l'Hon. Larivière, le 17 mars 1896, citée dans J. H. S. Reid, K. McNaught and Harry S. Crowe, *A Source-Book of Canadian History* (Toronto 1959), traduction, 361.
17/Mgr Langevin, cité dans Siegfried, *Le Canada, les deux races*, 43.
18/Laurier, *Débats de la Chambre des Communes*, le 3 mars 1896, 3034.
19/Sermon de Mgr Laflèche, 17 mai 1896, cité dans Siegfried, *Le Canada, les deux races*, 243.
20/Lettre de l'évêque de Rimouski, 12 juin 1896, citée dans Siegfried, *Le Canada, les deux races*, 54.

l'ensemble des évêques des commentaires plus acerbes que celui qu'il formulait à l'endroit de Mgr Langevin : « but the minority is in the hands of men who, as you know, have not shown any wisdom[21]. » Non, en dépit de l'influence indue que les évêques exerçaient et qui compromettaient son succès électoral dans la « priest-ridden province », Laurier ne dira mot, ainsi qu'il l'avait affirmé le 3 mars : « even though I have threats held over me, no word of bitterness shall pass my lips against that Church. I respect it and I love it[22]. »

Quant à Bourassa, devenu candidat libéral sur les instances de Laurier, la question des écoles du Manitoba revêtait à la fois un caractère ecclésiastique, social, et politique. Aux électeurs de son comté qui lui demandèrent de préciser sa position, il répondit : « Pour ce qui relève de l'Eglise, je ne ferai riens sans prendre l'opinion de notre évêque. Sur le terrain politique, je crois que le bon Dieu me donnera des lumières pour apprécier la valeur juridique d'une loi[23]. »

Arriva le 23 juin : Laurier receuillit quarante-neuf sièges dans la province de Québec, là même où pendant trente ans le clergé avait épaulé solidement le parti conservateur, là même où les catholiques appuyant les candidats libéraux se virent parfois refuser les sacrements. Le charme et le magnétisme de Laurier avaient conquis le peuple canadien. L'enjeu de l'élection n'était pas tant la question des écoles du Manitoba que la chance pour les Québécois d'élire un des leurs au poste le plus élevé au pays[24].

La première et la plus urgente des tâches à laquelle le nouveau gouvernement devait s'attaquer demeurait celle de régler le conflit scolaire au Manitoba. De toute évidence, Laurier n'allait pas proposer un autre bill réparateur. Il l'aurait peut-être fait en tout dernier ressort si ses « sunny ways » avaient failli de convaincre le gouvernement Greenway d'octroyer certaines mesures d'aide à la minorité. Une chose était absolument hors de considération : le gouvernement manitobain n'allait pas reconstituer des écoles séparées telles qu'elles existaient en 1871. Par ailleurs, Laurier entrevoyait la possibilité de faire inscrire dans le règlement des écoles publiques, des mesures qui favoriseraient l'enseignement de la religion catholique et du français, moyennant certaines conditions.

C'est à cet effet qu'il s'entretint d'abord avec Greenway et Sifton, puis avec Sifton, Watson et Cameron, venus à Ottawa au cours de l'été pour étudier le problème plus à fond. Ensemble ils élaborèrent le schéma de ce

21/Laurier à J. D. Cameron, cité dans Reid, McNaught, and Crowe, *A Source-Book of Canadian History*, 356.
22/Laurier, *Débats de la Chambre des Communes*, le 3 mars 1896, 3035.
23/Henri Bourassa, cité dans Rumilly, *Henri Bourassa*, 31.
24/Opinion de Dafoe.

qui s'appelera le Règlement Laurier-Greenway et dont nous reparlerons plus bas. Il restait à savoir si les minorités du Manitoba acceptaient ce projet. Tarte et Bourassa furent délégués au Manitoba pour s'en rendre compte. Leur mission consistait aussi à exercer les pressions nécessaires pour faire accepter le projet. Prendergast, ministre démissionnaire du gouvernement Greenway en 1890, n'etait pas récalcitrant devant les mesures proposées, étant d'accord avec les émissaires de Laurier sur l'impossibilité pratique d'obtenir plus du gouvernement manitobain. Même le farouche défenseur des droits intégrals des Canadiens-français, Mgr Langevin, se montra réceptif[25]. Toutefois, lorsque les stipulations du Règlement Laurier-Greenway furent révélées au public, le 20 novembre 1896, il s'éleva avec force contre le compromis des libéraux : « C'est aujourd'hui le jour le plus triste de ma carrière épiscopale... Je proteste de toutes mes forces contre l'emploi de ce règlement... Nous sommes peu nombreux et nous sommes pauvres. Ce n'est pas une raison pour insulter à notre misère[26]... »

Le Règlement comprenait trois séries de dispositifs : les uns qui réglementaient l'enseignement religieux, d'autres l'emploi de maîtres catholiques, un autre enfin, l'enseignement de la langue maternelle dans les écoles de la minorité. L'école publique subsistait toujours mais, dorénavant, on pourra y donner une demi-heure d'enseignement religieux par jour selon la foi professée par les élèves. Dans les écoles où l'assistance moyenne comptait au moins quarante enfants catholiques, dans les districts urbains – vingt-cinq pour les districts ruraux – les parents pourront obtenir un instituteur catholique. Dans les écoles qui comptaient au moins dix enfants ne sachant pas l'anglais, l'enseignement bilingue était autorisé. La rédaction du Règlement demeurait intentionnellement vague afin de permettre aux mennonites allemands de profiter des mêmes avantages que les Canadiens-français catholiques.

Laurier n'était pas dupe des implications que le Règlement comportait et jugeait le compromis sans vaine complaisance : « Je peux ajouter que ce règlement n'est pas aussi avantageux que je l'aurais désiré : mais je n'hésite pas à dire qu'après une agitation qui a duré six longues années où les passions humaines furent excitées au plus haut degré, il était impossible d'obtenir plus, et, dans les circonstances, le gouvernement du Manitoba ne pouvait accorder davantage[27]. »

Bourassa devint quelque peu méconnaissable si l'on compare l'attitude

25/Tarte prit bien garde de lui montrer le texte final du Règlement Laurier-Greenway.
26/Mgr Langevin, cité dans Groulx, *L'Enseignement français au Canada*, 333.
27/Laurier, *Débats de la Chambre des Communes*, le 26 mars 1897.

qu'il prit vis-à-vis le Règlement Laurier-Greenway en 1896 avec la position intransigeante qu'il afficha au sujet des écoles des Territoires du Nord-Ouest. Dans un article rédigé pour le *Ralliement*, il déclara : « nous pouvons accepter le compromis comme la meilleure politique possible en ce moment, sans nous lier à une approbation complète et entière et surtout finale, réservant toujours les droits de l'autorité religieuse à ce sujet[28] ». Il recommanda en outre de faire un essai loyal du compromis, quitte à ne ménager aucun effort pour améliorer le statut des minorités de l'Ouest. A l'égard de ceux qui boudaient le Règlement et, de ceux qui le trouvaient fort satisfaisant, Bourassa appliqua des termes dont il fut lui-même l'objet quelques années plus tard : « Ceux qui disent que le Règlement Laurier ne donne rien à nos compatriotes et coreligionnaires, et ceux qui disent que le Règlement règle définitivement la question sont des extrémistes[29] ». Les extrémistes de toutes tendances ne manquaient certes pas à l'époque... Pour sa part, le Grand Orange Lodge of Manitoba dénonça violemment le Règlement, qualifiant celui-ci de « betrayal of the national schools, an insidious recognition of denominational pretensions[30] ». En contre-partie, les évêques décriaient le règlement comme étant la continuation d'une injustice flagrante et d'un pacte entre deux gouvernements libéraux plus soucieux de recourir à des expédients politiques qu'aux principes moraux. L'impétueux Mgr Langevin écrivait au cardinal Ledochowski, le 25 novembre 1896, dans les termes suivants : « Une lettre Encyclique du Saint-Père serait le salut de nos écoles et j'oserai dire le salut de la province de Québec qu'un faux patriotisme ou un esprit de partisannerie outré... peuvent entraîner dans une très mauvaise vois[31]... »

Laurier également songea à en appeler à Rome pour faire cesser la pratique néfaste de certains évêques qui, ostensiblement favorisaient un parti politique plutôt qu'un autre et qui dictaient aux électeurs et aux élus les politiques à suivre, même en des domaines qui n'étaient pas de leur ressort. L'abbé Proulx de Saint-Lin et l'ex-zouave Drolet allèrent donc à Rome présenter la cause de la liberté de conscience et de la liberté constitutionnelle. Ils s'aperçurent à leur arrivée que déjà maints ecclésiastiques avaient traversé l'Atlantique et présenté à la hiérarchie romaine un plaidoyer justificatif qui donnait à Mgr Langevin, Mgr Laflèche et leurs amis, le plus honnête des rôles.

Bien que pourvus de lettres de créance du premier ministre lui-même, la délégation « officieuse » trouva maintes portes fermées et plus d'une

28/Bourassa, cité dans Rumilly, *Henri Bourassa*, 36.
29/*Ibid.*
30/Skelton, *Life and Letters*, ii, 10.
31/Mgr Langevin, cité dans Rumilly, *Henri Bourassa*, 40.

sourde oreille. Si à Rome, c'était presque le point mort, au Québec, les événements se précipitaient et la tempête s'annonçait violente. Du haut de la chaire, on dénonçait Laurier ; du haut de la chaire, on condamnait les journaux libéraux qui osaient soutenir le Règlement Laurier-Greenway ; du haut de la chaire, on interdisait la réception des sacrements aux fidèles qui persistaient à lire ceux-ci[32]. Laurier voulut empêcher que les choses ne s'enveniment davantage et, de concert avec quarante-cinq autres libéraux, dont Bourassa, envoya au Pape une « pétition[33] ». Celle-ci reprenait presque point par point le litige qui détériorait les bonnes relations entre le parti libéral et l'episcopat. Pression fut également faite pour qu'un observateur impartial vint du Vatican pour examiner à fond le problème scolaire du Manitoba, apaiser les consciences troublées des catholiques et faire arrêter les agiotages des cinq ou six évêques qui n'avaient cessé de soulever les esprits[34]. Ceux-ci s'employaient à causer des difficultés au sujet des écoles aussi bien à Rome qu'au Canada. Ils tentèrent de dévaloriser Laurier aux yeux des dignitaires ecclésiastiques, mais ce fut peine perdue, car Drolet leur lisait alors une lettre de Laurier dans laquelle il exprimait les sentiments les plus chrétiens :

My dear Drolet, you have known me for well over forty years; you know that I have never paraded my religious convictions, but that they exist... Whatever comes, « il faut marcher droit chemin... » It is a singular thing, that these violent acts... far from estranging me from the Church, draws (*sic*) me closer to it.[35]

Alors que la croisade cléricale battait encore son plein, Laurier exposa à nouveau les raisons qui l'avaient amené à opter pour le Règlement plutôt que pour toute autre solution : impossibilité de rétablir les écoles séparées à moins de révoquer le loi provinciale de 1890 ; impraticabilité de révoquer celle-ci à moins de faire fi des « présumés » droits provinciaux ; opportunité d'obtenir une amélioration voulue et consentie par le gouvernement du Manitoba plutôt que par une législation imposée de force par le gouvernement fédéral[36].

Il avait fait tout ce qui était possible de faire pour en arriver à un compromis honorable, mais l'opposition cléricale était irréductible[37] et, seule, la venue au Canada de Mgr Merry del Val allait faire cesser leurs

32/*L'Electeur, La Patrie*, le pamphlet rédigé par L.-O. David.
33/Skelton, *Life and Letters*, II, 205-07.
34/Mgr Merry del Val.
35/Lettre de Laurier à Drolet, le 15 décembre 1896, citée dans Skelton, *Life and Letters*, II, 205.
36/*Documents pour servir à l'intelligence de la question des écoles du Manitoba, avec quelques notes explicatives*, cité dans Groulx, *L'Enseignement français au Canada*, II, 117.
37/Mgr Langevin : « Pas de compromis ! »

clameurs. Arrivé au pays en janvier 1897, il s'employa à rencontrer tous ceux qui étaient mêlés de près ou de loin à la question des écoles du Manitoba[38]. Bourassa le rencontra à son tour et entendit le délégué apostolique lui dire : « Ce qui m'étonne, avec tant de querelles religieuses, c'est qu'il n'y a pas de schisme au Canada. Vous avez eu raison de dire, dans le mémoire envoyé au Saint-Père, qu'une question est plus importante que celle des écoles du Manitoba : le rétablissement de la paix[39]. »

C'était bien l'objectif que Laurier lui-même s'était proposé. C'était encore la façon de voir de Laurier que le prélat exprimait devant Russell :

But the bishops seem incapable of grasping the situation as it is, that as a matter of practical politics the central government cannot pass (no matter which side is in power) a remedial law and that the Church cannot allow generation after generation of children to grow up without any education at all, waiting until there is a Catholic majority in Manitoba which may never be[40].

Laurier avait enfin trouvé chez un dignitaire ecclésiastique un degré de compréhension qui était singulièrement absent chez de trop nombreux évêques canadiens. Toutefois, sa satisfaction ne fut pas complète puisque l'encyclique du 8 décembre 1897 déclara le Règlement Laurier-Greenway « défectueux, imparfait et insuffisant[41] ». En guise d'adoucissement, elle ajoutait cependant qu'il ne fallait pas refuser des satisfactions partielles, ni perdre de vue les règles de la modération, de la douceur et de la charité fraternelle[42].

L'encyclique produisit une détente que Laurier accueillit avec soulagement et dont il se servit ou réparer la brèche entre l'épiscopat, son gouvernement, et celui du Manitoba. Pour ce faire, des négociations furent entreprises avec le Dr Bryce de l'Advisory Board of Manitoba. Laurier désigna Bourassa pour représenter le gouvernement central. Ce fut un choix heureux car celui-ci s'inquiétait de ce que Laurier ne vienne à considérer le Règlement comme définitif. Ce rôle de négociateur l'autorisait donc à penser que le Règlement n'était qu'une entente préliminaire susceptible d'être élargie, amendée, et perfectionnée[43]. De la part de Laurier, c'était un habile moyen pour désarmer l'intransigeance de Bourassa et pour raffermir l'adhésion de celui-ci à la politique gouvernementale.

De tout autre que Bourassa, on aurait pu imaginer les paroles qui met-

38/Laurier, Greenway, Sifton, Tarte, Fitzpatrick, Langevin, Laflèche, etc.
39/Mgr Merry del Val, cité dans Rumilly, *Henri Bourassa*, 40.
40/Schull, *Laurier*, 366.
41/*Lettres apostoliques ou Encycliques*, brefs, etc., de S. S. Léon XIII, cité dans Groulx, *L'Enseignement français au Canada*, II, 127.
42/« Affari vos. »
43/Dans un article paru dans le *Devoir*, le 3 mars 1915, Bourassa réaffirma que tel était bien le but des pourparlers avec le Dr Bryce, à l'encontre des libéraux et conservateurs qui considéraient le Règlement comme définitif.

taient fin aux débats parlementaires destinés à régler la question des écoles du Manitoba : « A son arrivée au pouvoir, le gouvernement avait à régler cette difficulté de façon à rendre substantiellement justice à tous, et il y est arrivé... J'espère que nous entendons parler de cette question pour la dernière fois[44]. » Si l'on apposait cette prise de position à celle qu'il prit neuf ans plus tard au sujet des écoles des Territoires du Nord-Ouest, on aurait de la difficulté à les concilier. Alors que les principes impliqués dans le règlement des conflits scolaires du Manitoba et des Territoires du Nord-Ouest étaient sensiblement les mêmes, Bourassa se départit de son attitude conciliante et devint d'une intransigeance comparable à celle qu'il dénonça en 1896. Laurier, au contraire, demeurait constant dans son attitude : tenter d'obtenir le plus possible pour ses compatriotes et coreligionnaires mais toujours laisser la porte ouvert à un compromis honorable.

LES TERRITOIRES DU NORD-OUEST

Pour se faire une juste idée de la situation qui se présentait sous les yeux de Laurier et Bourassa en 1905, il faut revenir en arrière et résumer brièvement les étapes qui engendrèrent les conflits scolaires dans les Territoires. En 1875, le Parlement fédéral décida d'accorder aux Territoires du Nord-Ouest une forme rudimentaire de gouvernement autonome. Initialement, le projet de loi de 1875 ne comprenait aucune clause protégeant les droits des minorités. Ceci parut un danger à Blake et il insista auprès de Mackenzie pour qu'un article soit rédigé à cet effet. Ce fut l'article 11 :

Le commissaire en Conseil, s'il est autorisé à rendre les ordonnances concernant l'instruction publique, rend toutes les ordonnances à ce sujet ; mais dans les lois et les ordonnances concernant l'instruction publique, il doit toujours être décrété qu'une majorité des contribuables d'un district... peut y établir les *écoles qu'elle juge à propos*... et aussi, que la minorité des contribuables du district... peut y établir des écoles séparées...[45]

L'article 11 établissait donc le principe des écoles séparées dans l'Ouest et subordonnait toutes les ordonnances à cette provision. En 1885, conformément à ses pouvoirs, le gouvernement émit une première ordonnance qui servirait de base à son système scolaire. Deux régimes d'écoles séparées étaient prévus : l'une protestante, l'autre catholique. Un conseil, formée de deux catholiques et de deux protestants ainsi que du lieutenant-gouverneur, était chargé de l'organisation générale des écoles[46]. Toutefois,

44/Bourassa, cité dans Rumilly, *Henri Bourassa*, 42.
45/*Actes de l'Amérique du Nord britannique et Statuts annexes*, 195.
46/*Ibid.*, 111 ff.

chacune des confessions demeurait libre d'engager ses instituteurs de choisir ses manuels de classe, etc.

C'était un régime acceptable aussi bien pour la majorité que la minorité des citoyens habitant ces territoires. Lorsque d'autres ordonnances suivirent en 1886, 1887, 1889 et 1892, on s'aperçut que progressivement le gouvernement empiétait sur les droits des minorités. La dernière de ces ordonnances – celle de 1892 – supprimait les comités catholiques et protestants constitués en 1875 et les remplaçait par un Conseil de l'Instruction Publique duquel relevaient toutes les écoles des Territoires. L'enseignement de la religion était interdit avant 3:30 PM, même dans les écoles séparées[47], et l'anglais devenait obligatoire pour l'enseignement de toutes les matières enseignées au cours secondaire[48]. En fait, c'était abolir le caractère distinctif des écoles séparées : « Rien d'essentiel ne distinguait plus les écoles catholiques des écoles protestantes si ce n'était la distinction ironique d'écoles séparées[49]. »

En 1901, le gouvernement procéda à une refonte de toute la législation scolaire. Englobées dans l'Ordonnance 29, se trouvaient la majeure partie de la législation précédente plus certaines autres restrictions concernant les écoles séparées. L'article 22 faisant de l'école publique la seule base possible de l'organisation d'un district scolaire, était une répétition de l'ordonnance de 1886. L'article 41 ne permettait l'organisation d'une école séparée que dans les districts déjà organisés. Il en résultait que partout où les catholiques formaient la majorité dans un district, ils ne pouvaient organiser d'écoles séparées. Et comme ceux-ci s'étaient groupés en chateaux-forts, cela voulait dire, en pratique, qu'ils ne pouvaient plus constituer d'écoles selon leur gré. Black dit à ce sujet : « Only four separate schools had been organized since 1892 when Roman Catholic control and management of their separate school districts was abolished, though according to the 1901 census, 20 per cent of the North-West Territories was of the Roman Catholic faith[50]. » Des 1360 districts scolaires qui existaient en 1901, seulement 16 étaient pourvus d'écoles séparées[51].

Il était nécessaire, quoique fastidieux, de rappeler ces détails parce qu'ils nous aident à comprendre pourquoi les catholiques se sentaient lésés dans leurs droits et pourquoi Bourassa s'opposa à Laurier dans le règlement de la question des écoles des Territoires du Nord-Ouest en 1905. Venons-en maintenant aux faits qui concernent cet épisode.

47/*Ibid.*, article 85.
48/*Ibid.*, article 86.
49/Henri Bourassa, *Les Écoles du Nord-Ouest* (Montréal 1905), 16.
50/Norman Black, *A History of Saskatchewan* (Regina 1913), 461.
51/*Canadian Annual Review*, 1905, 50.

Lorsque Laurier songea à ériger les Territoires en provinces – « to put upon these Territories the stamp of Canadian nationality » selon l'expression consacrée[52] – il savait bien que la question scolaire allait susciter des difficultés : « Pourquoi essayer de réveiller la question des écoles séparées... Elle reviendra toujours trop tôt... et mon rôle sera de nouveau de combattre les extrémistes, et de maintenir la question là où l'Acte de L'Amérique britannique du Nord l'a placée... Rappelez-vous que la Confédération fut un compromis[53]... » Il n'avait certes pas à l'idée, à ce moment-là, que Bourassa serait du nombre de ceux qui lui causerait des soucis au sujet des écoles des Territoires du Nord-Ouest, puisqu'il lui demanda expressément sa collaboration : « Le gouvernement constituera deux nouvelles provinces à même les Territoires du Nord-Ouest. Le bill garantira les droits de la minorité catholique. Il se trouvera sans doute quelques fanatiques pour critiquer. Et j'aurai besoin d'hommes de caractère, parmi la députation canadienne-française, pour leur faire contrepoids[54]. » Bourassa accepta volontiers de prêter ses services. C'était d'ailleurs par l'entremise de celui-ci que Laurier se tenait en communication avec le délégué apostolique, Mgr Sbaretti, qui joua un rôle considérable dans la rédaction de la première clause 16. Quant aux ministres de son cabinet, ils ne furent guère consultés à part Fitzpatrick qui s'occupa des technicalités légales de cette clause. Bourassa lui en fit la remarque et Laurier de répondre : « Je ne déteste pas de les mettre de temps en temps devant le fait accompli[55]. » Cette omission s'avérera importante dans le cas de Sifton, et déjà Bourassa pressentait le danger d'un tel procédé puisqu'avant même que le ministre de l'intérieur ne s'insurge contre les dispositifs de la clause 16. Il demanda à Laurier : « Lui avez-vous fait connaître le texte préparé ? » Laurier : « Non, mais je lui ai dit nous ne pouvons pas faire moins que de conserver à la majorité ce qu'elle a[56]. »

Le 21 février 1905, Laurier présenta son bill d'autonomie à la Chambre des Communes. Relativement au problème du régime scolaire à instaurer dans les nouvelles provinces, il préconisa ni plus ni moins que le rétablissement des écoles confessionnelles, tout en conservant aux écoles publiques leur statut actuel : « nous avons incorporé dans la mesure législative à l'étude, deux propositions : l'une portant que la minorité a le pouvoir

---

52/Laurier, *Débats de la Chambre des Communes*, le 21 février 1905, 325.
53/Lettre de Laurier à Willison, le 11 juin 1904, citée dans Robert Rumilly, *Histoire de la Province de Québec*, XI (Montréal), 161.
54/Lettre de Laurier à Bourassa, sans précision de date, citée dans Rumilly, *Histoire de la Province de Québec*, XI, 175.
55/Laurier à Bourassa, cité dans Rumilly, *Henri Bourassa*, 192.
56/*Ibid.*, 193.

d'établir ses propres écoles, et l'autre, qu'elle a droit à une part des deniers publics[57]. » Puis continuant son discours, il exprima sans ambages le fond de sa pensée au sujet des écoles séparées :

S'il fallait manifester tout haut ma pensée au sujet de ces écoles, je dirais que jamais je n'ai réussi à m'expliquer qu'on puisse juger répréhensible un régime scolaire qui, après avoir assuré à l'enseignement profane sa juste part, permet d'inculquer à la jeunesse la doctrine de la religion fondée sur le Christ, et cela, indépendamment des divisions régnant parmi les adhérents de son culte[58].

Joignant le geste à la parole, il déposa devant la Chambre la constitution de l'Alberta et de la Saskatchewan, où se trouvait inscrite la politique qu'il venait de préconiser. L'article 16, que nous citons presque *in extenso* pour bien marquer la différence entre celui-ci et l'article 16 amendé, se lisait comme suit :

Les dispositions de l'article 93 du British North America Act, 1867, s'appliquant à la dite province comme si, à la date de l'entrée en vigueur de la présente loi, le territoire y compris était déjà une province, l'expression UNION au dit article, étant tenue pour signifier la dite date.
2 — Subordonnément aux dispositions du dit article 93 et en continuation de l'application du principe ci-devant consacré par l'opération de l'Acte des Territoires du Nord-Ouest, il est édicté que la législature de la dite province rendra toutes les lois nécessaires au sujet de l'Instruction publique et qu'il y sera toujours réservé (a) qu'une majorité de contribuables d'un district... peut y établir les écoles qu'elle jugera à propos... et (b) que la minorité des contribuables de ce district... peut y établir des écoles séparées...
3 — Dans la répartion des derniers publics... il n'y aura aucune inégalité ou différence de traitement entre les écoles publiques et les écoles séparées...[59]

Les dispositions de cet article constituaient non seulement un redressement de la condition injuste faite aux minorités mais une révocation des diverses ordonnances édictées par le gouvernement des Territoires. Fort d'une majorité de 70 voix en Chambre, Laurier escomptait faire passer le bill avec une aisance relative. Tel ne fut pas le cas cependant. A sa surprise et son désappointement, Sifton démissiona le 26 février sitôt revenu d'un voyage de santé. La raison de cette démission n'était pas très claire. Bien qu'il affirma à Laurier qu'il ne pouvait accepter les dispositions de l'article 16, il se peut aussi qu'il voulut mettre Fitzpatrick en mauvaise posture et s'accaparer de ce poste qu'il convoitait.

Laurier avait dit jadis : « Tant que j'aurai Tarte et Sifton avec moi, je serai le maître du Canada[60]. » Tarte avait déjà quitté le cabinet, Sifton

57/Laurier, *Débats de la Chambre des Communes*, le 21 février 1905, 1518.
58/*Ibid.*, 1519.
59/Article 16 du bill 69, cité dans Groulx, *L'Enseignement français au Canada*, II, 168.
60/Laurier, cité dans Rumilly, *Henri Bourassa*, 194.

venait de le faire, Fielding et certains autres ministres s'apprêtaient à les imiter. De plus, les journaux commencèrent une campagne de dénonciations qui n'avaient eu leurs pareils qu'au temps du règlement des écoles du Manitoba. Ils faisaient écho à l'opposition, pour le moins surprenante de certains ecclésiastiques protestants dont le plus loquace et le plus intolérant demeurait le Surintendant de l'Eglise méthodiste, le Rév. Dr Carman : « We must build on secure foundations and say to Rome, when it tries to force the tyrannies of a thousand years upon this young country : We don't want them here[61]. »

Qu'allait faire Laurier devant cette opposition grandissante qui menaçait le pays de disruption ? Une fois encore, il allait trouver un compromis, car l'œuvre qui lui tenait à cœur l'exigeait. En 1896, on s'en souvient, il avait déclaré : « I have devoted my career to the realization of an idea. I have taken the work of Confederation where I found it when I entered political life, and determined to give it my life. Nothing will prevent me from continuing my efforts to preserve that state of society...[62] » A Bourassa et Fitzpatrick qui tentaient de lui démontrer qu'en dépit des défections de certains membres de son parti, il pourrait quand même receuillir suffisamment de voix [40] pour passer le bill tel quel, Laurier répondit : « Peut-être, mais il subsisterait du malaise ; il y aura une agitation analogue à l'affaire des écoles du Manitoba[63]. » Non, il fallait ou céder ou tomber. D'après Le Nationaliste, Laurier devait maintenir ses positions jusqu'au bout, quitte à tomber noblement, mais le premier ministre réalisait que telle n'était pas la meilleure solution. Même le très catholique Fitzpatrick s'accordait avec Laurier : « Si le gouvernement tombe sur cette question, Borden et ses amis prendront le pouvoir ; pour les catholiques ce sera pis[64]. »

Le compromis devisé par Laurier et Sifton fut l'article 16 amendé. Nous citons une section de cet article afin d'élucider l'ampleur de la concession :

Rien dans ces lois ne devra préjudicier à aucun droit ou privilège au sujet des écoles séparées dont jouira aucune classe de personnes à la date de la passation du présent acte, aux termes des chapitres 29 et 30 des ordonnances des Territoires du Nord-Ouest passées en l'année 1901[65].

Si nous nous référons au premier article 16, nous constatons que celui-ci en était presque la contradiction. Alors que par l'article 16 présenté le 21 février, les minorités récupéraient tous leurs droits, l'amendement du 22 mars consacrait une situation scolaire où les minorités en étaient lésés.

61/Rev. Dr. Carman, citée dans Canadian Annual Review, 1905, 115.
62/Laurier, Débats de la Chambre des Communes, le 20 mars 1896.
63/Laurier, cité dans Rumilly, Henri Bourassa, 195.
64/Fitzpatrick, ibid., 198.
65/Actes de l'Amérique du Nord britannique et Statuts annexes, 223.

Ils l'étaient de fait sinon de droit, car les dispositions de l'Ordonnance 29 ne laissaient subsister pratiquement que seize écoles séparées sur un total de 1360 districts. Lors de la présentation de l'amendement, Laurier s'appliqua d'abord à réaffirmer les droits des minorités :

Alors qu'il s'agit d'admettre au sein de la Confédération deux provinces où il existe un système d'écoles confessionnelles, à l'instar de celles en vogue dans les provinces de Québec et d'Ontario, je m'appuie encore une fois – c'est ma conviction – sur la pierre angulaire de la constitution du Canada en affirmant que le Parlement fédéral, de par cette constitution a le devoir de conférer à la minorité des nouvelles provinces des droits et des privilèges similaires à ceux dont jouissent les minorités dans les provinces de Québec et d'Ontario[66].

Cette assertion voulait parer et contrecarrer toutes les objections de ceux qui contestaient le pouvoir du Parlement fédéral de sanctionner un système d'écoles confessionnelles. Se servant de l'article 93, paragraphe 1 – voir note[67] – ils affirmaient que la constitution ne permettait pas de continuer le système des écoles séparées puisque, selon eux, elles n'existaient pas avant l'Union – Union qu'ils disaient s'être effectuée en 1870. C'est à cet effet que le paragraphe 3 de l'article 16 précisait à la fois la date de l'Union et la loi scolaire qui régissait les écoles :

Là où l'expression « par la loi » est employée dans le paragraphe dudit article, elle sera censée signifier la loi telle qu'énoncée dans les dits chapitres 29 et 30, et là où l'expression « lors de l'union » est employé dans ledit paragraphe 3, elle sera censée signifier la date à laquelle cet acte est venu en vigueur[68].

Donnant les raisons pour lesquelles ce paragraphe fut substitué au paragraphe 1 de l'article 93, Laurier dit qu'en pareilles circonstances, s'ils remettaient en vigueur l'article 3 de la loi peut-être créeraient-ils une certaine confusion qui aboutirait à provoquer des procès tendant à faire définer le sens précis de la loi. « Nous avons donc cru préférable de donner à la loi une certitude absolue, et dans ce but nous y avons incorporé le texte des ordonnances sous l'empire desquelles la loi, dans sa teneur actuelles, a été établie[69]. » Un député fit remarquer à Laurier que l'ordonnance 31 établissant le mode de distribution des taxes n'était pas incluse dans le projet de loi et Laurier s'esquiva de la belle manière : « Nous avons cru qu'il valait mieux nous contenter d'établir ce principe sans imposer de

66/Laurier, *Débats de la Chambre des Communes*, le 22 mars 1905, 3030.
67/*Actes de l'Amérique du Nord britannique et Statuts annexes*, 190 : « Rien dans une telle législation ne doit porter préjudice à un droit ou privilège que la loi, lors de l'Union, attribue dans la province à une classe particulière de personnes quant aux écoles confessionnelles. »
68/Article 16, paragraphe 3, cité dans *Actes de l'Amérique du Nord britannique*, 223.
69/Laurier, *Débats de la Chambre des Communes*, le 22 mars 1905, 3039.

fardeau à la population des Territoires[70]. » Pour ceux qui connaissaient les motifs de Haultain, Sproule, Blain, D'Alton McCarthy et les autres de même acabit, une telle échappatoire était l'occasion rêvée pour inciter les gouvernements des dites provinces à affamer les écoles séparées et précipiter leur disparition. Se cachant sous la couverture des droits provinciaux, ils arrachèrent donc cette autre concession de Laurier. Bourassa ne mâcha pas ses mots dans son discours du 28 mars, en Chambre : « Les vrais criminels, ceux qui attentent à la vie nationale, ce sont les hommes publics qui s'efforcent de déguiser leurs sentiments réels et d'éluder leurs responsabilités en prétextant leur respect de la constitution[71]. » Puis, résumant un ton plus propre à la nature d'une assemblée parlementaire, il s'appliqua à démontrer que les rédacteurs de la Constitution avaient effectivement voulu préserver les droits des minorités :

Ils [les fondateurs] comprirent qu'en jetant les bases de la Confédération, cette entente des deux provinces faisait naître un principe et que ce principe devait dominer à jamais la loi et la constitution. Ce principe... c'est que tout citoyen du Canada, quelle que soit la province où il fonde son foyer, soit assuré que la justice et l'égalité y régneront et que la majorité n'y pourra jamais persécuter la minorité[72].

Bourassa rappela aussi en quels termes était rédigé la requête du 12 décembre 1867 pour annexer les Territoires et y établir des institutions parlementaires et scolaires : « Le bien-être... y serait sensiblement augmenté par la création d'institutions analogues, autant que les circonstances le permettront, à celles qui existent dans les différentes provinces du Canada[73]. » Poursuivant toujours son discours volubile, Bourassa fit appel à « l'honneur du Parlement et à la mémoire des hommes qui avaient fait la Confédération... les forçant à racheter leurs promesses et à prouver que ces hommes d'Etat ne se parjurèrent point[74]. » Il aborda ensuite le problème central des écoles séparées catholiques, analysant brièvement les conditions de leur existence. Tandis que les catholiques demeuraient obligés au paiement des contributions scolaires, aucune fraction du produit de ces contributions n'était plus destinée au soutien des écoles catholiques mais servait à l'entretien des écoles publiques qui, à leurs yeux, n'étaient plus propres à procurer l'instruction à des enfants catholiques que si elles étaient indubitablement protestantes. Bourassa ajouta : « Or j'affirme que le libre exercice de la religion catholique n'existe pas si le

70/*Ibid.*, 3040.
71/Bourassa, *Débats de la Chambre des Communes*, le 28 mars 1905, 3321.
72/*Ibid.*, 3373.
73/*Ibid.*, 3378.
74/*Ibid.*

père de famille catholique ne peut jouir sans entraves du droit de donner a son enfant l'enseignement que lui imposent sa croyance et sa conscience[75]. » D'aucuns auraient pu lui rétorquer que la liberté religieuse existait au sein de l'école publique, car la loi permettait l'enseignement religieux à partir de 3:30 de l'après-midi. Mais pour Bourassa et le clergé catholique, il n'en était pas ainsi. A cette époque, la doctrine catholique voulait que les principes religieux pénètrent toute l'instruction donnée à l'école. Tout – professeurs, inspecteurs, livres, activités, etc. – devait réfléter une attitude religieuse si ce n'était de « religiosité. » Bourassa termina son discours en lançant un appel presque pathétique : « Mon dernier mot est celui-ci : soyez justes envers les Canadiens-français. Je ne vous demande pas d'être généreux[76]... »

Quelque trois semaines plus tard, soit le 17 avril, Bourassa tint une assemblée « monstre » au Monument National à Montréal pour expliquer aux gens le projet de loi qui était devant la Chambre. A l'encontre de son discours pondéré et sagace du 28 mars, celui-ci prit un caractère hostile et acerbe. Non seulement y rappela-t-il les diverses ordonnances qui enrayèrent petit à petit les droits sacro-saints de ses compatriotes et coreligionnaires, il s'employa aussi à en démontrer toute l'illégalité ; illégalité que l'amendement Sifton allait sanctionner. Selon lui, toutes ordonnances n'étaient valides qu'en tant que conformes à l'article 14 des Actes des Territoires[77].

Nous avons cité plus haut l'article 14 ainsi que les ordonnances de 1892 et de 1901, pour mettre en lumière justement l'écart qui existait entre la loi initiale de 1875 et celle que le gouvernement Laurier voulait perpétuer. Bourassa dit fort à propos :

En acceptant l'amendement Sifton, le parlement fédéral annule sa propre législation et lui substitue celle de la législature des Territoires... il légitime l'illégalité de l'Ordonnance de 1901 et sanctionne à jamais les violations que cette ordonnance a fait subir à la loi organique qu'il avait lui-même adoptée...[78]

Lors de la présentation de l'article 16 amendé, Laurier avait tenté de prouver que la législation ainsi proposée dans l'article en question ne se départait pas de la loi fondamentale de 1875, mais Bourassa n'en croyait rien : « si Sifton, qui a démissionné parce qu'il ne pouvait accepter l'article 16, agrée l'amendement projeté, il est difficile de croire que les deux textes ont la même valeur et la même portée[79] ». Non, l'amendement de l'article

75/*Ibid.*, 3381.
76/*Ibid.*, le 28 mars 1906, 3403.
77/Bourassa, *Les Ecoles du Nord-Ouest*, 19.
78/*Ibid.*, 21.
79/*Ibid.*, 22.

16 était une capitulation, « un acte de faiblesse[80] ». « Tout ce que l'amendement Sifton garantissait en réalité, c'était la conservation de neuf écoles
séparées, de nom, dans toute l'étendue des deux provinces de l'Alberta
et de la Saskatchewan[81] » et le droit d'organiser des écoles séparées dans
des conditions analogues. Bourassa ne pouvait s'imaginer que lorsqu'on
aurait compris que l'effet de l'amendement serait de détruire ce que l'on
affirmait vouloir conserver. Le ministère persistât à « accepter cette mesure
néfaste et réduire à néant les principes de justice, de liberté et de droit
constitutionnel que Laurier avait proclamés avec tant de solennité dans
son discours du 21 février[82]. »

Laurier était déterminé à faire accepter un compromis – jugé honorable
dans les circonstances. Bourassa rejettait cette conciliation, la considérant
ni bonne, ni même possible « entre deux principes contraires, entre la
vérité et le mensonge, entre la justice et l'iniquité[83] ». D'ailleurs, ne s'était-il
pas réservé le droit de dissension lorsqu'il accepta la candidature dans
Labelle : « Je me réserve le droit de voter pour ou contre mon parti
suivant mes convictions », avait-il déclaré en 1896[84]. Lorsque vint le vote
final, en juillet 1905, seulement Bourassa et quelque six ou sept autres
députés votèrent contre la clause relative à l'éducation.

En cette occasion ainsi que dans bien d'autres subséquentes, Bourassa
fit preuve de beaucoup de courage et de détermination. Il n'était certes
pas facile de s'opposer aux décisions de Laurier alors que celui-ci était au
faîte de son prestige. Ni la crainte de perdre la faveur de l'électorat ni
l'hostilité de puissants personnages politiques ne l'empêchèrent de décrier
ce qu'il croyait être injuste. Le malheur fut que ceux à qui il servait ses
irréfutables arguments faisaient la sourde oreille. Laurier était bel et bien
aux écoutes, mais il lui était impossible de faire davantage pour ses compatriotes. Ayant connu les agitations et les turbulances qu'avait suscité le
conflit scolaire du Manitoba, il préférait la paix, la tolérance, et même le
compromis à d'autres querelles raciales et religieuses. Laurier et Bourassa
différaient vivement d'opinion sur le problème scolaire ; néanmoins, ils
conservaient l'un pour l'autre une admiration et une affection qui n'eut
jamais de relâche. Pris devant l'intransigeance de Bourassa et du clergé
ainsi que l'intolérance des groupes tory-orangistes, Laurier joua avec
succès le rôle du conciliateur et du champion d'un Canada uni. Si Bourassa
n'avait pas existé, il aurait fallu lui trouver un remplaçant.

80/*Ibid.*, 23.
81/*Ibid.*
82/*Ibid.*, 27
83/*Ibid.*, 3811.
84/Bourassa, cité dans Rumilly, *Henri Bourassa*, 30.

11

The Yukon: Northern Development in a Canadian-American Context

MORRIS ZASLOW

TO MOST CANADIANS, mention of the Yukon Territory brings to mind the exciting story of the mad dash from the four corners of the earth to the small circle of ridges and ravines through which flowed creeks lined with gravel flecked with gold – the movement known for all time as the Klondike gold rush. An economic historian, H. A. Innis, observed that "It is doubtful if, in rapidity, size and intensity, the Klondike gold rush has ever been equalled in the whole range of economic expansion,"[1] and a sociologist, S. D. Clark, has remarked that "Within this four-year period [1898–1902] the development of the Yukon passed through the full cycle of social disorganization and reorganization; for study of these social processes, few social laboratories could be more revealing."[2] A student of gold rushes, W. P. Morrell,[3] perceived in the gold mining camps of British Columbia and the Yukon an interesting contrast, in their methods of operation and their "styles" of activity, with other mining camps being

1/H. A. Innis, "Settlement and the Mining Frontier," in A. R. M. Lower and H. A. Innis, *Settlement and the Forest and Mining Frontiers* (Toronto 1936), 183.
2/S. D. Clark, *The Social Development of Canada* (Toronto 1942), 326.
3/W. P. Morrell, *The Gold Rushes* (London 1940).

developed in California and Alaska. He attributed this contrast to the differing political systems of British America and the United States, as did H. F. Angus, F. W. Howay, and W. N. Sage, the authors of that excellent study, *British Columbia and the United States*.

These judgments – selected from among many others – demonstrate a few of the differing vantage points from which the Klondike gold rush may be viewed and studied. The gold rush was a complex bundle of interrelated phenomena extending across the broad range of human behaviour. Because of its complexity, as well as because of the abruptness, scale, and dramatic intensity of its manifestations, the gold rush can be made to yield insights into problems that are characteristic of all the northern districts of Canada, and which, by marking them off from other, more settled portions of the country, give grounds for considering "the North" as a distinctive region of Canada. At the same time, because northern Canada is comprised of many districts that differ from one another in their geographical, historic, and sociological aspects, "the North" cannot be considered a true region if uniformity and homogeneity are regarded as essential qualities in the definition of a region. Thus at one and the same time, "the North" is – and is not – a true region of Canada. As for the phenomena exemplified by the Klondike gold rush, some are common to all parts of northern Canada, whereas others are peculiar to itself alone.

The Yukon Territory, one of Canada's most fascinating districts, still carries the marks of that cataclysmic event, even though the placer gold mining operation was finally terminated during the past year. Important as was the rise and fall of gold mining, it is not the sole, or even most important factor in the evolution of the Yukon Territory. This is to be found, more broadly, in the interaction between the settlers and the physical environment, as revealed in the social, cultural, administrative, and economic developments of the period.

The examination of the evolution of the Yukon Territory discloses the paramount importance of one particular aspect of this interaction – not that of the men on the spot to their environment, but that of the government that possessed the district to both the men and the environment. In the Yukon Territory we see the interaction between official Canadian policies and Canadian institutions and a community largely comprised of Americans and expressing the American frontier ideology. The outcomes – the imposition of a Canadian system of external controls upon the developing community, and the integration of the Yukon into the Canadian polity, economy, and society – are fascinating, little-understood sides of the region's history.

An important comparative aspect is seen in the history of the wider

Yukon region of Canada and Alaska during this period. Canada and the United States followed widely contrasted approaches towards the settlement and development of their frontier territories that were reflected in the histories of their colonial dependencies along the Yukon River during this period. Those histories are a unique opportunity to view the two opposed experiments in frontier administration under almost ideal conditions. Most of the elements in both situations were the same – the time, the physical environment, the type of settler, and his goals. The major variable, the contrasting effects of the colonial programmes of the controlling powers during the period of the Klondike gold rush, can readily be gauged. By examining this wider situation one may come to a better understanding of the salient features of Canada's programme of frontier control and development. From that one may better approach the regional trait beyond all others that is shared by all of Canada's northern territories – their colonial dependence upon Ottawa or the provincial capitals.

The Yukon region had been divided at the 141st meridian by the Anglo-Russian Treaty of 1825, but until 1895 almost identical conditions prevailed in the Alaskan and British American sectors. Both were dominated by the river as the sole means of travel and communications, both were frequented by the same nomadic hunting and trapping Indians of the Loucheux, Tukudh, or Kutchin tribes, to which were added a few white settlers engaged in the fur trade or the missions. British interests controlled the region until 1869. Entering the district from the east by way of the Mackenzie and Porcupine Rivers, the Hudson's Bay Company in 1847 established Fort Yukon at the junction of the Porcupine and Yukon Rivers. This post was almost a hundred miles inside Russian territory, although Company employees professed to believe they were still within the British boundary. Other trading posts had been established for a time along the upper Yukon River, really within British territory, but these were soon given up because of the hostility of the Indians and the difficulty of supplying them by way of the Liard River. Besides, the Company reached an agreement with the Russians that enabled it to dominate the trade of the upper Yukon from the coast. In the wake of the English traders, and each supporting the other, came Church of England missionaries who also made Fort Yukon their major westernmost base of operations.

The situation changed very quickly after the United States purchased Alaska in 1867. An official American party under Captain C. W. Raymond came up the river in 1869 and took possession of Fort Yukon, handing over the fur trade to Hutchinson, Kohl and Company, a San Francisco firm. The Hudson's Bay Company commenced a slow withdrawal up the Porcupine River, establishing three Ramparts Houses in succession, each a little further towards or inside British territory. However, after 1891 the trade of the Ramparts House – Lapierre House area also was attacked from the north by American whaling vessels based on Herschel Island. In 1893, during an economy drive to reduce expenses, the Hudson's Bay Company abandoned the entire operation west of the Mackenzie delta region. The Anglican missions followed suit, retiring from Fort Yukon in 1879 and leaving the western territory to the rivalries of American Episcopalians, Presbyterians, and Roman Catholics.

After the British interests had been driven from Alaska they proved unable to halt the Americans from advancing into British territory. The fur trade in Alaska came under the control of the Alaska Commercial Company which imported goods cheaply from the Pacific coast of the United States by way of Bering Sea and the Yukon River. In Canadian territory a number of small traders located along the upper Yukon and operated as clients of the Alaska Commercial Company. Other Americans began entering the territory after 1880, mainly from the south over the mountain passes, part of the wave of American gold seekers that had been swept into western America by the California gold rush. Drawn by rumours of gold, they moved from one likely location to another, sometimes in British territory, other times farther west in Alaska, the boundary being completely ignored. In the early 1890's another large American trading organization, the North American Transportation and Trading Company, entered the country. It was based at Dyea, at the head of Lynn Canal, the gateway to the interior, and operated its own vessels and outposts along the Canadian Yukon waterway. To all intents and purposes, the Canadian Yukon was a part of the American frontier, inhabited by American (or Americanized) miners and its trade monopolized by American mercantile interests. The sole British voice in the district was the Anglican missionary operation, headed by Bishop W. C. Bompas of Selkirk, who began organizing the diocese after 1891 from a base in the American mining camp of Fortymile, just inside the Canadian boundary.

The 141st meridian boundary held no administrative significance either; no effective system of government existed on either side of it. The interior of Alaska was in a state of anarchy, for nothing had been done to put the Organic Act of 1884 into effect in the interior. As for the Canadian portion of the Yukon, the first evidence of a government presence was the joint survey by G. M. Dawson and R. G. McConnell of the Geological Survey and William Ogilvie of the Department of the Interior in 1887–88. Ogilvie's advice to the Dominion government was to leave well enough alone for the present but to keep a watchful eye on the district with a view to future action. He argued that the imposition of Canadian laws and taxes would put the district at a disadvantage as compared with Alaska and would militate against the development of its mineral resources. Besides, he added, the miners were Americans and used to American rules, which were more suited to local conditions than were those of Canada.

The American system – or lack of system – that prevailed in both sections of the Yukon seemed designed for just such a situation as existed there in the 1870's and 1880's. The district judge held courts only at Sitka and Wrangell; the commissioners were located at these and at two other coastal settlements, Juneau and Unalaska. There was no law (or taxes) in the Yukon country, and the principal legal provision drafted with the region expressly in mind, the prohibition of the importation of liquor, was a dead letter. Such neglect was quite logical in terms of American political philosophy enshrined in the Constitution of the United States, that governments were the agents rather than the masters of the people. The principle that governments should be instituted by the people on the spot in keeping with their own needs had been further enshrined in the mid-century ideal of "squatter sovereignty." The United States government saw no need for the precipitate or premature imposition from outside of governmental institutions or controls upon a new territory in the absence of some major reason necessitating its intervention.

To meet this absence of external authority at this stage of Alaskan development the frontiersmen, particularly the veteran free miners, had been evolving their own system of rules and regulations in the hundreds of mining camps that flourished briefly in the half century after the California gold rush. In each camp the miners elected their recorder, fixed the recording fee, decided on the mining regulations that would be applied, and passed bylaws on other matters. Their regulations, derived from their past experience, were determined by majority vote. Though they were supposed to fall inside the broad limits of the appropriate federal legislation, sometimes, as with liquor prohibition, they completely ignored the federal enactments. Miners' meetings also heard suits between miners and decided on punishments for criminal acts. Penalties were usually fines or expulsion from the camp or district, but could extend as far as hanging. This system operated reasonably well without outside interference in the early days in Alaska, and by extension, in Canada. The miners settled their own problems and disputes and kept internal order. They paid no taxes, but neither did they ask for any services from government.

The system also had its disadvantages, particularly as the size and complexity of the camps increased. Occasionally persons simply defied the rulings of the miners' meetings and the miners could not always compel compliance. Since they tended to decide cases on the basis of their knowledge of the individuals concerned, rather than on the issues, the results sometimes favoured the popular person's suit; or a chivalric sense could overcome the members' sense of justice; or judgments were pronounced purely on frivolous grounds (particularly when the saloons became the major meeting places). As Joseph Ladue, a pioneer trader, commented: "The Miners on the Yukon are shrewd, experienced men, and sometimes they are tricky. I do not like the kind of government they set up for themselves, except in the very first stages. It is all by miners' meetings. They begin by being fair, but after a while cliques are formed, which run things to suit the men who are in them, or, what is just as bad, they turn the sessions into fun. Nobody can get justice from a miners' meeting when women are on one side."[4] Nor were miners' meetings infallible. Lacking legal experts they could not determine questions of law, or, sometimes, questions of fact. Ogilvie cited examples of miners' meetings committing serious mistakes in assigning claims, being deceived by false testimony, being swayed by secretly interested parties planted in the midst of the meeting to affect the result, or deliberately ignoring known rules of law to prevent the perpetration of a suspected fraud.

In 1893 the time seemed ready for the Canadian government to enter the Yukon to uphold Canadian authority, though as yet there were almost no Canadians or Canadian interests in the Yukon. From Ogilvie, back surveying the boundary along the Alaska Panhandle, from Bishop Bompas at Fortymile, from C. H. Hamilton, the manager of the North American Transportation and Trading Company, came requests for the Canadian government to take control. In 1894 it sent out a North West Mounted Police inspector and a staff-sergeant to look into the situation. Inspector Constantine came to Fortymile, collected some customs duties and mining fees, left the staff-sergeant to carry on, and returned to Ottawa to report that a large police force was needed to enforce the whole body of Canadian laws and regulations in the Canadian Yukon. In 1895 he returned with half the force he had asked for, a squad of 20 men, built a police post in the tradition of the prairie forts with buildings arranged in a square, and began to enforce Canadian laws to the best of his ability, while back in Ottawa the government proclaimed the existence of a District of Yukon.

Thus two diametrically opposed principles for the government of a pioneer environment confronted one another. The American philosophy, exemplified by the mining camps, was libertarian and laissez-faire, based on the principle of squatter sovereignty; the Canadian approach was

4/Cited in F. W. Howay, W. N. Sage, and H. F. Angus, *British Columbia and the United States* (New Haven and Toronto 1942), 350.

authoritarian or colonial. It began with the premise that the authority of the Crown and of the law predated the establishment of the frontier settlement, that the institutions of the frontier, as for any other section of Canada, were imposed by the fiat of the governing authority and remained applicable to the frontier until some provision was made for it to receive some portion of the authority of the central government and begin to legislate for itself. In the meantime it was the duty of the frontier to accept the regulations of the superior authority and the agents sent by the authority to administer the affairs of the region. Constantine and his men as agents of the federal authority in the Yukon District were not simply police officers; they were agents of every branch of the dominion government that had any interest in the Yukon region.

The affirmation of the authority of the Canadian government in the years 1895–97 quickly threw the system based on the miners' meetings into the discard, if only because it enabled those aggrieved by miners' decisions to disregard them with impunity and appeal for a new hearing according to Canadian law. Besides, Constantine was determined to make the miner accept his authority and he missed no opportunity to do so. "The men who live this sort of life are old miners from the Cassiar & Cariboo Districts of B.C. Men from Idaho, Montana, Nebraska, Nevada, New Mexico & Washington states – who have been used to no control except that of their own sweet will & who preserve order in their camps by stern law, if not justice in all cases."[5] He proceeded to send detachments of his men to collect customs duties, issue mining licences, register mining claims, and enforce other rules, at the same time asking Ottawa to institute regulations that would lessen the discrepancies between the two systems or improve upon the rules the miners imported from outside, as for example, by enacting a system of proper liquor licences to stop the manufacture of "home brew."

There were one or two incidents where the miners seemed inclined to question this assertion of Canadian authority, especially at Glacier and Miller Creeks, close enough to the border that they could argue against accepting Canadian jurisdiction until the boundary had been definitely located. Constantine accepted no excuses; he reported in August 1896, after one or two incidents, that "The action taken has shown the American miner who does not care for constituted authority, that they [sic] can't run the creeks on our side and has had a very quieting effect on gentlemen of that stamp."[6] Ogilvie was inclined to stress that the helpfulness of the

5/Charles Constantine to L. Herschmer, August 15, 1896, in "Superintendent's Letter Book, 1895–98," Constantine Papers, PAC, MG 30, E 2, vol. 4.
6/*Idem.*

Canadian authorities induced the American miners to accept the new system for the sake of convenience, rather than because of the compulsion implied in the reports of the policeman Constantine. As Ogilvie told a private correspondent on May 22, 1897, at the close of the NWMP's second winter in the Yukon and the end of the first winter's diggings on the Klondike creeks:

Owing to the diversity of character, nationality, traditions, and number of the locators on these creeks, the inevitable soon became apparent, confusion, and confliction, of which you have no doubt heard a great deal; but, I think, I know there is now and will be a healthier, and higher standard set up in the country. There is now a desire for the knowledge of mining laws, which twelve months ago was conspicuously absent, that augers well for the future peace and harmony of the camp; even hardened old timers have admitted to myself that "Miners Meetings" as a means of adjudication are generally unsatisfactory and often unjust.

The cry everywhere is "let us have law administered by disinterested men who are above influence and reproach" as a proof of this sentiment I have only to say no miners' meetings have been held in the District for over six months, though there were occasions when the temptation was sorely trying. Many old miners have stated to me "I'll never attend another miners meeting while I live". We have Magistrates and police men in the country who if they cannot stamp out vice and injustice, will at least preserve order, and prevent robbery and have a terror to evil doers, and I think I can assert confidently for the Canadian Government that their condition will be maintained as long as the need for it is apparent.[7]

Just as in British Columbia forty years earlier, the American miners found the practical convenience of accepting the authority of the state greater than the incentives to follow their older tradition of local autonomy. The question of whether the miners would continue to make their own rules or be governed by laws made in Ottawa and administered by its agents in the field was decided in favour of Canada before the influx of gold seekers began in earnest. With these came a renewed, more serious challenge to Canadian authority than that posed by the earlier free miners.

The rush that followed the news of the great gold discovery in the Klondike came in three waves. The first, in the autumn and winter of 1896–97, caused the abandonment of the camps at Fortymile, Circle City, and other nearby centres, bringing to the Klondike men who were already prospecting or mining in or near the Yukon basin. The news reached the outside world in the spring and early summer of 1897, in time for experienced travellers in the Canadian northwest or along the Pacific coast to reach the Klondike that autumn or early winter of 1897, if they hurried.

7/William Ogilvie to J. M. Wilson, Fortymile, May 22, 1897, typescript copy in Ogilvie Papers, PAC, MG 30, C 2.

Most would-be Klondikers spent that autumn and winter preparing for their journey, planning to reach the Yukon in the spring of 1898 when navigation reopened along the waterway. During the winter of 1897–98 they travelled by sea to ports on the Lynn Canal or Wrangell to begin the spring rush over the trails and passes to the headwaters of the Yukon. Boom towns sprang up at Dyea and Skagway as the many thousands began hauling their supplies back and forth over the passes to the tent and boat-building city along the margin of Lake Bennett. This largest group of gold seekers was overwhelmingly American, reflecting the effectiveness of American publicity media, the good communications with the Yukon by way of the ports on the Alaska Panhandle or Bering Sea, and the intense appeal that the opportunities in the Klondike held for footloose west coast Americans ready to take big chances to achieve great rewards.

These newcomers were not miners accustomed to the traditions of self-regulation, but they presented a challenge of another sort. They were adventurous, chauvinistic Americans in a highly jingoistic age. They were rebels, breaking loose from the shackles of convention and conformity in quest of a new life of adventure and fortune. Some in fact, were fugitives – from unsuccessful business activities, unhappy domestic situations, or the law. They played for high stakes, and did not appreciate being cramped, confined, regulated, or ruled by Canadian functionaries who could not be reasoned with since they had no authority beyond referring petitions and requests to Ottawa. Besides, their administration was extremely incompetent in the early stages, characterized by mixups and worse in the Dominion Lands Office where there was a certain amount of corruption in the allotment of claims. The Americans felt they had settled the country and organized its social fabric. They considered that the mining camps, the mining techniques, the businesses, and the city of Dawson all were American creations. They felt that the Canadian presence in the Yukon was only a geographical or diplomatic accident, that the country was the creation of American skills, labour, and capital and belonged to the people who could make the best use of it in the interests of civilization.

This not unfamiliar argument in our own time was even more strongly felt in the social Darwinian, white man's burden climate of the turn of the century. Such a feeling had inspired the British in their relations with the Boer republics of South Africa from the Jameson Raid to the Boer War. Some Americans in the Klondike (and more outside) felt they were Uitlanders too, as regards their position in the Yukon and the political disabilities under which they suffered – and some of them drew the same conclusions as the British were doing in South Africa.

Was there any chance of a takeover of the Klondike by the United States? The international situation did not rule this out completely, for Anglo-American relations were in a precarious state through much of the period. Even the building of Fort Constantine in 1895 had not gone unnoticed. The *San Francisco Examiner* and other west coast newspapers printed alarmist reports that Canada was building stone forts along the Yukon and sending in troops to occupy the ground in force and to undermine American claims to the disputed territory[8] (which some Americans assumed to be the entire Yukon country, just as most Canadians today seem firmly convinced that the boundary award deprived Canada of the whole of the Alaska Panhandle and gave it to the United States). This misunderstanding had barely been allayed when the touchy Venezuela-Guiana boundary dispute erupted, and the State Department intervened belligerently with the Olney Declaration. The *Examiner* carried a succession of articles on the military position of Canada[9] – whence might come British assaults upon the United States, and where the United States might best direct its counterblows. On the international front there was the excitement aroused by the Spanish-American War, an easy victory that increased American impatience with a situation like that of the Klondike, and the British involvement in the Boer War. Troubles over the location of the boundary in the vicinity of the Lynn Canal, and disputes over transit and transhipment rights in northwestern America were irritants closer to home that might have touched off a Canadian-American war. To these should be added the possibilities of on-the-spot insurrections that could bring American intervention in force in the Yukon. There are hints of conspiracies organized in Skagway as in the NWMP comptroller's references to "the occurrences of last winter when the futile attempt was made to organize a conspiracy to obtain possession of our Territory."[10] The counter-measures by the Canadian government indicate how seriously it took the danger. However, no attack or insurrection occurred. The British and Canadian governments took care to avoid letting their relations with the United States get out of hand. As for the chances of an uprising, Tappan Adney, perhaps the ablest of all the contemporary observers of the social scene, commented apropos of the attitude of the American settlers that "If there were not serious disorders it was due less to the quality of government than to the orderly character of the population, and

8/*San Francisco Examiner*, November 4, 5, 7, 9, 1895.
9/*Ibid.*, December 16, 1895, *et seq.*
10/F. White to F. C. Wade, October 11, 1902, in "Alaska Boundary, 1902–1942," F. C. Wade Papers, PAC, RG 18, vol. 4, entries for October 15, 1901 and January 25, 1902.

to the fact that men were there enduring the privations of an Arctic climate to make their fortunes and get away, not to help set in order the political house-holds of their Canadian friends."[11]

Instead, the American threat to the Klondike remained at the economic-social-cultural level, represented by the domination of the Yukon by American settlers and businessmen from within and American transportation and trading interests from outside. It was indicated in the predominance of American social modes and customs, including wide-open gambling, sale of liquor, and prostitution, that were characteristic of the American west but were completely alien to the Victorian respectability that prevailed almost universally in contemporary Canada.

On the other hand, the new wave of Americans was met with a stronger affirmation of Canadian authority than that proclaimed by Constantine on July 22, 1895. Americans arriving in the Yukon over the passes during the winter of 1897–98 were met by strong NWMP forces at the summits and subjected to stringent inspection. The police insisted that all persons entering the Yukon had to carry sufficient food (a year's supply, at a rate of three pounds per person per day) to remove any danger of starvation in that barren country. They used the occasion to examine the credentials of each intending immigrant, and turned back undesirables. They gave the immediate impression that the Yukon was under control, in complete contrast with conditions currently prevailing in the Alaska Panhandle. The police action obviously accorded with the best interests of the territory and of the newcomers and was accepted by most, though a few voices were raised against interference with the personal liberty of Americans to go where they chose. Others contended that the process was designed to blackmail Americans into paying tribute in the guise of customs duties, to compel them to purchase inferior Canadian goods, and to establish a Canadian claim to advanced positions in the territory under dispute, within ten marine leagues of the coast. The regulation respecting the food supply was disallowed by the dominion government, but it had done its work. The police had passed 30,000,000 pounds of food in the winter of 1897–98, "sufficient to feed an army corps for a year,"[12] and notwithstanding the enormous increase in the population, there was no food shortage in the Yukon during 1898–99.

The police also took other unaccustomed measures of control. The Canadian, rather than the American, practice respecting firearms was enforced in the Yukon, representing another marked difference with Alaska or even the contemporary western states. Under the domineering Superin-

11/T. Adney, *The Klondike Stampede*, cited in Clark, *Social Development*, 353.
12/S. B. Steele, *Forty Years in Canada* (Toronto 1915), 312.

tendent S. B. Steele the police also assumed control of the movement of the Klondikers down the Yukon River. After some loss of life on scows attempting to run the White Horse Rapids, Steele improvised and put in force a set of compulsory rules:

There are many of your countrymen who have said that the Mounted Police make the laws as they go along, and I am going to do so now for your own good, therefore the directions that I give shall be carried out strictly, and they are these ... No women or children will be taken in the boats ... No boat will be permitted to go through the canyon until the corporal is satisfied that it has sufficient free board to enable it to ride the waves in safety. No boat will be allowed to pass with human beings in it unless it is steered by competent men, and of that the corporal will be judge. There will be a number of pilots selected, whose names will be on the roll in the Mounted Police barracks here, and when a crew needs a man to steer them through the canyon to the foot of the rapids, pilots will be taken in turn from that list ... The rate now charged, 5 dollars, for each boat, seems to be reasonable.[13]

In the manner in which these rules were elaborated without discussion, without reference to any outside authority, and without any appeal being allowed against the rulings, Steele's action was the almost perfect affirmation of the authoritarian tradition in territorial administration in Canada.

The police performed a multitude of other services, including carrying the mail (an important activity when much gold had to be carried out of the Yukon) when the delivery by private contractors broke down. They patrolled the waterways, the gold-mining operations on the creeks, the city of Dawson and other communities, enforcing federal and territorial laws, and acting as agents for government departments that did not have their own officials in the territory. As Morrell observed: "The firm yet tactful and informal authority of the police won the admiring respect of American observers, who doubtless noted the absence of the political undercurrents apt to interfere with the course of justice in the Western States."[14] They were also vital to the security of the Yukon. They kept the criminal element under constant surveillance and ordered potential troublemakers out of the country. Their detectives infiltrated miners' and citizens' organizations to ensure that these were not used for purposes of subversion. Their numbers were raised to the 250 to 300-man level between 1898 and 1904, powerful enough to cope with small insurrections, besides which the government in 1898 sent in a 200-man militia contingent, the Yukon Field Force.

The civil administration also was greatly enlarged to parallel the increase in settlement. As chief executive officer and commissioner the

13/*Ibid.*, 311–12.
14/Morrell, *The Gold Rushes*, 389.

government sent Major J. M. Walsh to the Yukon in the autumn of 1897, and appointed a council of leading government officials to assist him in legislating for the Yukon District. He was given wide powers to alter mining and other regulations and to remove any federal government official, judges excepted, at his own discretion. These powers were withdrawn from his successors, and for the decade after his departure the Minister of the Interior kept close rein on activities in the Yukon. A judicial district was established and a judge was sent out to try cases in the area. A Dominion Lands Office was set up to regulate the all-important registration of mining claims, under the oversight of a gold commissioner. After a dispute with the Northwest Territories legislature, which asserted its right to legislate for the Yukon District, Parliament in June 1898 passed an act establishing the Yukon as a separate Territory (for a time it appeared as though it would be named "Klondike" instead of "Yukon"). In this way the dominion retained control in its own hands rather than sharing it with the autonomous government springing up in Regina. This step made possible the future advance of the Yukon towards separate self-governing status, but for the present it placed the Territory under the control of a regime less well attuned to pioneer conditions and aspirations than was that in Regina.

Between 1897 and 1900 the size and scope of the bureaucracy grew rapidly. The mining administration was represented by mining recorders at the major gold-bearing creeks. The legal system was reinforced with a variety of court officers, while two more judges were appointed to make a bench of three judges able to act as a supreme court as well as to process the multitude of lawsuits arising from mining disputes. A wide variety of inspectors, recorders, administrators representing most branches of government appeared in the Territory, including after 1902 agents of the territorial government in such fields as public works and education. Everything was quickly brought under regulations and controls in the Yukon, and the spirit of salutary neglect so typical of Alaska or the earlier Yukon was nowhere in evidence.

In its decisions respecting the political organization of the Yukon the dominion government was careful to avoid inflaming American opinion or aggravating the delicate situation in the Territory. It delayed granting self-government through fears that Americans might gain control of these institutions if they were allowed to participate; alternatively through fears that to give Canadians a monopoly of these institutions while the population was predominantly American would be regarded as discrimination and might awaken resentments akin to those aroused in the Transvaal. So the government retained control over the Yukon and refused to share it with the inhabitants for some years; and only gradually did it introduce measures of political reform while the complexion of the population changed in Canada's favour. Thus it introduced open council legislative sessions, granted two elected members to council (1901), then five elected against five appointed (1905), then all ten elected in 1908. The Territory received representation in the House of Commons by its own MP in 1902, while Dawson was granted an elected municipal government in 1901. In every case the electorates were limited to British subjects, but these were rapidly becoming the majority in the declining population of the Yukon.

All these steps were in marked contrast with the development of government control and authority in Alaska. Under the Organic Act of 1884, which specifically forbade the calling of a legislature or the granting of representation in Congress, Alaska was organized as a District, with an appointed governor but with administrative control exercised by the Secretary of the Interior. But no attempt was made to administer the interior of Alaska, and even the coastal settlements were most ineffectually administered, as was evidenced by developments at Wrangell and particularly at Skagway during the height of the gold rush in 1897–98. Alaskan authorities were quite powerless to curb the operations of a criminal gang in Skagway that preyed on Yukon-bound travellers, notwithstanding the presence there of a deputy marshal and for part of the worst period, of a detachment of United States marines. In the end, after a year of uncontrolled depravations, the citizens who wanted reform were compelled to organize themselves to take the law into their own hands. They were met head-on by the ringleader of the criminal element, "Soapy" Smith, who was shot and killed in a street gun duel in the best wild-west tradition. Following this drastic action the gang was rounded up by the suddenly-appeared agents of the law, to avoid their being lynched by the aroused citizens, and hustled aboard ship to face trial outside for their crimes.

The Klondike gold rush, the example of the Yukon Territory, and the advent of would-be miners to Birch Creek, Nome, and other sections of Alaska, at last brought action by the American government to institute an effective system of government for the interior where "non-interference with liberty by the central government has been but another name for neglect."[15] Under a law of June 6, 1900, prohibition was repealed, saloons and other businesses were licensed (constituting the first local taxation in the District) and a new criminal code especially designed for Alaskan conditions was enacted to replace that of Oregon which had been followed previously. A new civil code was provided, under which two of the three judicial divisions were in the north, at St. Michael and Eagle City. Provision was made for the establishment of municipalities with limited powers of taxation, while appointed commissioners were put in charge of

15/Adney, *Klondike Stampede*, cited in Clark, *Social Development*, 353.

the principal communities. However, it was not until 1908 that a gesture towards Congressional representation was allowed, when the people of Alaska gained the right to send a non-voting delegate to the House of Representatives, and only in 1912 was Alaska at last constituted a Territory, with a wholly elected Senate and House of Representatives able to legislate for and administer its local concerns.

In all these measures Alaska lagged behind the Yukon, which had received full representation in Parliament in 1902, an entirely elected territorial council in 1908, and possessed a much larger administrative and judicial establishment. Moreover, the sad tale of misgovernment at Nome indicated that the system of government provided from Washington was not an entirely satisfactory solution to the problem of colonial government. The trouble there arose from the appointment, through the influence of a North Dakota political boss, of a corrupt federal judge and court officials who concocted a scheme to enrich themselves by getting control of the mining claims. The case of Nome indicated the inability of the federal government to avoid making unsatisfactory partisan appointments or to exercise adequate supervision over its local agents. The Canadian government, though it could certainly not be accused of neglecting partisan appointments for the Yukon, nevertheless retained extremely close supervision over the Territory that prevented large-scale corruption at the local level. In fact, in 1899 it went so far as to prohibit government officials from involving themselves in mining properties. There was more danger of corruption originating or engineered from Ottawa, but there the glare of publicity on Yukon affairs (greater than upon Alaskan affairs in Washington), the system of governmental responsibility, and the vigilance of the parliamentary opposition, all combined to make an operation like that at Nome virtually impossible in the Canadian Yukon. Above all, the Canadian system of administration benefited from the firmly non-parisan traditions of the civil service, notably the all-powerful RNWMP and the large, impressive judicial system. Curiously, when it became fully developed after 1900, the Canadian system furnished the Yukon at one and the same time with a more powerful, authoritarian bureaucracy and more fully representative institutions than Alaska enjoyed.

The contest between Canada and the United States for the control of the Canadian Yukon turned strongly in Canada's favour particularly after 1900, largely because of the efforts of the police and other agencies of the government in the Yukon itself. At the same time, from outside the Yukon, other Canadianizing agencies were also attacking the American outpost in the Yukon Territory. The monopoly enjoyed by American trading concerns and port cities was challenged by vigorously advertising the advantages of securing outfits and supplies in Canada rather than in the United States, and by strict enforcement of Canadian customs regulalions to make these words come true. A serious effort was made to build, or have built, an all-Canadian access route to the Yukon to reduce the dependence upon American transportation media. Branches of Canadian banks in the Yukon handled the financing of mining operations and helped stabilize the economy, hitherto operating with gold dust as the sole medium of exchange.

To fight the monopoly enjoyed by Seattle and San Francisco in the marketing of the gold dust – which in turn gave those cities powerful commercial holds on the Yukon – a government assay office was set up in Vancouver to enable miners to convert their earnings into goods and credit in Canada rather than in the United States. Canadian manufacturing concerns were cajoled and given tangible incentives to compete for the supply trade, while companies were encouraged to set up branches and agencies in the Territory. Despite the tendency of American-controlled companies and American nationals to look to the United States for supplies, by 1902 Canadian firms were reported to be doing about 60 per cent of the Yukon trade.

The reconquest of the Yukon by Canadian business was actually helped by the economic decline and stabilization of its economy on a low level. As the returns from the Yukon diminished and the chances for large financial coups disappeared, business interests of San Francisco, Seattle, or Portland found the Yukon too small and awkward to compete for. They abandoned the field to Canadian firms that enjoyed the advantages of government protection and patronage and were content with more modest gains. The opening of the White Pass and Yukon Railway was a particular boon to Canadian business chances in the Yukon because it had the effect of segregating the trade of the Territory from that of the major part of Alaska. The railway also afforded a convenient, direct trade route between Vancouver and the Yukon that was quickly seized by the CPR and other shipping interests and rapidly displaced the more roundabout route via the Bering Sea and the Yukon River. Henceforth Vancouver became the principal trading and communications centre for the Yukon.

While encouraging Canadian participation to the full with a view to hastening the integration of the Yukon into Canadian life, the government did little to discourage the participation by Americans in its economic life. No attempt was made to prohibit American citizens (apart from those banned by the police) from settling anywhere or holding mining claims, as was the case with Canadians and other foreigners in Alaska. No effort was made to prevent an American-controlled company, the

White Pass and Yukon Railway (financed largely in Britain), from building the only railway link into the area from the port of Skagway, or to keep
American capital from playing an important role in integrating gold
mining operations in the highly successful Yukon Gold Company, organized by the Englishman A. N. C. Treadgold but financed by the Guggen-
heim mining interests of California.

The Canadianization of Yukon society also went forward rapidly after
1900. Canadian churches and fraternal organizations put forward determined efforts to convert the Yukon into a portion of Canadian society
as they conceived it. The presence of Canadian officials and institutions,
and the adoption by the federal government of policies reflecting the attitudes of southern Canada, were other potent forces in the remaking of
Yukon society. Church groups in particular complained endlessly against
the "un-Canadian" demeanour of Dawson – the gambling halls, saloons,
and houses of ill-fame operating openly and non-stop along the principal streets of Dawson. Left to themselves, the police and local government
were content with regulating these activities so as to insure that the games
were honest, the customers were not victimized, and no crimes were
committed. They argued that such activities were bound to take place in
the present state of the society, and so long as they were conducted openly
they could at least be policed and controlled. But the pressures of Canadian settlers wanting to bring their families to the Yukon, and the outcry
from groups and societies in southern Canada that could bring considerable pressure to bear upon the dominion government, would not let the
matter rest. The houses of ill-fame were banished to a back-street, then
expelled from Dawson across the Klondike River, and the gambling
houses and dance halls were closed. Above all, strict observance of the
sabbath – the hallmark of the Canadian way of life of the time which
differentiated it most sharply from that of the United States – was instituted
and enforced. By 1900 Dawson was a suitable place for orderly family
living, and by 1902 it was reported to be as Canadian as Toronto.

A measure of Canada's success in winning control of the Yukon was
the change in its population structure, as revealed in the censuses. At the
height of the gold rush, Americans probably numbered three-quarters or
more of the estimated 40,000 persons who reached the Yukon before
1900. Yet by the census of 1901, when the total population was given
as 27,219, the American group had declined to 8,700 persons, 32 per
cent of the total, most of their number having already departed for home
or for the new gold rush to Nome. The exodus continued with few
replacements, so that by the 1911 census there remained only 1,891
Americans in the Territory, 22 per cent of the whole. At the same time the

Canadian population, which was said to have constituted no more than 10 per cent of the advancing human wave, began to grow in relative importance if not in absolute numbers. Canadians tended to remain longer in the Yukon than the Americans, and to be replaced by other Canadians when they departed, the large government establishment furnishing a large source of employment and a stable economic base. By 1911 there were 3,850 Canadians in the Territory, double the number of American nationals, and 45 per cent of the total population of 8,512, making, with the 1,346 British, a Territory 61 per cent of whose population were British subjects.

Ironically, the triumph of Canadian interests in the Yukon was a pyrrhic victory, for the population continued to plummet even further, to the 4,000 level in the censuses of 1921 and 1931. Consequently, the political fortunes of the Yukon took a turn for the worse and its political lead over Alaska was eliminated. What had been regarded as a future province with all the powers of self-government associated with that status, had become by 1911 a Territory that scarcely seemed to warrant its present levels of administrative services and self-governing status. Indeed, it was a question whether or not the Yukon should be relegated to the common level of colonial administration that Canada provided for its undeveloped northern territories. From 1904 onwards the bureaucracy was considerably reduced, the judicial system was curtailed, and a plan was instituted to replace the elected council with a small appointed council. This fate was averted, but the council was reduced from ten to three members in 1919. At the same time, with the curtailment of a diversified civil service, many of its duties fell once more upon the shoulders of the smaller but still sizeable police establishment. The Indian Affairs administration – the very exemplar of the concept of Canadian trusteeship over her dependent territories and peoples – which had been almost entirely absent until this time, began to emerge in full force in 1914 as a means of regulating and controlling a native population that now accounted for half the Territory's inhabitants. By the 1920's the Yukon, reduced to a shadow of its former self, was hardly distinguishable from the settlements of the Mackenzie valley sector of the Northwest Territories. Only the river steamers, railway, and roads, the churned-up beds of the former Klondike creeks, and the decayed government buildings, amusement halls, business places, and dwellings of Dawson were left as a reminder of the glorious years when the Yukon stood on the threshold of becoming Canada's first northern province and was an object of feverish contention between Canadian and American cities, national governments, societies, and cultures.

12

The History of Newfoundland, 1900-49:
Background Notes*

G. O. ROTHNEY

NEWFOUNDLAND, 1900

IN THE NINETEENTH CENTURY, the world was in a state of transition from communication and trade by sea to communication and trade by land. Consequently the oceans were being replaced by the continents as the basis of political strength. The empires of Britain and France had depended upon sea power. The strength of the United States and Russia depended upon land power.

Newfoundland in 1900 was caught in the middle of this transition. Because she was an island and her people were mostly fishermen, she still belonged to the old world of the sea. Consequently she was still a British colony.

Her principal problems in 1900 were inherited from the old days of sea power. They had to do with the rights of French and American fishermen on her shores. French fishermen had been drying their fish on Newfoundland's shores as long as had the English, for France like Eng-

*As chairman of the seminar held at Memorial University in August 1967, Dr. Rothney made the following remarks to provide some background information about Newfoundland history.

land had been a great sea power. By 1713 the British navy was superior to the French, and Newfoundland had consequently become theoretically a British possession.

In 1713 British naval supremacy had been sufficient to put an end to French settlements in Newfoundland and to the French base at Placentia. But it was not yet quite great enough to stop French fishermen from drying their fish on the northern shores of the Island during the summer months.

Later on, when British sea power had in fact become great enough to eliminate this competition in the fisheries, the French saved themselves in Newfoundland by forming an alliance with the new continental nation which appeared in America in 1776. The combination of the French navy and American land power was too much for Britain. In 1783 she had to give the French and Americans the right to use the whole west coast of Newfoundland. The French could also use White Bay, while the Americans could also use the western part of the south coast and the whole coast of Labrador. French rights were the more serious of the two. American fishermen were not allowed to interfere with Newfoundland settlers, but from Cape Ray to Cape St. John, Newfoundland settlers were not allowed to interfere with French fishermen.

The establishment of American rights at Newfoundland in 1783 showed that the pull of the continent had begun to make itself felt there, though it was not yet nearly as strong as the pull of the ocean, represented by Britain and France. With the west coast dominated by the French, the pull of the continent was still not great enough in 1867 to bring Newfoundland into the new dominion of Canada. Yet the fact that it was growing was proved by the completion of the railway from St. John's to Port aux Basques in 1898, and the growth of population in the neighbourhood of Codroy and Stephenville.

Newfoundland's greatest problem in 1901 was how to end the French fishing rights on the west coast, blocking as they did the development of agriculture and industries which would bring her into greater contact with the continental mainland. A second problem was how to meet the competition of American fishermen backed by continental wealth and efficiency.

In wishing to solve the problems of French and American competition, Newfoundlanders were united. They were divided, however, about the way in which this was to be done. They were divided most of all by the question of how the railway and other land communications and services were to be financed on the basis of Newfoundland's limited maritime economy.

The steady drift of people away from east coast districts such as Ferryland to west coast districts such as St. George made the question of the French Shore critical. Settlers on that coast were tolerated only so long as they did not interfere with the French fishery.

In order to get a railway built across the island, a Tory government at the end of the nineteenth century had allowed not only the railway but also most of Newfoundland's other means of communication to come into the possession of one man, Robert Reid. Robert Bond felt that this was wrong in principle. When he became premier in 1900, Bond therefore hoped to obtain a revision of the contracts with Reid, but under responsible government he had to obtain the support of the majority of the members of the Assembly. To do this, his supporters had to join with those of Edward Morris. Together they formed a new Liberal party in 1900. Morris was not so strongly opposed to the Reid contracts as was Bond, so a compromise was necessary.

When the St. John's *Telegram* forecast that during the twentieth century the Liberal party would meet little opposition from the Tories of 1901, it was right. The great political battles of the future were to be caused by divisions among Bond's supporters themselves. Generally speaking, the leaders of the future would be those who best understood that Newfoundland's economy could not be based solely upon the sea, as in the past.

Newfoundland's structure of government, like that of Canada, was based on the British parliamentary system. There was no separation of the executive and legislative branches, as in the United States. It was responsible government because the executive was responsible to the elected legislature. But it was also colonial government because the governor was appointed in London by the British Colonial Office, and still had the power of veto.

NEWFOUNDLAND, 1901–14

As the twentieth century began, the new Liberal government felt that its principal problems were (1) the contract which had given R. G. Reid control of most of Newfoundland's communications; (2) the right of French fishermen to make use of the west and part of the north shore of the island; (3) the competition of American fishermen. The first two of these problems reflected the expanding activities of the people living on the east coast of Newfoundland. The third problem, however, reflected the conflict of this expansion with that of people living under the continental government of the United States.

In Newfoundland after 1900 the world-wide trend towards greater geographical, economic, and political unity made itself felt through the desire of the government in St. John's to bring the French Shore from Cape St. John to Cape Ray under its complete control. This meant getting the British government to persuade the French government to give up its rights under the Treaty of Versailles of 1783. In 1904 the French accepted this suggestion. In the same way, the Newfoundland government wished to establish its right to make regulations with regard to Americans fishing on the coast. This right was established by a decision of the Hague Tribunal in 1910.

Politically, Bond's Liberal party had an overwhelming majority in the House of Assembly. But it had been formed by a coalition with Morris in 1900. Could Bond hold it together now that the Tory party had become so weak? The solution of these problems involved difficulties arising out of Newfoundland's colonial relationship to Britain. It was this relationship which eventually caused Bond's downfall.

If greater economic unity were to be established in Newfoundland, government control of land communications was needed. In 1901 the government bought back the railway and other means of communication (although it allowed the Reid Newfoundland Company to operate them). Further steps in the utilization of the land (in contrast to the sea) were the development of the paper plant at Grand Falls, encouraged by the Bond government, and the development of branch railway lines, encouraged by the Morris government.

The trend of the times towards greater personal equality, brought Edward Morris to power in 1909, supported by a "People's Party" which he had formed after breaking with Bond in 1907. Whereas Bond, in the traditional way, tried to keep down government spending, Morris promised to increase teachers' salaries and introduce numerous social services, including old age pensions. These measures were small by modern standards, but they began the movement toward the present welfare state. It was time, too, when the small men in society were beginning to organize to protect their interests. The Longshoremen's Protective Union and the Fishermen's Protective Union appeared, both democratic organizations which hoped to bring about greater economic equality among the people of Newfoundland.

On the purely constitutional side, the governor's refusal to grant a new election to Premier Bond in 1909 raised an issue which was to create great controversy again in Canada in 1926. It could be argued that the Assembly represented the people and that, since democracy means rule by the people, it was essential from a democratic point of view to allow the Assembly to meet. This Bond was unwilling to do, in view of the fact that the election of 1908 had resulted in a tie.

On the other hand, the undemocratic feature of the governor's position was that he was in no way responsible to the people of Newfoundland or to their representatives. He was appointed by the government of another country. Bond did not want the humiliation of meeting the Assembly and not being able to control it, although Morris had no prospect of being able to control it either. The real reason why the governor refused Bond's advice and thus forced his resignation was the fact that the British government was irritated by Bond's attitude towards the Americans and wished to be rid of him. (See "Politics and the Crown: The Case of the 1908 Tie Election in Newfoundland," by S. J. R. Noel, *Canadian Journal of Economics and Political Science*, May 1967, 285–91.) This being the case, the real issue was one of colonialism, and the governor's position was undemocratic. However, the issue was confused by Bond's refusal to meet the assembly as premier, and his unyielding obstruction when he met it as leader of the opposition. The electorate upheld the governor's appointment of Morris as premier. The day when governors would no longer be appointed by and take their instructions from the government of Britain had not yet come.

NEWFOUNDLAND, 1914–18

By 1914 Newfoundland was a "dominion" within the British Empire, but her governments had taken part in international affairs only in connection with North Atlantic fisheries. Because of fishery disputes they had sometimes quarreled with the governments of France, the United States, of Britain, and Canada, but they had had no trouble with the government of Germany. However, the disputes over the Newfoundland fisheries had been settled by satisfactory treaties. Most Newfoundlanders believed that this settlement was guaranteed by the power of the British navy. Therefore, when the French and the British went to war with the German emperor in 1914, the Newfoundland government did not think of them as old rivals, but as partners who had guaranteed the survival of Newfoundland's fisheries.

When the Asquith government declared war on the German government on August 4, 1914, Newfoundland as part of the British Empire was automatically involved. The Morris government at once decided upon full participation in the British war effort. In 1914 the governments of Canada and Newfoundland were completely united with the British government in foreign policy.

As in other countries, the war caused the Newfoundland government to move towards greater equality of individual sacrifice. The prohibition of alcoholic liquor, the tax on business profits, and conscription of men for the Royal Newfoundland Regiment were all regarded as democratic measures.

A crippling war debt and the loss of 1,500 men in her own armed services was the price that Newfoundland paid for imperial solidarity, the belief that the destinies of Great Britain, Canada, and Newfoundland were the same. In a world growing smaller they had acted together against the government of Germany, in a war fought mainly on the continent of Europe.

NEWFOUNDLAND, 1918–29

Newfoundlanders had put forth a major effort during the war from 1914 to 1918. The prime ministers, Morris (1909–1918) and Lloyd (1918–1919), regarded the United Kingdom emotionally as the "Mother Land" or the "Home Land." Yet as soon as the war was over Newfoundland was on her own again. She was regarded by Britain as an independent member of the British Commonwealth of Nations, although the United States and France regarded her as too small to be an independent member of the League of Nations.

As in Britain and Canada, so in Newfoundland a "National Coalition" had been formed during the war. William F. Coaker had represented the organized fishermen in the ministries since 1917, much as organized farmers had been represented in the Canadian government and organized labour in the British government. For those who remained at home, the crisis actually brought increased importance and prosperity to the "working class."

With the war over, prices soared. Newfoundland fishermen, like Canadian farmers and British labour, suffered severely from the sudden rise in the cost of living. As did T. A. Crerar in Canada and the labour representatives in the British coalition, Coaker had to decide whether it would be best for him to remain in the government or to go into opposition. This would depend upon which group in the country gained control of the coalition.

From the end of the war in 1918 to the beginning of the depression of 1929, Newfoundland politics revolved around Coaker and his Fishermen's Protective Union. He was never quite strong enough to be prime minister himself and therefore needed the assistance of the more usual type of politician. Yet parties during this period were always judged by whether they were for or against Coaker. Those whom he supported were invariably regarded as the real "Liberals," and those whom he opposed were the "Tories," backed by the St. John's merchant class.

In Newfoundland, as in Britain and Canada, the coalition government after the war came under the control of its more wealthy and conservative supporters. Labour withdrew its support from the British government late in 1918; Coaker left the Newfoundland government and Crerar the Canadian government in 1919. High prices caused a political revolt among farmers and fishermen alike. Ontario and Newfoundland went to the polls at almost the same time in 1919. In both cases a "Tory" government was defeated. E. C. Drury, leader of the United Farmers of Ontario, formed a coalition with labour representatives after the election, and became premier. In Newfoundland, Coaker of the Fisherman's Union party formed an alliance before the election with an ambitious and opportunistic politician, R. A. Squires. As a result the Cashin government, supported by the St. John's merchants, was defeated, and Squires became premier.

In this way the fishermen's movement in Newfoundland became absorbed in a "Liberal party," much as did the farmer-based Progressives in Canada. At the end of the twenties both these Liberal parties were in power, with Robert Forke sitting in Mackenzie King's cabinet, and Sir William Coaker in that of Sir Richard Squires. In Britain, too, Labour was in power by the end of the twenties, and there too it was dependent upon the support of the Liberal party. The difference was that British Labour maintained its independence as a distinct party. In the United States, on the other hand, where "prosperity" lasted longest, the party of conservative big business, the Republican party, was still in power in October 1929 when the Great Depression began in earnest. But even Coaker could not protect the Newfoundland fishermen from the international economic crisis. The little dominion, on her own, was much too small to have the resources with which to plan effectively, even though the Privy Council in London had given her a huge "northwest territory" in 1927 by ruling that the "Coast of Labrador" (placed under the Governor of Newfoundland in 1809) meant the entire eastern watershed of that peninsula!

NEWFOUNDLAND, 1929–39

Newfoundland's total trade was greater in 1929–30 than ever before. The United States was her chief trading partner, and the export of pulp and paper was up. But the fact still remained that if her outside markets were to collapse, Newfoundland could not supply herself from her own resources. No government could make Newfoundland self-supporting. By 1931 the price of fish had dropped. In 1932 it was still declining.

In Newfoundland, as in Canada and the United Kingdom, the party of the "left" was already in power before the United States itself was struck in 1929 by the full force of the Depression. The total collapse of prosperity which followed throughout the North Atlantic world caused the fall of the Liberal government in Canada in 1930, of the Labour government in Britain in 1931, and (for the same reasons) of the Liberal government in Newfoundland in 1932. In each of these cases the first reaction of the people was a forlorn effort to save themselves by imitating the extreme economic nationalism of the United States – the "Canada First" policy of Canadian Conservatives in 1930, the "National" government of the United Kingdom in 1931 and the "United Newfoundland" government of Frederic Alderdice in 1932. But economic nationalism was the opposite of what was needed, particularly in the Island of Newfoundland, which was far from self-sufficient. Being much the smallest of the three countries mentioned, Newfoundland was the one in which the local economy collapsed completely.

Frederick C. Alderdice, a St. John's merchant and former premier, emerged as the central figure of the depression period. When the full force of the economic crisis struck, it was to him as leader of the opposition and of the United Newfoundland party that the people gave the opportunity of finding a solution for Newfoundland's isolation. The only solution was to join some larger economic unit, in which self-sufficiency through planning, or something near it, would be a possibility.

Canada's Conservative government had too many problems of its own, and in any case Newfoundlanders had been opposed to Confederation too long for such a sudden change. Her conservative government, and a highly conservative royal commission which advised it, thought back instead to the old days of sea power and the British connection. Britain was still a stronger power than Canada, and during World War I there had been unquestioning sentiment in Newfoundland about "Imperial solidarity," "rallying to the support of the Mother Land," and "our Great Empire." In those days Newfoundland had done all she could to support Britain. Now on the basis of the same sentiment she asked Britain to support her.

Britain's National government agreed, but the price which Newfoundland had to pay was humiliating. Her people had to give up the right to vote which they had enjoyed since 1832. It must be admitted, however, that this suggestion was supported by many Newfoundlanders themselves, particularly in St. John's, most of whom thought they would be better off under the rule of a "Commission Government" appointed in London (1934). Instead of blaming the isolation of Newfoundland and her inability to supply her own food and clothing, the blame was put on the "waste and extravagance" of politicians like Sir Richard Squires – although in the United States Roosevelt was just beginning to show (as World War I had already done) that extensive government spending was essential to the economy, even if it looked like "waste and extravagance."

By 1939 the Commission had brought many reforms to the island, and close association with the government of the British Empire had saved the situation. But no amount of old-fashioned economics could make Newfoundland "self-supporting" again. And because they no longer had the vote, Newfoundlanders could not change their government, as the Americans had done in 1933 and the Canadians were to do in 1935. For less conservative policies, they had to await the coming to power of the British Labour party after World War II.

NEWFOUNDLAND, 1939–45

Newfoundland's strategic importance in the eighteenth and nineteenth centuries had been as a base from which to control the fisheries along her coasts and also out on the Grand Banks. The island had never been of strategic importance, however, so far as land warfare was concerned. It lacked the necessary population and other resources. In fact, its fate depended upon what happened elsewhere. The French conquest of Newfoundland in 1708 was based on Quebec. The British conquest of Nova Scotia was based on the mainland colonies in what is now the United States, at a time when Newfoundland was dominated by the French. The British acquisition of the island in 1713 was the result of British victories elsewhere. The British conquest of Cape Breton Island in 1758 and of Quebec in 1759 was based on Halifax, not Newfoundland. In 1762 St. John's was seized by a fleet based on France, but far from being a threat to British North America, the harbour was soon recovered by an expedition based on New York and Halifax. The colony of Saint-Pierre-et-Miquelon, which was ceded to France in 1763, was of no strategic significance at all, for it could be seized by ships from Newfoundland at any time. Had it been of any strategic significance it would not have been ceded.

Newfoundland, therefore, did not affect the outcome of the American Revolutionary War, or of the Napoleonic Wars, or of the War of 1812–14 with the United States. In the days of empires based on sea power, Newfoundland and the fisheries which it controlled were prizes to be fought for. But sea power itself was based on the ports of much more populous countries.

The coming of air power and the development of trans-Atlantic planes changed all this. By the time of the outbreak of World War II it was possible to fly across the ocean. This had not been the case at the time of World War I. In 1939 the airplane was able, in effect, to attach Newfoundland to the mainland at last. She now for the first time acquired strategic importance herself. Her airports could become what her seaports never were, the ports of a continent. This curiously enough was at a time when she was once again governed directly not from the continent but from Britain.

The tiny colony of Saint-Pierre-et-Miquelon continued to be a shelter for French fishing ships, having been ceded once more by Britain in 1815, following her last war with France. Only in the case of hostility between the governments of Britain and France would it be necessary again to seize the French islands. Among the old-fashioned military commanders in France there was one exception, a modern young officer named General Charles de Gaulle, who would see to it that if this unthinkable necessity ever seemed likely to arise, Frenchmen would remedy the situation themselves.

In World War I Newfoundland as an independent dominion had organized a more extensive war effort than she could afford. In World War II her contribution was under the direction of the British government, and was kept within practical bounds. One result of the way in which the world had shrunk since 1918 was the fact that the defence of Newfoundland and the construction of its bases were largely taken over by her continental neighbours, Canada and the United States. Since by Newfoundland standards these governments paid construction workers extremely well, there was no problem about recruiting for war work. This time there was no military conscription, with the diversion of energy which it caused in World War I. Most Newfoundlanders could contribute more usefully in other ways. However, there were volunteers in all of the services overseas.

The most sensational happening of the war in Newfoundland waters was the seizure of Saint-Pierre-et-Miquelon in 1941 by General de Gaulle's Free French forces. De Gaulle had had Churchill's support ever since the fall of France in 1940. Earlier, in 1941, the Free French and the British had together conquered Syria and Lebanon from the Vichy French. De Gaulle, therefore, could count upon the sympathy and support of the British administrators in Newfoundland. The United States government was hostile, however, Roosevelt still being under the mistaken illusion that the Vichy authorities could be turned into useful allies. The seizure of Saint-Pierre by de Gaulle's naval commander at the end of 1941 made it impossible for the Germans to make use of the French colony during their great submarine offensive in 1942. It also provided the Americans, in spite of themselves, with an additional source of naval protection for their ships in the western Atlantic.

The use of Newfoundland's facilities made by Canadians and Americans under the pressure of war necessity demonstrated in a dramatic way that the island's future lay with the continental mainland. It was the prelude to Confederation.

NEWFOUNDLAND, 1945–49

Wartime spending, especially by the governments of the United States and Canada, had brought "prosperity" to Newfoundland such as she had never known before. Her "isolation" had been ended with a vengeance. But, as the war drew to a close, the problem was how such a situation could be made permanent.

The coming to office of the Attlee ministry in Britain in 1945 made it certain that a change in the government of Newfoundland could be expected soon. The Labour party had not approved of Commission government even in the beginning. In any case the suspension of self-government had been intended to last only until the financial crisis of 1934 was over. But the Labour ministers knew also that a mere return to independent dominion status would provide no protection against the return of economic depression. The alternative seemed obvious, but it was considered important to find some way by which the Newfoundland people could make the decision in democratic fashion for themselves.

One of the achievements of the Attlee Government in Britain was the manner in which, between 1945 and 1949, it put Newfoundland back into the mainstream of modern history. The logical sequel to the opening of the west coast, the vast improvement in means of communication, and the experiences of the Depression and war years was to join Canada, thus recognizing in a rapidly shrinking world the need for ever larger areas of political and economic planning. This was done with meticulous care for democratic procedures.

In 1945 there were 321,817 people in Newfoundland. One of these was Joseph R. Smallwood, a former journalist who was raising hogs in Bonavista Centre. In 1945 he announced that he had become a "Confederate," the first public man to do so for many years. The campaign for Confederation was led by this native Newfoundlander. It culminated in the referendum of 1948 and achieved its objective on March 31, 1949. It resulted immediately in the introduction of Canada's nation-wide social services, thus making possible greater individual equality and democracy than had ever existed in Newfoundland before. In Newfoundland Smallwood was the man chosen to inaugurate this new age as the first provincial premier. In Canada the prime minister who concluded the negotiations was Louis Saint-Laurent. In Britain the statesman who made it all possible was Clement Attlee. It was only forty-nine years since Robert Bond had become president of Newfoundland's Executive Council and started his campaign to end French and American interference with the development of the west coast. In 1949, the process of converting that area into the front door, through which Newfoundland faces her sister provinces in one dominion under the name of Canada, was finally completed.

13

Newfoundland's Quest for Reciprocity, 1890-1910

PETER F. NEARY AND SIDNEY J. R. NOEL

FAR-REACHING INTERNATIONAL entanglements and conspiratorial domestic politics are the curiously mixed commonplaces of the Newfoundland past. This is true of every period of the island's history from the earliest days of European settlement, but in no period is the importance of and the interplay between the two more readily apparent than in the years from 1890 to 1910. These years stand out so prominently primarily because of Newfoundland's persistent and even aggressive attempts to escape the economic consequences of the isolation she had earlier imposed upon herself by choosing to remain outside the Canadian Confederation. Not surprisingly, in view of her geographic position, it was in a closer economic relationship with the United States that Newfoundland hoped to find the guarantee of her future prosperity. The chief architect of this policy, and the dominant political figure in Newfoundland throughout most of this period, was Robert Bond (1857–1927), and any study of the island's external relations at the turn of the century must therefore begin with him.

In some respects Bond was a typical member of the St. John's ruling élite: the son of a wealthy merchant, he was sent to an English public school for his education, and entered the House of Assembly at the age of twenty-five as Liberal member for Trinity. Yet he was far from being a typical Newfoundland politician. He was exceptional in that for him the appeal of politics lay not so much in the mundane business of administering domestic affairs and dispensing local patronage as in the heady realm of international relations. The dominant thread in his political career is the pursuit of policy at this grand level. He was also a "nationalist" in the sense that his consistent aim in seeking to strengthen Newfoundland's economic position through closer ties with the United States was to preserve the island's political independence.

Given the economic and political circumstances of Newfoundland in the latter part of the nineteenth century, it is easy to see why an ambitious and talented young politician like Bond should have turned towards the United States. Newfoundlanders had rejected Confederation in 1869 and the prospect of union with Canada remained unattractive to them. On the other hand, even so insular a people as Newfoundlanders could not fail to be impressed by the anomaly of their isolation in times which favoured the growth of large states. To see the price they paid for independence they had only to compare their record of material achievement with that of their Canadian neighbours, and nowhere was that comparison more striking than in the field of transportation. Twenty years after Confederation Nova Scotia and New Brunswick had long since been linked by rail with the centre of the continent, while in Newfoundland the relatively modest project of a trans-island railway was still a doubtful starter. And yet, when all the economic arguments were weighed, the people of Newfoundland were still determined to maintain their political independence – always, of course, within the framework of Empire. Here then was a great problem for the Newfoundland politician: how to make political independence compatible with economic progress. The answer which Bond supplied was not really new – it was indeed, for all practical purposes, the policy to which the British North American colonies as a whole had resorted after the break-up of the old colonial trading system in the 1840's – but it was new in the sense that Newfoundland had not before pursued it independently.

Prior to 1885 Newfoundland had been content to see her negotiations with the United States merged with those of British North America as a whole, but in that year she made a direct approach to Washington in an effort to secure a separate fisheries and commercial agreement.[1] This effort had to be abandoned, however, when Great Britain entered into negotia-

1/A. M. Fraser, "Fisheries Negotiations with the United States, 1783–1910," in R. A. MacKay, ed., *Newfoundland: Economic, Diplomatic, and Strategic Studies* (Toronto 1946), 355.

tions for a similar agreement covering Canada as well. These wider negotiations also proved abortive, and in 1890, when a temporary agreement of 1888 regulating the activities of American fishermen in British North American waters expired, on the initiative of Bond (who was at this time Colonial Secretary in the administration of Sir William Whiteway, having obtained office for the first time in the previous year), direct negotiations between Newfoundland and the United States were resumed.[2] The negotiators were the American Secretary of State, James G. Blaine, and Bond. The *quid pro quo* which Newfoundland had to offer the United States in return for favourable trading arrangements was the settlement of a long-standing dispute over the fisheries article of the Anglo-American Convention of 1818 as they affected the island, and the granting of special privileges to American fishermen.

The Bond-Blaine negotiations, which took place in Washington, resulted in the drafting of a comprehensive agreement covering both reciprocal trade and American fishing rights in Newfoundland waters.[3] But this agreement was vigorously opposed by Canada and, in consequence, vetoed by the Imperial government, which in February 1891 informed Newfoundland that her negotiations with the United States must proceed *pari passu* with those of Canada.[4] The Canadian government, unable itself to obtain a satisfactory agreement of the type that Bond had negotiated, was unwilling to see its prospects of doing so further diminished by a separate arrangement between Newfoundland and the United States. Moreover, it feared, probably with good reason, that by making Newfoundland more economically dependent on the United States, the agreement which Bond had obtained might end all hope of bringing the island into Confederation or, worse still, might in time encourage in Newfoundland a movement in favour of annexation to the United States. In this latter regard it should be noted that there is evidence to suggest that Blaine foresaw the disruptive effect which the proposed agreement would have on relations between Canada and Newfoundland and that he entered into negotiations with Bond with this mischief in mind.[5]

Outraged at having the plum of reciprocity so rudely snatched from it at Canada's behest, Newfoundland retaliated by prohibiting the sale of bait to Canadian fishermen. Canada answered this with a heavy duty on the import of other Newfoundland fishery produce, whereupon Newfound-

2/*Ibid.*, 359–61.
3/For this agreement see 61st Congress, 3rd Session, Senate Document 870, IV, 77–79.
4/Fraser, "Fisheries Negotiations," 368.
5/See T. Dennett, *John Hay: From Poetry to Politics* (New York 1934), 423.

land imposed a restrictive duty on the import of Canadian flour.[6] In an effort to end this unseemly squabbling, a conference was held between Canada and Newfoundland at Halifax in November 1892; its failure served only to aggravate matters.[7] Newfoundland-Canadian relations were thus at an extremely low ebb when in the spring of 1895 the Newfoundland government, faced with imminent financial collapse and the refusal of the Imperial government to lend practical aid, found itself in the humiliating position of having to supplicate for entry into Confederation.[8] Negotiations opened at Ottawa in April 1895, but quickly broke down when the Mackenzie Bowell administration, with characteristic ineptitude, sought to take advantage of Newfoundland's desperation by driving an excessively hard bargain. Ultimately the colony was saved from collapse only by the timely success of Robert Bond (who had been a delegate at the Ottawa negotiations) in floating a loan in the City of London; but neither he nor his countrymen could easily forget the niggardly attitude shown by Canada at a time of crisis. A lesson had been learned, and thereafter Newfoundlanders turned more than ever towards the United States, where the thwarted Bond-Blaine convention had afforded them "a tantalizing glimpse of riches behind the American tariff wall."[9]

In 1900 Bond, on becoming prime minister, reopened the reciprocity question by asking the Imperial government to ratify the 1890 convention or, if Washington considered it defunct, to permit Newfoundland to begin negotiations for a new agreement.[10] His request came at an opportune moment. After a full decade Canada could no longer credibly blame Newfoundland for her own failure to come to terms with the United States; and though Sir Wilfrid Laurier, like Macdonald before him, feared that a separate agreement between Newfoundland and the United States would further imperil the prospects of bringing the island into Confederation, his protests were in vain. With British approval, Bond opened discussions with the State Department in Washington in August 1902.

By mid-October agreement had been reached, but a new stumbling block to Bond's ambition now appeared in the form of Senator Henry Cabot Lodge, the acknowledged spokesman of the New England fishing interests and chairman of the powerful Senate Foreign Relations Committee. While the negotiations were still in progress, Lodge let it be known

6/H. A. Innis, *The Cod Fisheries* (New Haven 1940), 451–52; Fraser, 376–82.
7/Fraser, "Fisheries Negotiations," 382–85.
8/See Harvey Mitchell, "Canada's Negotiations with Newfoundland, 1887–1895," *Canadian Historical Review*, XL (December 1959), 277–93.
9/C. S. Campbell, *Anglo-American Understanding, 1898–1903* (Baltimore 1953), 260.
10/*Ibid.*

that he would not support an agreement with Newfoundland that was not acceptable to American fishermen.[11] Accordingly, he urged Hay to consult with the representatives of the fishing industry at Gloucester, Massachusetts, the New England centre most likely to be affected by any agreement with Newfoundland, before concluding talks with Bond. He urged him also to delay signing the proposed agreement until after the congressional elections scheduled for November 4. That this latter suggestion should have been made by Lodge is not surprising since his son-in-law, Augustus Gardner, was the Republican candidate in the Massachusetts congressional district which included Gloucester. In the event Hay delayed signing the agreement until November 8, by which time Gardner had been safely returned; but he rejected the remainder of Lodge's advice on the grounds that to satisfy the demands of the New England fishing interests would make any agreement with Newfoundland impossible.

Under the agreement which Bond and Hay had negotiated Newfoundland was to obtain free admission to American markets for a wide range of fishery and mineral products.[12] In return American fishing vessels were to have "the privilege of purchasing herring, caplin, squid, and other bait fishes at all times, on the same terms and conditions, and subject to the same penalties as Newfoundland vessels"; and "the privilege of touching and trading, buying and selling fish and oil, and procuring supplies in Newfoundland, conforming to the Harbour Regulations, but without other charge than the payment of such light, harbour, and customs dues as are, or may be, levied on Newfoundland fishing-vessels." In addition the convention listed a number of manufactured goods and foodstuffs that Newfoundland was to admit from the United States duty free. To protect American deep-sea fishermen, fresh cod was specifically excluded from the list of Newfoundland fishery produce which the United States was to admit duty-free, but despite this conciliatory gesture to American fishermen, the convention was vigorously opposed in New England. The result of this opposition was that, though the convention was reluctantly consented to by Great Britain, it was blocked in the American Senate by Henry Cabot Lodge. Indeed it was not until January 1905, and only then at the specific urging of President Roosevelt, that Lodge reluctantly agreed to report out of the Foreign Relations Committee a drastically amended version of the agreement, totally unacceptable to Newfoundland.[13]

11/See Dennett, *John Hay*, 424; J. A. Garraty, *Henry Cabot Lodge* (New York 1953), 234–39.
12/Senate Document 870, IV, 79–82.
13/See *Journal of the Executive Proceedings of the Senate*, XXXV, 495, 499–502.

For Bond the blocking of the convention in the Senate was a bitter disappointment but hardly a surprise. As early as January 1903 he had anticipated this result and when it became clear in 1905 that Lodge was completely adamant, he was ready to retaliate. What he now attempted to do was to bring the New England opponents of the agreement to heel by disrupting the operations of American fishermen on the Newfoundland coast. He did this in two ways. In the first place he secured during the 1905 session of the Newfoundland legislature an amendment to the Foreign Fishing Vessels Act of 1893. This act had required foreign vessels, American included, to obtain licences before engaging local crew or purchasing "bait, ice, seines, lines, and all other supplies and outfits for the fishery."[14] The amended act abolished this licensing system, empowered Newfoundland customs officials to board and inspect foreign vessels at will, and prescribed that the mere presence on board any such vessel of any of the items formerly obtainable under licence was to constitute *prima facie* evidence of their illegal purchase.[15] The implication of these amendments for American fishermen was abundantly clear. By 1905 their operations on the Newfoundland coast were confined almost entirely to the lucrative winter herring fishery at Bonne Bay and Bay of Islands, where they were permitted under the Convention of 1818 to fish within the three-mile limit.[16] In this fishery the American vessels were accustomed to, and virtually dependent on, the hiring of Newfoundland crew and when necessary, the completion of their catches by the purchase of fish, under license (herring was regarded as a bait fish under the 1893 act), from local fishermen.[17]

The second part of Bond's plan of counter-attack was the adoption by Newfoundland of an entirely new interpretation of the Convention of 1818 which threatened American fishermen with complete banishment from Newfoundland waters. The substance of this new interpretation was that while the convention of 1818 accorded American fishermen the liberty to fish on "the Coasts, Bays, Harbours, and Creeks" of Labrador, it accorded them the same liberty only on the "Coast" from the Rameau to the Quirpon Islands of Newfoundland itself. Arguing that this variation in phraseology had been deliberate, Bond thus maintained that it had been intended in 1818 that American fishermen should not fish in any of the bays, harbours, or creeks on the Newfoundland treaty shore.[18]

14/Senate Document 870, II, 184.
15/*Ibid.*, 197–98.
16/See Raymond McFarland, *A History of the New England Fisheries* (Philadelphia 1911), 199–210.
17/Parliamentary Papers, 1906 (Cd. 3262), 1–5; J. D. Rogers, *Newfoundland: Historical and Geographical* (Oxford 1911), 233.
18/Parliamentary Papers, 1906 (Cd. 3262), 61–66. The terms "treaty shore" and

In moving so decisively against American fishermen Bond sought to direct his fire not against the United States as such, but against the New England fishing interests. Thus, speaking in the Newfoundland House of Assembly in April 1905, he appealed for the support "of all those within this Colony and beyond its borders whose judgment is influenced by considerations of justice and patriotism."[19] His appeal was premised on this distinction:

With the Administration of the United States we have no shadow of a cause for complaint. They have treated us with the greatest courtesy whenever we have approached them, and have manifested both a friendly and just attitude towards this Colony. It is not the fault of the Administration at Washington that we are where we are to-day in the matter; the fault lies solely at the door of those who for petty personal interests ... have deceived those who represent them in the Senate of their country.

A dramatic disruption of the Americans' trade, Bond hoped, would teach them the value of the concessions Newfoundland was prepared to make in order to obtain reciprocity, and thus compel them to reverse their stand on the issue. It was a daring policy and in the circumstances not an unreasonable one. An influential body of opinion in the United States was likely to sympathize with Newfoundland. Bond could also take comfort from the fact that several American newspapers were openly on Newfoundland's side and that the emasculation of the agreement in the Senate had sharply divided opinion in Washington.[20] Moreover, within Newfoundland his position seemed very strong. In 1904 a long-standing dispute over French fishing rights in Newfoundland had been settled to the island's advantage and in the wake of this settlement Bond and his Liberal party had won a decisive renewal of their mandate, maintaining their unprecedented majority of 1900 by winning 32 of 36 seats.

Yet events were soon to show that Bond had miscalculated wildly. Far from responding as he had hoped, the Roosevelt administration rallied to the defence of American fishermen; the Imperial government, for its part, was in no mood to allow the rapprochement it had carefully nurtured over the previous decade with the United States to be suddenly endangered by a belligerent minor colony. It therefore dissociated itself from Newfoundland's actions and set about appeasing the United States. On the Newfoundland coast itself the ingenuity of American fishing captains in obtaining fish by engaging crews outside the three-mile limit prevented

"treaty coast" were used to refer to that part of the Newfoundland coast on which American fishermen enjoyed liberties under the Convention of 1818.
19/*Ibid.*, 60.
20/In view of the relatively small importance of the convention to the United States, surprisingly strong feelings were aroused in Washington by its defeat. (See Dennett, *John Hay*, 426–29.)

a crisis from developing during the 1905–6 winter fishing season, but when in May 1906 Newfoundland closed this loophole by a further amendment to the Foreign Fishing Vessels Act, an angry protest was heard from New England.[21] The fishing interests were at last beginning to feel the pressure of Newfoundland's policy. Unfortunately for Bond, however, this pressure was soon alleviated by the action of the British government. Thoroughly alarmed by the vehemence of the diplomatic protests from the United States, it withheld Imperial assent to the new amendment. More severely still, the Colonial Secretary, Lord Elgin, informed the Governor of Newfoundland, Sir William MacGregor, that in order to avoid "a highly undesirable and even dangerous situation" it was necessary to arrange a *modus vivendi* with the United States for 1906–7 winter fishing season.[22] This was duly arranged on October 6 by an exchange of notes between London and Washington which, in essence, guaranteed American fishermen all the privileges they had enjoyed before 1905.

At this point, any likelihood that Newfoundland might succeed in forcing the New England fishing interests to accept reciprocity vanished. To be effective her action had to be swift and absolute. The *modus vivendi* ensured that it would be neither. In retrospect it is easy to see that Newfoundland should therefore have accepted defeat as gracefully as possible and adopted a policy of conciliation. But by the autumn of 1906 Bond had so deeply committed himself and the Liberal party to a policy of restricting the American fishery that any retreat was bound to be both humiliating and politically damaging. Yet to persist in the face of British hostility was to court disaster. Already the cost of antagonizing the Imperial authorities had been higher than Bond realized. Newfoundland's independent attitude in dealing with foreign powers had long been a sore point in London, and it is therefore not surprising that the thought again arose that Newfoundland might be less troublesome if less independent.

As early as May 1906 the Governor-General of Canada, Lord Grey, who had already shown signs of a remarkable lack of restraint in interfering in Canadian domestic affairs, now turned his attention to Newfoundland, writing to Lord Elgin on the assumption

that H.M.G. agree with me that it is desirable that Newfoundland should become a province of the Dominion as soon as possible. Sir W. MacGregor understands the importance in view of the prospect of cleaning the slate between Canada and the U.S. [a reference to negotiations in progress between Canada and the United States for the settlement of all their outstanding

21/Fraser, "Fisheries Negotiations," 388–89.
22/Parliamentary Papers, 1906 (Cd. 3262), 18.

differences], as well as for general considerations of preventing any action on the part of the government of Newfoundland which may prejudice the friendly treatment by the U.S. of the points at issue between us. He appears to think that a visit from me would assist the party in Newfoundland who favour confederation.[23]

Grey subsequently visited Newfoundland on the pretext of spending a holiday there, and upon his return to Ottawa reported to Elgin on the prospects for union.[24] Among those in favour of it, he found, were two prominent individuals – the governor and the Roman Catholic archbishop of St. John's – and three influential business interests – the Bank of Montreal, the Canadian iron ore companies, and the Reid railway monopoly. The opposition, he believed, came from "the few two-penny ha'penny industries at St. John's" and from "Bond himself." Thus, Grey concluded, Confederation could be brought about in one of two ways: either by persuading Bond that it was necessary for his political survival, or by persuading Edward Morris (1859–1935), Bond's most prominent Liberal colleague, to break with his leader and head a movement for union. "Morris is R.C.," Grey wrote, "much liked and respected, and I believe at heart confederationist. Whether he has the little bit of courage required to break with Bond, of whom he, and I believe all his colleagues are to some extent afraid, I know not, but that he has the power of knocking out Bond and winning the Island to confederation if Bond remains obdurate, I feel pretty certain."

Within Newfoundland the political situation gave Bond's enemies good reason to feel optimistic. Although economically the country was prospering as never before, the Liberal party's hold was beginning to weaken. The government's attempt to attain reciprocity by coercion had caused considerable alarm, and those most affected by it – the west coast fishermen – were openly hostile.[25] The sale of fish to the visiting Americans was for them a profitable business. The Americans paid well for their purchases and in cash, thereby relieving the local people from the iniquities of the traditional truck system. A disruption of the American fishery swiftly applied might have won popular support and been successful, whereas the long drawn-out campaign which Bond was forced into by the Imperial veto could only backfire on its protagonist.

Bond, however, refused to accept the inevitable. His reaction to the imposition of the 1906 *modus vivendi* was to test its validity before the courts.[26] In spite of the grave warnings of Lord Elgin, a case was instituted

23/Grey Papers, Public Archives of Canada, Grey to Elgin, May 23, 1906.
24/*Ibid.*, Grey to Elgin, August 16, 1906.
25/Parliamentary Papers, 1908 (Cd. 3765), 54–56, 131–41, 146–47.
26/*Ibid.*, 13–14, 20, 25–27.

against two Newfoundland fishermen who had signed on as crew members aboard an American vessel outside the three-mile limit. Both were convicted and fined, leaving an embarrassed Imperial government to pay their fines in order to forestall an appeal to the Privy Council, whose confirmation of the court's decision would have given the Newfoundland government authority to frustrate the *modus vivendi* by a policy of wholesale arrests. Newfoundland thereupon offered to refrain from pursuing the matter, if Britain would arrange with the United States to prevent any further attempts to employ Newfoundlanders on American vessels. It was only by delaying a negative reply to this offer until the 1906–7 winter fishing season was over that Britain was able to avoid a serious flare-up.[27]

Bond's decision to persist in his retaliatory policy marked a critical turning-point both in the course of the fisheries dispute and in the political fortunes of the Liberal party. There was no longer any hope of forcing the issue of reciprocity: the only vital issue now turned upon the broad legal question of the extent of American fishing rights in Newfoundland waters under the Convention of 1818, and, specifically, the liability of American fishermen to colonial law, a question which the whole controversy had elevated to prominence. By making a solution of these matters difficult to achieve, Bond only played straight into the hands of those who wished to destroy him.

These "anti-Bond" or "anti-Liberal" forces were essentially those which Lord Grey had identified, with the notable exception of the Roman Catholic Archbishop of St. John's, Michael Howley, whose support for Confederation was subordinate to his high personal regard and political support for Bond and his strident advocacy of the Liberal government's policy *vis-à-vis* the United States.[28] Governor William MacGregor's main concern appears to have been to curry such favour with his superiors as would secure for him the pension he felt he deserved but to which under the strict letter of Colonial Office regulations he was not entitled.[29] He evidently thought that by undermining Bond and supporting Confederation he could ingratiate himself with those who were sufficiently well-connected to help him personally. The active opposition to the anti-confederate Bond of the Bank of Montreal, the major financial institution in

---

27/F.O. 371/185, 40047, MacGregor to Elgin, November 23, 1906, and F.O. 371/387, 1728, Elgin to MacGregor. The authors wish to thank the Controller of H. M. Stationery Office for the access granted them to Crown-copyright records in the Public Record Office.

28/See letter by Howley in *Evening Telegram*, January 14, 1907: "Newfoundland ... is on the brink of the greatest crisis that has ever occurred in her history." He appealed for national unity in the face of "an insatiable American rapacity on the one hand, and a compromising British diplomacy on the other."

29/The Colonial Office records contain an elaborate correspondence on this subject. Ironically, in the end the avidly sought pension was refused.

the island since 1894 and the holder of the government's account, and the Canadian iron ore companies, which had been mining ore at Bell Island since 1895, was only to be expected.

As for the Reids, their unremitting hostility towards Bond was of long standing. On attaining power in 1900 Bond had carried out an election pledge to revoke the major terms of the notorious railway contract of 1898 which had been overwhelmingly in their favour. Moreover, the Reids no doubt saw in Confederation a hope of ridding themselves of what had proved to be an unprofitable and already deteriorating railway. For Bond the Reids were particularly formidable not only because of their wealth (they had financed the entire opposition campaign in 1900), but also because they controlled the St. John's *Daily News* and, more importantly, the *Western Star*, the only newspaper published on the west coast of the island. The latter's thunderings against the government, by virtue of coming from the very centre of the American fishery in Newfoundland, carried considerable force both at home and abroad.[30] Opposing Bond in a different way were the highly placed advocates of Confederation, working quietly and privately towards union, strongly represented in Canada by Lord Grey, in Newfoundland by Governor MacGregor, and in Washington, after January 1907, by an energetic new British ambassador, James Bryce. Their reports to London contributed to a general hardening of the British attitude towards Newfoundland at a time when Bond was about to encounter his last chance to extricate himself from the quagmire: the 1907 Colonial Conference in London. By making use of this occasion, with its opportunities for personal diplomacy, to come to terms with the Imperial government, Bond might yet have escaped the worst consequences of his policy towards the United States. But in the event his reception in Downing Street was not encouraging.

By this time the British government was strongly in favour of submitting the entire fisheries dispute to the International Court of Justice at the Hague, a procedure Bond objected to in a speech before the conference on the grounds that the Convention of 1818 was not ambiguous, whereas to submit Newfoundland's statutes to arbitration "would be derogatory to the Crown, and in contravention to the constitutional right of the self-governing Colonies."[31] Later, however, under pressure from the Foreign Office, and perhaps realizing he was to be given no

30/See Parliamentary Papers, 1908 (Cd. 3765), 92–99, 102–6, and *The Times*, November 14, 1906. By the spring of 1907, MacGregor had adopted the tactic of sending to the Colonial Office batches of newspaper articles that were uniformly hostile to the government, without mentioning who owned the newspapers in question – an absolutely vital point where the Newfoundland press was concerned.
31/Parliamentary Papers, 1907 (Cd. 3523), 600.

choice in the matter (for if a *modus vivendi* could be imposed against his wishes so also could arbitration), he finally agreed.

This was Newfoundland's contribution to a settlement. Yet without the co-operation of Canada it was likely to prove futile, for even though Canada was not directly concerned in Newfoundland's quarrel with the United States, she was necessarily concerned with any question affecting national jurisdiction in the North Atlantic fisheries. Under the Convention of 1818 the United States had been given the same fishing rights in what later became part of Canada's territorial waters as in part of Newfoundland's; therefore Canada also had to be persuaded to accept arbitration. This proved to be no easy task. The dominion was still smarting from the consequences of the Alaska Boundary Award of 1903, and inclined to look with suspicion upon any arrangement that could conceivably lead to another American coup. Consequently, when the Colonial Conference ended on May 14, Sir Wilfrid Laurier still had not consented to arbitration, and though both he and Bond remained in London for further consultations, no agreement could be reached.[32] Meanwhile the possibility of a quick settlement vanished, leaving the British with no alternative but to negotiate yet another *modus vivendi* with the United States, this time for the 1907–8 winter fishery. To Bond this was anathema. He vehemently protested, maintaining that Britain should either refer the dispute to the Hague Tribunal or support the colony in the enforcement of its laws.[33] But Lord Elgin on June 18 brusquely set aside his contentions:

It is the duty of His Majesty's Government to deal with international relations, and while we should prefer in a matter of this kind to rely upon Colonial legislation, we shall not hesitate if necessary to use such other means as are open to use to obtain sanction for the arrangements which we consider essential for the preservation of relations of peace and amity with a friendly nation, and for the settlement of disputes in an orderly fashion.[34]

Two days later, with this new crisis deepening around him, Bond sailed for St. John's.

He was to find that affairs had not stood still in his absence. The colony had followed the progress of the negotiations in London with mounting anxiety, for failure almost certainly meant a revival of the quarrel with the Americans and another humiliating imposition of the Anglo-American *modus vivendi*. The most severe strain naturally fell upon the Liberal party, and within the party it inevitably focused upon Edward Morris, for he alone, as Lord Grey had correctly perceived, had the political strength

32/Sir Edward Grey Papers, Public Record Office, Grey to Bryce, June 7, 1907.
33/Parliamentary Papers, 1908 (Cd. 3765), 184–88.
34/*Ibid.*, 189.

to force a major split. Morris was, however, a much more complicated and devious character than Grey had imagined him to be. Born on Lime Street in the slums of St. John's the son of a poor Irish immigrant, he had early developed into the twentieth-century prototype of the successful Newfoundland politician. Intensely ambitious, clever, with a genius for the rough-and-tumble of local politics, uninhibited in his quest for power by such considerations as party loyalty, and a convincing purveyor of economic fantasies, his career was destined to end fittingly in 1918 with a Lloyd George peerage and a seat in the House of Lords. As Bond's strength declined, Morris's increased proportionately, a change noted with satisfaction by the advocates of Confederation, who hoped to use him as their standard bearer. On July 20 Morris took the crucial step.

Revealingly, he chose to resign from the cabinet without committing himself on either the American fisheries question or Confederation. In his letter to Bond he advanced but one purely local reason for his action: a misunderstanding with the minister of public works over who should take credit for the granting of a pay increase to road labourers. The full impact of his resignation was not immediately obvious, since the House of Assembly was not in session and there could be no dramatic confrontation between the rebel and former colleagues. Yet there could be no doubt that the split in the party was no mere surface crack, but an irremediable fissure that would be found in time to cut deep into the constituencies, where Morris's appeal had always been most potent.

Nor were the Liberal prospects improved by the turn of events in the fisheries dispute in the months following Bond's return from London. By the time Canada finally agreed to arbitration,[35] the opening of the 1907–8 winter fishery was only two months away. Already, on August 10, Newfoundland had been informed by the Colonial Office that

the provision necessary to secure a *modus vivendi* during the interval until the decision of the Hague Tribunal is obtained should be the act of the Colonial Government and Legislature, but, in the absence of any assurance to this effect, His Majesty's Government must proceed to take whatever measures are necessary to provide for it, as Imperial interests of great importance are involved.[36]

Though still adamantly opposed to an Anglo-American *modus vivendi*, Bond, under pressure from a section of the Liberal party, offered to arrange a compromise which would permit American fishermen to purchase fish, but maintain the prohibition against the hiring of Newfound-

35/The actual arbitration took place at The Hague during the summer of 1910. On all important points the International Court upheld the Newfoundland contentions.
36/Parliamentary Papers, 1908 (Cd. 3765), 157.

land crews.[37] But since nothing less than complete acceptance of the *modus vivendi* could satisfy the United States, his offer was rejected.[38] On September 6 the two powers completed the agreement, thereby guaranteeing American vessels the right to employ Newfoundlanders.[39] Then on September 9 the British government issued an order-in-council (under an act passed in 1819) which, by providing that legal process against Newfoundland citizens could not be served on board American vessels, and that neither these vessels nor their boats or tackle could be liable to seizure, was designed to assist the officers of the Royal Navy in their task of enforcing the *modus vivendi*. At the same time, having wielded the stick, Britain dangled the carrot: the order would be revoked, Lord Elgin promised, if Newfoundland would unreservedly accept the *modus vivendi*.[40] Still Bond refused, angrily protesting that the order-in-council was undermining the colony's case before the Hague Tribunal by yielding to the Americans in advance the very point that was to be decided. Furthermore, he added, the law officers of the crown in Newfoundland advised that an order-in-council "cannot be operated against the Laws of the Colony."[41]

With Newfoundland apparently as intransigent as ever, and with the New England fishing fleet inexorably on its way, a new crisis seemed imminent. In Washington, the British ambassador was fearful of the consequences: if Newfoundland attempted to prevent her fishermen from shipping on board American vessels, he warned Lord Grey, there might be an outburst of popular feeling which would embarrass the American government, and encourage the Senate, if that body was maliciously disposed, to raise difficulties regarding the terms of the arbitration. He therefore urged the Governor-General to do anything he could to prevent Bond from disrupting the *modus vivendi*. Laurier had already declined to intervene directly but he now passed on to Grey a suggestion from Chief Justice Fitzpatrick that pressure might be put on Bond through the Bank of Montreal. On October 1, having been in touch with Edward Clouston, first vice-president of the Bank, Grey sent this report to Elgin on the prospects of getting rid of Bond at the next general election:

The case against Bond that could be made by a clever fighter is one that if properly pressed ought to carry the Island. I wish we had a clever and hard

37/F.O. 371/389, 28346, C.O. to F.O., August 23, 1907; Parliamentary Papers, 1908 (Cd. 3765), 159–60.
38/F.O. 371/389, 28990, memorandum communicated by Whitelaw Reid, August 29, 1907.
39/Parliamentary Papers, 1908 (Cd. 3734), 2.
40/*Ibid.* (Cd. 3765), 166–69.
41/Fraser, "Fisheries Negotiations," 398.

fighter in Sir E. Morris – and Sir Wilfrid wishes he were a Protestant – for he is afraid that the fact of his being an R.C. will enable Bond to rally the Orangemen behind him.[42]

The bankers, however, had evidently been more encouraging, for Grey's letter continued:

The Canadians who have interests in Newfoundland can be relied upon to do whatever is possible to stiffen Morris and to assist him in the battle against Bond. All the money he wants to enable him to conduct an educational campaign will be forthcoming, so I have been privately informed.

In this context there can be no doubt that "educational" was but Grey's transparent synonym for "political." Thus, although in St. John's the political surface remained ostensibly unruffled, with Morris eschewing public controversy and the legislature not due to reassemble until January 1908, already the Morris bandwagon was quietly beginning to gather steam.

Meanwhile, the vanguard of the New England fleet was beginning to arrive in Newfoundland waters. Fearing a hostile incident, the Imperial government, at the last moment, hurriedly sought to have Bond's earlier offer to allow the sale of fish under licence substituted for the *modus vivendi*; but when the State Department objected, the matter was dropped.[43] Since the Imperial order-in-council gave Newfoundland fishermen no immunity from prosecution after disembarking from American vessels, the colonial government could still have seriously disrupted the American fishery had it wished to do so. But rather than provoke a conflict, which would have been to invite the intervention of the Royal Navy, Newfoundland chose instead to permit the sale of fish under licence even though the *modus vivendi* was not withdrawn. This action served the dual purpose of preserving at least the fiction of the colony's right to regulate the fishery (this was regarded as important if the case before the Hague Tribunal was not to be prejudiced), and allowing the Americans to obtain fish without having to contravene the Foreign Fishing Vessels Act of 1906 by employing Newfoundlanders.

Although this arrangement worked satisfactorily, it was unavoidably damaging to the beleaguered Liberal party. The more extreme advocates of restricting the Americans were bound to regard it as a capitulation; whereas the opposition could point with scorn to the futile policy which had made it necessary. "The appeals of the west coast fishermen during the last two years for free fishing have been refused by the Government."

42/Grey Papers, Public Archives of Canada, Grey to Elgin, October 1, 1907
43/F.O. 371/390, 34428, Bryce to Grey, October 17, 1907.

complained the *Daily News*, "and a concession is only made now because such a step is part of the Government's policy of trickery and deception."[44] Only if the Imperial government rescinded the order-in-council, as Bond requested on November 1,[45] could the Liberals have hoped to salvage so much as a minor victory; but even that was denied them when Bond's petition was turned down.

As the year 1907 drew to a close there was thus no glimmer of improvement in the Liberal party's position. In the general election of 1908 the Liberals could manage no more than a tie with a new party (ironically labelled "the People's Party") led by Morris, who, predictably, had contrived to accept the Confederationists' money but not their politically unpopular policy. The end for Bond – and for reciprocity – came in May 1909 when, after an extended constitutional crisis in which Governor MacGregor had acted partisanly and decisively against the Liberals, Edward Morris took office as prime minister.[46]

Now that Newfoundland is a province of Canada, it is easy to assume that the "completion" of British North America in 1949 had about it a certain inevitability. This, however, would be far from the truth. Even granted that the continued independence of Newfoundland was not economically feasible, there remains the possibility that it might have joined, or entered into some closer economic relationship with, the United States. There was briefly, in 1949, an attempt to rally support for something called "economic union" with the United States, but the necessary foundations for such a relationship did not exist in an island that since 1934 had had its constitution suspended in favour of administration by a commission appointed by, and responsible to, the Dominions Office. Administratively, as well as culturally and economically in this period, Newfoundlanders had had been closely tied to Britain. Yet the idea of a closer economic relationship with the United States remained alive. Had either of the reciprocity agreements negotiated by Bond come to fruition the subsequent history of Newfoundland might have been very different. Two possibilities are that reciprocity might eventually have led Newfoundland to seek admission as a state of the union, thus ending forever the Canadian hope of bringing Newfoundland into Confederation; or that reciprocal trade might have so strengthened the Newfoundland economy that the virtual bankruptcy

44/*Daily News*, October 12, 1907.
45/F.O. 371/390, 37074, MacGregor to Elgin, November 1, 1907.
46/See S. J. R. Noel, "Politics and the Crown: The Case of the 1908 Tie Election in Newfoundland," *Canadian Journal of Economics and Political Science*, XXXIII (May 1967), 285–91.

of the 1930's need not have occurred, dominion status need never have been surrendered, and Newfoundland might have survived to the present time as an "independent" entity within the American orbit.

In fact, of course, the reciprocity attempts of 1890 and 1902 both failed, to the ruination of Bond's career. Power then passed into the hands of less scrupulous leaders and the events were set in train which led to economic collapse, the surrender of dominion status, and, finally, Confederation with Canada. The question of Newfoundland's relations with the United States, therefore, is of more than passing importance in the modern history of the island. Indeed any study of Newfoundland's relations with Canada in the period 1890–1910 in particular, and any general attempt to explain Newfoundland's long delay in joining the Canadian federation, must be concerned with Newfoundland's attempts to negotiate reciprocal trading agreements with the United States.

14

Newfoundland and Confederation, 1948-49

PETER CASHIN, HAROLD HORWOOD, AND LESLIE HARRIS

DR. GORDON ROTHNEY: We have as members of our panel, Major Cashin, Harold Horwood, and Dean Leslie Harris from Memorial University. Major Peter Cashin's father – Michael Cashin – was the first to leave the Bond Liberal party. He crossed the House in 1905 because he disapproved of the anti-American legislation that Bond was putting through. This shows a great deal of political sense because it was this legislation which in the end caused Bond's downfall.*

Michael Cashin was the member for Ferryland. Ferryland is south of St. John's, which means it is "up" from St. John's – it is "up south" – up the "southern shore" of the east coast, where settlement is very old. In the days of King Charles I, the capital of Newfoundland was Ferryland. But Cromwell's Puritan Republic put an end to that, and the Ferryland District went into decline until the Cashins revived it about the end of the nineteenth century.

After resigning from the Liberal party, Michael Cashin sat alone as an Independent until Edward Morris joined him two years later. A year after that, together with some others, they formed the People's Party which

*See the two preceding papers in this volume, pp. 198–202, 210–25.

came to office in 1909 as a result of the tie election of 1908. In that government, Cashin became a cabinet minister, and was minister of finance in Newfoundland for about ten years, which meant that he was minister of finance all through World War I – a great responsibility.

During the war, a coalition government was formed which put an end to the old Newfoundland party system. In 1919, Edward Morris having entered the British House of Lords the previous year, Michael Cashin formed a new political party, the Liberal Progressive party, which survives, really, to the present day. This was the real origin of the present Progressive Conservative party in Newfoundland, though Cashin in 1919 called it the Liberal Progressive party. The word "Progressive" at least is still there.

This party was defeated in the election of 1919, however, by a new Liberal party (not to be confused with the Bond Liberal party) which is basically the Liberal party of today. Thus the two parties really began in 1919. What existed before 1919 has nothing to do with the parties that have existed since that time.

It was in 1923 that Peter Cashin, for the first time, was a candidate. He had been on the mainland before the First World War, working for the CPR out in the West, and then in 1914 had immediately volunteered and was in France or on active service throughout the war. He entered politics, as I said, and supported the Liberal Progressive party. In 1924, after his father had retired from politics, this party came to power, and Major Cashin was the member for Ferryland on the government side of the House. By this time, the party was calling itself Conservative. But soon, inheriting his father's political sense, Cashin realized that the government was following policies which were going to lead to its defeat and so he left the party around 1926. He crossed the floor of the assembly and joined the Liberals. In the following election, which occurred in 1928, he accomplished one of the greatest political feats in the history of Newfoundland. He turned Ferryland, which had been as Conservative a district as you could find, over to the Liberal party. In other words, he took his district with him, and then became minister of finance in the Liberal government which took office in 1928.

When the Depression came, the Liberal government of Sir Richard Squires became involved in what might be considered some very questionable practices. In 1932 Major Cashin, on an issue relating to the question of honesty in the government, resigned from the cabinet. It was this resignation that precipitated the crisis which brought down Squires' Liberal government and led to the appointment of a royal commission to look into the affairs of Newfoundland. Cashin thus played a key role around 1932.

As a result of his revelations, a riot occurred which saw the sacking of the Colonial Building in 1932. I do not think he led the riot, but he did provide the ammunition.

Then came those days of Commission government. In 1946, after the war, the British Labour government, following the pattern it had set in India, decided to have a National Convention elected to recommend possible forms of future government to be put before the people. Two people attending this seminar were elected to that National Convention. Major Cashin was elected in St. John's West, as was Michael Harrington. Mr. Harrington is the editor of the *Evening Telegram*, the larger of the two daily newspapers in St. John's. St. John's West had three members at the convention and these were two of them. Both opposed Confederation. During the campaign, at the time of the referendum in 1948, the opponent of Confederation who emerged as the greatest orator on that side – and I think it is absolutely safe to say this – was Major Cashin.

I have the results from Ferryland, which I cannot help reading to you, which show how effective Major Cashin was in his own district. This was the official report of the chief electoral officer: "Ferryland, number of registered electors: 3,791. Number of persons voted July 22: 3,965." In the next column, the percentage vote that turned out is listed as 104.59 per cent. I would like to see that matched anywhere else. By a small margin, Confederation carried. Ferryland had been the most anti-Confederate district in the whole island, with an 84.56 per cent vote for responsible government.

Then in 1949 the first provincial election in Newfoundland was held, in which two people at this seminar were elected. Major Cashin became an Independent for Ferryland, for he would have nothing to do with either mainland party. He had been elected for Ferryland first as a Conservative, then as a Liberal, and then as an Independent. Harold Horwood was elected as the first member for Labrador by an overwhelming majority, as a Liberal and a supporter of Confederation.

In 1951 Major Cashin was elected in St. John's West as a Progressive Conservative. After the election he became leader of the opposition in the assembly. But he soon found there was a bit of a dispute as to who was running the Conservative party in Newfoundland, whether it was George Drew or Peter Cashin. Again he resigned from the party and became an Independent until he retired from politics in 1953. Since that time he has been Director of Civil Defence in Newfoundland. There are very few "living documents," as Gerald Graham would say, who are so important in the history of this province as is Major Cashin.

MAJOR CASHIN: First, let me thank you for having me here, because, as you all know, this is an educational institution. My education didn't go beyond the tenth grade. In those days, way back in 1906, people had to work, and I remember my father coming up to Brother Culhane, then president of old St. Bonaventure's College, where I had been a student boarder for almost six years, and telling him: "I am taking Peter out of school and putting him to work." It may interest you to know that the charge for a student boarder at that time was something in the order of fifty dollars per quarter. I had nothing to say about this move, but to be frank or honest about it, I was tickled pink to get out of school. Being associated in the family business at Cape Broyle, and having watched the elections of 1908 and 1909 in which I did not have a vote, I got the feeling that sometime I should be a politician. Little did I think at that time that something else was in store for me.

In 1910 I left Cape Broyle and went to Montreal, moved west in 1911, worked at the harvest in Saskatchewan for a couple of months, and finally landed in British Columbia. I worked for a few months as bookkeeper in a whaling plant on Queen Charlotte Island; then back east again in 1912, where I settled down working for the CPR at Fort William, Ontario, next door to the City of Port Arthur. In early 1915 I returned to Newfoundland, joined the Newfoundland Regiment, went overseas, and was seconded to the British Machine Gun Corps. I am thankful that I was not at Beaumont Hamel on July 1, 1916, or chances are I would not be here now.

I'll get right down to brass tacks. I don't want to talk about my father or anything else at the present time. I'll only say he was a tough old politician and a tough boss. I don't know what he would be thinking if he could see me here tonight. Incidentally, I recall that in 1934, the first year of Commission government, I was in business. Sir William Coaker came to town and rang me up. He asked me if I would drive him from wherever he was downtown to see some relatives of his. I said "Certainly," and went and picked him up. Going down Bonaventure Avenue, he said to me: "Peter, I was talking to your father when I was in London." Now my father had been dead eight years, and I wondered what was wrong with Coaker. I knew he didn't drink, but there must be something wrong somewhere. I listened while he told me about a "séance" he had attended in London. The first fellow that he asked for was Collishaw, a great friend of Coaker's who had helped him in many ways. Coaker told me he was talking to Collishaw. He didn't tell me where he was, but that he was very busy and was working all the time. Then he asked Collishaw had he seen Cashin. "Yes, he is right here, would you like to speak with him?" Father came on the line, or whatever system they have there. Coaker asked Cashin how he was getting along, and he replied that he was very busy and getting along fine. Then Cashin asked Croaker what was wrong with the boys down there, that they let a bunch of Englishmen come in and take over. Finally Coaker asked Cashin had he seen John Crosbie. "Yes," Father said, "he is around here getting into serious trouble, and it takes all my time to keep poor Crosbie out of trouble." That ended the conversation.

I would like to go over briefly the fall of 1928, when I contested the district of Ferryland with Sir Richard Squires as leader of our party. To me, there is no such thing today as a real Liberal party or a real Conservative party. We were the Squires party as far as I was concerned. It was Liberal-Tory, although Sir Richard always said it was Liberal in many ways. Though I was elected, I had the toughest fight of my political life. People were opposed to me; women who were voting for the first time were more easily influenced then. My opponents concentrated on the women's vote. "All the devils in hell" were not in a class with me. I lost a lot of personal votes and was just lucky in getting elected. We took over the government from Alderdice around the end of October 1928, as well as a deficit of some two million dollars, and carried on. In early 1929 Sir Patrick McGrath rang me. He was a great political friend of my father's and I knew him very well. I have stated elsewhere that McGrath was our ablest man, our ablest Newfoundlander. He was an invalid all his life. I went down to see Sir Patrick that night in his old meeting room on Gower Street. We talked about the recent election. McGrath had been out of the country during that election – he didn't want to be tangled up in politics any more. If he stayed here, he would be bound to get into it. When I was leaving his room that night, he said to me: "Peter, if you want any help with your budget, I will help you." I knew that McGrath wrote budgets for everyone. It didn't matter what side, he wrote them. He was just that type of man.

I was delighted when he offered to do this for me, and the next day started to gather details of everything necessary for a budget. It was an education to watch him work, and see how he handled such matters. He was afflicted with epilepsy; he had it all his life and had learned to live with it.

We had a good budget that year, 1929–30. McGrath and I argued over one point, which was that I claimed we would have a surplus on current account of between $140,000 and $150,000. He couldn't see it and neither could I at the time. I knew we were owed a lot of money by outside concerns – DOSCO being one of them – but McGrath didn't know anything about this then. In the fiscal year 1929–30 we collected the largest revenue in the history of responsible government in Newfoundland – $11.5 million I think it was. Unfortunately, McGrath did not live to see the $140,000 surplus. I was down to see him one night. He had rung me up and asked me if I would come and meet Sir Newton Moore. Sir Newton, a Conservative member of the British House of Commons, was also president of DOSCO, the company on Bell Island – now abandoned by the company and owned by the Newfoundland provincial government. They owed our government a substantial amount of money – we settled it down at McGrath's. McGrath settled everything in Newfoundland in those days.

Incidentally, I asked Sir Patrick would he mind me bringing Coaker. Now Coaker and McGrath couldn't look at each other politically, but McGrath said "sure," and I brought Coaker along with me. I didn't know what might happen. McGrath welcomed him and we sat down and discussed this DOSCO business and agreed on a temporary cure. After that, Sir Newton, born an Australian, now a Conservative member of the British House of Commons, started to talk English politics with McGrath and Coaker. McGrath answered them very quickly – I will never forget it, he said: "Sir Newton, you are going to have a Labour government in Britain this fall. Ramsay MacDonald is your next Prime Minister" – Sir Newton did not agree, but McGrath's words came true. McGrath died around the middle of June 1929, at the age of sixty. I lost a wonderful friend, and Newfoundland lost her most brilliant son.

We went into the fiscal year 1930–31 with that surplus. In that same year we raised a loan of some $6 million at 5 per cent, at par, the biggest price we, or any other dominion, received. I think it was 99.8 or something like that. Well, our credit looked good and we carried on. The next thing we knew we were in trouble.

Our next request for a loan of some $8 million was turned down flat – there were no bids. The Bank of Montreal, which had been acting as our financial agents for years, never advised us about the money market. This happened around May 1931. That winter we requested the bank to loan us temporarily $1.5 million which would be repaid when we received our loan of some $8 million later in the year. We also arranged with the bank to use this $1.5 million as we required it. They gave us $500,000 at first; when we asked for the balance of $1 million they wouldn't look at us – that's the Bank of Montreal. You could see the handwriting on the wall. We went to Montreal and New York. New York told us the Bank of Montreal did all our business; they should help us. The 1929 depression, which started in New York in October 1929, had now hit Canada with full force. We eventually arranged with the Imperial Oil Company to loan us $2 million temporarily to pay our interest charges coming due the end of June 1931. Our backs were to the wall.

The next thing we knew, some three or four months later, who came to see us urgently but the four Canadian chartered banks doing business in Newfoundland. Representatives of these banks requested us to go off the gold standard and make Canadian paper money our legal tender. They had told us a few months previously that Newfoundland was bankrupt. Well, I now had the privilege of telling them that it appeared to me that they were also bankrupt. About that time, the people of Newfoundland had around $25 million in savings accounts in those banks and, under Newfoundland law, these people could claim gold for that money. Around this particular period Canadian currency was worth about 80 cents on the dollar in us funds. Gold currency was worth something like $20.67 per ounce. What was happening was this: business people here in Newfoundland, who were financially well fixed, could go into the bank and demand gold to pay their obligations in the us. Gold jumped to $35 per ounce us funds, and the businessmen here in Newfoundland would make almost a 100 per cent profit on the transaction. Also at this particular period we had people in the us bringing, say, $100,000 to Newfoundland in American paper money. They would deposit it in our banks and receive a premium of around 20 per cent, and thus get credit in a savings account for $120,000. They could leave that money in the bank, and in a month or so, go to the bank and demand it in gold. Then they would return to the United States and make a premium amounting to another $25,000 or more. In all, a trip to Newfoundland would net a profit of around $50,000, or about 50 per cent on the entire transaction. These figures are roughly correct. However, it can be seen that the Canadian banks doing business in Newfoundland at that time made a profit on the $25 million in the savings accounts of our Newfoundland people of about $20 million or 80 per cent. We ultimately went off the gold standard and the four banks refused to underwrite our loan of $8 million. We knew that many of our business people owed these same banks substantial amounts of money and were hinting to us that if we did not go off the gold standard, they might have to close their banks in Newfoundland. It would be interesting to know at this time how much the Canadian banks and the British government made in Newfoundland on exchange when the American forces moved in here in 1941, spending hundreds of millions of dollars in the construction of military and naval bases and airfields, employing thousands of Newfoundlanders who were paid in Canadian funds, whilst the

Americans doing similar work were paid in American funds. In addition to this, the Commission government had requested the American authorities not to pay our labourers more than 35¢ per hour. I claim that the Canadian banks as well as the British government made about $100 million on United States exchange during the war period.

Certain things were happening within our government at this time, in 1931–32, which I could not tolerate or be a party to. I have been severely criticized for my action at this time, and I was nicknamed the "buster of governments." But I put the question to you: if you were made responsible for the safekeeping of large amounts of money and you went to your office the following morning and discovered that your cash till had been rifled, what would you do about it? Would you stay with the people who tampered with it? I couldn't do that, not even if I wanted to. I resigned and the Liberal Progressive party found itself politically dead. When the facts were eventually revealed, the opposition organized a march of citizens on our House of Assembly. It developed into a riot and resulted in a general election in the early summer of 1932. I did not stand in that election.

The Alderdice party (Conservative) won the election with a huge majority – only two members were elected by the Squires party; Sir Richard Squires went down to defeat himself. The Conservatives had told the electorate that they would straighten out our finances and put Newfoundland on her feet. They were due for a big surprise because they were unable to adjust our financial situation.

When I was minister of finance in 1931, I had suggested that we should reduce our interest charges from an average of 5 per cent to 3 per cent, which would mean a saving of about $2 million annually. The members of the opposition and some members in our own party would not go along with me in this particular matter. They stated that such an action would mean default. I never got an opportunity to ask these members why they had agreed to do just this when they became members of the Commission government. In fact, this was one of the first pieces of legislation enacted by the Commission when they took over the administration of government in February 1934. I have been accused of being an anti-confederate. I wasn't opposed to Confederation as such; but I was opposed, violently, to the methods which were used to bring it about. There are only two ways to do anything – the right way and the wrong way. Either carry out the law to the letter, or do it the other way by breaking the law. They broke the law and that was why I opposed Confederation in 1934. In my opinion Newfoundland was cheated out of not less than $300 million because of this.

I'll put it this way. When we went into Confederation in 1949, our per capita debt was around $220 a head. I think my friend, Mr. Horwood, often heard me say this in the House of Assembly. The Canadian national debt was around $1,400 per head, a difference of some $1,200 dollars per head, a difference in our favour of not less than $1,000, or a total difference of not less than $300 million. Our population was around 350,000 people. I claim that money difference would be in our favour if we had gone into Confederation on an equitable basis. No less an individual than Mr. Pickersgill has stated on various occasions that Canada gained more by Newfoundland coming into union with Canada than Newfoundland gained. Now let us look at what actually happened. In 1945 the war was over. Please forgive me for using the personal pronoun so much. I am compelled to, because I was more or less alone. A few old political friends of mine and a few others suggested that I start some kind of movement to drive out the Commission government. The Newfoundland treasury showed a surplus in actual cash of some $40 million. Our people were all working – the American bases on the island of Newfoundland continued to employ several thousands of Newfoundlanders. Do you realize that we would not have had Confederation today if the Commission form of government had continued? At least that's the way it looks to me. Together with a few friends who helped me in many ways, I started a radio campaign – none of those people who backed Confederation later made any effort whatever to join me in a campaign to dethrone "commission government." It would appear from the actual facts such people desired a continuation of Commission government. I made a few speeches on radio station VONF, the government station. Well, you can realize I wasn't allowed there very long. I called VOCM, at that time "The Voice of the Common Man." The late Joe Butler treated me royally. He owned the station and didn't charge me very much – I didn't have much to pay anyhow. I spoke over VOCM every Saturday night at 10.00 PM. The campaign went over big. We were getting letters from all over Newfoundland giving us encouragement to carry on. We decided to circulate a petition requesting our own government be restored. We did that and had some twenty-five or thirty thousand names on the petition, which we proposed to take to the bar of the British House of Commons. Then Governor Walwyn returned to England and the British government sent a new governor named Macdonald. He started immediately to carry out what I believe were his instructions from the British Dominions Office. One of his first actions was, I understand, preaching from the pulpit of one of our local churches. This started a real sectarian battle unprecedented in Newfoundland or, for that matter, in any other British possession. Macdonald was elevated to a peerage by the British government. He passed away a few years ago and undoubtedly received his just reward in the other world.

And so we had the National Convention when the British government, advised by Macdonald and the Commission government, ascertained that our petition was meeting with such enthusiasm by the people generally around the country. All we would have to do was to bring such a petition to the House of Commons in London. At least that is what we were legally supposed to do to have responsible government restored. We never got that far. Macdonald stated we were going to have a National Convention, which was the greatest fraud I have ever witnessed. The British government did not take the recommendation of the Convention, which opened with all the fanfare and pomp of the opening of either the British or the Canadian House of Commons. They had dressed Macdonald up to look like a real governor or king. After all this political camouflage, as I said a few moments ago, the British government did not take the recommendations of the Convention and treated our members like so much dirt.

Now someone said something critical at this seminar about the late Sir William MacGregor, who was governor of Newfoundland when Morris came into office in 1909. I spent the loneliest ten days of my life at MacGregor's home in Scotland in 1916. He was a great friend of my father's and I could not turn down his invitation. His household was operated more like an army, as far as discipline was concerned. Everyone had to be up in the morning at a certain hour, breakfast at another hour, lunch at another, tea at four, dinner at 7:30. He lived by the clock and was a wonderful old gentleman.

The National Convention met the first week of September 1946. Myself and Mike Harrington here, and the late Ches Crosbie, were elected in St. John's West. The late Cyril Fox was appointed chairman of this farcical convention. He divided us up into groups. I was appointed chairman of the finance committee, Smallwood was given something else, someone else was given something else, and it wound up, I think, with myself and the present premier writing all the reports made in that convention. The forty-five members knew nothing whatever about government work. Not that Smallwood and myself knew it all – we had to do the best we could. Suddenly one afternoon, Smallwood wanted a delegation sent to Ottawa immediately – but we voted it down and carried on the best we knew how. The next thing was a delegation to London, and I happened to be on that.

We met with a committee of the British government with Lord Addison as chairman. Addison was the political chief of the Dominions Office. We were surprised at the presence of Governor Macdonald and Sir Albert Walsh. Well, anyone with a cork-eye could see that we were practically into union with Canada. One of the members of that committee was sympathetic to our views as well as our demands. We never laid eyes on him after that first meeting. He was literally banished. We returned to Newfoundland knowing full well that the British government had sold us up the river. We finished our duties in the convention early in 1948, and our recommendations to the British government were looked upon as a joke. As usual, the British violated the terms of that convention.

In the autumn of 1948 myself, Fred Marshall, and Jack Higgins took our petition and presented it to the members of the House of Commons through Sir Alan Herbert. Again, we were literally laughed at. I met Anthony Eden in the lobby of the House of Commons. He asked me what were we doing over there and I told him we had come over with a petition from the people of Newfoundland concerning the Confederation matter. He said, and I quote: "Sure, that's fixed up long ago." He almost told me where it was fixed. We went into Confederation by a very small margin – 49 per cent against and 51 per cent for.

In the course of the convention, I as usual got into trouble and landed up in the Newfoundland Supreme Court on a charge of civil libel. My plaintiffs in this case were Sir Edward Emerson, Chief Justice, Mr. Harry Winter, Assistant Judge, and Mr. Alex Winter, registrar of our court. I talked with a lawyer friend of mine and asked him what he thought of it. He told me he would advise me to plead my own case. I did just that. I refused to give an undertaking that I would retract certain statements I had made in a meeting of the Convention. The lawyer for the judges was no less an individual than our present Chief Justice, Mr. R. S. Furlong. We went to draw a jury of nine. I was told I could object to a certain number of jurors. I told them that I was a public man and would not object to any juror. They could pick any juror they wished, provided he was a Newfoundlander. The case went before Judge Dunfield. He wanted me to employ some lawyer. I think I remember telling him that I got into this mess myself, and that I was going to fight my way out of it if I could.

The first thing that happened when the court opened was that they put me in the witness box to give evidence against myself. I thought it was wrong – still think it was wrong – but I spent 2½ hours on the witness stand and Furlong failed to break me. Incidentally, Chief Justice Furlong is a relative of mine. After lunch on that historic day for me, Furlong had to put his clients, the plaintiffs, on the witness stand and I had the privilege of cross-examining them. Judge Dunfield addressed the jury after I had spoken 1½ hours to them, then Mr. Furlong, and finally Judge Dunfield. The result was that the jury of nine men disagreed, and they had the right to appeal. I haven't heard anything about it since. The judge had to clear the court and thousands of people were outside the courthouse. They literally went wild when I appeared. It was the greatest political move I have ever made. I am sure the old governor, Macdonald, must have had a fit when he was told the result. I was, and still am, convinced that Macdonald was the individual who influenced these three court officials to take action against me. His idea was to get me out of his path for six or more months on the road to Confederation.

Now let us get down to the "Terms of Union." The delegation was selected by the Commission government and Governor Macdonald. The members of that delegation did not really represent the people of Newfoundland. They were carefully selected by Governor Macdonald, and some wanted Confederation at any price. The first visit to Ottawa in the summer of 1947 by a delegation selected from the convention spent three months at Ottawa more as guests of the federal government than as representatives of Newfoundland. The Terms of Union submitted by the Canadian government at that time were ridiculous. Financially these terms were an insult to our intelligence. Over a period of some twelve years the Canadian government would pay the Newfoundland treasury some $29 million. Under the final financial terms they paid us some $42,750.000. Then after a period of eight years a royal commission investigated our financial situation and made recommendations as to what sum Newfoundland would require to carry on on an equitable basis. The commission recommendation was for an amount of some $8 million. This looked better. The Diefenbaker government agreed to this amount and eliminated Term 29, which reads:

Review of Financial Position

In view of the difficulty of predicting with sufficient accuracy, the financial consequences to Newfoundland of becoming a Province of Canada, the government of Canada will appoint a Royal Commission within eight years assistance, if any, that may be required by the Government of the Province of Newfoundland and to recommend the form and scale of additional financial assistance, if any, that may be required by the government of the Province of Newfoundland to enable it to continue public services at the level and standards reached subsequent to the date of Union, without resorting to taxation. [And so on, and so on ...]

But this term does not commit anyone to anything, not one thing. Anyhow I say now, that when that $8 million was granted (and I read it in the estimates for last year) clearly it meant that the $42 million that we received over a twelve-year period should have been $96 million. In other words, another $54 million which the Canadian government morally owes the Newfoundland government.

Now a lot of people have said that I was opposed to Confederation. I have already told you that I was opposed to the illegal manner in which Confederation was brought about. Do you know that up to the time of Confederation I had never voted in Newfoundland during a general election for either myself or anyone else? The first vote I had was in Saskatchewan in 1911. I was working in Montreal in the early part of 1911. I remember Sir Wilfrid Laurier returning from England and an imperial conference in London early in the summer of 1911. Thousands of people were down on the Montreal piers to welcome him home. When he landed, I listened to him speak in both languages and receive a tumultuous reception. I said to myself, if I ever have a vote in Canada I will vote for that fellow. That same fall there was a federal election in Canada. I was working at the harvest in Saskatchewan when the election took place. I had been living in Canada for about nine months and, as I was a British subject was entitled to vote. I voted for Laurier's candidate. He had gone to the country on a platform of reciprocity with the United States. His party was defeated by the then real Tory party, under the leadership of Sir Robert Borden. That was the last time either a real Tory party or a real Liberal party existed in Canada. Then I went out to British Columbia and was working in a whale factory as a bookkeeper. This was on Queen Charlotte Island. We had 40 Newfoundlanders, 40 Japanese and 40 Chinese working in that plant. Early in the summer of 1912 there was a provincial election in B.C. A candidate came to visit us one day – went to the manager telling him he was a candidate and knew that these 40 Newfoundlanders had a vote. The manager sent the chap to me, telling him that a young fellow named Cashin, the bookkeeper, was a Newfoundlander and knew all the Newfoundlanders well. He came down to the office and we talked and I took him around to meet the Newfoundlanders. The next thing I knew I was the deputy returning officer – I received all the papers, ballots, etc. We Newfoundlanders agreed amongst ourselves to vote for the candidate who called to see us. No other candidate came near us. We felt that if this man thought it worth his while to come and see us, and no other had come, we should vote for him, and we all did. The Newfoundland voters had cast their ballots in about half an hour. I received fifty dollars as returning officer, and the manager of the plant wanted me to give it to an Indian. We had a few strong words and I quit the job. I was on the road again.

I ended up in Fort William late in 1912, and worked for the CPR until 1915, which is when I returned to Newfoundland and joined the Newfoundland Regiment. I went overseas as a corporal and later was seconded to the British Machine Gun Corps, spent two or three years in the army in France, and returned to Newfoundland in early 1919. I went to Fort William that summer and worked with the CPR again for a few months, but I had an attack of sciatica and returned to Newfoundland in early 1920. I was elected in Ferryland for the first time in the spring of 1923, taking over my father's seat; he was elected in St. John's West in a terrific political battle. It was one of the toughest elections in the history of Newfoundland. And there it goes! I had taken on his political mantle and it was anything but an easy job to follow in that man's political shoes. I am sure he would get a jolt if he could see me here this evening.

Now what do I think of Confederation? I think that is the question you would like me to answer. I told you that I was not against Confederation so much as against the methods which brought it about, and they are too numerous to mention.

Confederation has been wonderful for Newfoundland, although many things have been done which I do not agree with. We own the Labrador – we own "Churchill Falls." If we didn't have Confederation, we as a country could never develop it because Quebec could block us and Quebec in turn would be backed by the federal government of Canada. Now development is actually under way, many thousands of workers will be required to complete that development and then operate it – it means many millions of dollars annually to the Newfoundland government. Now that we are in Labrador – now that we actually have that valuable asset, there is and there will continue to be for many years to come plenty of employment for our people. Newfoundlanders generally have created the impression that they are not particularly interested in continuous work – they like to work and pile up what is called a "stake," quit without any excuse whatever, blow in that "stake," and then return and expect to get another job and repeat their previous action. That is not going to work any more – that day is gone. Let me try to say to the young men and women of this island, there is no excuse which anyone can offer for our workers not to wish to go to Labrador. In ten years from now Labrador will be settled down. If our people do not avail themselves of the possibilities of settling there, the French Canadians from the province of Quebec will control it – and Newfoundland may lose the sovereignty of this precious territory. If the Newfoundland people want to retain the sovereignty of Labrador, then they must work hard and continuously. Many of our people today are living luxuriously on government relief. Some do not want to work. Many Canadians, and this includes Newfoundlanders, are of the view that the federal treasury is inexhaustible. That is absolutely false. The federal government at Ottawa has its problems just as much, if not more so, than we have. So I say to my many Newfoundland friends, particularly the young men and their families: get in touch with the employment officer or your local member of the House of Assembly, get moving, forget living in a welfare state, be independent, play your part in retaining Labrador for Newfoundland.

There is only one thing that can happen if our Newfoundland workmen do not wish continuous employment and refuse to move to Labrador, that is to sell Labrador, our portion of it, to the province of Quebec. Speaking of that, I think it was around 1925, Walter Monroe, then prime minister, led a delegation from his cabinet to discuss selling our interest in Labrador to Quebec. Mr. Taschereau was then premier of Quebec. Monroe felt we could settle the dispute without having to go to the Privy Council. We ascertained on the return of the Monroe delegation that Monroe offered to sell our interest in Labrador to Quebec for some $20 million or $25 million, retaining our fishing rights on the coastline. Mr. Taschereau turned down the offer and so the case went to the Privy Council. Early in 1927 the decision of that legal body handed down its decision in favour of Newfoundland.

When our request for an $8 million loan was rejected in 1931, I was one of a delegation who went to Ottawa and met with Prime Minister Bennett to discuss the possibility of selling Labrador for some $110 million either to the federal government or the Quebec government. The other members of that delegation were Sir William Coaker, Dr. Barnes, and Dr. Mosdell. We had a few meetings with Prime Minister Bennett and he was seriously interested. However, the depression had hit Canada violently and Mr. Bennett wrote me a short note, advising me that they, too, were having their financial difficulties and regretted that at that time they could do nothing about the matter; and so I feel glad today that our mission to Ottawa in 1931 was a failure. There was a French Canadian named Champlain who was going back and forth between St. John's and Quebec; each time he arrived here he would tell us that Taschereau wanted to buy Labrador – sometimes Champlain used to tell us he had Labrador sold. Joe Champlain was a weird character. Several of our businessmen-politicians had been giving Joe money to keep him working. It was a great joke at that time. Champlain was apparently telling those individuals he would see that there was a share in what he would be getting from Quebec. Now we own Labrador, not alone through the judgment of the Privy Council decision of 1927, but through the Terms of Union with Canada when we joined that country in 1949. If Quebec wants the Labrador now, it can come to the Newfoundland government and put a proposition to that government to buy it. What price would we take for it? My price would be $1 billion. That would be the least, and I would have to take some time to figure out if the area is worth more. I think it will be the main source of revenue for our province in the not too distant future. During the last ten or fifteen years the federal government has been pouring in millions of dollars into Newfoundland. The government is having its own difficulties, and will have to pull in its horns and tighten its belt. Newfoundland, which has been booming for the past ten or fifteen years, will feel the effect the same as any other province. Taxes will be raised and we in Newfoundland will have to pull in our belts also. We must take it easy for a while and plan our policies for the future.

I have stated that our provincial government under Smallwood's leadership has made many costly mistakes: I haven't time to discuss them now. The government has put into effect legislation for the development of our province. In this respect I mention "Brinco" legislation, as well as the introduction into Newfoundland of the great Rothschild banking house, and the establishment of our Memorial University, which is costing many millions of dollars. Smallwood's government may have rushed this job too much, and in its eagerness to get the university established as soon as possible may have over-spent, so some waste and errors are bound to occur. I have made up my mind at the present time that I am finished with politics, although there are times when I feel like going at it again.

Young men today are not the political type. We had fifteen years of Commission government controlled by the Dominions Office in London. You know about that Commission government – how it treated our people. Six cents a day to live on. I know what I am talking about in this respect. In Ferryland district when I was a boy there were thirty or forty cows as well as hundreds of hens. Before they were granted any relief whatever people were told to sell their cows and hens or otherwise they could eat them. Three Newfoundlanders were members of that Commission and tolerated this kind of treatment of our people. They assisted the English commissioners and the Dominions Office in starving many of our fine people. Thank God, I can claim some credit for helping drive them from office. I wondered why there hadn't been a rebellion long before I returned to Newfoundland. But that's what was happening. During the fifteen years of Commission dictatorship our people, particularly our young people, did not worry much about politics – they were too busy trying to grab something to eat and actually live. Looking over the situation as I see it today, I cannot see anyone around that could take over the leadership of government and successfully administer our public affairs. There may be one or two individuals who wish to try it, but they are like a hockey team; if their coach and manager fails in his leadership the team will fail miserably. I am of the opinion that Joe Smallwood will remain in public life for some time to come. If he could back some potential leader, remain as a member of the House of Assembly as an ordinary member, seating himself close to his new leader, he may be able to teach him something in a few years. Otherwise, I claim that it would be tragic if anything happened to Smallwood at this time. The next four years will test our government's real abilities. In addition, we need and should have a good opposition, which would mean better government. That is up to the people themselves – particularly independently minded people. At the present time it is difficult to get good men to enter political life; they generally do not wish any change because most of them are making big money out of government, and out of government contracts which they do not wish to lose. Their desire is not to rock the boat.

Before I conclude I would like to tell you my first experience on my entry into public life. My father, who was contesting the district of St. John's West in this particular election (1923), came to Ferryland with myself and Phil Moore, his former colleague. As the roads were blocked with snow, we went to Ferryland in our little steamer *Cabot*. A public meeting had been arranged for 8:00 PM. When we steamed into Ferryland that evening, we had to tie up our ship to an ordinary stage-head. There was no public wharf in the capital of the district. Little did I think I would use this as a political weapon. However, the meeting started on time. Ned Healey, an elderly man, was chairman, and Ned could talk better politics than myself. Father was the first speaker. He talked on everything, particularly the fishery. In his winding-up remarks he told the people that if I did not do the proper thing if elected, he would come up there the next election and "beat hell" out of me. That remark tickled the audience in the old Star Hall. Now, in his speech he had touched on everything and left nothing for me to say. So it suddenly struck me that there was no public wharf in Ferryland, and I quickly decided to work this on him. After a few brief remarks, I turned to the chairman and said: "My respected father has told you, the people of Ferryland, that if I do not measure up and do the proper thing, he will come up here the next election and beat hell out of me. Well, Mr. Chairman, when we steamed in here this evening, there was no public wharf. Now Father has represented this district for thirty years and you elected him eight times, but there is no public wharf in Ferryland, the capital of the district, and the place where Baltimore landed. I make this solemn promise this evening – if you elect me as a member for Ferryland, I will fight and get a public wharf in Ferryland." The audience went wild when I turned to my father on the platform and said "I think the boot is on the other foot now."

After the meeting closed, we staged a little social party in the old Carter residence, then occupied by Mike White and family. We served the usual refreshments and the men enjoyed themselves thoroughly. I often heard Father say: "There's more votes in a bottle of rum than a road grant." When we met after the party he came to me and said: "What in hell did you refer to that public wharf for?" He said, "You will never get that wharf." It took me five years to get it. Father did not live long enough to see the job completed. I have always felt that his St. John's West campaign sapped up a lot of his failing strength. It is interesting to know that the three Ferryland men who nominated him in 1893 nominated me in 1923. One of these persons, Mr. Patrick Farrell, was grandfather to Professor Ashley of Memorial University.

Before concluding this extemporaneous talk, I take this opportunity of expressing to you, Mr. Chairman, my personal thanks for such a wonderful introduction. You may have to shoulder the responsibility for driving me back into public life – I hope not. I also wish to express my thanks to all the personnel of this distinguished gathering of educationists for the courtesies that have been extended to me, and wish you each my profound thanks.

DR. ROTHNEY: Major Cashin, at the end of his talk, brought in Labrador. The coast of Labrador, after all, is what prevents Newfoundland from being just another "Maritime province." The other Maritime provinces don't have a northwest territory.

We have here this afternoon, Harold Horwood, the first member for Labrador to sit in the House of Assembly in all its history. Labrador was not represented before Commission government. Harold Horwood was elected in 1949 after having campaigned with Joseph Smallwood for Confederation the previous year. He was on the opposite side politically to Major Cashin, and I think that after listening to Major Cashin he must be very anxious to say some things that we are all anxious to hear.

HAROLD HORWOOD*: Oddly enough, I agree with most of the things Major Cashin has said. I came here fully prepared to disagree with almost everything. There is only one major point, and this is one on which there will probably always be a big division of opinion. That relates to the part that Governor Macdonald played in bringing Confederation to Newfoundland.

I was connected with the confederate movement from 1946 when Joe Smallwood came to town, looking for disciples, trying to organize things

*MLA, Beachy Cove, St. John's East; associate editor, *St. John's Evening Telegram.* Author of *Tomorrow Will Be Sunday* and *The Foxes of Beachy Cove.*

in the Confederate Association. I was a very young man at the time –
twenty-two years of age. But it happened that I was president of the largest
labour organization in eastern Newfoundland and this attracted Mr.
Smallwood. He figured that the presidents of labour organizations would
have some political pull. He gathered a number of us who would consent
to go into his organization, and so introduced a group of labour organizers
and labour union presidents into the Confederate Association. I was one
of the first, so that I was with him in 1946, during the period of the
National Convention and during the campaigning we conducted after
the National Convention. The real fight to get Confederation occurred
after the National Convention finished its work and the referendums were
announced.

I agree with Major Cashin that the governor may have been largely
responsible for the referendums being held, though Major Cashin himself
undoubtedly stimulated the public uproar that caused the governor to
recommend the national convention's being called in the first place. I don't
think the Commission government had reached the stage where it would
have spontaneously recommended to the government of Great Britain
that anything be done about Newfoundland's political status, had not
Major Cashin started this campaign – one of the most successful one-man
campaigns that has ever been conducted.

I hope that somewhere some of the tapes from radio station VOCM are
available. I remember very vividly the speeches that Major Cashin made
at that time. I listened to him every night while he was on and they were
among the most effective, most violently oratorical things that you could
ever listen to. It was almost unbelievable that a man could do this sort of
thing on radio. As a result, he created a very large popular demand, and a
very large popular indignation against the Commission government which
was totally undeserved. This government, from the point of view of purity
of administration, purity of intention, and so on, was undoubtedly the best
one we have ever had. It was not the most inspired government, but a
very good government, by the highest kind of British civil service standards. However, Major Cashin succeeded in making it look like a pack of
rogues and inspired a large public demand to have something done about
restoring self-government to Newfoundland. Indirectly, Major Cashin
needs to be ranked as *the* "Father of Confederation," for that reason.

There is a popular belief among the people who were anti-confederates,
during and after the Convention, that when it was called, the whole thing
was pre-decided in some way between the government of Canada and the
government of Great Britain and that Governor Macdonald, who, incidentally, was the only Socialist governor we ever had here, was sent out

here to implement this confederate plot. I am perfectly sure that nothing could be further from the truth. If there were any machinations at all between Governor Macdonald and the government of Canada, or between the government of Canada and the government of Great Britain, then those of us who fought the campaign for Confederation in Newfoundland would have known about it. I was as close to the centre of that campaign as anyone ever was except Smallwood himself. I was one of his three "bright young men," the other two being Phil Forsey, who's dead, and Greg Power, who was subsequently finance minister and who is now a private chicken farmer. None of us, incidentally, supported Smallwood for very long, although Power stayed with him longer than the rest of us. But we were the core of the Confederate Association. If there had been anything going on I am perfectly sure we would have known about it. If Smallwood had known about it, I would have known about it, and I didn't. As a matter of fact, we were afraid that Governor Macdonald was hostile to Confederation and we actually suspected that he was blocking the moves to get Confederation on the ballot paper after the National Convention was over.

I won't go into the convention itself; you know what happened, it's on the record. The forty-five members met. They were expected to meet for perhaps a couple of months, to make recommendations and then the thing would be over. But the convention turned into the most violent public political battle which had ever occurred here. Instead of sitting for two months, the convention sat for something like two years. The delegates' job was to consider forms of government and to recommend to the government of Great Britain forms of government that might be placed before the people in a national referendum.

Smallwood was personally responsible for turning the convention into the political battle that it became. The government radio station, VONF, decided to broadcast all the proceedings *verbatim* every night. The convention sat throughout the afternoon and adjourned at six o'clock. At eight o'clock VONF came on the air and broadcast the whole afternoon's proceedings, until midnight or however long it took. Practically every person in Newfoundland sat all night with his ear glued to the radio, listening to what had gone on in the National Convention that day.

Smallwood, very cleverly, turned the convention into a campaign for and against Confederation. All the other issues were secondary. It didn't matter whether or not we were solvent, or whether or not we could support ourselves financially. These supposedly basic issues were all submerged. The battle for Confederation started there and continued after the convention adjourned.

I don't know to how many people he promised senatorships, but it was his method of lining up supporters – I think he would admit this himself now after all these years. He went around to everyone and promised them senatorships if they would join the Confederate faction. He had been back and forth to Ottawa.

He had gone to Ottawa with the first delegation to discuss Confederation. The Canadian government agreed to receive the delegation and Smallwood met there members of the Liberal party, including Louis St. Laurent, Jack Pickersgill, Senator Gordon Fogo, and C. D. Howe. These were the people, Pickersgill, Fogo, and Howe, who actually implemented Confederation for us at that end. Subsequently, when the convention adjourned, as Major Cashin has said, twenty-nine members voted for just two forms of government being placed before the people in the referendum, that is, responsible government and Commission government. Sixteen voted for three forms of government, responsible government, Commission government, and Confederation on the terms that the government of Canada had agreed to with the delegation which went from the convention to interview them.

The day after the convention adjourned, we launched our campaign for Confederation with a speech by Gordon Bradley, who had been chairman of the convention and who was one of the pro-confederate people in it. Bradley went on the air with a very violent speech which he didn't write himself, denouncing the twenty-nine people who had voted for only two forms of government as the twenty-nine dictators trying to prevent the people of Newfoundland from making a free choice for themselves. He urged the people to send in a petition appealing to the government of Great Britain to add Confederation to the other two forms of government on the ballot paper.

The petition was a surprise to all of us. I don't know what the voting strength of Newfoundland was at the time, perhaps 70,000 voters, but we had 40–50,000 names on that ballot paper. I worked on the committee that handled the petition. I personally campaigned from house to house in the Mundy Pond area, which was the most anti-confederate area of St. John's. I got the names of a lot of people who certainly had no sympathy for Confederation but who agreed it should be on the ballot paper. The petition was collected in about a week and it was taken to Government House here and placed in charge of Governor Macdonald for transmission to His Majesty's government in Great Britain.

About two weeks later we discovered that the petition never left Newfoundland. Whether the governor sent the results of the petition on to the government of Great Britain, we never will know. Certainly Smallwood was furious when he learned that the petition had never left St. John's. Later, he was enormously relieved to learn that the government of Great Britain had indeed decided to include Confederation on the ballot paper.

Up to that point we had no inkling whatsoever that anything was fixed or prearranged or that there had been any talk or discussion between Canada and Great Britain with respect to the future of Newfoundland. I believe that Smallwood was personally responsible for launching the confederate campaign in the beginning. I don't believe anyone approached him and asked him to do it. It was his own idea. I believe that it was something that he thought of himself and that he created the campaign himself, in the National Convention and subsequently.

We then had the two referendum campaigns. The form of the referendum was that there would be three forms of government on the ballot paper. If any one of the three forms got an over-all majority, then the government of Great Britain would pass the necessary legislation for that form of government. If no one of the three gained an over-all majority there would be a second referendum, a run-off between the first and second place forms to decide which one we would have. Almost from the beginning the first referendum campaign took a rather ugly turn. It was quite obvious that there was a decided division along religious lines, even in the first referendum.

We started with no organization whatsoever. There were Smallwood and half a dozen of us here in St. John's, including a few delegates to the convention who launched the organization. We had no organization outside. We met in Smallwood's living room one night and decided we would launch the confederate organization as such. We sat around picking out the known sea lawyers, as they are called in all the various out-ports of Newfoundland, and we counted one hundred and one of them. Smallwood wired each one of these one hundred and one men, inviting him to become vice-president of the Newfoundland Confederate Association. And so we had our one hundred and one vice-presidents. This was the only organization we had at the beginning. We hired a room down on Water Street.

Now I must digress for one moment to tell you about the "Water Street Millionaires" – there were supposed to be twenty-one of them. I don't know whether there were or there weren't, but that's what we said. The "Water Street Millionaires" were, almost to a man, opposed to Confederation. Many people of Newfoundland felt that Confederation would create such a violent economic strain and disruption that their businesses would be in jeopardy. As it subsequently turned out, a great many of them, especially small manufacturing businesses (the tradesmen and the merchants actually benefited greatly), went under. A lot of them who didn't go under, including a number of the merchants, were afraid they would. Thinking of competing with T. Eaton Company and the national supermarket chains and that sort of thing was enough to make them apprehensive. So they, almost to a man, opposed Confederation.

I remember the night that Smallwood announced that we had hired an office down in the lion's den on Water Street as headquarters for the Newfoundland Confederate Association. But the association consisted only of Smallwood, Forsey, Power, and myself, as well as a few people who drifted in and out from time to time. It was about the loneliest place in Newfoundland, this office.

I had a very big map I remember, ten inches to the mile. I pasted it up on one wall and went down to Dicks and Company and bought numerous coloured pins. I stuck these pins of various colours in all the major towns all over Newfoundland. They didn't mean a thing in the world. The bigger the town, the more colours I used. The big towns would have all six colours and smaller places would have only one. People coming in saw this map, you see, and this was the confederate organization. In Cornerbrook we had six different colours. It did wonders for morale.

But the big problem we had was the need for money. We first of all appealed to the fishermen and workers of Newfoundland to enter the organization and to pay a one-dollar initiation fee, as the CCF used to do in Saskatchewan and other parts of Canada. In this grass-roots organization everyone paid his dollar. We never fooled ourselves that we could collect enough money to do anything worth talking about, but we felt we might be able to finance ourselves for a month or two at any rate. It didn't turn out that way though we did collect four or five hundred dollars in one- and even in two-dollar lots.

We had very few people we could appeal to locally in St. John's. There were two people on Water Street who were interested in senatorships, one of whom subsequently became a senator. The other didn't because he had trouble with his income tax. (You can't very well make a man a senator after he has been convicted of income tax evasion.) But there were two of them who undertook to buy senatorships from us. It was a speculation which assumed there was a possibility that we would win, and if we did win there was a chance of getting a senatorship. I wrote the first receipt for the first instalment for the first senatorship – $250. This looked like an awful lot of money to us.

But we did sit down and talk about fund-raising. Smallwood himself is completely hopeless when it comes to funds, always has been, and always will be. He knows nothing about finances. All he knows about money is how to spend it. But we had a couple of people with us who did know about finances. Forsey was a good financial man. He became minister of supply in the first provincial government and consequently party fund collector. He became known as "Ten Percent" Forsey. Forsey had some others with him. Ray Petten was one. He subsequently became a senator and was a most valuable member of the Confederate Association. He was a small out-port merchant (with the Fishermen's Union Trading Company). Petten was with us from the beginning, and he and Forsey and some other people, who also knew something about funds, put their heads together and came up with some advice on how to collect money. It was perfectly obvious that we could not collect enough in Newfoundland from two potential senators and a few sympathizers. As a result, we had to go to Canada.

We went first, of course, to the fountainhead, C. D. Howe, who controlled the purse strings and everything else in the Liberal party. And he said, in effect, "Well, you know, with all the sympathy in the world I don't think anyone in my position could be publicly associated with helping to finance a political campaign in another country. But why don't you talk to Senator Gordon Fogo?" Now I believe Senator Fogo was the actual treasurer of the Liberal party at the time, so we talked to him. He said, in effect, "Send a man up to see me and I will see what I can do, but I can't do anything out of the Liberal treasury. I will see if I can do something privately." In the meantime we had sent a fellow named Charlie Penny, who had been an insurance salesman, on a trip right across Canada to interview expatriate Newfoundlanders, some of whom were fairly wealthy. We had a list of maybe a couple of thousand of them, and we figured that the ones he saw would be able to put him in touch with some others. Right from Halifax to Vancouver he went to interview former Newfoundlanders, to solicit their support and try to get some money from them. Charlie did collect some money – almost enough to finance his trip from Newfoundland to Vancouver and back again, but not enough to do anything toward financing the campaign. So Petten, to his enormous credit, put up some money of his own on loan, to keep us going. He backed notes at the bank and various things of that sort. When he went to Ottawa and saw Fogo and Howe, they gave him a list of private people, not members of the Liberal party, not outstanding members anyway, who might be induced to contribute to the campaign in Newfoundland. Most of these, it turned out, were brewers and distillers and vintners – people who were in a rather sensitive position, and who, if the word were dropped from the Liberal party that they should do a favour for somebody else, would be very apt to do the favour. The result was, we collected what must have been approximately a quarter of a million dollars altogether – not at one fell swoop, of course. Petten went back several times to his list of contacts, but he did keep us going.

There were very large expenses here. I think we must have spent several times what the Responsible Government League spent, because they were tapping "Water Street," which is made up of notoriously tight-fisted people. These twenty-one millionaires weren't going to put their money on the line. They might give a few thousands here and there. Petten spent most of the time on the mainland, and kept us supplied with campaign funds.

We ran a weekly newspaper, which cost us about $5,000 per week. We got the best cartoonist in Canada to do cartoons for us at $500 each. The cartoons were very effective. The humour in the paper (it was an extremely humorous paper, though it may not have seemed humorous to the people who were on the other side) was bitingly sarcastic and extremely well done. It was written by the three best writers in Newfoundland, Power, Smallwood, and myself. Smallwood did most of the writing. Power wrote most of the humour. I limited myself to small "news items," largely in imitation of Smallwood's style.

We put on an enormous drive on radio. We had people on morning, noon, and night continuously blasting confederate propaganda over the radio. We succeeded in getting a few fairly prominent people even during this campaign, although not very many. Most people were unknown like ourselves. But the basic thing of course was the money. We had the money to do it, though sometimes we were very short of it.

The *Telegram* refused to print our newspaper, the *Confederate*, as we used to call it, except with the money laid on the line before the presses started to roll. They would set it up and put it on the presses, but before they would press the button to start the press, they had to have the cash in their hand. There were times when it was a bit difficult, but we managed to come through with it.

Now I haven't said much about the issues. The first referendum campaign began to take a rather ugly turn at an early stage. There began to be a religious division in the electorate, with the Roman Catholics lining up for responsible government and a fair section of the Protestants, but not nearly all of them, lining up for Confederation. Some supported it because the Catholics were against it. The reason for the Roman Catholic opposition to Confederation was quite simply that the Archbishop of St. John's, Archbishop Roach, who was not only Archbishop of St. John's but Metropolitan in Newfoundland as well, you see, came out solidly against Confederation. He campaigned against it quite openly, and made use of the Roman Catholic newspaper, the *Monitor*, as a medium of political propaganda. Now I think if he had not done that we might very well have lost the issue completely, and might have had responsible government win outright on the first ballot paper. It was very close the first time.

During the first campaign, Commission government only got 22,000 votes (responsible government 69,400; Confederation 64,066; Commission government 22,311). The gap between Confederation and responsible government was substantial. We barely got under the wire in the first referendum. When the vote was taken it became quite obvious that the country was divided along religious lines, because nearly every Roman Catholic district returned a large majority for responsible government, in Ferryland something like 90 per cent.

The second major mistake of the anti-confederate people – the Responsible Government League – was to try and capitalize on this further. In the paper that Don Jamieson (Liberal MP for Burin-Burgeo since 1966) and Geoff Sterling ran and owned, the *Sunday Herald*, now called the *Newfoundland Herald*, they boasted about the way the vote had split along religious lines. On page 1 they ran a little item saying that for the first time in history the nuns had left their convents and had gone out to vote.

The day that this came out, I went around to practically every store in St. John's and bought every copy of the *Newfoundland Herald* that was on sale. I brought them back to confederate headquarters, tore off all the front pages, and circled the item in large blue carpenter's marking pencil so that nobody could miss it. Then we got a list of every Orange Lodge officer in Newfoundland and I mailed each one a copy of the front page with no comment.

Gordon Bradley and some other members of the Loyal Orange Lodge Association put their heads together and decided that they would also issue something which subsequently became known as the *Orange Letter*, the details of which I am not familiar with. But there was an appeal launched by the grand lodge, if there is such a thing, to the lesser lodges to prevent Newfoundland from being taken over by a "papist plot": the "papist plot" being responsible government.

The second campaign was very bitter. It approached violence on more than one occasion. I remember the time when we were in St. John's, which was an anti-Confederate town. Although the city itself had a population approximately half Roman Catholic and half Protestant, the area, if you included the environs (known as the "externs"), was predominantly Roman Catholic. It was also, of course, the headquarters for responsible government propaganda. The people fighting the issues were right there.

You had here rabble-rousers like Major Cashin, who were very adept at rousing rabbles.

One little incident that is worth remembering during the second referendum campaign was the placarding of the Protestant churches. Things at this time had reached a point where Smallwood himself was carrying a revolver in his pocket because his life had been threatened several times. He had applied for a permit to carry a revolver for self-defence and though the police refused it, he carried it anyway. We also organized a small goon squad, the leader of which rose subsequently to a very responsible position as head of a government board here for a few years. We had an ex-criminal, or rather a reformed criminal on the squad, who was expert in gutter-fighting techniques. Finally it included a couple of guards from His Majesty's penitentiary who were schooled in dirty fighting, too.

The conclusion to the campaign was a monster rally in the Church Lads Brigade Armoury in St. John's. It was rather a daring thing to do here in St. John's, right in the heart of the opposition to Confederation. That was the night that Major Cashin or somebody brought people down from Blackhead Road to stand outside and boo. We filled the armoury that night right to the doors and we had something like three or four thousand people on the street listening through loudspeakers. It was a series of real rabble-rousing speeches with Smallwood doing the wind-up. Actually, when he walked out through the door, the mob attacked him. He was rescued and was perched on top of a car which drove away through the crowd at about ten miles an hour, knocking people aside as it went. Nobody got hurt fortunately. Smallwood's clothes were torn and his glasses broken, but he was rescued.

This was marvellous propaganda. This was just wonderful. You know, Smallwood had been seriously attacked; his life was in danger. They had tried to lynch him – he was the next best thing to a martyr. I remember his saying to me, "You know, Harold, the one thing we don't have that we really need, is a martyr."

But, back to the business of the church. One Sunday morning, the Protestant people of St. John's arrived at church and discovered that their churches had been pasted up the night before with large posters reading: "CONFEDERATION MEANS BRITISH UNION WITH FRENCH CANADA."

Now there had been a movement for union with the United States – economic union – which was part of the responsible government propaganda. It never amounted to anything for there was no reality in it. One of the strings in the responsible government bow was the promise of economic union with the United States. We had countered by calling union with Canada "British Union," and we made the Union Jack our emblem in the second campaign. The idea was that the responsible government advocates wanted to tear down the Union Jack, whereas we wanted to keep it flying. This was fairly effective propaganda, too. So, we used the slogan BRITISH UNION! The Responsible Government League replied with "Confederation means British Union with French Canada," and posted it all over the Protestant churches. No Roman Catholic churches were touched, and we immediately made the most of this, too. We photographed the things. It was a holy horror; it was almost sacrilege. It was just unbelievable that people would stoop to anything so low. But the Roman Catholics didn't know, and it was not known for fifteen years, that a group of Confederates had had the posters printed, and had gone out and pasted them up on the Protestant churches! If you had said so at the time, nobody would have believed it. What actually happened was that we had a double agent – a member of the Responsible Government League who was also a confederate, and he, with the connivance and help of Phil Forsey, oversaw the production and posting of the slogans by a group of the lunatic fringe from the league.

By the date of the second referendum, we succeeded by these devious and highly suspect methods in getting enough additional Protestants (in addition to the sixty-odd thousand we had in the first referendum), to give us a bare, squeaking majority of 2 per cent. It was two point something by which Confederation beat responsible government, in the second referendum (52.34 per cent). Mackenzie King hesitated about accepting this, but Pickersgill persuaded him to accept the thing and to agree to it for the government of Canada. King's hesitation was genuine. I think he genuinely hesitated about accepting this majority of two point something per cent, until Pickersgill pointed out to him that he had never won an election by as great a majority as this.

Well, is there anything else about the issues? The issues, apart from this religious thing, which was a very effective red herring, were really questions of sentiment or economics. I don't want to insult the people who supported responsible government, but I really think the basic issue was one of sentimentality as opposed to economics. It was perfectly clear – we made it perfectly clear to everybody so there was no doubt about the fact – that we would be better off financially if we were in Confederation, regardless of the terms we could get. The terms didn't really matter. The financial terms were really bookkeeping, between the two governments. But the people of Newfoundland would quite clearly be enormously better off as citizens of Canada than they could ever hope to be as an independent nation of one third of a million people. We made this perfectly clear and almost everybody knew it before the second referendum was finished.

The appeal on the other side was, "We mustn't sell our pine-clad hills." This is what it amounted to, you know, selling Newfoundland down the river. The sentimentality I refer to involved having your own government, or of standing where your father stood, and that kind of thing. I'm not intentionally trying to caricature it, for I respect it. Since Confederation I've gone back to it a lot myself. I look back nostalgically to the sort of country we had and don't have any more. But this is basically what it was. The other issue, aside from this red herring of religion, was, then, the basic one between the sentimental, the desire to preserve Newfoundland's traditions and a separate Newfoundland individuality which is very real, and the cold economics of being financially better off as part of Canada.

DR. ROTHNEY: Thank you. We lived through the referendum campaigns, over again today. It's the first time for most of you, but for Newfoundlanders, it's the second time. We have with us a third panel member, Leslie Harris, Dean of Arts and Science at Memorial University and an historian by profession. I think he was a school teacher in 1949 in Newfoundland. After hearing from the two active participants of the battle, we'll now hear some extemporaneous remarks from a specialist who is also an historian from Newfoundland.

LESLIE HARRIS: I will not dwell at all on the Confederation campaign of 1947–8, since I could add very little to what has already been said by two first-hand witnesses. However, I will say that the issues and the emotions, which have been the twin themes of this discussion, are really inextricably bound up together and always have been. Indeed, it is very difficult to say when an issue ceases to be purely emotional and becomes a practical one, nor are there many practical issues that do not at some time acquire emotional overtones.

Now I think we must look at the 1948–49 campaign for Confederation against a background of the previous campaigns for there are enough similarities of pattern to justify comparison, although the last one resulted in Confederation and the others resulted in its rejection.

The first campaign for Confederation, fought between 1864 and 1869, was very similar in many respects to the campaign of 1948. Let us begin with a parallel that is very close indeed if we accept Major Cashin's charge that Governor Macdonald was sent to Newfoundland in 1946 to foster deliberately the idea of Confederation and that he was largely responsible for its having been brought about.

It is true that on Mr. Horwood's evidence, and in the absence of any positive proof to substantiate Major Cashin's claim, it may be possible to exonerate Governor Macdonald, but certainly there is no proof lacking that in 1864 Governor Musgrave was thoroughly committed to the Confederation of Newfoundland with Canada. The British government had directed Musgrave to foster and encourage the idea of Confederation and to use whatever means he possessed to bring it about. Musgrave was not transferred to Victoria until he was convinced that Newfoundland would enter Confederation. It is clear, then, that the British government at that time was committed to Confederation, as indeed were the Canadians, though perhaps not as enthusiastically. For the British had a particular reason for wishing Newfoundland into the Canadian Union; namely, to be rid of the bother of having to deal with another unprofitable colony which was, moreover, perpetually in trouble of one sort or another and the source of perennial delegations from a House of Assembly that always seemed to have something of which to complain. To be rid of Newfoundland was a consummation devoutly to be wished and here was the golden opportunity.

Despite the fact that Musgrave's successor, Lieutenant-Colonel Hill, was far less active in the cause of Confederation than his predecessor had been, it appears that a resolute legislature could have done in Newfoundland precisely what the legislatures in Nova Scotia and New Brunswick did. When the delegates Shea[1] and Carter[2] came back from the Quebec Conference a majority of the assembly were actually Confederates. But there were some rumblings of public discontent and a cautious Prime Minister, certain that the people would respond favourably, decided to test the question in a general election rather than have it pass through the legislature and be presented to the population as a *fait accompli*.

The general election of 1865 did indeed result in a victory for the Confederates but once again Carter and Shea, perhaps fearing the eruption of sectarian strife, deferred the ultimate decision because the majority was small and they wanted nothing less than an overwhelming majority. This they hoped to achieve in 1869. But the election of that year finally removed

1/Sir Ambrose Shea (1817–1905) entered the House of Assembly in 1848 representing Placentia. In 1864 he attended the Quebec Conference, and gave his support to the idea of Confederation. On his return he was received with hostility by his constituents and in the 1869 election the following verse was sung:
> Remember the day
> When Carter and Shea
> Crossed over the way
> To barter away
> The rights of Terra Nova

2/Sir Frederick Bowker Carter (1819–1900) was the fourth premier of Newfoundland (1865–70; 1874–78). In 1864 he went with Sir Ambrose Shea to the Quebec Conference. Like Shea, he was a convinced Confederate.

the matter from consideration, for there were returned to office a decided majority of anti-Confederates. This remarkable change was largely the result of the rise to political prominence of Charles Fox Bennett, a very able propagandist and a man with much at stake.[3]

Bennett was one of the genuine entrepreneurs in Newfoundland who had looked beyond the fisheries and trade to other means of accumulating wealth. His most recent enterprise had been in the field of mining speculation. He had acquired a vast tract of land which contains most of the copper, lead, and zinc in Newfoundland, concessions to which today are being developed by a number of companies based in the Burlington Peninsula and at Buchans. He had already opened copper mines at Tilt Cove and was a man of wealth and ability.

One of the terms of Confederation which had been suggested at the Quebec Conference was that all natural resources and crown lands should become the property of the federal government which would pay a per capita subsidy to the provinces in exchange for the relinquishment of their rights in these fields. Bennett saw in this proposal the imminent disintegration of his vast mining empire and was determined to prevent its happening.

Hurriedly departing for Britain, he sought assistance from business associates and members of the merchant community with trading interests in Newfoundland. Among them was Walter Grieve, a retired partner of an important St. John's firm, who decided to return to Newfoundland with Bennett and to assist him with his campaign. Having acquired a steamer, one of the first ever used in Newfoundland, Bennett and Grieve carried their propaganda to virtually every village of Newfoundland.

The focus of their campaign was the Irish Roman Catholic community which had always been an extremely important one from the point of view of Newfoundland's political and constitutional advancement. Dr. William Carson's abilities and dedication notwithstanding, his campaign for representative government probably owes more than has been generally acknowledged to the Irish.[4] They alone must be given a major share of the credit for the achievement of responsible government in 1855.

3/Charles Fox Bennett (1793–1883) came to Newfoundland from England as a boy and about 1827 began a brewery. This incursion into business was but the first of many successful ventures. His interest in mining and the natural resources of Newfoundland had been expressed early. His personal connections with England as well as his business interests made him a strong supporter of maintaining close ties with that country. In the election of 1869 his party defeated that of Sir F. B. T. Carter and he became prime minister.
4/William Carson (1770–1843) was born in Kirkcudbrightshire in Scotland, received his medical education in Birmingham, and moved to Newfoundland in 1808. With Patrick Morris he became involved in the agitation for political reform. The introduction of representative government in 1832 was partly a result of his efforts.

The Irish had been a deprived and, to a degree, a persecuted community in Newfoundland as in their homeland. Most of them had come to the island as servants and sharemen. Some had been abandoned there by unscrupulous fishing masters, after their return fares and half their wages had been withheld in compliance with laws designed to compel their return to Europe and to prevent the colonization of Newfoundland. Most were poor, many were indebted, all were denied access to place and privilege, to government jobs, or to any form of official patronage.

By 1832 important developments had occurred. The climate in the British parliament had changed in the direction of reform and Roman Catholic emancipation had become a political reality in Britain and consequently in Newfoundland. Under the leadership of a new and radical bishop, the Right Reverend Michael Anthony Fleming, the Newfoundland Irish were soon prepared to demand those rights and privileges to which, as a majority of the population, they felt themselves entitled. To accomplish this Bishop Fleming had had to replace those priests, trained primarily in continental Europe and who tended to support the establishment, with political activists trained at the Irish seminary at Maynooth.

The change in the composition of the priesthood and the coming of Bishop Fleming were two of the most significant political events in Newfoundland's nineteenth-century history, for under the leadership of Fleming and his priests, the Irish community gave strong popular support to men like William Carson, Patrick Morris,[5] John Kent,[6] John Valentine Nugent,[7] and Robert Parsons[8] in the struggle for representative government, and that having been won, for liberal control of the Assembly.

The task of taking complete command of the Assembly was accomplished in the 1836 election. The next battle was for responsible government and this was won in 1855. On this occasion the leader was an Irish Catholic, Phillip Francis Little, who had come to Newfoundland from Prince Edward Island.[9] Again the Church and the priesthood, now under

5/Patrick Morris (1789–1849) came to Newfoundland from Waterford in Ireland in 1800 and led, together with William Carson, the agitation for representative government which was attained in 1832. In 1836 he was elected to the Assembly representing St. John's. In 1840 he was appointed to the Executive Council.
6/John Kent (1805–72) was born in Ireland but came to Newfoundland at an early age. He was actively involved in the agitation for reform prior to 1832 and was elected to the first Assembly. He became prime minister in 1858 but was dismissed from office by Governor Bannerman in 1861.
7/John Valentine Nugent was an Irish schoolmaster who, allegedly, was forced to flee Ireland because of his violence in politics. In Newfoundland he became an active member of the Liberal movement and was elected on several occasions to the Assembly. His legal training and his scholarship were valuable assets to his party.
8/Robert J. Parsons was the editor of the *Patriot*, a newspaper that usually supported Liberal views, and which was quite influential in mid-nineteenth-century St. John's.
9/Philip Francis Little (1824–97). Mr. Little arrived in Newfoundland in 1844 and

the direction of Bishop Mullock, gave outstanding support to the cause which was opposed by the Anglican establishment of Church and State, led by Hugh Hoyles[10] and Bishop Field, as well as by a substantial segment of the merchant community.

Having acquired political power, the Irish were soon able to acquire a measure of economic control as well. They were particularly successful in getting a share of government jobs and in controlling a share of patronage proportionate to their numerical strength in relation to the total population.

In any case, the Irish rightfully felt that a self-governing Newfoundland was predominantly their achievement. This they wished to preserve, not only for sentimental reasons, but because they feared that in a larger Canadian community their hard won equality would be lost, for they would be grossly outnumbered by both Anglo-Saxons and French. The Church, too, may well have feared the loss of separate schools, to say nothing of domination by French ecclesiastics.

In was clear, therefore, that Bennett's propaganda would fall on fertile ground. That he was aware of this is evident from the manner in which he used the very word "Union" to arouse Irish antipathy to the idea of Confederation. Bennett gave "Union" the connotation that it has in the Anglo-Irish context. He declaimed over and over again that here was but one more example of the perennial British passion for subjugating the Irish to their will and for destroying Irish independence. Newfoundland's union with Canada, he asserted, was another scheme which could be directly equated with Ireland's union with Britain.

There were, of course, other arguments. Bennett maintained that Confederation would mean increased taxation. This was an argument designed primarily to appeal to the more affluent section of Newfoundland society. For the tax structure of Newfoundland was primarily a system of indirect taxation, the burden of which fell most heavily upon the fishermen and upon craftsmen and tradesmen associated with fish production.

Again, Bennett easily demolished two arguments that were virtually irrefutable in the mainland context. He pointed out, quite properly, that railway connections, which were so important to the other colonies, meant little to Newfoundland since she was separated from Nova Scotia by one

in 1850 entered public life, soon becoming a leader of the Liberal party. In 1855 he became the first prime minister of Newfoundland. In 1866 at the age of forty-two he retired and moved to Ireland.

10/Sir Hugh William Hoyles (1815–88) began his career as a lawyer in 1836. Ten years later he became solicitor to the House of Assembly and in 1848 was elected as a Conservative representative for the Fortune district. In 1861 he became prime minister and held the position for four years. In 1865 he became chief justice of Newfoundland and held the post until his retirement in 1880. He was the first native-born prime minister and the first native-born chief justice.

hundred miles of water. And he declaimed with passion that while Canadians, New Brunswickers, and Nova Scotians might wish to unite to combat potential American aggression, Newfoundland had no quarrel with the United States, nor any desire to have her youth snatched from their homes to serve as cannon fodder in a war which was of no concern to them.

The combination of common sense and strong emotionalism was a powerful one. The proferred terms of union were certainly not very attractive but even had they been much more so they would hardly have affected the issues at that particular time. The Confederates lacked a strong leader; the anti-Confederates had a leader. The Roman Catholic population of Newfoundland, almost to a man and Shea notwithstanding, opposed Confederation.[11] And since they were concentrated in specific electoral districts they had absolute control of a substantial portion of the Assembly. Under those circumstances a decision by general election was virtually certain to be a decision against Confederation. Thus for nearly twenty years the idea of union lay dormant.

Then in the 1880's the Newfoundland government, driven by a desperate financial problem, turned to Ottawa to seek Sir Charles Tupper's help. Tupper was not very encouraging. In any event, the next season in Newfoundland happened to be very good, with good weather, good fishing, and good markets. The difficulties were soon forgotten but the mere fact that an approach to Ottawa had been made was sufficient to assist materially in bringing about the subsequent defeat of the government.

The next Confederation campaign of any consequence was in 1895. This time there were no really outstanding leaders on either side and the most noteworthy thing about the campaign is the anti-Confederate song which is still sung from time to time.[12] The terms offered by Bowell were so parsimonious that no government could have considered them for a moment even though Newfoundland, still reeling from the Great Fire of

11/It should be noted that this does not include the Catholic population of the St. George's-Port au Port area of Newfoundland's west coast. For they, because they lived on the "French Shore," had not participated in the struggles of the east coast community for political reform nor, indeed, had they been part of the electorate until late in the nineteenth century. Thus they had none of the sentimental attachment to responsible government exhibited by their co-religionists on the east coast. Their contacts had, indeed, been closer with Canada than with St. John's. This may explain why, in 1948, theirs was the only Roman Catholic district to defy the position of the Church and to vote for Confederation.

12/The chorus is as follows:
Hurrah for our own native isle, Newfoundland
No stranger will hold one inch of her strand
Her face turns to Britain, her back to the Gulf
Come near at your peril, Canadian Wolf.

1892 and the Bank Crash of 1894, was in a desperate financial situation.

Again the electorate left no doubt as to where it stood and again there was clear evidence that the Irish part of Newfoundland's population was solidly anti-Confederate. Moreover, in the twenty years preceding 1895 many Newfoundlanders had developed a strong sense of anti-Canadianism.

There is not time to trace this development from its genesis but we may take the Bait Act of 1886 as a case in point. The Newfoundland legislature realized that their great advantage over foreign competitors on the off-shore fishing grounds was that the essential bait fish had to be taken in coastal waters. They therefore passed legislation forbidding the sale of bait to foreigners. Although this was aimed primarily at the French, Canada nevertheless protested vociferously, in part because she feared the consequences for her own fishery, but more particularly because she objected to the implication that Newfoundland could legislate in a field impinging upon Empire foreign policy which was jealously controlled by Britain.

Prompted by Canada, the British government disallowed the legislation. The following year, 1887, was the year of the first imperial conference. The Newfoundland prime minister attended the conference and carried with him to London a new Bait Act, hoping that he could persuade the other dominions to support him in preventing its disallowance. In fact only Canada failed to support him and in the event the Act was allowed despite Canada's objection.

During the next twenty years Newfoundland sought from the United States an agreement which would allow the free admission of Newfoundland fish into the American market in exchange for certain reciprocal rights for Americans to fish in Newfoundland waters. The United States on a number of occasions was agreeable to such an arrangement; but on every such occasion the vigorous opposition of the Canadian government was brought to bear upon Great Britain with the object of preventing the approval of any such agreement which did not also include Canada. The most important and significant incident of this type was the one known as the Bond-Blaine Treaty, which was actually signed by the American secretary of state and the Newfoundland prime minister but which was not ratified, mainly because of Canadian objections.[13]

13/Sir Robert Bond (1857–1927) was a member of the House of Assembly for thirty years, never suffering personal electoral defeat. Having served as Speaker of the House, colonial secretary, and leader of the opposition, he became prime minister in 1900 and continued in that office until 1909. In 1913 he combined with William Coaker in an attempt to defeat Sir E. P. Morris' People's party. This attempt failing, he retired from public life in 1914.

These incidents were widely reported and contributed to a positive anti-Canadianism. Moreover, Newfoundlanders generally knew little of Canada. There were certain trading connections and the south and west coasts of Newfoundland were familiar with the Maritime provinces, but in general Canada was a *terra incognita* and Canadians were people who were obsessed with the idea of thwarting our legitimate aspirations *vis-à-vis* the United States.

By 1948 the attitude towards Canada had changed remarkably, in part as a consequence of the Second World War, which had brought many Canadians to Newfoundland, and in part because of improved communications including a Trans-Canada Airlines service to Newfoundland. Canada's attitude towards Newfoundland had also changed. There is a perennial fiction, which runs as a theme through much of the history written in Newfoundland, that this island occupies a remarkably valuable strategic position in military and naval terms. In fact it was not until the Second World War that this fiction came to bear a resemblance to fact. By 1940 Newfoundland's unique geographical position mid-way between the principal east coast centres of American population and the principal centres of European population, and directly adjacent to the principal North Atlantic shipping centres, gave her a large importance as a terminus for undersea cables, as a base for airplanes whether employed in conveying trans-Atlantic cargoes or as a refuelling stop for trans-Atlantic flights, later on as a radar site, then as a site for strategic air command bases, and ultimately as a potential missile site. Although her importance as a military base has decreased sharply with the development of inter-continental ballistic missiles, the Confederation campaign came about when Newfoundland was still strategically significant.

For this reason Canada was much more interested in bringing Newfoundland into Confederation in 1948 than she had been at any previous time. John A. Macdonald had not been much concerned about Newfoundland. He would have liked to round out Canadian territory, but in any case he believed that within a few years Newfoundland would fall "like a ripe plum" into the Canadian lap. Tupper was only mildly interested in the 1880's and Bowell was extremely cool to the idea in 1895. Now, in 1948, some responsible Canadians were interested and some were positively eager to bring union to a consummation.

The British government had not changed its position; it reacted in precisely the same way as it had in 1864. In that year it had sent a Confederate governor to Newfoundland, with instructions to use all the influence at his command to aid the cause of Confederation. In 1946 it again appointed a governor who, at least according to Major Cashin's story, was a confederate. More significantly, it overruled the decision of the National Convention and placed Confederation on the ballot paper. This may have been a decision based solely on the democratic principle that Newfoundlanders should be permitted to say for themselves what they wanted. But it certainly suggests an eagerness on Britain's part to be rid of what they may have come to consider an incubus.

Prior to the National Convention, Newfoundlanders themselves were completely apathetic. I think that Major Cashin's story about the public wharf in Ferryland is apropos. People do want a chicken in every pot if they can get one, and a wharf in every harbour, and a breakwater on every point. If they can get these things without paying too dearly for them, they are reasonably content. In general they are more likely to be moved to political action by local rather than by national issues.

Under the Commission government, dictatorial as it was, prosperity reigned supreme, thanks to the American bases, the effects of the war, and the unprecedented high prices paid for Newfoundland's basic products. While the boom continued the people were content to ignore the fact that they were not governing themselves. Indeed, until Major Cashin began his series of radio talks, very few people even considered that they were living under a dictatorship. Even the Major's fiery oratory roused but a few for when the National Convention was elected, only 20 per cent of the electorate turned out to vote.

The appearance of Premier Smallwood on the scene made a difference. He did for the Confederate movement in 1947–48 what Charles Fox-Bennett did for the anti-Confederate movement in 1869. Many of the issues were still the same, particularly as far as the Irish were concerned. The Canadian government's attitude had changed somewhat, but this did not particularly influence the decision except that it gave the Confederates access to campaign funds they would not otherwise have had. I am not generally a subscriber to the "great man" theory of history, but I believe that this is one instance in which social forces were created and events shaped to meet the desires of one man.

15
Les Archives et le régionalisme

BERNARD WEILBRENNER

LE RÉGIONALISME, c'est un individualisme transposé au niveau de la collectivité. C'est aussi l'ensemble des mœurs, des usages, des coutumes, de la culture d'un milieu limité à une région. C'est enfin le caractère distinctif qui a été imprimé par ce milieu sur les objets et les êtres qui en sont sortis.

LES ARCHIVES RÉGIONALES ET LE PRINCIPE DE LA TERRITORIALITÉ

Pour les archives, un certain régionalisme est normal, voire essentiel. Le principe de la territorialité des archives, qui est généralement reconnu, prévoit justement que les archives, reflet et émanation d'un territoire donné, appartiendront, de droit à la société qui leur a donné naissance, et seront conservées là où elles ont été créés.

Ce principe a donné lieu, surtout ces dernières années, à de vastes programmes de microfilmage : les pays colonisateurs, refusant la plupart du temps de remettre aux anciennes colonies les archives qui les concernaient, ont offert à la place des copies sur microfilms. Tous les pays nouvellement indépendants procèdent, grâce aux photocopies, au repatriement de leurs trésors nationaux que constituent leurs archives. Plusieurs changements de frontières ont aussi donné lieu, en Europe, à des transferts d'archives.

La situation n'est pas tellement différente au Canada, où les dépôts canadiens ont tenté et tentent encore de rétablir l'intégrité de leurs archives publiques par des microfilms de complément photographiés dans les anciennes métropoles : Londres ou Paris.

Ce qui est vrai au niveau des pays l'est aussi au niveau des états qui font parti d'ensembles plus vastes, Union ou Confédération. Les Etats-Unis rassemblent et publient dans leur *Territorial Papers* les documents concernant les Etats américains en gestation. Les Etats confédérés du Canada demandent aux Archives fédérales les archives qui les concernent : pour le Québec ou l'Ontario, ce sont les dossiers crées sous le gouvernement de l'ancienne province de Québec, du Haut et du Bas-Canada et de l'Union. Dans le cas des provinces de l'Ouest, ce sont les dossiers concernant l'administration des terres publiques que le gouvernement fédéral s'était réservée pour plusieurs années. Pour Terre-Neuve, c'est plutôt du côté de la Grande-Bretagne que l'on se tourne, le lien colonial s'y étant maintenu jusqu'à ces dernières années.

Le régionalisme devient vraiment un problème à l'intérieur même des états. Il est alors lié de très près au système administratif existant. Ce problème est sensiblement le même dans toutes les provinces canadiennes. Je me référerai surtout au Québec à titre d'exemple, mais sans doute mes observations pourront-elles être analogues sinon identiques à celles que l'on pourrait faire pour une autre partie, ou région, du pays.

Au Québec, les bureaux d'enregistrement des transactions immobilières sont répartis sur tout le territoire. Ils sont situés au cœur de la région qu'ils desservent, et le citoyen peut facilement aller consulter les registres qui concernent sa localité. Les archives des municipalités et des commissions scolaires locales ou régionales sont, de la même façon, conservées au centre administratif de la municipalité ou de la commission scolaire qui crée ces archives.

Les archives judiciaires sont conservées dans les quelque trente palais de justice d'autant de districts judiciaires. Le principe de la territorialité des archives y est scrupuleusement observé. Si un nouveau district est créé, on y verse les archives concernat la région concernée.

Le système pour les greffes des notaires et pour les archives de l'état civil est un peu plus compliqué. Les notaires conservent dans leur étude les minutes qu'ils rédigent. Mais cinquante ans après leur retraite, leur greffe doit être déposé aux archives judicaires du district dans lequel ils ont exercé leur profession.

Les registres des baptêmes, mariages et sépultures sont faits en double dans les paroisses. Le double est envoyé, chaque année, aux archives judiciaires du district. En plus, les paroisses préparent, depuis 1926, des rapports périodiques qu'ils envoient au Service de démographie du Québec, à Québec. Les hôpitaux, les municipalités, les médecins, sont aussi appelés à faire des rapports aux archives judiciaires et au Service de démographie, notamment pour les personnes ne pratiquant pas de religion reconnue.

Quant aux autres services administratifs du gouvernement du Québec, la situation est plus confuse. Il existe de fortes tendances vers une administration décentralisée. Le Ministère du commerce et de l'industrie a défini une dizaine de zones économiques, avec leur chef-lieu, mais le regroupement de tous les services administratifs du gouvernement suivant ces frontières est loin d'être réalisé. Chaque ministère découpe la carte du Québec suivant ses désirs et choisit des centres administratifs suivant ses besoins. Et ces centres administratifs ont fort peu d'autonomie, de sorte que leurs archives sont de peu d'intérêt. D'ailleurs, l'utilisation de plus en plus poussée des appareils électroniques, exige, au nom de l'efficacité, une concentration de plus en plus grande des informations et des processus administratifs : c'est particulièrement vrai dans le domaine des allocations sociales, dans celui des permis et licences, même dans celui de la santé et de l'éducation. La cybernétique devient un puissant facteur de centralisation administrative. Comme aussi la volonté d'uniformisation. Au niveau régional et local, on parle plus volontiers d'animation sociale ou d'enquêtes sociologiques, et de promotion des corps intermédiaires.

LES ARCHIVES ET L'ESPRIT RÉGIONALISTE

Nous avons peut-être abordé la question du régionalisme sous un aspect un peu trop limité. Voyons maintenant l'esprit qui a présidé à la fondation et au développement des archives et qui anime encore celles-ci.

Nous étudierons donc les dépôts qui ont été créés dans le but avoué de conserver des documents pour des fins de recherche plutôt que pour des fins administratives, même si la distinction est parfois subtile entre les dépôts qui ont des archives surtout utiles à l'administration et ceux dont les documents sont surtout utiles à la recherche. Nous examinerons brièvement les archives du gouvernement fédéral et des gouvernements provinciaux, les archives des universités, et les archives des sociétés historiques.

Les Archives fédérales furent créées en 1872. Déjà, en 1857, la Nouvelle-Ecosse avait ses propres archives. Mais si les Archives fédérales furent longues à devenir réalité, il serait injuste de ne pas faire état de tous les efforts qui avaient précédé leur création. Dès les années 1700, l'intendant de la Nouvelle-France avait songé à ériger un édifice pour les archives. Les instructions royales prévoyaient la préservation des dossiers administratifs du gouvernement, et les principales séries ont été préservées, en dépit des incendies et autres catastrophes, depuis 1663. Sous le régime militaire, le conquérant, soucieux de maintenir les prérogatives anciennes de la couronne française au profit de l'anglaise, exigèrent le retour au gouvernement des anciennes archives publiques. Peu de temps avant l'acte constitutionnel de 1791, une enquête générale sur les archives avait eu lieu. En 1824, la Quebec Literary and Historical Society était fondée, à Québec, et par la suite, le Parlement s'intéressa aux archives historiques et se tourna très tôt vers la France et l'Angleterre pour obtenir des copies de la correspondance des gouverneurs, des récits de voyages etc... Un effort considérable sera fait, avec l'aide des Etats-Unis, de la Société Historique de l'Etat de New York notamment. L'abolition de la tenure seigneuriale, en 1854, provoquera un intérêt grandissant pour les archives, à la fois pour leur valeur légale et financière, et pour leur intérêt historique. Quand Louis Hyppolite Lafontaine abandonne la politique, il travaille à la cour seigneuriale, et commence des travaux historiques sur les institutions judiciaires du Canada.

C'est donc une longue préparation qui amène finalement la création d'une institution qui s'appellera le Bureau des Archives en 1872. Début bien modeste, avec un archiviste qui sera seul pour dix ans. Mais aussi, début surprenant par un aspect : ces archives publiques ne s'occuperont pas, ou si peu, des archives publiques du pays : on y assemblera plutôt des copies de complément, de source privée, ou de gouvernements étrangers : France et Angleterre. L'inspiration de la Quebec Literary and Historical Society semble avoir été acceptée d'emblée par les Archives du Canada. Ce ne sera qu'en 1903 que les archives publiques, jusque-là sous le contrôle du « Keeper of the records » au Secrétariat du Canada, passeront aux Archives sous l'autorité de l'archiviste fédéral.

C'est vers les années 1912 que l'on voit que les Archives du Canada s'inspirent des techniques et des principes internationaux de classement d'archives, grâce à l'influence d'un Canado-Americain, O. W. Parker, qui avait son apprentissage sous la direction de Waldo Leland, sous les auspices de la Carnegie Foundation.

C'est plutôt sous l'influence de l'Angleterre que l'on veut mettre en place les structures d'un Public Record Office en 1914. Mais en 1956, c'est plutôt sous l'influence américaine que l'on érigera un dépôt intermédiaire.

L'originalité des Archives publiques du Canada, qui différencie cette institution d'organismes similaires en France et aux Etats-Unis, c'est qu'elles acceptent aussi bien les archives publiques du Canada que les archives privées et les copies d'autres dépôts publiques de France, d'Angleterre et d'ailleurs : plusieurs raisons peuvent être évoquées ici : (1) l'origine du dépôt, alors que ses seules archives étaient d'origine privée ou étrangère ; (2) la création tardive, aux Etats-Unis, d'archives nationales ; (3) l'absence d'une bibliothèque nationale. Un autre aspect intéressant, c'est que, dès les débuts, on essaie de satisfaire toutes les régions du pays. On tente de grouper à Ottawa les documents qui intéressent l'Ouest, le centre, les Maritimes. On a même pendant un certain temps des bureaux régionaux et des dépisteurs qui parcourent le pays à la recherche des documents.

Pendant ce temps, les provinces s'occupaient un peu de leurs archives. Le Québec en particulier mettait ses documents à la disposition du public en les publiant. C'est dans le premier quart du xxe siècle que les archives obtiennent un peu d'autonomie : c'est sans doute sous l'influence du premier congrès international des bibliothèques et des archives, en 1908, de la parution de volumes sur les archives, et aussi parce que la documentation commençait à créer des problèmes d'espace de rangement dans les ministères.

Au Manitoba, dès 1886, on remettait les archives à la bibliothèque parlementaire. L'Ontario publie des rapports sur les archives â partir de 1903. La Colombie Britannique consacre elle aussi l'unité de la bibliothèque et des archives de 1908. Au Québec, dès 1917, de nombreux inventaires sont publiés ; les archives sont créées en 1920 ; elles logées dans un édifice séparé en 1931.

C'était, pour les provinces comme pour le fédéral, un intérêt pour les documents « historiques » de toute provenance qui se manifestait. Il faudra presque attendre les années cinquante pour voir un intérêt sérieux se manifester pour les archives administratives en tant que telles.

Dans les universités et les sociétés historiques, l'intérêt pour les archives était assez ancien, à preuve les riches collections amassées par le Séminaire de Québec et par la Quebec Literary and Historical Society. Mais dans bien des cas, il s'agissait d'un intérêt pour les vieilles choses, intérêt d'antiquaire plutôt que d'historien. De nos jours, les universités s'intéressent plutôt à devenir des centres de recherche et de documentation, tandis que les Sociétés historiques ont un intérêt marqué pour l'histoire locale.

Quelle a été l'influence de l'esprit régionaliste dans tout ce développement des archives ? Il est certain que l'un des objectifs était la conservation des documents racontant l'histoire d'une région du pays, mais cette histoire n'était pas conçue comme restreinte. On la considérait très tôt à l'échelle du continent, et partie de l'histoire de l'occident. Voyons par exemple ce que dit Douglas Brymner en 1889 devant l'American Historical Association (voir *Rapport des Archives du Canada, 1889*) : « My ambition aims at the establishment of a great storehouse of the history of the colony and colonists in their political, ecclesiastical, industrial, domestic, in a word, in every aspect of their lives as communities... Ottawa might become on this continent the Mecca to which historical investigators would turn their eyes and direct their steps. » La même année, l'*Atlantic Monthly* décrivait les archives du Canada « unrivaled on the Continent for materials in Western History. »

Nous pourrions mentionner aussi que durant les années trente, des sociétés historiques furent créées en France et en Angleterre dans le but de facilitier la communication des archives privées relatives au Canada.

A noter aussi que c'est sur l'initiative et avec de fortes subventions du gouvernement canadien que fut organisée à Paris, en 1929, une très importante exposition sur les anciennes colonies françaises, où les documents canadiens dominaient mais une place honorable était faite à ceux de la Nouvelle-Angleterre, de la Louisianne, des Antilles, et de la Floride.

Quand l'intérêt commença à se dessiner pour l'histoire économique au Canada, les Archives du Canada jouèrent un rôle important, grâce aux publications d'Adam Shortt, et de A. R. M. Lower. Même si les Archives publiques du Canada jugèrent devoir fixer des limites à leur politique d'acquisition, ce ne fut jamais, je crois, dans un dessein inspiré par le régionalisme.

Du côte des archives provinciales, il y a naturellement des soucis analogues aux archives fédérales. L'Ontario notamment est à la recherche de documents sur tout son territoire. Mais le manque de dynamisme a peut-être été la principale raison qui a pu faire qualifier de régional l'esprit qui les animait. Comme je l'indiquait au début, les archives provinciales ont déjà fort à faire à rétablir l'intégrité de leurs archives. Le choix des archives administratives à conserver absorbera bientôt beaucoup de leur énergie. Certaines tentatives de centralisation se manifestent également.

Du côté des archives universitaires, plusieurs tendances se font jour. On ne sera pas nécessairement collectionneur d'archives historiques. Les documents littéraires, parce que peu recherchés par les autres dépôts, forment parfois l'essentiel de ces archives. Ce sont plutôt des archives qui alimenteront un centre de recherches. Le régionalisme est, ici, un aspect secondaire, même si les universités jouent un rôle de plus en plus important dans l'économie générale des archives.

Nous voici enfin aux archives des sociétés historiques. La plupart d'entre elles sont carrément d'esprit régional. Les documents concernant la région sont d'importance capitale pour elles, les autres, négligeables.

Mais là encore, si l'on peu déplorer un intérêt trop marqué pour l'histoire anecdotique, on sent de plus en plus un énlargissement, dans les sociétés les plus actives, des intérêts et de la documentation : à l'histoire religieuse, politique, au peuplement et à la généalogie, viennent s'ajouter des préoccupations côté social, économique, géographique, linguistique, etc. En général donc, on peut dire que les archives, malgré la réputation qu'elles ont peut-être, ne souffrent pas outre mesure d'esprit régionaliste.

LES ARCHIVES RÉGIONALES FACE À LA CENTRALISATION

Quel doit être le rôle de archives dans le contexte du régionalisme ? Les archives doivent être au service de la collectivité, au service de la recherche. Leur premier devoir est-il envers les gens de la région ?

Il faut, je crois, aborder cette question du point de vue d'un large humanisme, et d'une façon analogue à l'histoire. Ce serait une digression que de vouloir discuter du problème de l'histoire, de l'histoire locale, régionale ou nationale, et de leur orientation, leur valeur respective. Mais vous serez peut-être d'accord pour accepter comme base de discussion que l'intérêt premier de l'histoire, c'est la compréhension de l'homme à travers les situations concrètes où il a été placé. Cependant, l'histoire, légitimement, peut donner, aux peuples et aux gouvernements, les grandes lignes d'une politique, une sagesse, une expérience collective. L'histoire peut être utilisée pour encourager un sens de solidarité, un nationalisme, qui est sain et un antidote utile contre un individualisme extrême : que l'histoire est l'école principale de l'homme, en tant qu'être essentiellement politique et social.

Ainsi peut-il en être des archives. Les archives nationales doivent sans doute encourager le sentiment de fierté des habitants du pays, non pas dans un contexte de supériorité, mais dans un esprit de fraternité humaine. Les archives nationales doivent être au service de l'Etat dans la mesure où celui-ci se préoccupe des valeurs humaines qu'elles conservent. Mais elles doivent peut-être plus encore être au service désintéressé de la recherche, au Canada, de l'homme *canadien*, une variété de l'homme tout court. Les archives provinciales, similairement, sont au service de l'Etat, et de la recherche, Les archives régionales ont la même responsabilité à l'échelle locale.

Mais quel est l'avenir des archives régionales ? La recherche connaît de moins en moins de frontières. Les efforts se portent de plus en plus sur des études qui utilisent des méthodes quantitatives plutôt que qualitatives d'examen. L'historien traditionnel n'est plus le seul chercheur à fréquenter les archives : sociologues, économistes, démographes, politicologues se disputent la matière brute que constituent les archives.

Les archives régionales ont une double raison d'être : (1) les chercheurs, les étudiants peuvent consulter *sur place* des documents ; (2) ces documents qui leur sont plus facilement compréhensibles, parce qu'ils se rapportent à des objets, à des personnes et à des lieux qui leur sont familiers : l'empathie, qui est au cœur de la connaissance historique, comme l'a admirablement démontré le professeur Irenée Marrou (*De la connaissance historique*) est alors plus pénétrante, plus complète.

Mais les archives provinciales ou nationales présentent aux chercheurs des ensembles plus vastes, plus diversifiés, nécessaires à la recherche à un plus large niveau et situés plus centralement. Ne devrait-on pas centraliser les archives complètement ? Le rêve du chercheur pourrait s'y réaliser : un centre bien équipé où se trouveraient réunies toutes les sources qu'il désirerait consulter ?

Mais cette centralisation pourrait devenir excessive. A une récente conférence internationale d'archivistes, un archiviste disait, avec une pointe d'humour, que la prolifération des microfilms allait enlever beaucoup de charme aux recherches : il avait pour sa part trouvé grand profit et grande joie à sa randonnée à travers l'Europe à la recherche de ses sources.

Si les microfilms allaient se multipliant à un rythme accéléré, c'en serait bientôt fini de ces voyages : chaque chercheur serait enchaîné à son pupitre où on lui apporterait tous les documents. L'histoire, et l'on pourrait dire la même chose de toutes les sciences de l'homme, l'histoire est tout autant, sinon plus, un art qu'une science, et l'élément humain y est de première importance. La visite d'une région peut être un complément essentiel à l'étude des documents qui y ont été produits. L'existence des archives régionales s'en trouve justifiée.

A vrai dire, le problème peut, de nos jours, être presque résolu grâce aux méthodes relativement peu dispendieuses de copie, comme le microfilm. Tous les documents régionaux, sauf ceux d'un intérêt plutôt local, peuvent être réunis sous forme de copies, dans un lieu central, sans en déposséder les archives locales. Et les archives régionales peuvent élargir leur champs d'intérêt en faisant copier soit dans un dépôt central, soit dans un dépôt régional voisin, les documents qui permettent d'établir avec ceux qu'elles ont en leur possession des comparaisons utiles.

Là où les archives régionales ne sont plus justifiées, c'est là où elles ne peuvent être maintenues et communiquées d'une façon convenable, là où une multitude d'efforts sont dépensés inutilement pour satisfaire la vanité de quelques coteries. La création d'un nombre raisonnable de dépôts régionaux bien équippés et bien administrés dans les diverses régions des provinces et du pays sera un signe de santé. J'y vois pour ma part une condition presque indispensable à une revitalisation de l'enseignement de l'histoire.

Le régionalisme, souvent, est considéré un terme péjoratif. Il n'est pas nécessaire qu'il en soit ainsi. C'est, dit-on, la vertu du Canada que d'accepter la diversité. Le régionalisme est l'un des éléments de cette diversité. Il sera une richesse s'il ne se replie pas sur lui-même, s'il n'est pas teinté de xénophobie, s'il met au sommet de ses préoccupations l'humain, même s'il conserve une légitime affection pour les particularités de son coin de pays.

16

Canada and Canadian History
as Viewed from the United Kingdom

GERALD S. GRAHAM

IT HAS BEEN suggested that as a Canadian living in England I could address myself to this hazardous subject with the advantage of perspective. This may be true. Despite lack of constant, intimate contact there are some advantages in viewing the Canadian or North American scene across a large ocean. One may conceivably see problems in starker outline than the local inhabitants who live with them. On the other hand, the outside observer runs the grave risk of misunderstanding them, and an even greater risk if he begins to suggest solutions. Yet, when I inquired of colleagues in Canada as to ways and means of dealing with "Canada and Canadian History as Viewed from the United Kingdom," they replied almost to a man: Seminars wilt under the assault of clichés, but come to life under the needle.

The art of needling Canadians, needless to say, is an old one. Take the famous Samuel Butler, who some time in the 1880's visited Montreal, and wrote a poem, in which each verse concluded: "Oh God, Oh Montreal." It appears that the poem was written in some anguish after the Montreal Museum of Art had put a fig leaf on the statue of a renowned Greek discus thrower. Now that the Canadian government has put a maple leaf on the national flag in an effort to safeguard national chastity, I have no doubt Butler, were he alive today, would write with equal fervour: "Oh God, Oh Ott-a-wa."

The poets were once the most provocative wielders of irony. When Rupert Brooke visited Canada shortly before World War I he was unimpressed. "It is an empty land," he wrote in *Letters from America*, "To love the country here ... is like embracing a wraith." In the past decade, however, such erotic symbolism has tended to be replaced by the garish realism of the satirist. The recent flood of television interviews, books, articles, and reviews on Canada has outmoded the sharpest poetic barbs, and made clichés of traditional pin-pricks. In the colour supplement of *The Observer* of June 25, 1967, Ronald Bryden described his school life in the forties, somewhere near Niagara Falls. Canadian sex, he learned, was largely a summer activity. "In winter you built yourself up, with milk, chocolate bars and sport ... You tended your body with showers, liniment and cream ... Then you looked forward to summer, and the annual exodus to the 'cottage' in the wooded lakeland of northern Ontario." There, in the long warm sub-Arctic twilights, you lay in wait for the daughters of adjacent cottagers or the inmates of girls' summer camps, fresh from the superior boarding schools in Toronto.

Unhappily I cannot speak of my youth in the twenties with equal authority. My generation was too shy. An earlier generation may have been even more inhibited, but less cynical and less self-absorbed. "The really remarkable thing about Canada," wrote Lord Robert Cecil to Hugh Cecil in October 1905, "is the incompetence of the Canadians. There they have been for 150 years in a country of exceptional richness, and look how little they've done with it ... the English out here seem to be for the most part purely money-makers, and the rest idolators of Empire."[1]

But the species of "Empire idolator" is now almost extinct, and in retrospect fire-breathing Toronto imperialists and Montreal railway barons seem positively benevolent compared with the new breed of devouring carnivora infiltrating over the border. "The American weapons," wrote Nicholas Monsarrat in June 1967, "are hard cash, commercial skills, raw energy and the printed and spoken word. Thus armed, they are steadily digging up and eating Canada, with good-humoured relish and total appetite. They are everywhere as thick as starlings – starlings with scoop-shaped claws and crops to match ... Bright-eyed and bushy-tailed, they set a pace which has all other competitors outrun. They make British salesmen look like limping pedlars. They make Canadians feel like lodgers ... "[2]

1/Balfour Papers, deposited at Whittingehame, East Lothian.
2/*Sunday Telegram*, June 25, 1967.

Some twenty years ago, fear of engulfment by monolithic American culture was principally responsible for the appointment of a Royal Commission on National Development in the Arts, Letters and Sciences, with Mr. Vincent Massey as Chairman. This commission reported that the failure of determined attempts to evolve distinct cultural interests could be largely explained by the propinquity of an over-powering neighbour. The corrosive effects of American radio, television, magazine journalism, and of industrial penetration and influence – all these – induced a distorted sense of values that was inherent in a society rich in material things. The suggestion is, of course, that Canadian culture, in becoming increasingly North American, has become less urbane, less British. But may I remind you that the day of gracious learning, the age of contemplative learning, is passing away even in Britain, under the assault of acquisitive multitudes, which since World War II have filled the expanding network of secondary schools. The unhurried days of the widely read and luxuriating don are over. In Britain, as in Canada, university teachers are today becoming involved in public life to a degree unthinkable to a scholar at the beginning of this century. I quote from an editorial in *The Times Literary Supplement* of May 18, 1967: "Dons seem to have thoroughly outlived their musty, otherworldly reputation of some years ago. No longer are they popularly viewed as absent-minded ancients dragging out their arid, lengthy lives amid the loaded shelves, the port, the slim girl students' ankles. They are now among the most courted bastions of our weekend culture. They are fun."

But the public betrayal of a traditional calling is by no means confined to the "lively young don." Middle-aged professors in British universities work part-time for departments in Whitehall, they advise foreign governments, and administer social welfare schemes for the benefit of the nation. They act as consultants to industry, prescribe for investment trusts, and sit on boards concerned with cultural activities such as the British Council. They broadcast, and the more quick-witted are televised in discussion and debate. And according to *The Times Literary Supplement*, "those whose memorable names disguise grey, furrowed faces or contralto stutters can always compensate with extra column inches in the weeklies."

Perhaps the greatest single change in university life within the last half century has been the enormous amount of specialized research accomplished by these uncobwebbed academics in the arts as well as in the sciences; and this development is probably as true of Canada and the United States as of Britain. Forty or so years ago the older universities would have no part in turning the civilized pursuit of knowledge by study and research into a comprehensive factory system geared to produce worker-experts in specialist fields. Thanks to the growing prestige of science, today many universities have come to accept the originally German notion that a university is "above all a workshop of scientific method."

This trend has been encouraged in the last twenty years or so by the social revolution. Canada has now sixty-three universities – more than any other country in the Commonwealth, and as far as the liberal arts are concerned, perhaps thirty more than are necessary; India comes next with thirty-five, Britain third with thirty-four. (I have heard very recently that aggrandized technical colleges have brought the British total to forty-three.) The consequent increase in the number of MA and PHD candidates within these proliferating universities has not only accelerated competition for fields of research, it has inevitably affected the purity of academic purpose. With the decline of the old class of teacher-scholar, a new working class has arisen – not working class in the social sense, but in the strictly professional sense – men who feel no impelling call, but whose purpose it is to learn the techniques of documentary research as a bricklayer learns to lay bricks, or as an engineer learns to build a dam. On the golden road to promotion or a better job, books and articles, whether or not they are written to be read, are more easily identifiable than good lectures. And as university teaching in the arts has become increasingly a profitable occupation, the sense of dedication which usually accompanies mild poverty (as with the craftsman) has gradually dwindled.

The "poor scholar" is a definition with as much tradition behind it as "the absent-minded professor." Both generalizations lack validity today, and I should not be surprised to learn that a good many members of our profession were overpaid. Who knows, a vow of poverty, to be imposed on every lecturer up to the rank of associate professor, might discourage industrious entrants who are more interested in a secure and respectable job than in dedicating themselves to their subject!

At the same time, the growth of a professional attitude towards scholarship is not to be deplored. The average quality of work by present-day scholars probably surpasses that of their predecessors in the arts. On the other hand, I don't think I am being over-sentimental when I say that one impelling drive today – one principal motive of research – is the promotion to be won, *not* the eccentric will to discover the truth about something, while enjoying the process. Research, however trivial, has become a more remunerative activity than teaching. With high salaries, extra leaves of absence to write extra books, with enormously increased research funds and research assistants, the young Canadian lecturer is encouraged to see his future in terms of writing rather than teaching, and he begrudges the time spent on teaching anything but his speciality, and not infrequently the time spent on graduate students who will follow eventually in his footsteps.[3]

The balance of university subjects has already been affected by a growing emphasis on learning for specific tasks. Even the arts faculties are becoming more and more departmentalized, as more and more teachers are appointed to teach specialized fields. And at a time when universities have become increasingly dependent on the state, there are bound to be suspicions that government may bring pressures to bear in favour of a curriculum that provides more highly trained men for particular jobs; in other words, state scholarships for future servants of the state.

In regard to the content and structure of undergraduate courses, obviously no university can be indifferent to the requirements of the civil service or the professions. Most of our departments would go out of business if our graduates were not acceptable to such professional bodies.

None the less, the possibility of Canadian universities becoming professional trade schools, to the neglect of broader studies that encourage intellectual curiosity and foster the spirit of zealous inquiry, was certainly a gnawing fear in the mind of my old friend, the late Harold Innis of Toronto. He felt deeply that universities, and particularly scholars within universities, should avoid too close an association with either government or business. He saw no future for a university as a public service institution. And if he were alive today, he would certainly ask that staff should have precedence over buildings, and insist that the true balance between education and learning could not be obtained by half-baked or perfunctory research, by subsidized machine work, unreflective and uninspired, the creation of grim skills without a craftsman's love.

But there is another, more ominous danger to which even the dedicated and totally involved scholar is not immune. In a world more deeply than ever before at the mercy of mass media of communication, mankind is increasingly at the mercy of bureaucratic agencies. The most austere and honest university teacher may be taught to serve false gods, and sometimes evil purposes. Indeed, the historian, anywhere in the world, is probably the most vulnerable of all. In any climate his productions can so easily be tainted with untruth, and, if needs be, warped to produce the antithesis of objective thought. With nationalism in full cry in so many lands, never has so much depended on the personal integrity of the scholar. Patriotism may not be the last resort of the scoundrel, as Samuel Johnson put it, but nationalism remains the deadly enemy of historical truth. One has only to examine certain contemporary European or Asian textbooks, to appreciate

3/Gerald S. Graham, "In Defense of the Ivory Tower," an address given at the University of New Brunswick on Founders' Day, March 1967, 6–7.

how persuasively lessons of the past can be distorted to produce national pride and national prejudice.

Canada has not entirely avoided this danger, although it is far less acute than in the time of my boyhood when the presence of the bogeyman on Canada's southern border was the basic fact in Canadian history. Even today, most of you will probably agree that fear of the United States represents the dynamic core of urgent Canadian nationalism. Certainly, the Canadian state seems to have been shaped less by historic kinship with Americans and Britons than by historic antagonisms, less by similarities and affinities than by antipathies.

To what extent have these negative forces affected the course of Canadian history?

One hundred years ago, lacking the self-reliance that comes with economic self-sufficiency and close political unity, less than 2,500,000 Canadians had, perforce, to depend for meagre security on the weight and bargaining power of British diplomacy. In terms of population, apart from the St. Lawrence Valley, the country was little more than a series of fly specks dotted across mountain and plain from Atlantic to Pacific. In terms of status, the nation was an anaemic midget on a stage dominated by two great powers, and in those days no one was so naïve as to think she could play the part of interpreter. In North American parlance, Canada was "the little guy" in the middle, to be kicked or cuffed or ignored as circumstances dictated.

It used to be assumed that Canadian interests were sacrificed in almost every Anglo-American treaty since 1783. Certainly, during the last quarter of the nineteenth century the weary imperial titan was deeply anxious to placate the United States; and policies of appeasement, which British governments practised, sometimes meant yielding on certain peculiarly sensitive Canadian issues such as fisheries and boundaries. Most of the concessions, particularly in regard to boundaries, were, in terms of natural law, quite unfair, but considering the vulnerability of Canada, they were not unwise. Canada had much more to lose from a just war than from an unjust treaty. Canadians, including the Prime Minister, John A. Macdonald, might curse the timidity of British diplomats, but Macdonald knew right well that Canadians, if they had been left to their own resources, could not have maintained their national existence at all.

Out of the conflicts of power during those years, a British colony had managed to survive, and even take on significant shape. Indeed, its national development was guided and accelerated by conflict and fear. Fear of the United States stimulated imperial loyalty, just as distrust of the mother country encouraged North Americanism. Because there was a real balance of forces. Canada was able to avoid American absorption on the one hand, and any extreme form of colonial dependence on the other. Amid the play of power politics, she was able to ensure that the North American continent beyond the Gulf of Mexico should be shared between republic and monarchy.

But Canada had yet to emerge as a fully fledged sovereign state. Her interests and status were still bound up with the power and prestige of the mother country. Consequently, recognition of Canada's independent existence as a self-governing entity came slowly. The first substantial advance came with World War I. By advertising the sacrifices of a distinct British North American nation, the war of 1914–18 provided the first step up the ladder of international status. The meetings of the Imperial War Cabinet in 1917–18 contributed little in this direction, but they gave a significant psychological stimulus to national pride. Canada was consulted and to a certain extent she helped to decide policy. But on the whole, the invitations were by grace and favour; they were aimed at winning and invigorating Canadian and Dominions support for an all-out war effort. Canadian representatives were told that their country was sharing equally in the councils of the Empire; that the nations of the Empire stood equally shoulder to shoulder, bound by the same fate.

As long as the German peril existed, Canada was happy to accept this humble but dignified role; indeed, when the menace of German arms had been extinguished, a united Empire front was sufficient to win for Prime Minister Borden, against the opposition of the United States delegation, a seat at the Peace Conference, and this hard-won battle was confirmed by admission to the League of Nations along with the right of membership in the Council. None the less, despite or possibly owing to the enormous sacrifices she had made between 1914–18, Canada was soon ready to turn her back on Europe; and in the interest of splendid isolation did nothing to make peace-making under the aegis of the League of Nations effective. Protected by a powerful neighbour and isulated from Europe by a great ocean, she was able to insist on a liberal interpretation of Article x of the Covenant, thus relieving herself of any military obligations overseas. If actual war should threaten, declared the Prime Minister in 1922, the Canadian Parliament would be asked to decide whether circumstances dictated Canadian participation.

This indifference or distrust of Europe was, perhaps, the most conspicuous development of the post-war era. And in resisting the trend, Borden showed himself a far more astute statesman than his Liberal successor, Mackenzie King, who had inherited Laurier's limiting view of foreign policy. Both Borden and King were agreed that if a war broke out and threatened the survival of the United Kingdom, Canada would probably become involved. But Borden recognized that the only likely source of major conflict lay in Europe, and therefore Britain's affairs must be of primary concern to Canada, whereas Mackenzie King believed that his country could ignore such a potential empire commitment, and rest relatively secure within the fireproof structure of the North American continent.

It must be admitted, however, that this distaste for Europe and British entanglements was bolstered by a general hankering for everlasting peace that was shared by many people in Britain as well as in other Dominions; and the combination of isolationism or anti-Europeanism and pacifism was responsible in Canada for a rapid scaling-down of defences. The new armament industries were gradually discarded, and before long the country became once again almost as dependent on outside supply as Gambia or Sierra Leone. In 1939 Canada was to pay the price for failing to understand that Europe could not be ignored; despite 3,000 miles of ocean, she remained an unwilling prisoner of the western world in spite of herself.

For the moment, however, the doctrine of North American immunity was intact; there was peace in Europe, and although it was a false and faltering peace, it was sufficient to enable Mackenzie King by a series of cautious retreats from British imperial responsibilities to underline Canada's status as a distinct national entity. In 1923 when a new treaty with Turkey was eventually negotiated, Canada declined to sign or ratify it on the grounds that she was not represented. In 1925 she refused to participate in the negotiations preceding the Treaty of Locarno, and the final abandonment of a common foreign policy for the Empire revealed itself in Clause IX of the Treaty which specifically excluded the dominions from its provisions, and in so doing recognized that a dominion might adopt a passive role in any European conflict involving the mother country. The Imperial Conference of 1926 endorsed this declaration of independence. By the end of the twenties, Canada appeared to have reached the borders of the Promised Land of Sovereignty – a status of equality with Great Britain which was confirmed by the famous Statute of Westminster in 1931.

Legally this legislation had real meaning; Canada had become in law an equal partner in a commonwealth. Yet she remained essentially a British-protected state. Equality in law is not the same thing as equality of function. A legislative grant of independence was insufficient to make the long-sought image of nationhood a reality. The unhappy period of self-conscious adolescence continued, but it was expressed during the thirties in a kind of defiant North American nationalism. Having thrown off the imperial yoke, it was important to demonstrate this fact to the world, by seeking closer relations with the United States. "The cardinal thesis of the [nationalist] school," wrote the scholarly editor of the *Montreal Star*, George Ferguson, "was that, at all costs, Canada had to fight its way out from under the traditional influence of British imperialist and colonial rule; and that one of the best ways of doing it was to use the influence of the United States as a counter-balance against the pressure from Westminster."[4]

The importance of membership in the Commonwealth was deliberately under-rated officially and unofficially. That emporium of bureaucracy – Ottawa – has always afforded ample opportunities for the creation of collective opinion and the insinuation of a common establishment attitude. Involvement in British foreign affairs, it was whispered, meant danger to status, and risk of war. Canada, it was argued, should continue to cut commitments inside the Commonwealth. A British Commonwealth bloc, declared the Prime Minister, Mackenzie King, would excite resentful opposition throughout the world.

In short, there was a sharp reaction from the old British Empire. The long struggle by which Canada had maintained her separateness against American "Manifest Destiny" was tacitly forgotten. "A whole new generation of politicians, publicists, journalists and professors," wrote Professor D. G. Creighton of the University of Toronto, " – the professional nationalists of the 1930s – arose to extol the sufficiency and normality of our North Americanism." I remember that decade well. Cynicism became the sign of maturity and originality; the denigration of empire and the condemnation of militarists became fashionable exercises in which university intellectuals took a leading part. Historians devoted themselves to the Whig or Liberal interpretation of Canadian history, recounting the glorious story of Canada's liberation from the silken meshes of British imperialism. Such was the negative character and tone of Canadian nationalisim in the pre-war years. The "thirties" were flaccid, ineffective, and sick years of good intentions, when the evil peril of Naziism could be reduced to common room proportions, and when bustling, bright, and provocative scholars could seek bubble reputations by intellectual exercises that ignored the world the locusts were already devouring.

It took another world war to dissipate this academic malaise. Despite the murmurings of isolationists who favoured "passive belligerency" and the efforts of the Premier of Quebec to exploit the anti-imperial

4/D. G. Creighton, "Nationalism in Canadian History," *The Listener*, LXI, no. 1577 (June 18, 1959), 1048.

sentiment of his province, a North American nation, not a British dominion, rejected neutrality and went to war of its own volition on September 10, 1939.

The salient feature of the period between the wars had been the remarkable progress towards national autonomy. Yet despite her enhanced status as an equal partner in the Commonwealth, Canada had less influence on high policy matters between 1939 and 1945 than during World War I. Her role as interpreter between the two great kindred powers was a very minor one; neither Britain nor the United States called her to their councils. There was a partnership in name, but in practice the main direction of military affairs within North America was provided by the United States. This unilateral surrender of part of her sovereignty was in considerable degree the result of unpreparedness, for which the Prime Minister, Mackenzie King, must be held largely responsible.

None the less, when peace came, largely in consequence of the revolution in her industrial life, the so-called "arsenal of democracy" stood in fourth place as a trading and industrial nation. And until the recovery of devastated Europe and Asia – especially Japan – she was able, because of the resources at her disposal, to exercise a considerable influence in the councils of the powers. Indeed, Canada was sometimes lauded as the embodiment of international idealism – the example of a small power capable of playing a civilizing role in world affairs.

During this period, for reasons of national expediency, she preferred the international stage to the British Commonwealth club room. Canadian governments were prepared to accept the Commonwealth as "a worthy association of well-wishers," whose prime ministers met regularly and decorously as at mothers' meetings, but Mackenzie King and his successors found it politically safer to propound a foreign policy in terms of universal security rather than through an association that remained suspect in the eyes of French Canada, until recently diluted and sterilized by African and Asian membership.

It is important, therefore, not to over-idealize the external policies of recent Canadian governments. Short of moral pretentiousness, Canadian foreign policy has been based on two major considerations. One is the inevitable subordination of any distinctly Canadian policy to the requirements of American foreign policy, with the consequent need to assert Canadian nationalism in the international arena where smaller powers may at least make themselves heard. The other is the political necessity of preserving unity in the face of an actual sectional and racial division, which constant exposure to "Americanization" had not broken down. It was essential, and still is, that Canadian policy should have the widest, and at the same time the least divisive appeal to a heterogeneous nation, of which the proportion of British stock was less than 50 per cent. Because of racial divergencies it was safer to support policies of universal security through the United Nations or NATO than to play a possibly hazardous role as senior dominion at the Commonwealth conference table.

When the storm over Suez rocked the Commonwealth in 1956, official emphasis remained, as before, on peace, not the enforcement of peace – on declarations of righteous principle and not the pursuit of righteous action. The popular acclaim which greeted Mr. Lester Pearson's eager intervention as "honest broker" was much welcomed in Ottawa, but it was not accompanied by any increase of international influence. Without the will or the power to back up moral judgments, any serious approach to leadership in international affairs was and remains a delusion. Moral strictures on the part of Canada's Secretary of State for External Affairs could not alter the fact that the use of force, even through the United Nations, was not a basic Canadian interest. In the past ten years, the approach has continued to be vigorous, and the pursuit of status by exhortation and example is still fervent, but tidy compromise by peaceful negotiation is not the key to the solution of every international problem. Law and order exist in this world only if interested nations are prepared to enforce them. International problems will not be solved by the idealist or the amateur who ignores or mocks the power element in contemporary statescraft.

Let us not, therefore, glorify Canada's special interest in international peace-keeping, when the government is not prepared in the last resort to back up intervention with the armed men necessary to make the effort effective. Mr. Pearson naïvely regarded the North Atlantic coalition "less as a defense coalition and more as a foundation for a closely cooperating political and economic community"; and he was largely responsible for Article II of the North Atlantic Treaty which demanded joint action in economic and cultural fields as well as military. This clause is pure eyewash. NATO happens to be basically a military alliance, and no partner can expect to claim powers of leadership or count on strengthening its position in the forum of the United Nations by means of peace-loving aims supported by a few peace-keeping patrols.[5]

Of course, there are risks, as Mackenzie King had well realized, in playing too active an international role. An eager-beaver pursuit of even the worthiest ends could be embarrassing to the United States, and might

5/See Dean Acheson, "Canada: Stern Daughter of the Voice of God," in *Neighbors Taken for Granted, Canada and the United States*, Livingston T. Merchant, ed. (New York and Toronto 1966), 141–42.

invite interference. Canada lies comparatively aloof from the perils of an uneasy world, but "3,000 miles of unguarded frontier" is in itself a reflection of her dependence on her neighbour. There is no alternative to close collaboration with the United States, and no doubt, in the minds of some people, no alternative to eventual union with the republic. Canada has been and remains incapable of providing for the military and naval extensions required to defend her essential interests. Inevitably Washington is bound to regard Canadian shores as simply northern extensions of the Atlantic and Pacific coastlines of the United States.

Geography has forced the two countries into a military partnership, which, under American direction, can have no fixed limit. The United States, for the sake of her own security, is determined that the North-West Territories should not give ready access to the invader who plotted a course over the Arctic. This policy has inevitably meant a further sacrifice of Canadian sovereignty, and there is little that Canadians can do about it. The vital decisions for Canada (as also for Britain) are, and will continue to be, made in Washington.

There is also the obvious and significant fact that the way to an expanding economy and great riches has been the path of least resistance. Any Canadian government would find it impossible to accept curbs on economic development – resulting possibly in a lower standard of living – in the interest of cultural nationhood. The life of Canada is too closely interwoven with that of the United States to permit anything approaching a positive independence. In trade, transportation, investment, and living standards, the two countries are irretrievably bound together.

Yet Canadian governments have collaborated on the whole amicably and effectively with their American counterparts. In peace-time, they have been able, thanks to vast natural resources, to play the client rather than the sycophant, not hesitating on occasion to remind Washington that the small neighbour should not be taken for granted as a poor relation. Indeed, during the lustrous mid-fifties, the last remnants of the old colonial inferiority complex seemed to have been dropped behind the United Nations' footlights in New York. Canadians began to talk of their new maturity with a confidence suggesting that the twentieth century might still be theirs.

During that balmy Indian summer, literary critics wrote about the "dynamic and fruitful tension between the dual cultural and religious traditions" – the happy willingness to accept and live within an uneasy balance of ever-changing domestic fortunes. But the effort to find strength through tension could not be sustained, and the eager pursuit of international recognition was insufficient to make the long-sought image of national greatness more than an illusion.

Like Britain, Canada must come to terms with her diminished role in the world. This, she has already been learning the hard way – a process that is painful to pride, but altogether wholesome if it eliminates further rhetoric in regard to Canada's unique role as professional flower child on the international stage. Tolerance and political ingenuity are native characteristics which may very well stem from Canada's divided cultural inheritance, but influence and respect in the world arena are deeply affected by the success of Canadian governments in exercising these qualities to master their own domestic conflicts. To make any impact in the international field, a country needs a national identity. Failure at home has inevitably blunted the pruning hooks and limited the range of Canadian foreign policy. The curse of domestic division remains. The political and emotional foundations of Quebec separatism have not been broken and the federal compromise which seemed essential to enduring nationhood is once again in jeopardy.

Today Canadians are rightly concerned because a fringe group of separatists – probably a little more than a tenth of the Quebec voting strength – wish their provincial brethren to contemplate economic *hari-kari* for the sake of cultural pride. In this adventure, they have the support of General de Gaulle, whose recent performance in Quebec revealed the mania, but not the professional skill of that Monsieur Blondin who many years ago trod the tightrope over Niagara rapids. Such emotional incitements could lead to episodic violence, but in the long run they must surely alienate the bulk of a Canadian population which has grown to over 20,000,000 (partly as a result of the influx of Poles, Hungarians, Germans, Ukrainians, and Italians) and whose Anglo-Saxon proportion is now far less than 50 per cent.

The process of producing from the melting pot a distinctive human being with a maple-leaf birthmark, or, at least, something that will develop into a 100 per cent North American, has naturally been accelerated in every region except Quebec (which has, incidentally, its own concept of 100 per cent based on three and a half centuries of national life in the St. Lawrence Valley). Consequently, because of a fairly steady European dilution, the average English-speaking Canadian of 1967 bears little resemblance to his predecessor who fought for king and country in 1914, or even the emerging nationalist of 1939.

Today, Canadians remain sensitively conscious of the fact that their country lacks the cultural solidarity of Australia or even the United States;

and they are also aware that the wall of special privileges erected in 1774 (the Quebec Act) has become within the last few years an ever increasing barrier to common nationhood. Yet the onlooker from overseas might well be puzzled by the amount of introspection, self-absorption, and punishing self-criticism that existed long before "Québec Libre" became the shrill rallying cry of a frightened minority. Why this fierce striving for national identity? Why try to force the homogenizing process by injections of synthetic nationalism? The vexatious problem of national unity remains to be solved, but not by university professors; that is a problem for skilled professional politicians, not academic bridge-builders.

As for the country's future role and status in the world, why not leave something to fortune? After all, Canadians have achieved immense prosperity and a dignified international status, and although the idea of a distinct national identity may be a myth, they do exist as a recognizable people, or peoples, distinct from Americans. There *is* a Canada built in defiance of geography, in defiance of history, and shored up by a series of compromises that bridge a cultural gulf far less forbidding in depth and breadth than that confronting statesmen in the United States today, and which may face Great Britain tomorrow. Let Canadians thank God for their so-called illiberal immigration laws which have saved them from the greater peril of savage racial, not just cultural, conflict. The American experience has shown Great Britain the enormous price that may be paid for the well-meaning but stupid assumption that people of all colours and civilizations can in a day learn to love and live with each other in an over-crowded country and, if not, can be made to do so by legislation.

Mutual trust and understanding between French- and English-speaking Canadians is still far away, and sometimes one wonders whether an *entente cordiale* is beyond the reach of men of goodwill. Not infrequently today one hears the cry for leadership: that a solution would be obtainable through a man of sufficient vision and inspiration to make the country's government effective at home and respected abroad. "The crying need for Canada," Lord Tweedsmuir wrote to George V in the year before he died, "is for some national leader who would really guide the thought and touch the imagination of the whole country." In Ottawa, the lack of skilled statesmanship at the top is very apparent, but in present times unless professional skill were allied to commanding genius it would scarcely be enough. We are living in an age when political leadership is both scorned and distrusted. In the circumstances it would take a Messianic titan built to the extravagant proportions of the elder Pitt, Churchill, or de Gaulle, to burst above the accepted level of events, and take charge of Canadian destinies. Canadians, like Britons, tend to prefer the apparently safe and solid, if mediocre, to the imaginative and impulsive. The election of the flamboyant and scholarly Pierre Trudeau as prime minister in June 1968 is the exception that proves the rule.

On the other hand, calculations founded on Canada's past and present regional or cultural difficulties may become irrelevant in the light of more ominous considerations. On a vast continent which modern technology seems intent on ironing to pancake level, French and English Canadians may find it preferable to stick together, however painful the process. In this rapidly shrinking world provincial sovereignties, even more than unlimited national sovereignties, are concepts which run counter to the prevailing tendencies of our times.

Index